Ambivalence,
Modernity, Power

Nuala Finnegan

Ambivalence, Modernity, Power

Women and Writing in Mexico since 1980

PETER LANG

Oxford · Bern · Berlin · Bruxelles · Frankfurt am Main · New York · Wien

Bibliographic information published by Die Deutsche Bibliothek
Die Deutsche Bibliothek lists this publication in the Deutsche
Nationalbibliografie; detailed bibliographic data is available on
the Internet at ‹http://dnb.ddb.de›.

British Library and Library of Congress Cataloguing-in-Publication Data:
A catalogue record for this book is available from The British Library,
Great Britain, and from The Library of Congress, USA

ISBN 978-3-03910-507-6
Cover Image: Photograph by Elsi Pérez Jarillo.
Cover Design: Tracey Brockwell, Peter lang Ltd.

© Peter Lang AG, International Academic Publishers, Bern 2007
Hochfeldstrasse 32, Postfach 746, CH-3000 Bern 9, Switzerland
info@peterlang.com, www.peterlang.com, www.peterlang.net

Printed in Germany

Contents

Acknowledgements   7

Introduction   9

Chapter One
Place, Nation and History in Sara Sefchovich and Silvia Molina   29

Chapter Two
The Disintegrating Self: Narrative and Survival in Susana Págano
        and Brianda Domecq   75

Chapter Three
Angeles Mastretta and the Curse of the Popular   135

Chapter Four
Class, Gender and Questions of Feminism in Guadalupe Loaeza
        and Rosamaría Roffiel   179

Chapter Five
Postcolonial Journeys: Transnational Spaces in Silvia Molina
        and Sara Sefchovich   247

Conclusion   .   309

Bibliography   319
Index   341

Acknowledgements

I am deeply indebted to many people who have helped and encouraged me during this long journey. I am also fortunate to have had financial support from the College of Arts, Celtic Studies and Social Sciences, University College Cork and would like to acknowledge its generosity. I thank also Alexis Kirschbaum and Helena Sedgwick at Peter Lang for their efficiency and understanding. Elsi Pérez Jarillo kindly granted permission to use the photograph on the front cover.

I have benefited immeasurably from constructive feedback offered by many friends and colleagues. I owe a particular debt of gratitude to Claire Lindsay but also to Pat Crowley, Jane Lavery, Deborah Shaw and Anne Walsh. To all my wonderful colleagues in Hispanic Studies, I thank them for their interest in the project and their encouragement. Friends who offered valuable support include Debbie O'Shea, Mairead ní Loinsigh, Silvia Ross, Cinta Ramblado, Kathryn Hargreaves and Clare Connelly. Thanks are also due to Orla Borreye, Karla Kowalski and Cecilia Gamez who have helped me in different ways sourcing material.

I have been privileged in the last few years to supervise a number of doctoral projects and to work with a group of talented enthusiastic students. I am particularly indebted to two of them: Lorraine Kelly who devoted much time to collecting material for me in Mexico and Ana Cruz García who, apart from her work on the bibliography, has been a source of constant support, encouragement and invaluable help. They have also inspired me in ways they are probably not aware of and I am immensely grateful to both of them. I would also like to mention the many other students on my final year undergraduate course, 'Women and Popular Fiction in Mexico' and the students of 'Third World Feminisms' in the Women's Studies programme who have contributed significantly to my thinking on the various subjects covered in the book.

I am particularly grateful to Kay Doyle who has been a wonderful rock of support and calm efficiency, as usual. I also thank Jo Richardson for her insightful comments and her patience.

Finally, a few words of gratitude to my family. To my Dad, Mum and sister Emer for their support and John without whose love and encouragement, no project would ever be finished.

This book is dedicated to my boys, Cian, Conor and Eoghan, who show me every day the importance of story-telling.

Introduction
Ambivalence, Modernity, Power: Women and Writing in Mexico since 1980

By the late 1980s, gender roles in Mexican society were more complex than ever before. Many voices bear eloquent testimony to the changes evinced in the roles of women in Mexico over the last three decades. They include the poignant and undeniably powerful presence of Ramona – the 'feminised' voice of *Zapatismo* –, the forceful voice of Claudia Colimoro, prostitute and political hopeful in the 1991 Mexico City parliamentary elections, and the many feminist activists involved in the Convención Nacional de Mujeres por la Democracia, *fem* and Colectivo Cine Mujer. This book takes as its starting point the *boom femenino*, or the explosion in publishing by women writers in Mexico since 1980. It argues that the texts produced by these writers continually interrogate ways of conceiving gender and that they resist any fixed, limited or absolute representation of the feminine. The book aims to account for the *boom* with close attention to the globalisation of publishing, and the myriad other ways in which literature is disseminated, commodified and absorbed. It examines the work of seven writers, all of them well-known in Mexico and many of them best-sellers both at home and abroad.[1] The campaign for political, cultural and economic *modernización*, aggressively implemented from 1982 onwards, activates the voices of women in the cultural arena for virtually the first time. These voices are enabled by the modernising project and are thus also deeply implicated in it. In this way, women writers occupy a richly ambivalent position in relation to the modernising forces which have shaped Mexico over the past three decades. It is this ambivalence which generates a literature that is full

---

1   The book examines the work of the following seven writers, listed here in alphabetical order: Brianda Domecq, Guadalupe Loaeza, Angeles Mastretta, Silvia Molina, Susana Pagano, Rosamaría Roffiel and Sara Sefchovich.

of 'interstitial sparks', or disjunctive sites, through which resistance and opposition emerge out of the uneven processes of modernisation.[2] The book aims to arrive at an understanding of how women writers negotiate their positions in a modernised intellectual sphere through a combination of text-based readings and close analysis of the contexts of reception and production.

Globalisation and the Crisis of Literature

The book is very much rooted in a cultural studies approach in that it recognises the necessity of examining all the players in the literary process, not just the writer and the text. It therefore examines the impact of the shifting dynamics of the publishing world on specific women writers in Mexico.[3] I explore the pressures for translatability, the rise of multinational publishers and chart the trajectory of publishing houses like Joaquín Mortiz, first established to encourage experimental writing and later subsumed by multinational publisher, Planeta.[4] The book also addresses the impact of canon formation and

2   The term, 'interstitial sparks' is used by Alberto Moreiras who discusses them in the context of Martín Hopenhayn's formulation of the 'interstitial or peripheric as a disjunctive site that holds the possibility of a singularisation of thinking beyond negativity'. See Alberto Moreiras, *The Exhaustion of Difference: The Politics of Latin American Cultural Studies,* (Durham, North Carolina: Duke University Press, 2001), p.43 and Martín Hopenhayn, *No Apocalypse, No Integration: Modernism and Postmodernism in Latin America* (Durham, North Carolina: Duke University Press, 2001), p.155.

3   As Jean Franco notes, 'literature itself is now mass-mediatised. With the globalisation of the book industry and the publication of translations and best-sellers, the stake in popularity and translatability has grown. The market is not tolerant of writing that is too experimental or "untranslatable". Some writers now court rather than reject commercialism'. 'What's Left of the Intelligentsia: The Uncertain Future of the Printed Word', in *Critical Passions: Selected Essays* (Durham, North Carolina: Duke University Press, 1999), pp.202–3.

4   Danny Anderson provides a fascinating insight into the changing publishing criteria of Joaquín Mortiz in his article, 'Creating Cultural Prestige: Editorial

curriculum inclusion on the fluctuating and unstable position of women in the cultural market-place in Mexico. This position underwent dramatic changes in the 1980s as a result of the socio-economic crisis generated by the oil scare and the subsequent devaluation of the *peso* in 1982. The crisis precipitated a tremendous change in work practices for women, leading to the creation of a body of female consumers eager to read fiction, for the first time in Mexico's history. Furthermore, the fragmented and diverse *boom femenino* forms part of a wider and much documented fragmentation of the Mexican political system including the ascendancy of the political parties, Partido Revolucionario Democrático (PRD) and the Partido de Acción Nacional (PAN) in the 1990s, *zapatismo* and the new social movements, and culminating in 2000 with the toppling of the Partido Revolucionario Institucional (PRI) which had been in power since the 1920s. Indeed, it could be argued that the current body politic in Mexico is more splintered than ever in the aftermath of the infamous 2006 election which caused widespread civil unrest amid accusations of electoral fraud and appeals to the Federal Electoral Tribunal (TRIFE).[5] The fragmentation of form, content and authorial position with regard to fiction produced by women since 1980 is registered, therefore, in almost all areas of cultural production during this time.[6]

Why the *boom femenino* occurred at all during the tumultuous 1980s is itself an interesting question given the widely held notion that literature's oppositional clout has been irrevocably diminished as a result of the blurring of the differences between 'high' and 'low' art,

Joaquín Mortiz', *Latin American Research Review*, Vol.31, No.2 (1996), pp.3–41. I draw extensively on his research in Chapter Three.

5   Felipe Calderón was formally declared President in December 2006 after the Federal Electoral Tribunal (TRIFE) confirmed his victory over the PRD candidate, Andrés Manuel López Obrador by the narrowest of margins. For a good account of the election, see Joseph Kliesner (ed.), 'The 2006 Mexican Election and Its Aftermath', *Political Science and Politics*, Vol.XL, No.1 (January 2007), pp.11–48.

6   For a detailed discussion of fragmentation in the context of Mexican literature, see Carol Clark D'Lugo, *The Fragmented Novel in Mexico: The Politics of Form* (Austin: University of Texas Press, 1997).

as well as the onslaught of mass media.[7] However, even in the face of the collapse of the central historic subject and the inescapability of difference, I contend that writing is part of a cultural process in which the dynamics of power shift continually, and thus to quote Argentine writer, Luisa Valenzuela, is 'always, already political'.[8] What is more, while the globalisation of the market-place cannot necessarily be overcome or erased, 'spaces of co-existence may be implemented, folds within the global system, where an exterior to totality emerges as the site of a possible, concrete freedom'.[9] It is to these possible freedoms, then, that the book turns to examine the ways in which both these texts and their intertexts emit a forceful political charge. The book is not, however, an attempt to argue that some form of cohesive oppositionality emerges from this body of work. It is widely acknowledged that market rationality fosters segmented audiences that need not, in turn, relate to each other.[10] Indeed it pits cultural players against each other as competitors in often hostile and destructive ways, as is evidenced by many Mexican women writers' attitudes to notions of 'women's writing' and 'feminism'.[11] What is overwhelm-

7   Jean Franco points out that this was especially true in Mexico in the mid-1980s, when the price of books became exorbitant, halting what Carlos Monsiváis and José Emilio Pacheco termed 'democratisation from below'. *The Decline and Fall of the Lettered City: Latin America after the Cold War* (Cambridge, Massachussetts: Harvard University Press, 2002), p.11.

8   Cited in Steven Bell, Albert H. Le May, Leonard Orr (eds), *Critical Theory, Cultural Politics and Latin American Narrative* (Indiana, University of Notre Dame Press, 1993), p.21.

9   Alberto Moreiras, *The Exhaustion of Difference*, p.43.

10   Jean Franco, George Yúdice and Juan Flores (eds), *On Edge: The Crisis of Contemporary Latin American Culture* (Minneapolis: University of Minnesota Press, 1992), p.xi.

11   Recent publications from Kay García, *Broken Bars: New Perspectives from Mexican Women Writers* (Albuquerque: University of New Mexico Press, 1994) and Gabriella de Beer, *Contemporary Mexican Women Writers: Five Voices* (Austin: University of Texas Press, 1996) contain ample evidence of this kind of competitive sentiment. This ranges from frustration to outright animosity. As Mastretta explains, 'how often can you attend a conference about literature "written by women?" Please, don't let them organize another conference on that subject. They are going to drive all of us women crazy, with everyone talking about literature "written by women." Can't we talk about

12

ingly apparent, however, is that discussions about these women's work and their place within a globalised culture industry – whether from the perspective of consumer, reader, publisher or critic – almost inevitably lead back to questions about gender and feminism. Thus the book addresses a series of questions that have been central to much feminist research over the past four decades. How in the face of the diluted oppositional value of the aesthetic and the irreducible and ruthless logic of the market-place, can writing by women make a difference? In particular, specific questions arise over whether spaces have emerged for contestatory political and cultural practice and what form they might take. As cultural products are integrated into a (global) market rationality, with their effectiveness measured in sales receipts and media ratings, they are less articulated to social move-ments which, in turn, impacts on cultural politics.[12] This does not mean, however, that no cross-over is possible. Indeed, as Jean Franco notes, 'the genre and mode in which women write constitute their positionality within a debate whose terms are seldom explicitly articulated'.[13] This book is an attempt to explicitly articulate those terms as they operate in Mexico from 1980 onwards.

something else?' *Contemporary Mexican Women Writers: Five Voices*, p.230. Carmen Boullosa has protested on various occasions against her inclusion in any kind of category of 'women's writing': 'Que yo sea mujer es un mero accidente biológico. [...] Yo creo que hay sensibilidades chatas, sensibilidades agudas, inteligencias agradables, inteligencias torpes [...] y que eso no tiene nada que ver con el sexo del escritor'. Cited in Roselyn Costantino, 'Resistant Creativity: Interpretative Strategies and Gender Representation in Contemporary Mexican Women's Writing', Ph.D, Arizona State University, 1992, p.173. Mexican poet, Myriam Moscona articulated the same point of view in a recent discussion at the Centre for Mexican Studies, University College Cork. 1 May, 2007.

12   *On Edge: The Crisis of Contemporary Latin American Culture*, p.x.
13   'Going Public, Reinhabiting the Private', in *Critical Passions: Selected Essays*, p.52.

Literature, Feminism, Power

Alberto Moreiras's book, *The Exhaustion of Difference* captures elo-quently the sense of fatigue surrounding the bewildering array of critical perspectives on ethnic, cultural, class and generic differences. Moreover it hints at another exhaustion, an exhaustion with the 'gen-der question', more specifically with women, and most certainly with literature produced by women. Indeed, one of the reasons why it has become necessary to raise explicitly feminist questions in relation to cultural production in Mexico generally is that, despite the boom in publishing by women and the wide dissemination of their texts, there is a tendency visible in much critical writing on the subject of Latin America to erase it systematically as a separate and distinct category. Beneath overarching discussions on Latin American cultural studies, questions of gender lie quietly put to one side, except for when they intrude upon 'bigger' questions, like those of subalternity. Much of the critical theory being generated under the rubrics of Latin American Cultural Studies, Latin American Subaltern Studies and Latin Amer-icanism is notable for its evasiveness with regard to the question of gender and the 'woman's question'.[14] Subaltern Studies is an illus-trative case in point. John Beverley, a founding figure of Latin Amer-ican Subaltern Studies and author of *Subalternity and Representation: Arguments in Cultural Theory*, displays a constant slippage in his terminology. On the one hand, he employs Ranajit Guha's definition of the subaltern, 'a name for the general attribute of subordination [...] whether this is repressed in terms of class, caste, age, *gender* and office or in any other way' (my emphasis) as the original formulation

---

14   Recent studies illustrating this trend include Román de la Campa, *Latin Americanism* (Minneapolis: University of Minnesota Press, 1999), Alberto Moreiras, *The Exhaustion of Difference: The Politics of Latin American Cultural Studies*, John Beverley, *Subalternity and Representation: Arguments in Cultural Theory* (Durham: Duke University Press, 1999), Neil Larsen, *Determinations: Essays on Theory, Narrative and Nation in the Americas* (London: Verso, 2001), and Martín Hopenhayn, *No Apocalypse, No Integration: Modernism and Postmodernism in Latin America*.

from which much of Latin American subaltern studies springs.[15] And yet, it emerges in his work almost uniformly to mean 'poor'.[16] Thus the work of 'clearly' subaltern women such as Rigoberta Menchú, among others, is subsumed into this category. In many ways, this is an understandable lapse, but unfortunately, it leaves the privileged female intellectual from Latin America unaccounted for.

Ileana Rodríguez's detailed and compelling introduction to the *Latin American Subaltern Studies Reader*, exhibits a similar slippage. She isolates the formative task facing the group, 'Our question concerns the necessity of redefining the concept of oppression to make it more comprehensive. "Subalternity" seemed a more all-encompassing term than "class" in expressing the fullness of the disenfranchised community'.[17] Here, then, when addressing notions of ethnicity and gender, 'what to do' with women and members of ethnic minorities who are not poor, would seem to remain beyond subaltern parameters. They remain, however, 'disenfranchised' in very specific, harmful ways. While all the women writers studied in this book come from privileged backgrounds, many are of European origin, and all are to some extent or other, members of an intellectual elite, they have also encountered both hostility and resistance, struggling in some cases to have their work published and/or accepted. Their position, therefore, within debates about subaltern, marginalised identity is far from simple. A further question arises: how do I, a critic working in a peripheral European country and therefore on the fringes both of the mainstream academy and of the writing context itself assign myself the power to talk about these women writers. In other words, who is

---

15 *Subalternity and Representation: Arguments in Cultural Theory*, p.26.

16 Beverley talks about subaltern studies as a secular version of the 'preferential option for the poor' of liberation theology, sharing with liberation theology the essential methodology of 'listening to the poor'. Indeed he cites a passage from Richard Rodriguez's famous autobiography, *Hunger of Memory*, 'Los pobres', as a perfect illustration of the subaltern providing, as it does, a '"necessary antithesis", to invoke Guha, of a dominant subject', *Subalternity and Representation*, p.28.

17 *The Latin American Subaltern Studies Reader* (Durham and London: Duke University Press, 2001) p.5.

the subaltern here?[18] Of course, as Beverley points out, the very idea of 'studying' the subaltern is catachrestic or self-contradictory given that as a form of elite academic discourse, it is itself complicit in the social construction of subalternity. Nevertheless, the complexity of a politics of location[19] in which the Western critic operates from within a less privileged context than her 'objects of enquiry' who themselves inhabit multiple locations – both geographically and metaphorically – becomes apparent.

One of the problems implicit in Beverley's formulation is that a far too easy binary relationship is established between us (US, and to a lesser extent, the European academy) and them (poor Latin Americans). In this way, it also deeply immerses itself in the perpetuation of destructive binary oppositions while under the illusion that it is undermining them. It is clear that Beverley is aware of the dangers of locking the debate within limiting binary parameters. Indeed he sum-

18 The emphasis on class differences in debates between 'First' and 'Third' world women activists is well documented. Debra Castillo cites the exchange between Bolivian mine worker's wife, Domitila Barrios de Chungara and the chair of the Mexican delegation to a Tribuna del Año Internacional de la Mujer, during which she asks, 'Ahora, señora, dígame: ¿tiene usted algo semejante a mi situación? [...] Nosotras no podemos, en este momento, ser iguales, aun como mujeres'. *Talking Back: Toward a Latin American Feminist Literary Criticism* (Ithaca: Cornell University Press, 1992), pp.13–14. Nira Yuval-Davis describes what she calls the 'dialogue of the deaf' between 'First' and 'Third' world women at international conferences. She also notes that there is little attention paid to the fact that many of the 'Third World' women present at global feminist conferences frequently come from highly privileged environments and are often actually members of a powerful national elite, something that is rarely the case with Western feminists. *Gender and Nation* (London: Sage Publications, 1997), pp.116–21.

19 This phrase was, of course, made famous by American poet, Adrienne Rich, in her 'Notes Towards a Politics of Location', *Blood, Bread and Poetry: Selected Prose 1979/1985* (London: Virgao, 1987), pp.210–31. It provoked much debate about the importance of location and standpoint with regard to epistemology and has been very influential in feminist theory. As Caren Kaplan writes, 'the term "politics of location" has been picked up as a useful way to articulate the concerns of regional, particular, and local interests in a number of different fields and disciplines', *Questions of Travel: Postmodern Discourses of Displacement* (Durham, North Carolina: Duke University Press, 1996), p.162.

marises various critiques of Subaltern Studies in order to engage with the issues they raise:

> Subaltern and postcolonial studies represent a North American problematic about identity politics and multiculturalism, and/or a Commonwealth problematic about postcoloniality, which has been displaced onto Latin America, at the expense of misrepresenting its diverse histories and social-cultural formations, which are not easily reducible to either multiculturalism or postcoloniality.[20]

There is a clear sense, then, of the difficulties inherent in deploying such fraught terminology but there is little awareness of the evasion of gender concerns with regard to theories of subalternity. Historically, of course, the 'woman question' has always proved problematic for the left and the betrayal felt by feminist activists in the West in the 1960s has been much documented.[21] It seems that new conceptualisations of Latin American cultural production are evading, once again, questions of gender particularly when they relate to the bourgeois subject. This study critiques the current trend to sideline the gender question and tentatively suggests strategies that might account for the bourgeois female subject that have until now, in my opinion, remained undertheorised.

20 *Subalternity and Representation*, p.17. For a fuller elaboration of critiques of Subaltern Studies, see Hugo Achugar, 'Leones, cazadores e historiadores: A propósito de las políticas de la memoria y del conocimiento', *Revista Iberoamericana*, Vol.180 (1997), pp.379–87, and Mabel Moraña, 'El boom del subalterno,' *Revista de Crítica Cultural*, Vol.14 (1997), pp.48–53.

21 Michèle Barrett offers a valuable account of Marxist-feminist politics in general in her study, *Women's Oppression Today: Problems in Marxist Feminist Analysis* (London: Verso, 1980). Robin Morgan's study, *Sisterhood is Powerful: An Anthology of Writings from the Women's Movement* (London: Vintage, 1970) documents the tensions that arose between women activists in the Civil Rights and Peace Movements in the US in the 1950s and 1960s. It is widely known that women-only groups emerged in France as a result of the intense disillusionment felt by the many women active in the student revolts. For a good overview of the period, see Linda Nicholson (ed.), *The Second Wave: A Reader in Feminist Theory* (London: Routledge, 1997).

The Bourgeois Female Subject

In the light of the gap in critical theory, it becomes necessary to account theoretically for the subject position of women writers in Mexico who are, as Jean Franco states, both 'privileged and marginalized at one and the same time'.[22] She laments the fact that many women writers do not begin the process of dismantling their own position of privilege.[23] Technically 'natives' of the 'Third World' and thus fossilised in many conceptualisations of the relationship between 'First' and 'Third', these women are clearly subordinate on one level and yet uniquely privileged on so many others.[24] One potential tool for enabling access to the bourgeois female subject is uncovered through the notion of supplementarity as discussed by Jacques Derrida, and taken on board more recently in Homi Bhabha's challenging writing on the subject in his study, *Nation and Narration*. His discussion

22 'Going Public, Reinhabiting the Private', in *Critical Passions*, p.52.
23 'What's Left of the Intelligentsia: The Uncertain Future of the Printed Word', in *Critical Passions*, p.218.
24 As already mentioned, the tensions between 'First' and 'Third' world women have been the subject of much critical attention. Chandra Talpade Mohanty's writing on the subject is effective in its spirited denunciation of the extreme form of 'universalism' evident in Robin Morgan's anthology *Sisterhood is Global* and in her passionate invective against the Western feminist agenda. See 'Under Western Eyes: Feminist Scholarship and Colonial Discourses', in Mohanty, Ann Russo and Lourdes Torres (eds), *Third World Women and the Politics of Feminism* (Bloomington: University of Indiana Press, 1991), pp.51–80. The widespread use of domestic servants further perpetuates the feminist dilemma in that the 'freedom' enjoyed by women activists (including writers) is frequently predicated on the continued subservience of lower-class or indigenous women, an irony of which many of them are very aware. This continues to be a problem for feminism and clearly, not just in the 'Third' World. See Nira Yuval-Davis, *Gender and Nation*, p.120. Angeles Mastretta treats the subject of the reliance on domestic servants in her essay, 'Guiso feminista', *Puerto libre* (Mexico City: Cal y Arena, 1993), pp.89–95. What is interesting about many of the discussions over 'first' and 'third' world women, is the extent to which Latin America is absent altogether or appears only in the form of limited grass-roots activism.

focuses largely on questions of temporality and nationhood but the central insights are crucial for the purposes of this discussion:

> A supplement, according to one meaning, 'cumulates and accumulates presence'. [...] the *double entendre* of the supplement suggests, however, that it intervenes or insinuates itself *in the place of...* If it represents and makes an image it is by the *anterior* default of a presence... the supplement is an adjunct, a subaltern instance.[25]

The notion of cumulation and accumulation of presence is noteworthy for the way in which it enables the bourgeois female subject to come on board the intellectual boat so to speak, but not necessarily in any antagonistic way. The inclusion of the term 'subaltern instant' is also powerfully suggestive as it reinstates the notion of subordination so central to any definition of subalternity, and yet limits that subordination temporally. The subaltern instant penetrates the discourse of the bourgeois female subject but she is no way defined by it and therefore retains the freedom to slip beyond that instant into another. It is perhaps another way of answering Gibson-Graham's eloquent question, 'how do we retain the concept of "change" as a feminist category – *distinct from the subaltern although not unrelated*?' (my emphasis).[26] Bhabha continues his discussion, clarifying the supplementary position further:

---

25   *Nation and Narration* (London: Routledge, 1990), p.305. Bhabha draws on Jacques Derrida's ideas on supplementarity in writing. See *Of Grammatology*, trans. by Gayatri Chakrovorty Spivak (Baltimore: Johns Hopkins Press, 1976). Derrida's argument that writing is a supplement to speech is developed extensively in his discussion of eighteenth-century French writer, Jean-Jacques Rousseau. My use of the term places it in a very different context than that invoked by either Bhabha or Derrida.

26   Gibson-Graham pose this question in her/their article on women's involvement in mining in central Queensland, Australia. '"Stuffed if I know!": Reflections on Post-modern Feminist Social Research', in Linda McDowell and Joanne P. Sharp (eds), *Space, Gender, Knowledge: Feminist Reading* (Oxford: Oxford University Press, 1997), pp.124–47, p.125. To avoid confusion, it should be pointed out that Gibson and Graham are different researchers but publish their work together under the combined name. I shall henceforth refer to them in both the singular and the plural.

Its strategy of intervention is similar to what parliamentary procedure recognises as a supplementary question. It is a question that is supplementary to what is put down on the order paper, but by being 'after' the original, or in 'addition to' it, gives it the advantage of introducing a sense of 'secondariness' or belatedness into the structure of the original. The supplementary strategy suggests that adding 'to' need not 'add up' but may disturb the calculation.[27]

It would seem to me that this passage offers an extraordinarily suggestive conceptualisation of the way in which the bourgeois female subject actually operates within the intellectual sphere in a Third World country. It also accounts for the somewhat additive curriculum model in which women writers are belatedly added to an original list.[28] Her writing adds to the already existent, not as a simple 'add on', but in a way that forcefully upsets the calculation of the original. In this way it bears a resemblance to what Jean Franco identifies as the 'unsettling' effect achieved by many Latin American women writers:

> many Latin American women writers understand their position to be not so much one of confronting a dominant patriarchy with a new feminine position but rather one of unsettling the stance that supports gender power/knowledge as masculine. The 'unsettling' is accomplished in a variety of ways, through parody and pastiche, by mixing genres and by constituting subversive mythologies.[29]

This notion of 'unsettling' has deep roots in the work of Jacques Lacan who concludes his story about being made fun of on a boat as a

27   *Nation and Narration*, p.305.
28   A powerful recent example of this tendency occurred in Ireland with the publication of the *Field Day Anthology of Irish Writing* (Vols.1–3), in 1991. This extensive collection, covering more than a thousand years, was marked by the virtual absence of female writers. This was hastily rectified with the commission of *Field Day*, Vols.4 and 5 devoted exclusively to the uncovering of the Irish female literary legacy. See Séamus Deane (ed.), *Field Day Anthology of Irish Writing* (London, Derry, New York: Faber and Faber, W.W. Norton, 1991). For an account of the controversy, see Patricia Boyle Haberstroh and Christine St. Peter (eds), *Opening the Field: Irish Women, Texts and Contexts* (Cork: Cork University Press, 2007).
29   Franco, 'Going Public: Reinhabiting the Private', in *Critical Passions: Selected Essays*, p.57.

child with the revealing statement, "I was rather out of place in the picture"'. John Beverley interprets the story as 'about subalternity and representation – in this case, about how the subaltern represents the dominant subject to itself, and thus unsettles that subject, in the form of a negation or displacement: "I was rather out of place in the picture".'[30] However, as Bhabha points out, the power of supplementarity is not necessarily in the form of negation of the pre-constituted social contradictions but rather 'in the renegotiation of those times, terms and tradition through which we turn our uncertain, passing contemporaneity into the signs of history'.[31] What is perhaps most evocative is his insistence that the supplement does not 'simply confront the pedagogical, or powerful master-discourse with a contradictory or negating referent. It does not turn contradiction into a dialectical process. It interrogates its object by initially withholding its objective'.[32] Returning again to the refusal of the supplementary to adopt a strictly oppositional relation to the master-discourse, it evokes the ambivalent positioning of Mexican women writers as they stake out their locations within the intellectual sphere. Bhabha concludes: 'Insinuating itself into the terms of reference of the dominant discourse, the supplementary antagonises the implicit power to generalize, to produce the sociological solidity'.[33] It is in these lines, thus, that the political potential of the supplement is fully realised. By insinuating herself into the terms of reference, the Mexican woman writer participates in a project of unsettling dominant discourse, compensating for the minus in the origin. It is on this process of 'unsettling' that much of my argument will focus.

---

30 *Subalternity and Representation*, p.26. For Lacan's account of the incident, see *The Four Fundamental Concepts of Psycho-Analysis* (New York: Norton, 1981), pp.95–6.
31 *Nation and Narration*, p.306.
32 *Nation and Narration*, p.306.
33 *Nation and Narration*, p.306.

Ambivalence, Modernity, Power

I have chosen, what might be termed, 'keywords' to frame my discussion of the Mexican *boom femenino*. These three words – ambivalence, modernity and power – permeate the readings of all seven writers in five separate chapters. Ambivalence is popularly defined as the simultaneous coexistence of contradictions (often emotional). In many cases this leads to a state of uncertainty or fluctuation between two opposites.[34] I use the term here, conscious of its etymology from the Latin *ambi* ('both') and *valentia* ('strength'). Used in this context, it evokes notions of strength and vigour as well as connoting fluctuation and contradiction. Over the course of my research into the writing by Mexican women, it seemed to capture effectively the impossible situation of many of the fictional characters explored in these writers' texts. Furthermore, by linking it in a more general way to the writers' own position vis-à-vis traditional structures of cultural power, it seemed extraordinarily apt.[35] Elissa J. Rashkin employs the term in her study on Mexican film-makers, sounding a note of caution against the frequently optimistic portrait of changing women's roles and pointing out that:

> the many women who have entered the work force since the 1970s have not done so out of personal ambition but out of necessity. With the increasing dependence of the Mexican economy on male migration to the U.S., many women have been forced to sustain their families by entering the unstable informal sector or working in low-wage border industries. Thus the notion of women's increased economic mobility must be taken with caution understanding that the increased privileges enjoyed by a few women are

34 The English term 'ambivalence' is from the German, *ambivalenz* (based on the model of *equivalence*) which was coined by the German psychologist Eugen Bleuler and stems from his work with schizophrenic and autistic patients. It has passed from being a psychological term to one of broader usage.

35 I was first struck by the appropriateness of the term while researching for an article on Brianda Domecq's novel, *La insólita historia de la Santa Teresa de Cabora*. See 'Reading Ambivalence: Order, Progress and Female Transgression in *La insólita historia de la Santa de Cabora* by Brianda Domecq', *Revista Canadiense de Estudios Hispánicos*, Vol.29, No.2 (Winter 2005), pp.413–27.

paralleled by a far more widespread social and economic instability whose effect on the majority of women has been ambivalent at best.[36]

Nikki Craske also employs the term in her examination of the role played by women in national discourses during the 1980s.[37] Her analysis links ambivalence directly to the modernising processes at work in Mexico during the 1980s, most notably, the regime of Carlos Salinas de Gortari (1988–1994). Modernity therefore is also a key term in this re-conceptualisation of women's roles in the economic, political and cultural arenas.[38] As I noted earlier, *modernización*, or the implementation of neo-liberal economic policy created opportunities for women within the work-force that were hitherto denied. It is widely acknowledged that neo-liberalism depends largely on the feminisation of the global work-force with the concomitant results of poor working conditions and lack of job security. In many ways, the women writers who have emerged from the modernising period in Mexico have benefited sufficiently from that agenda to envision a life beyond the domestic sphere. Craske points out that, 'Salinas used women as a symbol of modern Mexico, emphasising their increased political participation and various policy initiatives to demonstrate Mexico's commitment to democratisation'.[39] He devoted much energy to the promotion of progressive images of women as modern workers

36 *Women Filmmakers in Mexico: the Country of Which We Dream* (Austin: University of Texas Press, 2001), p.18.
37 'Ambiguities and Ambivalences in Making the Nation: Women and Politics in 20th Century Mexico', *Feminist Review*, Vol.79 (2005), pp.116–33.
38 I use the term, modernity, as a term to describe the general process whereby Enlightenment values (progress, freedom, democracy) are imposed or adopted. In a recent study, Jorge Larraín defines the entire historical period since Independence in Latin America as 'a process of the construction of modernity' and concludes that, 'It may be well that Latin American modernity is not the same as the European one, but neither is it totally disconnected from it. Latin American modernity is a hybrid that is neither purely endogenous nor totally imposed from without'. *Identity and Modernity in Latin America* (Cambridge: Polity Press, 2000), p.140. The term, *modernización*, on the other hand, refers more specifically to the neo-liberal economic policies in force in Mexico to various degrees since the 1940s.
39 'Ambiguities and Ambivalences in Making the Nation: Women and Politics in 20th Century Mexico', p.127.

and contributors to the Mexican state. On the other hand, neo-liberal reforms depend on 'women's reproductive roles being largely maintained in their traditional forms'.[40] There is, therefore, an essential ambivalence in the neo-liberal project that encourages women to participate actively in the making of profits for the nation while it leaves their roles as home-makers and mothers unprotected and unsupported. In this way, ambivalence is inextricably linked to women's role in modernity, an argument that has relevance on a wider scale and does not just apply to late twentieth century Mexico. Both of these concepts lead inexorably to questions of power and control. I choose to retain these categories as central to my arguments and to the premise of the book, in keeping with a feminist position that sees political change as a fundamental goal. In this way, the position of women writers within an increasingly complicated 'literary apparatus'[41] is central to the ways in which the books are bought, read and interpreted (in that order). The undeniable power exercised by literature in the competition for cultural legitimacy is not to be underestimated. In this way, women writers play a crucial role in re-aligning detrimental power structures that marginalise and exclude.

The book is divided into five chapters. Chapter One takes the nation as its primary focus and examines the ways in which Sara Sefchovich and Silvia Molina engage with, consume and enthusiastically devour the nation construct. Chapter Two isolates narrative as a crucial tool in the preservation of feminine subjectivity in the work of Brianda Domecq and Susana Págano. These texts grapple with the notion of empowerment through narrative while they exemplify, on a parallel level, the robust engagement of both authors with a national canon that seeks to constrain and exclude. Chapter Three avoids primary textual analysis to focus instead on the reception

40 Nikki Craske, 'Ambiguities and Ambivalences in Making the Nation: Women and Politics in 20th Century Mexico', p.127.
41 This term is taken from Alberto Moreiras, *The Exhaustion of Difference*, p.2. Katie King uses the phrase, 'apparatus of literary production' to refer to the emergence of literature at the intersection of art, business and technology. Cited by Donna Haraway, 'Situated Knowledges: the Science Question in Feminism and the Privilege of Partial Perspective', in *Space, Gender and Knowledge: Feminist Readings*, pp.53–72, pp.67–68.

of Angeles Mastretta's first two novels. In this chapter, I investigate the different 'players' in the literary 'game' including the writer, the reader, the critic and the publisher. In this way, I aim to shed new light on the ways in which cultural authority is being negotiated in contemporary Mexico. Chapter Four moves to the primary texts of writers, Guadalupe Loaeza and Rosamaría Roffiel. In my study of their work, I examine an intertextual link to Rosario Castellanos that illuminates their exploration of the meanings of class in modern urban Mexico. Chapter Five returns again to the work of Silvia Molina and Sara Sefchovich. In this chapter, however, I look at the way in which spaces outside Mexico are privileged in their texts and assess the extent to which this dialogue between the national and the transnational implies a potentially fruitful alliance.

As outlined in the previous section to the introduction, the book investigates new theoretical terrain as a possible way of addressing very pragmatic feminist questions relating to literature, women and cultural power. One of the many dilemmas of a poststructuralist feminist position includes the tension produced by the emphasis in poststructuralism on the fundamental instability of meanings and the political necessity for feminism for the category of women to make sense in some way. And yet, as Gibson-Graham underline/s, 'we need to pose the question if we accept that there is no unity, centre or actuality to discover for women, what is feminist research about? How can we negotiate the multiple and decentred identities of women?'[42] She/They suggest(s) 'imagining a research strategy' for feminism through metaphors of creation and interaction. She/They note(s), in a striking similarity to Bhabha that these metaphors can, 'produce alternative discourses that entail new subject positions, *supplementing or supplanting those that currently exist*' (my emphasis).[43] Through an analysis of the creative work of certain women writers in Mexico, I explore the new subject positions of these Mexican women writers examining the ways in which cultural power is crystallised in new sites as a result. Various categories are chosen – nation, family, narrative, class and space – and configured as lenses through which to

---

42   'Stuffed if I know!', in *Space, Gender, Knowledge: Feminist Readings*, p.125.
43   *Ibid.*, p.141.

focalise cultural production by women in Mexico. Each of the categories informs and shapes the other forming a series of interconnected and fundamental questions central to feminist research. To return to Moreiras, I am interested in the 'interstitial sparks' generated by the collision between conflicting notions of womanhood and modern Mexico as constructed in these texts.[44] Of course, as Moreiras reminds us:

> If there is tendentially no conceivable exterior or outside to the global system, then all our actions are seemingly condemned to reinforce it. So-called oppositional discourse runs the most unfortunate risk of all: that of remaining blind to its own conditions of production as yet another kind of systemic discourse.[45]

If there is no space outside of modernity and the forces of globalisation then it is even more important that we examine the circumstances through which women writers have staked out influential positions within Mexico and the provocative new subject positions they offer through their texts. The fragmented, contradictory, unstable picture that emerges from this study bears testimony to its unstable conditions of production. The words, 'fragmented', 'contradictory', 'fleeting' and 'unstable' have become an established part of the poststructuralist and postmodernist lexicon. However, if these 'established' concepts, which themselves ironically underline the theoretical hegemony of the supposed instability of meaning that poststructuralism upholds, are to make any sense for a modern feminist project, they must form part of a wider oppositional politics that might enable new female identities to emerge and to exist alongside older ones that continually re-invent themselves. What is crucially important is that analysis of cultural production continues to happen while being filtered through an optic of gender, in ways that will draw attention to

44 The use of the term 'interstitial sparks' is one of many concepts by Moreiras, Beverley and others that I invoke in this study. While it is clear that my study critiques the limitations of what might be termed 'Latin American Cultural Studies texts' certainly as they pertain to questions of gender and power, it is firmly located within the debate around Latin American cultural studies and is intended as another voice in dialogue with those already in the arena.
45 *The Exhaustion of Difference*, pp.40–1.

the continuing struggles of women in Mexico to be heard, recognised and valued.

Chapter One
Place, Nation and History in Sara Sefchovich and Silvia Molina

'In a country like this',[1] writes Angeles Mastretta, shortly after the publication of her best-selling novel, *Arráncame la vida* (1985), and so conveys a sense of the frustration, pride, awe and anxiety that so often forms a part of the ambivalent relationship between citizens and their 'imagined community'.[2] Emanating from her words also is a distinct awareness of responsibility along with anxiety, felt more widely perhaps by women writers, as they negotiated their place within an intellectual sphere that was only just at the end of the 1980s, beginning to expand its boundaries to admit them.[3] In this chapter, I

1   Phrase taken from an interview with Angeles Mastretta: 'Creo que la literatura *en un país como éste* es un lujo y que por eso es una doble responsabilidad [...] tienes todavía más la responsabilidad de contar lo que mucha más gente no va a contar, de recuperar otras voces, las voces de gente que no va a poder hablar jamás'. (my emphasis). Ron Teichman, 'Angeles Mastretta: Con la precisión del arrebato', *Nexos* (April 1987), p.7.
2   This phrase belongs of course to Benedict Anderson's now classic thesis on nationalism and national identity, *Imagined Communities: Reflections on the Origins and Spread of Nationalism* (London: Verso, 1983). Much feminist research takes issue with Anderson noting his lack of consideration of gender and the place of women within the symbolic system. See for example, Anne McClintock, 'No Longer in a Future Heaven: Gender, Race and Nationalism', in *Imperial Leather: Race, Gender and Sexuality in the Colonial Context* (New York: Routledge 1994), pp.352–90. See also, Yira Nuval-Davis, *Gender and Nation* and Caren Kaplan, Norma Alarcón and Minoo Moallem (eds), *Between Woman and Nation: Nationalism, Transnational Feminisms, and the State* (Durham: Duke University Press, 1999).
3   Margo Glantz reminds us of the 'aparición de una vasta producción de literatura femenina' since 1968. Talking about Josefina Vicens, Amparo Dávila, Emma Dolujanoff, Luisa Josefina Hernández, Elena Garro and Rosario Castellanos in the 1950s and Poniatowska, Mastretta, Fernández de Alba, Seligson, Jacobs,

would like to examine novels by two other women writers, who were jostling for authorial position during this period, Sara Sefchovich's *Demasiado amor* (1990) and Silvia Molina's *El amor que me juraste* (1998). Sara Sefchovich is a sociologist and researcher and has published numerous essay collections and three novels. Her first novel, the subject of this study, won the Premio Agustín Yáñez and her second, *La señora de los sueños* (1993) was also a best seller and has been translated into seven languages. *Demasiado amor* appeared in 1990, just at the end of the crisis-ridden 1980s and at the beginning of the tumultuous nineties. Published eight years later, Silvia Molina's award-winning novel, *El amor que me juraste*, is set during 1994 and thus the time-frame of both books is remarkably similar. It should also be pointed out that *El amor que me juraste* is just one in a long line of successful novels published by Molina since 1977. *La mañana debe seguir gris* won the prestigious Premio Xavier Villaurrutia in that year and her other novels, *Ascensión Tun* (1983), *La familia vino del norte* (1987) and *Imagen de Héctor* (1990) were also critical successes. It is clear then that both writers inhabit the Mexican intellectual sphere from the mid-1970s onwards and are active participants in the *boom femenino* in Mexican literature from that time.

As has been explored in the introduction, this time-frame exerts particular significance in this study. It is widely accepted that the oil scare and the devaluation of the peso in 1982 triggered an unprecedented political, economic and social crisis that had ramifications throughout civil society. This led, as Roger Bartra asserts, to a serious erosion of the ruling party, the PRI's popular base and produced serious splits and shifts within the unity of the 'revolutionary family'. It is out of these splits and shifts that the 'women's voice' finally be-

Esquivel, Molina, Boullosa in the 1980s, she asserts, 'la proliferación de la literatura femenina responde a una proliferación de nuevas formas, de cambios radicales en el país. Las infancias han cambiado: las narradoras que tardan de recrearla quizá debieran enfrentarse a lo desverbal, a lo ingobernable, a lo que se desdibuja y trata de configurar otro diseño, cuya lectura sería importante descifrar'. 'Las hijas de la malinche', in *Esguince de Cintura: Ensayos sobre narrativa mexicana del Siglo XX* (Mexico: Consejo Nacional para la Cultura y las Artes, 1994), pp.182–3.

gins to emerge in Mexico, emphatic and determined to explore their very differently-positioned subjectivities with regard to Mexico and *mexicanidad*. This voice resonates throughout the labour market, the intellectual and cultural sphere and even begins to penetrate the formal political spectrum. Women's increased presence in the labour force leads to a disposable income that enables them for the first time to become both consumers and producers of culture. They are, therefore, deeply implicated in the modernisation project of that decade and owe their voice to the gaps created in the traditional make-up of Mexican civil society.[4] As a result, there is an ambivalence inherent in the nature of the women's voice that begins to emerge, a new freedom that is enabled and empowered through forces that were also in many cases, deeply repressive. This ambivalence haunts the pages of both these texts penetrating content, form, structure and location. It is the nature of this ambivalent relationship to the nation in particular that I would like to examine in this chapter.

I would specifically like to answer the many questions that arise from an exploration of these two novels in the context of discourses about the nation, history and the place of women in 1980s Mexico. The texts lend themselves to discussion together not just because of the ostensible preoccupation with love evident in both their titles. They are written a decade apart and yet share in common an almost obsessive concern with place and its relationship to identity, both imagined and real. In a country, for example where the myth of 'discovery' has been so wholly deconstructed both literally and figuratively, what does it mean to produce narratives that are almost pathologically dedicated to discovering and exposing themselves? Is their frantic attempt to re-inscribe the nation a type of imperialist nostalgia for a glorious past? Furthermore, they both interrogate the

---

4   As Roger Bartra asserts, 'Faced with the terrible blows of the open economic crisis of 1982 and the symptoms of a latent political crisis, the leaders of the system – especially the technocrats – have proposed a "new" policy that can be summed up in one word: modernisation'. 'The Crisis of Nationalism', in *Blood, Ink and Culture: Miseries and Splendors of the Post-Mexican Condition* (Durham and London: Duke University Press, 2002), p.107.

nation in innovative ways contesting its systems of cultural representation and women's roles both as boundary and metaphoric limit.[5] Explored through the discourses of travel writing, it becomes clear that both these texts profoundly rupture the framework of power relations governing the travel genre, subverting its conventions and reinventing the parameters.

Demasiado amor

Demasiado amor tells the story of Beatriz, an orphan of lower middle-class origin who initially works as a clerical worker, but who later becomes a successful prostitute in Mexico City. It uses a fragmented epistolary format that alternates chapters addressed to a male lover with letters sent to the narrator's sister in Italy. The letters to the sister tell the story of the negotiation of the sisters' shared dream of a *casa de huéspedes* by the sea, and also make reference to the various events in her sister's life including her marriage and the birth of her children. The chapters addressed to the lover detail the couple's weekend journeys through Mexico and their experiences of local culture, food, markets and landscape. The story ends as the relationship breaks down and Beatriz's business escalates to the point where she dedicates her life to the service of the many clients who inhabit her apartment, which has been converted into a kind of naturalist paradise and where the clients engage in meditation and conversation. At the end of the novel, the reader learns that the travel sections addressed to 'tú' are actually notebook entries that she has sent to her sister in Italy as a chronicle of her life with this man.

Reading the narrative through discourses of travel writing shows how *Demasiado amor* represents an emphatic break with the

5   See Anne McClintock on women's role within discourses of the nation. 'No Longer in a Future Heaven: Gender, Race and Nationalism', in *Imperial Leather: Race, Gender and Sexuality in the Colonial Context*, pp.352–90.

conventions of that genre. It is this breakdown that ultimately leads the protagonist to the highly problematic utopian otherworld that forms her haven in the closing pages. What remains imperative in any examination of this novel, is an analysis of how the travel sections function and to what extent they interpellate the reader within their ideological framework. The travel sections are largely written in the second person, the narrator describing how 'tú' led her to consume various places, foods, ceramics, monuments and buildings. The sections are in some cases relatively straightforward,[6] but in other cases, constitute a form of linguistic bombardment of the reader with interminable lists of things and places. In these sections, any notion of realist description is thoroughly deconstructed as the reader wades through an exaggerated enumeration of places typically familiar to an average tourist. Consider the following as an example of the more straightforward sections:

> Me arrastraste a Yucatán en la frontera y a Monterrey en la frontera y en todas partes hacía calor, calor húmedo y calor seco. A Veracruz para que viera yo el golfo y a Mazatlán para que nadie me contara del Pacífico y a Cancún para conocer el Caribe y a Baja California donde el mundo tiene su orilla (p.25).[7]

These measured descriptions disappear gradually, the pace of the narrative accelerates and the text becomes quite frenzied:

> Fuimos a Chacala y a Chacalilla, a Caleta y a Caletilla, a Iguala y a Igualapa, Tonala y Tonalapa, Xochimilco y Tochimilco, Michoacán y Mechoacán, Taxco y Tlaxco, Pinotepa Nacional y Pinotepa de don Luis. Fuimos a lugares con

6   In her fascinating reading of the novel, Alicia del Campo analyses the content of the travel sections according to three distinct categories: lo indígena, lo popular y lo moderno. 'Reterritorializando lo mexicano desde lo femenino en el contexto neoliberal: *Demasiado amor* de Sara Sefchovich', *New Novel Review*, Vol.2, No.2 (1995), pp.61–75.
7   All references are from *Demasiado amor* (Mexico City: Planeta: 1991) and will appear after the quotations in parentheses. Much of my argument on the novel is taken from my article, '"En un país como éste": Contesting the Nation, Resisting Modernity in *Demasiado amor* by Sara Sefchovich', *Bulletin of Hispanic Studies*, Vol.83, No.4 (2006), pp.367–84.

nombres extraños como Maní en Yucatán, Mar Muerto en Tehuantepec, Purísima del Rincón y San Francisco del Rincón, que se llaman así por estar en un rincón entre Guanajuato y Jalisco, a Polotitlán de la Ilustración en el Estado de Mexico, a San Felipe Torres Mochas, Arista de Luz, Lugar de Cinco Vientos, Espíritu Santo, Flecha de Aire, Marfil y Cañada de Negros (p.104).

As well as detailed outlines of places, there are also lists of things, objects, lavish descriptions and virtuoso linguistic displays that are meticulous and polished:

Me llevaste a visitar alfareros, ceramistas, orfebres, textileros. Me compraste tallados, estofados, moldeados, borados, laqueados, pintados, esculpidos, deshilados, tejidos, decorados, soplados, horneados, cincelados, teñidos, martillados, recortados y picados (p.112).

At first glance, the text seems to have little in common with other travel writing by women so comprehensively examined by Mary Louise Pratt in her study, *Imperial Eyes*.[8] Absent are many of the characteristics attributed to travel writing by women in the colonial era with their focus on relationships, domestic details and their preference for a 'sentimental' type of narration.[9] The narrative in the travel sections in *Demasiado amor* actually emerges from the male lover's lead-

8   Pratt's study examines the work of Maria Graham and Flora Tristán in depth and while it clearly deals with writing from a very different time period, many of its insights are relevant to *Demasiado amor*. See Mary Louise Pratt, *Imperial Eyes: Travel Writing and Transculturation* (London: Routledge, 1992), Sara Mills, *Discourses of Difference: An Analysis of Women's Travel Writing and Colonialism* (London: Routledge, 1991), and Sidonie Smith, *Moving Lives: Twentieth Century Women's Travel Writing* (University of Minnesota Press, 2001). See also Claire Lindsay's excellent discussion of domestic travel writing in Latin America, *Locating Latin American Women Writers* (New York: Peter Lang, 2003).

9   Indira Ghose asserts that the differences between travel accounts by women and men are not differences of essence but rather of foci and interest, a notion also underscored in Pratt's work. See Indira Ghose, *Women Travellers in Colonial India: The Power of Female Gaze* (Oxford: Oxford University Press, 1998). Furthermore, the focus on relationships and domestic detail highlighted by Pratt is present in *Demasiado amor* though not in the travel sections *per se* but rather in the letters exchanged between the sisters.

34

ing of Beatriz, and his showing her the splendours of their native country. Indeed in this way, the book conforms more closely to the type of text attributed to male travel writers. Caren Kaplan observes the close connections between metaphors of travel and (Euro-American) modernism, linking the two notions through the concept of the 'gentleman traveller'. She writes that the 'traveller who occupies a primary place in this formation can be characterised as a Western individual, usually male, "white" of independent means, an introspective observer, literate, acquainted with ideas of arts and culture and, above all, a humanist'.[10] Sefchovich plays with the idea of the 'gentleman traveller' in this text juxtaposing details about his range of cultural knowledge with graphic depictions of his sexual control over the narrator:

> Dos días y dos noches que me tuviste desnuda, echada sobre la cama, parada junto a la ventana, a gatas sobre el tapete, debajo de la regadera, sentada en el escusado, subida en el lavamano, volando sobre las sillas para hacerme el amor (p.12).

This description is clearly at odds with Kaplan's notion of the 'gentleman traveller' with its emphasis on the imposition of male sexual power and the wielding of control. The more 'humanist' aspects are nonetheless upheld in other areas of the text:

> ¡Cuántas historias te sabías! [...] Otro día me contaste de Lizardi y Prieto que escribieron cosas divertidas, de Altamirano que hacía llorar y de Rabasa que hacía pensar. Un día me leíste a Azuela, otro a Rulfo el triste y otro más a Fuentes el elegante (pp.125–6).

In these and other similar passages he is presented as the archetypal bourgeois male subject, both educated and enlightened who plays the role of teacher and educator to Beatriz. He is also searching for an enlightened past: 'Me acuerdo cuando te dio por recorrer los hoteles que algún día fueron famosos y distinguidos. Como si tuvieras una deuda pendiente con el país que fue éste hace cincuenta, hace cuarenta años' (p.7). In some ways, this seems typical of the kind of imperialist

10   *Questions of Travel: Postmodern Discourses of Displacement*, p.50.

nostalgia for a glorious past and in particular for the Mexico of the 1940s and the start of the economic miracle which was to last until 1968.[11] This lamenting of an era that is gone, 'tu peregrinar por la nostalgia de años que se fueron hace mucho y de gente que ya se murió pero que algún día fue muy rica?' (pp.7–8), and more specifically, the attraction of rich people, permeates the text and is paralleled in the letter pages by the protagonist and her sister's struggle for money. Furthermore, the idea of a debt with the past raises interesting questions in itself about modern Mexico's ambivalent relationship with the past, an ambivalence that permeates the novel throughout. Indeed as Kaplan points out, 'the production of "tourist experiences" depends upon a specifically modern world that is marked by an ambivalent relationship to the past'.[12] Dilemmas about modernity thus infuse the novel not least through the dialectical relationship formed between the traveller (and his companion) and the communities to which they travel.

Furthermore, the colonial discourse that is so central to the travel genre, is always present and most acutely perceived through the authoritative male voice who 'shows' his female companion her *patria*. This mastery of landscape – so pivotal to early examples of travel writing – is perhaps rather distorted here. Instead of panoramic descriptions of landscape, there are instead exhausting lists of places, monuments, churches and regional cuisine:

> Me trajiste por los altos de Chapas y los bajos de Tabasco, por los altos y los bajos del mismísimo Jalisco, del mismísimo Querétaro. Un día te pedí que me llevaras a Puerta del Cielo y me llevaste a Cadereyta, te pedí ir a Tepeji del Río y me llevaste a San Juan del Río. Un día me dijiste que íbamos a Atotonilco y me llevaste a Guanajuato, que íbamos a Atotonilco y me llevaste a Hidalgo, que íbamos a Atotonilco y me llevaste a Jalisco (p.104).

11   See Héctor Aguilar Camín and Lorenzo Meyer for an excellent overview of this period. *In the Shadow of the Mexican Revolution: Contemporary Mexican History, 1910–1989*, trans. by Luis Alberto Fierro (Austin: University of Texas Press), 1993.

12   Caren Kaplan, *Questions of Travel: Postmodern Discourses of Displacement*, p.58. See also Dennison Nash, 'Tourism as an Anthropological Subject', *Current Anthropology*, Vol. 22, No.5 (October 1981), pp.461–81.

This bewildering assault on the reader which is repeated continually in the novel clearly indicates mastery on one level – if only over language – but is further compounded by the overdetermined use of the second person singular tense to convey the sense of 'leading' and 'showing' the way to the beauties and hidden mysteries of Mexico:

> Porque tú me enseñaste este país. Tú me llevaste y me trajiste, me subiste y me bajaste, me hiciste conocerlo y me hiciste amarlo. Me llevaste a Guanajuato y a San Miguel de Allende (p.24).

In a later passage, he conquers her, treading the territory in an almost clichéd portrayal of the imperial conquistador, 'En Jalapa me llevaste [...] En León me compraste zapatos y dijiste que así debía ser. En Taxco me compraste aretes y dijiste que así debía ser [...] Y siempre dijiste que así debía ser' (p.37). What is more, the alignment between the ability to travel and consume the national territory, and the ability to consume goods is carefully established, consumption being a central trope of the narrative as a whole. What resonates most in these passages, though, is the foregrounding of the *tú* voice, particularly given the cumbersome grammatical form (–aste, –iste) of the second person singular in Spanish. The emphatic ending of the *tú* voice therefore announces with authority and power its own central presence. Furthermore, the to-ing and fro-ing of the syntax and the rhythm of the second person preterite ending also replicates a sense of movement and travelling back and forth. Yet, I contend that by its very definition, the *tú* form complicates its own authoritative status as it always requires the presence of the enunciative 'I' for legitimacy. The use of the familiar *tú* form also evokes a sense of intimacy with the other speaker, the female narrator. This draws attention to the dialectic relationship, and even from the beginning punctures the notion of absolute mastery over either text or landscape, a mastery that is thoroughly deconstructed by the end of the novel.

The War between Pronouns

This process of deconstruction begins early in the text and is located primarily in the struggle over and between pronouns, a 'travelling' between the *tú* and the *yo* voices that leads ultimately to a radical break with any notion of authority. Initially the conflict is signalled by the disjunction between what 'he' sees and what 'she' sees, a disjunction that becomes more pronounced as the text progresses. The *yo* voice becomes stronger, however, as the narrative continues: 'Me acuerdo de la maleza. [...] De todo me acuerdo, de todo. De las velas gordas, perfumadas y de colores de Cuernavaca. [...] De todo me acuerdo. [...] De todo eso me acuerdo, de todo' (pp.30–1). Here, the female narrator gradually affirms the importance of her memory and inserts herself into the narrative: 'Siempre supiste cómo me gustaban las tardes [...] De todas mis memorias contigo, las que me conmueven son las de esas tardes llenas de luz, a esa hora en que todo guarda silencio. Recuerdo siempre los sonidos' (p.36). The brief wielding of control, however, is reversed when the *tú* voice returns for the rest of this section, 'me llevaste de día a un museo [...] me llevaste de día a oír mariachis [...] me llevaste de día al Zócalo y de noche a oír canciones de amor' (p.37). These passages at times read like curious sections from a language exercise class in which all permutations of a given idea are rehearsed, as though the rehearsal of all possible linguistic forms, all possible voyages, all possible forms of identity are carefully worked through and then discarded, one by one.

The wavering between subject positions, from *tú* to *yo* to *nosotros* occurs throughout the first three-quarters of the novel. At times we are immersed in the second person narrative, at others we are drawn to her visions, her versions of events. At still other times, the reader is compelled to view them as a single unit:

> En todas partes comíamos frutas, mandarinas y mangos, guayabas y guanábanas, mameyes, capulines, y tejocotes, jícamas y papayas, zapotes de tres colores y chicozapotes de color café, membrillos y limas, naranjas, manzanas, plátanos, sandías, piñas y melones. Comimos tunas. [...] Vimos arreglos de frutas y tapetes de frutas [...] Vimos mujeres que cargaban jícaras con fruta,

canastas con fruta, rebozos con bordados de fruta y macetas con dibujos de frutas (p.90).

In passages such as these, the subjects are sutured together and the distinct visions presented in the other passages become fused. The overall impression at first, aside from the exhaustion of wading through the various lists, is the fluidity of the subject position, from his to hers (yours to mine), to theirs (ours) as the reader navigates the heterogeneous, fragmented image of Mexico that emerges, an image that is never fixed, never static but always shifting from place to place. Rather than functioning as an allegorical illustration of the vicissitudes and evolution of their relationship, however, in this case, the journey is the relationship, the 'voyage without objective' reminiscent of Jean Baudrillard's travelogues, the frenzied consumption of a nation and its assets. In this sense the narrative conforms closely to Baudrillard's notion of the trip with no end, and firmly locates it within a post-modern framework of travel deconstructed to the point of absurdity:

> You have to travel, keep on the move. You have to cross oceans, cities, con-tinents, latitudes. Not to acquire a more informed vision of the world – there is no universality any more, no possible synthesis of experience, nor even, strictly speaking, is there any pleasure of an 'aesthetic' or 'picturesque' variety to be had from travel – but in order to get as near as possible to the world-wide sphere of exchange, to enjoy ubiquity, cosmopolitan extraversion, to escape the illusion of intimacy. Travel as a line of flight, the orbital voyaging of the age of Aquarium.[13]

Certainly the travel descriptions constitute a linguistic line of flight and the text debunks any notion of a uniform aesthetic pleasure to be gained from travel in a way that also seems to invoke Baudrillard's utterly chaotic world. The text resists, however, absolute descent into chaos and thus challenges a purely postmodern reading of its aesthetic vision. I shall return to this link between nation, consumption and lan-guage in the concluding section of the chapter.

13   Jean Baudrillard, *Cool Memories* trans. by Chris Turner (London: Verso, 1981), pp.168–9.

Initially, thus, the wavering subject positions signal a profound discomfort with fixed locations and static images, an unease that is palpable in the many descriptions of the 'emergency situation' that is Mexico at the end of the 1980s. When Miguel de la Madrid took over the presidency in 1982 shortly after the nationalisation of the banks, he delivered a dramatic speech to the nation, a speech that was punctuated by the word 'crisis'. Indeed words such as 'perish', 'paralysis', 'acute' and 'severe', among others reverberate throughout in a way that encapsulates the sense of anxious helplessness pervasive during the time:

> We live in an emergency situation. It is not a time for hesitation or feuds; it is the time for decisions and responsibility. We shall not allow ourselves to succumb to inertia. The situation is intolerable. We shall not allow our fatherland to perish in our hands. We will act with decisiveness and firmness.[14]

It is little wonder that a text produced during such a national crisis will itself construct such a fraught relationship between protagonists and nation. It is also, however, from out of this emergency, as noted earlier, that new authorities, new 'I' voices emerge to contest the older systems of domination and hegemony. On a parallel level, it is clearly a time of opportunity for real, not just fictional, voices to materialise and explains in part the dramatic rise of women's voices in the cultural arena during this time. In the rest of this section, I would like to document how the new 'I' voice establishes itself within Sefchovich's text.

14   *In the Shadow of the Mexican Revolution*, p.220.

Mexico Uncovered

Amid myriad accounts of trips in which the descriptions seem to spiral out of control, a turning point occurs with the incisive insertion of 'no' into the travel narrative, a 'no' that heralds the breakdown, not just of the voyages as they had been unfolding, but of all linguistic and social order. It starts off in a muted and understated fashion: 'Pero un día las cosas se empezaron a poner difíciles. No quisiste llevarme a conocer los prostíbulos de Ciudad Juárez y yo me enojé. No quisiste llevarme a beber a los antros de Tijuana y yo me enojé. No quisiste ir a bailar' (p.145). What starts as a logical, if somewhat incongruous series of references to his sudden unwillingness to 'show' her the spectacle of Mexico, becomes an irrational and arbitrary series of refusals on his part without explanation:

> No entramos a Iguala y no nos quedamos a desayunar en un restorán del camino, no nos detuvimos en Tulancingo para comer en un restorán. [...] No me dejaste comer raspados de colores y camotes en los carritos de las esquinas. No me dejaste montar en Ixtapán ni nadar en el mar abierto de Mazatlán. No me dejaste probar el pozol de los indios de Chiapas ni el chocolate de las indias de Oaxaca ni el pulque de los indios de todas partes (p.147).

His absolute authority is ominously underlined in the text by several references to his violent hobbies: 'Y yo no quise ir contigo a Yucatán a ver maltratar a los cebúes, ni a Matlapaní a ver degollar a los gallos, ni te acompañé a cazar liebres y venados en Chihuahaua, ni a las corridas de toros en las plazas ni a las peleas de gallos en los palenques' (p.147). The violence of the activities in the above passage further upholds his sense of mastery and the control he wields throughout the travel sections of the narrative. The realism of the narrative such as it existed, unravels as the negatives become more prominent: 'No pudimos detenernos en todas partes, en tantas selvas que había en el sur y tantos bosques que había en el norte, en tantos desiertos que había en el norte y tantas lagunas que encontrábamos en el sur' (p.152). But just as the reader starts to become accustomed to what is seemingly a random series of negatives, the reasons become apparent:

> No pudimos ir a Mulegé porque los gringos que llegan en sus barcos ocupan todos los hoteles, ni quedarnos en Acapulco porque los gringos que llegan en sus aviones ocupan todos los hoteles ni por lo mismo quedarnos en Huatulco ni en Cabo San Lucas ni en Cancún (p.152).

Thus what starts as a gentle critique of the deterioration of their travel conditions, leads into a frantic indictment of that process of *modernización* partly in place from the beginning of the 1970s, but which was energetically implemented by Miguel de la Madrid from 1982 onwards after the national crisis.[15] Pinpointing the 'gringos' as the reason behind the sudden halt in Beatriz and her lover's activities also poses an interesting dilemma for the/this *gringa* critic (herself a tourist in all these places) who is suddenly converted into the silent accused of the novel. The critiques quickly become sharper:

> Y entonces, precisamente cuando las cosas se empezaron a poner difíciles, descubrimos que la blusa deshilada no era de Aguascalientes sino del mercado de Tepoztlán, descubrimos que el rebozo de Santa María no cabía por el aro de un anillo porque no era de seda sino de imitación, que el marco no era de plata sino de latón, el sarape no era de lana sino sintético, el mantel no era del mercado sino de una tienda, el pantalón de manta no lo hicieron los indios sino una gringa de San Miguel, las macetas no eran de mayólica ni las mesas de laca ni la vainilla era pura porque tres veces recorrimos Papantla y no la pudimos encontrar (p.155).

This collapse of the myth of authenticity and purity, the illusion sustained in the previous pages leads in turn to the dramatic eruption of *lo feo* into the previously idyllic landscape:

> ¿Qué pasaba? ¿Qué nos sucedía? Cuando llegamos al Templo de la Consagración había desaparecido el Cristo de Marfil. Cuando llegamos al templo de Potzontepec habían desaparecido dos coronas de oro […] Faltaban marfiles en las catedrales, Cristos en las misiones, reliquias en las iglesias, muebles en los conventos, joyas en los museos, libros en las bibliotecas, piedras en las ruinas, faroles en las calles y hasta fuentes en los jardines.

15 This process was, of course, infamously continued by Salinas de Gortari in 1988 which culminated in the signing of North American Free Trade Agreement (NAFTA) and the violent *Zapatista* uprising, of which more in the next section.

> Un día llegamos a Tlacolula y había desaparecido el barquito de la fachada. Un día llegamos a Tula y habían desaparecido dos diosas. De Palenque, La Venta, Yucatán y Quintana Roo se habían llevado estelas, monolitos, cabezas, códices, y piedras. Un día llegamos a Actopan y los ricos tiraban el muro del Convento para construir sus casas. Un día llegamos a Guadalajara y los ricos tenían su casa amueblada con lo que sacaron de una iglesia [...] Y yo antes no me había fijado en nada de esto, en nada (p.156).

In the above passage sometimes blame is assigned (to 'los ricos' for example), in others, it seems to have simply happened ('había desaparecido'). The rot also extends to the bodies of the narrators themselves who become diseased:

> Y entonces pasó que un día nos dolió la garganta, un día tuvimos jaqueca y otro una infección intestinal. Un día fue una hemorragia, otro una caída, el tercero caspa y el cuarto salpullido. Un día nos dio una gripa muy fuerte y otro un cansancio atroz (p.155).

While this clearly signals, again, the total breakdown of any pretence at realist narrative, it is also a powerful reminder of the diseased body politic of Mexico in the 1980s. The juxtaposition of typically middle-class afflictions (sore throats, migraines) and the illnesses that commonly afflict the poor of a country (intestinal infections from poor hygiene, flu, skin diseases or rashes) reminds the reader of the utter collapse of the lines between middle-class and poor during these years. In fact the presence of the poor is acutely perceived throughout the text as evidenced in this early passage:

> Contigo vi a los indios, a los dueños del mundo, los tarahumaras tan flacos, los mixes tan pequeños, los de Cuetzalan vestidos de blanco, los de Janitzio pidiendo limosna, los de Oaxaca con sus ropas bordadas de flores, los de Chiapas tan desolados, los de Guerrero tan sensuales, los que venden serpientes y frutas en las orillas de los caminos, los que veneran al peyote en un cerro, los que tejen, los que amasan, los que rezan en un templo, los que venden en un mercado, los humildes, los agresivos, los enojados, los alegres y los tristes, *los pobres, siempre los pobres* (p.25, my emphasis).

In research concluded in December 1987, Aguilar Camín and Meyer point to the paradox that six years of economic crisis had made Mexican society more egalitarian, in the sense that now Mexicans were

43

'more equal in their poverty'. According to their calculations, 'the number of poor [...] had increased from 40 percent of the population to nearly 60 percent'.[16] This paradox is embedded in the narrative in sections like the one above, confounding realism while confirming collapse and decay. The phrase, 'un cansancio atroz', uttered by Beatriz in the earlier passage, aptly sums up the reaction of much of Mexico to the government's inability to cope with the worst economic crisis of its history.

If the intrusion of the 'no' may be read as an emphatic rejection of the power relations inherent in the previous sections, then what emerges to take its place here? What follows is a slow obliteration of the *tú* voice as it becomes subsumed into a solemn united *nosotros:*

> Vimos quemar llantas, pescar langostas y ostiones en tiempo de veda, barcos camaroneros encallados, una fuga de amoniaco, corrupción en los ingenios, maquiladoras en el norte y refugiados en el sur, leche rebajada con agua, contrabando de madera, fruta que se pudría en vagones y bodegas y demasiadas cosas más. Todo eso lo vimos y lo notamos, lo sentimos, por primera vez. ¿Por qué? ¿Qué nos sucedía que veíamos lo feo por doquier? (p.160).

Finally *lo feo* erupts from beneath the dazzling linguistic displays of national beauty and the beauty is exposed as illusion and myth. The rot is here defined as modernity, as exemplified in the incidence of corruption, gas leaks, the presence of *maquiladoras*, and the arrival of refugees in the south. For the first time, the narrative emerges from the frozen static time of its landscape descriptions preserved for touristic consumption, to enter into the chaotic modernity of Mexico in the 1980s. The references to 'real' elements of Mexico's present enter the text in force. They include the proliferation of *maquiladoras* on the northern border from the 1970s onwards and the gas leaks, mentioned in this passage (*fuga de amoniaco*) may be read as an allusion to the horrific tragedy of San Juan Ixhuatepec (San Juanico) in 1984 which caused untold death and destruction.[17] In addition, there is also a

16   *In the Shadow of the Mexican Revolution*, p.228.
17   Pemex's official explanation of the tragedy stated that there had been, 'un estallido como consecuencia de la fuga de gas'. For an excellent analysis of the

reference to the presence of large numbers of Central American refugees fleeing El Salvador and Guatemala, a trend which forced Mexico centre-stage to take the role of peacemaker in the region.[18]

Interestingly, it is from the unified perspective of *nosotros* that the filth and rot is contemplated. The position of the master – always under threat in the narrative from the encroaching *yo* and *nosotros* voices is finally, irrevocably altered. Thus the singular, authorising narratorial voice has been forced to contemplate the other side of the idyll and is then disappeared almost completely from the narrative as the *yo* voice takes over:

Empecé entonces a mirar, a notar, las tierras empinadas y agrestes, desgajadas, cortadas. Vi que la tierra en este país, que es el lugar sagrado que da el sustento, que organiza el tiempo, que sirve para trabajar, descansar, fecundar, morir y ser enterrado, era pobre y triste, era seca y pobre. Era ésta una tierra de milpas y chozas, de maíz chaparro y quelites, de frijol y chile, de tunas arrancadas al nopal y leches arrancadas al maguey. Sólo entonces lo vi. [...] Vi los lugares donde nunca llueve y como en ellos se secan la tierra y las gentes y vi también los lugares donde siempre llueve y cómo en ellos se inunda la tierra y se enferman las gentes. Vi la tierra que no alcanza para todos y también la tierra ociosa, sin trabajar y vi la fiebre y el calor, la pobreza, la tristeza y el miedo, la gente que duerme junto a su machete, la gente que cree en brujerías, la gente que vive con fantasmas. Todo eso vi (pp.162–3).

controversy surrounding the San Juanico tragedy, see Carlos Monsiváis, 'San Juanico: los hechos, las interpretaciones, las mitologías', in *Entrada libre: crónicas de la sociedad que se organiza* (Mexico: Ediciones Era 1987), pp.123–50, p.136.

18   Aguilar Camín and Meyer elaborate on these key aspects of life at this time including the Central American conflict and the new tensions it generated between US and Mexico. They outline how Mexico attempted a multi-lateral policy with Venezuela, Colombia and Panama in Contadora at the beginning of 1983. They also note the growing integration of the Mexican and US economies including the development of the *maquiladora* industry and the new automobile factories in Saltillo and Hermosillo, the incorporation of the Televisa group into the US communications network as the largest Spanish-language TV network in North America (Spanish International Network), and the recognition of PAN by the Republicans as the force that was closest to embodying the US ideal for its Mexican neighbour. See *In the Shadow of the Mexican Revolution*, pp.222–5.

With this betrayal of its people by the earth, the narrative suddenly uncovers the people within it for the first time, not the folkloric classification of peoples presented before, but people who live circumscribed by conditions of poverty, heat and fear that are beyond their control. The narrator questions herself:

> ¿Por qué entonces empezaba ahora a ver y a notar las cosas feas, las que no funcionaban, las que morían, las que se echaban a perder? ¿Por que empecé a sentir dificultad? No lo sabía, no lo supe entonces y tal vez nunca lo sabré. Pero en mí, algo muy fuerte sucedió, algo cambió (p.165).

It is tempting to read this, of course, as a 'toma de conciencia', a profound *desgarramiento* with the past, and in purely psychoanalytic terms, as the eruption of the repressed into the stark reality of the present. And yet, the narrative anchors itself at this point as a vicious indictment of a system that has broken down and failed in all its aspects: linguistic, political, sociological and telluric. It is this break-down that triggers the crisis in the relationship and leads to the escape to the utopia that occurs at the end of the novel. In postmodern terms, this is an apocalyptic vision of a world in tatters, where all the grand narratives have been demystified and destroyed. The rejection of the idealised heterosexual love union in 'el gran amor es imposible de soportar' (p.184) is followed by the almost inevitable rejection of God and the organising principle of religion, 'Yo lo había convertido en Dios y al Dios hay que arrastrarlo por los templos' (p.185). Retreat into an orgiastic utopia becomes the answer for the protagonist. Pleasure and intimacy are foregrounded and become the comfort and refuge from a system that has failed: 'Soy un personaje de la vida real porque conmigo se puede gozar, entrar en intimidad, sentirse bien, irse y atre-verse a volver' (p.178). The notion of pleasure returns again in the final pages: 'lo que se ve, se huele y se oye son nuestros placeres' (p.182). The emphasis on a different *nosotros* alludes to a world that includes her clients, friends and partners in a veritable paradise world of pleasure. On one level, this is clearly ironic as the central pro-tagonist is a prostitute, the crudest possible example of a modernised system of exchange and demand. And yet, the narrative also resists

this postmodern closure and forms a trenchant critique of the system –
the nation – in order to formulate the possibility of resistance.

History, Nation, Voice

This resistance is crystallised metaphorically through Beatriz's frank
rejection of middle-class familial relations. These have been parodied
throughout the text in the gentle juxtaposition of her unorthodox
promiscuous lifestyle with her sister's ultra-traditional life with her
husband and children in Italy. The following example contains ex-
clamations that might normally be reserved for reactions to Beatriz's
own life but here they are transposed onto her sister's utterly
conventional life with ironic effect: '¿Qué te pasa? ¿Hasta dónde pien-
sas llegar? ¿No te parece un exceso?' (p.169). The notion of excess is
ironically attached to the sister's conservative lifestyle and yet is
strangely absent from the parts of Beatriz's life where it might logic-
ally be applied, as, for example, to the list of lovers/clients attended by
her (pp.169–70). As the narrative closes, Beatriz reflects on the hypocrisies of bourgeois morality:

> Me seguí pensando en lo que dices de la vida estable y de sentar cabeza. ¿Tú
> crees que yo estoy hecha para eso? Fíjate, tengo un cliente que de plano me
> trajo a su esposa para que yo le enseñara como hacer divertida su vida mat-
> rimonial. Tengo otros que traen a sus hijos para que 'la pasen bien antes de
> casarse' (así dicen). Veo las caras de mis compañeras de oficina o de las
> meseras del Vips. ¿De verdad crees que ése es el camino? (pp.167–8).

This attack on the family leads to the envisioning of an alternative
familial relationship in which Beatriz and her clients are the principal
actors, 'Yo recibo de ellos un gran cariño. Son mis amigos, *son mi
familia*, me hacen feliz' (p.182, my emphasis). With this statement,
the narrator imagines a new family unit, radically different from the
conventional nuclear structure of her sister's family in Italy.

That Beatriz's 'vision' is different from the dominant view proffered through the *tú* voice is clear from early on. In an early description, the gulf between the two opposing world-views is striking:

> Por que tú me enseñaste este país. Tú me llevaste y me trajiste, me subiste y me bajaste, me hiciste conocerlo y me hiciste amarlo. Me llevaste a Guanajuato y a San Miguel de Allende donde decías que era la ruta de la Independencia pero yo sólo veía azulejos. Me llevaste a Oaxaca donde hablaste de Juárez el héroe y de Díaz el dictador, pero para mí era sólo un lugar lleno de huipiles y animales de madera pintada. Me llevaste a Orizaba y a Córdoba para contarme de Maximiliano pero yo sólo vi la neblina y los mariscos. Me llevaste a Michoacán por aquello de Cárdenas pero yo sólo me acuerdo de las guitarras y el cobre. Me llevaste a San Luis Potosí a ver un ayuntamiento en manos de la oposición pero yo sólo vi las enchiladas rojas y el agua de Lourdes. Me llevaste a Juchitán por lo mismo pero sólo vi a las mujeres gordas y fuertes que trabajaban sin parar (pp.24–5).

This fascinating passage constitutes an homage to the diversity and heterogeneity of Mexico, a veritable linguistic enactment of what Bartra terms, the crisis in Mexican revolutionary nationalism.[19] Indeed her vision is an almost stream-of-consciousness listing of words, a word association game, connecting up the dots between Cárdenas, guitars and copper, and between San Luis Potosí, political resistance, *enchiladas* and holy water from Lourdes. The language is carefully processed, polished, deliberated upon and the symmetry is almost irritating with each word placed meticulously. A triangular pattern is established, consisting of an 'official' historical figure or place contraposed with two completely contrasting elements. It is difficult not to read this in psychoanalytic terms, as a way of the subconscious or the repressed erupting to the surface to disturb the linear nature of the first concept (person or place). In this way, a bizarre re-working of the surrealist image occurs as further evidence of the surfacing of the subconscious.[20] It is also, however, a rather problematic enactment of

---

19   See 'The Crisis of Nationalism', in *Blood, Ink and Culture*, pp.104–32.
20   The artists of the surrealist movement attached tremendous importance to the perfectly constructed surrealist image. Lautréamont's acclaimed example of the surrealist image *par excellence* utilises this triangular structure: 'beau comme

dual histories, suggesting an opposition between history and *herstory*, a concept central to so much feminist research. In this case it is problematic because it simply reinforces the binary positions so often assigned to male and female: hers is the frivolous sensual memory while his is the logical, rational route of history and progress. Hers is the memory of objects and things and serves as a reminder of how she is deeply immersed in the economy of her country, informally as a prostitute, and formally as a tourist. Her refusal ('pero yo sólo vi') however, to countenance his view constitutes an interesting rejection of official histories and a resolute instatement of an alternative vision.

This fragmentation of Mexico's history, its literal splitting in two with one component in the first section of the image and two in the second, ruptures any possibility of historical continuity as attested by del Campo:

> La historia de México se presenta como una sucesión de anécdotas borrosas que no permiten visualizar una continuidad histórica con sentido, sino que se remiten más bien a trozos de información disperses e inconexos. La historia mexicana emerge, al igual que su territorialidad, como una entidad fragmentada desde la cual no es posible hacer sentido o establecer proyecciones futuras.[21]

Does this novel present, therefore, a fluid reconfiguring of the power dynamics inherent in the imagining of a nation? Do passages such as the one quoted above offer a new way of conceptualising the nation or do they simply lock it into a problematic binary relationship? And finally, if we accept that it is fluid, can it possibly be progressive given Beatriz's insertion as the female consumer and consumed?

In fact, Beatriz's different world-view raises many interesting questions about the position of female subjects in relation to configurations of nationhood and citizenship. Yuval-Davis's work on gender and nation leaves no doubt as to the different positioning of

---

[…] la rencontre fortuite sur une table de dissection d'une machine à coudre e d'un parapluie', Peter Nesselroth, *Lautréamont's Imagery: A Stylistic Approach* (Geneva: Droz, 1969), p.13.

21   'Reterritorializando lo mexicano', p.68.

female population vis-à-vis the national system.[22] In the text, the limits of both the family and the nation are radically called into question. The attack on the conventional family unit is accompanied by an attack on the notion of Mexico itself, a link which has wide theoretical currency. Anne McClintock reminds us that nations are figured through the iconography of familial and domestic space with nations evoked as 'motherlands' and 'fatherlands'. She goes on to outline how the family trope is important for nationalism in at least two ways: 'First, it offers a "natural" figure for sanctioning national *hierarchy* within a putative organic *unity* of interests. [...] The family offered an indispensable metaphoric figure by which national difference could be shaped into a single historical genesis narrative'.[23] In Latin America, of course, this 'familial' notion of the nation has particular resonance in the quasi-feudal system of land ownership and the relationship between the *patrón* and his tenants. In many cultural and historical constructions of this relationship, the *patrón* is figured as a benevolent father, looking after his family.[24] In this text, the only traditional family unit is displaced to Italy and we are left with a series of wandering, eccentric subjects performing various identities. The link between personal and national identity is rendered explicit in the following example in which Beatriz talks about one of her clients, 'un tipo que se disfraza, algunas veces de soldado, otras de cura y otras veces se envuelve en la bandera nacional y se ríe tanto que no lo podrías creer' (p.169). This constitutes a self-conscious reflection on

22 Nira Yuval-Davis, *Gender and Nation*.
23 'No Longer in a Future Heaven: Gender, Race and Nationalism', in *Imperial Leather*, p.357.
24 In Mexican cinema history, this figure is immortalised through the character of the *patrón* in *Allá en el rancho grande* (1936). See also *El compadre Mendoza* (1933). Examples of this kind of construction in literature are too numerous to mention, but Isabel Allende's Esteban García, from *La casa de los espíritus* and his plaintive insistence, 'Yo era como un padre para ellos' underlines how close a link existed between the roles of *padre* and patron. Isabel Allende, *La casa de los espíritus* (Barcelona: Plaza y Janés, 1998), p.63. For a good overview of the historical roots of this, see Alan Knight, *The Mexican Revolution: Porfirians, Liberals and Peasants*. Vol.1 (Cambridge: Cambridge University Press, 1986).

the performance of national identity as her client dresses up as a soldier and a priest, representing two opposite extremes of acceptable masculinities. As he finally wraps himself up in the Mexican flag to laugh out loud, the reader is left in no doubt as to the target. The derision at the masculinist discourses of power filtered through the problematic and fraught trope of the nation, is finally dismantled. The riposte continues with a gentle mocking of the left in Beatriz's reference to one of her clients, a Marxist professor, 'que me explicó detalladamente en qué consisten los principios de la visión marxista de la estética' (pp.169–70). In this sentence, the ironic charge is all the more acute given his participation in the economic exchange between client and prostitute. Finally, she turns her attention to the gringos, 'lo peor que conocí fue un gringo que hace todo de manera tan aguada que me aburrí muchísimo' (p.170), a gentle but nonetheless sharp deflation of mythologies of sexuality and power as filtered through the relations of domination between US and Mexico.

The text resolves itself with a complete reversal of its opening dependence on the *tú* point of view:

> Te odié [...] Te odié [...] Te odié [...] Te odié porque por tu culpa olvidé yo mis sueños, por tu culpa me olvidé yo de mí, por tu culpa pasé noches en vela [...] Te odié por tantas iglesias, y tantos hoteles y tantos parques, paisajes, soles, lluvias, noches, mercados, jardines, caminos (p.171).

In these sections the voice of *tú* becomes almost one with the country he is revealing to her. At other times, they are kept separate:

> Te odié porque me enseñaste este país con toda su tristeza, con todo su dolor, con sus ríos muertos y sus selvas destruidas, con sus tierras flacas, con su gente pobre y con su hambre, con los ojos enormes de sus niños (p.172).

The final words have a piercing clarity: 'Pero sobre todo te odié porque nunca me preguntaste nada de mí' (pp.171–2). The statement reverberates with the resentment at being left completely out of constructions of the nation and her determination to insert herself back into an alternative vision of how that should look. The alternative vision takes the form of total escape from modernity and an idyllic immersion into a sensual otherworld:

Esos días todos estan encantados, viéndome pasear por el lugar. Hay veces que me quedo todo el tiempo acostada, entre las sábanas blancas y ellos vienen a mí. En otras ocasiones camino por la casa y los voy atendiendo donde estén, en el piso del comedor o de la sala, en el baño, en los pasillos o las escaleras del segundo piso. Y es que los vecinos se han ido todos y los departamentos están sin ocupar. Yo pago las rentas. Muchas veces son tantos los clientes que esperan, que no alcanza el lugar en la casa y entonces se meten a esos sitios vacíos. Allí, algunos esperan de pie, otros sentados, fumando, meditando o dormitando, haciendo el amor entre sí. [...] Y aquí estoy yo, dispuesta siempre. [...] Sólo se escucha el aleteo de las mariposas que se posan en una oreja, en el pelo. Sólo se ve la neblina del incienso densa y perfumada. Sólo se huelen nuestros cuerpos, nuestros líquidos, nuestros deseos. Lo que se ve, se huele y se oye son nuestros placeres. [...] Te escribo para decirte que por fin se ha cumplido mi sueño de tener una casa de huéspedes y de escuchar todo el tiempo el sonido del mar (pp.182–3).

Clearly, this vision is deeply problematic on so many levels in that it fixes her position as the ultimate object of consumption by her voracious clients. That it should be problematic, however, should not surprise us. How can a subject escape from a modernity in which she is so wholly implicated? Beatriz is painstakingly constructed as a modern figure *par excellence* – a tourist who consumes the country aggressively pursuing its ceramics, its cuisine, its monuments. In this way she functions as the quintessential agent of modernity as outlined by Kaplan. What is portrayed as her independent decision to earn her living as prostitute is also presented as a progressive grasping of economic opportunity:

¿Y sabes qué es lo mejor? ¡Que ya no hago ese horrible trabajo de oficina que me traía a la casa en las noches para acompletar! Así como lo oyes, ya no necesito eso, estoy ganando más con los señores que atiendo. ¿Qué te parece? ¿Verdad que está bien así? (p.56).

Her lifestyle is clearly presented as a choice, a way of retaining financial independence in a manner more satisfactory than her clerical work had allowed her. The section in which she outlines her decision functions as a perfect example of the complicitly ambivalent position into which so many women have been placed as active participants in the globalised labour market:

El tipo lo hace despacito, sin prisa, sin fogosidad, sin alterarse, a su ritmo. Yo sólo le sirvo de trinchera pero a mí eso me da igual. Lo que sí estuvo un poco feo es que cuando se iba y le pedí el dinero, se molestó, pero finalmente sacó la cartera. ¿Por qué será que algunas gentes tienen tanta dificultad en desembolsar un poco de dinero? ¿Por qué será que les gusta recibir pero no dar? ¿De verdad creerán que tienen derecho gratis a una mujer a la que acaban de conocer? ¿O imaginarán que ella lo hace por su linda cara? No se darán cuenta de lo difícil que es tener que hacer esto? En fin, así es (p.46).

In this passage, a tension is set up between the illusory control she imagines she wields over her own decisions and the fact that she is so immersed in a ruthless system in which she is totally commodified. Perhaps the most interesting feature of life in the utopian otherworld is how the money exchange has almost completely disappeared. After so much careful attention has been paid throughout the text to the financial exchange between prostitute and client, what emerges is a kind of orgiastic type of existence in which the guests have sex with each other as they meditate, smoke and sleep. Her need for material goods/money is absent and she presents herself as fulfilled in her dream of listening to the sound of the sea. In this way, the final picture presents a strangely amodern (as opposed to pre or post modern) world in which the notion of consumption has certainly been diminished but which continues to anchor women in an almost clichéd position of passive/dominated object of pleasure. As Roger Bartra notes in his discussion of changing female positions in the 1980s:

> this apparent dispersion of domination does not of course eliminate it: on the contrary, the new spread of functions is a faithful, enlarged photograph of the polarity underlying domination. The stage has changed, and the actors have multiplied, but the tragedy reveals the same wounds, and they are still bleeding.[25]

---

25 'From the Charismatic Phallus to the Phallocratic Office', in *Blood, Ink and Culture*, p.136.

53

El amor que me juraste

Silvia Molina's best-selling, prize-winning novel, *El amor que me juraste* was published in 1998, and shares much in common with *Demasiado amor* by Sefchovich. This book, like Sefochovich's, bears testimony to the impossibility of lasting love. Like *Demasiado amor*, it is also a travel narrative, albeit superficially a much more conventional one than Sefchovich's, and it too makes use of the epistolary format.[26] It is set against the tumultuous political backdrop of Mexico in 1994, as the forces of globalisation converged in the signing of NAFTA, and the grassroots exploded in the form of the *Zapatista* rebellion in Chiapas. These, and many other events from that year, are discussed and integrated into the plot of the novel. Both books are centrally concerned with how women confront and challenge the ways in which male power is exercised in their lives and thus raise crucial questions about authority – literal, figurative and narrative – and women's place within the frameworks of national, cultural and political hegemony. As in *Demasiado amor*, the concept of women's complicity in the uneven processes of modernisation in Mexico is also pivotal in this text, and is explored primarily through the trope of the family.

As the promotional paragraph on the back of the English edition states:

26   The epistolary format has long held fascination for women writers and feminist researchers. Its 'intimate' and more 'personalised' nature was seen as an appropriate form of expression for women. Indeed Juan Bruce-Novoa notes in a discussion of Elena Poniatowska's text, *Querido Diego te abraza Quiela* that, 'Beloff's unanswered letters are a metaphor for the history of women's literature in the male-dominant culture', 'Subverting the Dominant Text: Elena Poniatowska's *Querido Diego*' in Susan Bassnett (ed.), *Knives and Angels: Women Writers in Latin America* (London: Sed Books, 1990), pp.115–31, p.128.

Marcela the heroine of the novel, is a modern, professional woman in her forties sifting through her disappointment after a brief but intense, extra-marital affair. As the novel opens, Marcela is in the town of San Lázaro, the home town of her forebears, not only to pick up the pieces of her life, but also to discover the secret past of her parents. Set in Mexico in 1994, Mexico's last elections, the Mayan insurrection in Chiapas and the assassination of presidential candidate Luis Donaldo Colosio serve not only as backdrop, but they also parallel the emotional vicissitudes in Marcela's own life.[27]

Based on the stalest of conventions, therefore, the notion that travel helps one 'find oneself' and come to terms with the past, Molina embarks on her own narrative 'journey'. As will be seen, however, this is no clichéd tale but rather a dynamic and energising voyage that questions, like *Demasiado amor* before it, its own status as novel and the subject positions of its protagonists.

Applying characteristics of travel writing to Molina's narrative seems to reveal a relatively conventional example of the genre, with panoramic lyrical descriptions of the landscape:

Por el hueco que había quedado entre las cortinas del cuarto, entraba ya la luz de la mañana. Me levanté y las descorrí. Miré la bahía: el mar turquesa estaba quieto como un estanque. Los barcos camaroneros habían salido y sólo unas cuantas barcas y lanchas seguían allá, atadas a los muelles, tripuladas por gaviotas.

Hacia el lado del Parque Principal había muy poco movimiento, aún no abrían los almacenes de ropa y abarrotes ni las tiendas de artesanías; solo los meseros de los restaurantes sacaban las mesas a las aceras y las iban vistiendo para el desayuno con manteles de colores brillantes y llamativos como el naranja y el amarillo. La calle estaba casi vacía, excepto por los hombres que barrían el parque y uno que otro caminante.

Vi las cúpulas de mosaicos azules y blancos de las iglesias de San Gabriel y San Juan, y los laureles de la India de la Plaza de San Fernando. Los tordos habían partido temprano, como los pescadores. A veces una que otra familia de gaviotas cruzaba el cielo, y alguna audaz bajaba de pique al mar (p.56).[28]

27   *The Love You Promised Me*, trans. by David Unger (Connecticut: Curbstone, 1999).
28   All references are to *El amor que me juraste* (Mexico City: Joaquín Mortiz, 1998) and will appear after the quotations in parentheses.

There is also ample evidence of the 'manners and customs' approach so characteristic of early examples of travel writing but which is also central to the ethnographic tradition of *indigenista* writing in Mexico.[29] The simplicity of the language, along with the lyricism and vivid nature of the evocation, resonate here with effect:

> Habíamos desayunado en el mercado municipal, tacos de cochinita pibil y horchata de arroz. Era un lugar inmenso, limpio y oloroso a fruta, a oregano, a laurel, a achiote, a cebolla morada, a mar.
>
> Todavía ahora, a pesar de las cadenas comerciales de autoservicio, los indígenas bajan al Puerto para llevar al mercado fruta y hortalizas, y ponen sus tendidos de chile habanero, frijol, arroz y maíz sobre mantas blancas, y los venden por cuartillos de litro y no por kilo. Las mujeres te hablan de 'tú' en su medio español mientras amamantan a sus niños: '¿Tú lo llevas un cuartillo?' (p.154).

Interest in domestic detail is central to the narrator's evocation of San Lázaro but nor is her account free of the colonial discourse so intrinsic to the genre. In the discussion on *Demasiado amor*, it was clear how much this kind of writing is infused by questions of domination, mastery and appropriation, questions that are very much alive in this text as the narrator surges through the territory, appropriating it for her own personal fulfilment:

> No me reconocía en ninguno de esos fantasmas sino en lo que de veras pude palpar: me entendía en las calles de San Lázaro, en ese paisaje, en ese viento que vuela el pelo a las mujeres, en ese calor que sólo se soporta bajo el ventilador, en las aguas inmóviles de la bahía, en el salitre de las paredes de las casas, en el mármol de los pesos, en las tejas de Marsella. No era la gente lo

29   See Sara Mills, *Discourses of Difference: An Analysis of Women's Travel Writing and Colonialism*. For an excellent overview of the *indigenista* literary tradition in Mexico, see Joseph Sommers, 'Changing View of the Indian in Mexican Literature', 'Novels of a Dead Revolution', 'Literatura e historia: las contradicciones ideológicas de la ficción indigenista', 'El ciclo de Chiapas: nueva corriente literaria', and 'La novela mexicana, la revolución y la Alianza para el progreso'. Full details of these may be found in the bibliography. This ethnographic tradition was made famous in the modern era by Oscar Lewis's *The Children of Sánchez: Autobiography of a Mexican Family* (New York: Random House, 1961).

que me daba sentido, sino el lugar. El abuelo no desheredó San Lázaro, pero yo lo recuperé con el sentimiento de una exiliada que vuelve a su patria. Si mi padre hubiera vivido, le habría descrito, demasiado cambiada, la ciudad que dejó (p.163).

Here colonial discourses begin to penetrate the writing as it deploys an authoritative narratorial presence that articulates and names the landscape with masterful words that take upon themselves to describe both the people and the place of San Lázaro. The power to represent, initially conceptualised as a scopic power (in that it describes the position from which she sees the landscape), raises many interesting questions about the power that inheres in the ability to name, list, describe. From the start, Marcela contemplates the powerful past of her family with a mixture of disdain and admiration:

Mi visión de la familia paterna no era idílica sino más bien inasible. Me costaba trabajo imaginarla caminando por las mismas calles empedradas y limpias que yo recorrería al atardecer, cuando el sol bajara; me parecía increíble que hubieran vivido en aquellas casonas coloniales del centro, las que seguían de pie a duras penas, como la del número 57 de la calle de Hidalgo (p.53).

She recalls their grandeur and wealth but also their arrogance:

Veía a las mujeres altivas (mi madre lo decía: 'los Souza eran altivos') con sus vestidos incómodos subir al carruaje tirado por caballos o tomar el tranvía jalado por mulas para ir de paseo, o regatear a los indios el precio del agua de lluvia; y con el bisabuelo, el menú para la cena a la que iría el gobernador (p.53).

Much of the narrative concerns Marcela's need to come to terms with her dead father's betrayal of her family. It was discovered only after his death, that he had another family and children, information that comes to light from the various archives she consults and, most importantly, through the sense of him and his family that she perceives on the streets of San Lázaro. We learn that Marcela's forebears are descended from the powerful Souza family, originally from Santa Cruz de Tenerife in the Canary Islands. This information about her grandfather and great-grandfather is filtered through the prisms of nobility (the street name, *Hidalgo* is, of course, a reference to the glorious 'father' of Mexican independence), prestige and power. After reading some of the archival data concerning her great-grandfather's sending for a wife from the Kingdom of Aragon, there follows an italicised passage marking the incursion into her thoughts of her ex-lover Eduardo's memories of his own landowning past:

> *Me pedís, señora, que os cuente cómo es esta villa a la que he venido a dar y quiero traeros. Cuenta para vuestra devoción con las iglesias de Jesús, San Joseph, San Andrés y la iglesia y convento de San Francisco de suyo antiguo. Paralelas al mar tiene las manzanas de casas de españoles construidas de cal y canto, muy dignas de verse por sus herrerías, el labrado de sus canteras y el trabajo de sus puertas, que aquí hay oficiales en esas materias muy entendidos y os aseguro, señora, que ni en todo vuestro pueblo encontraríais muebles como aquestos que visten estas casas pues llegan de todas partes de Europa en los barcos que aquí atracan* (p.55).

This extract from Eduardo's correspondence with Marcela conveys a breathtaking sense of privilege and wealth and gently underscores the colonial past and European heritage of the places they now revisit. Because of its slightly disjunctive positioning, the reader is jolted from the evocations of San Lázaro and drawn on a journey through the life of another privileged member of the country's elite.

Marcela continues to outline her family's descent from grace, their decline in fortunes as their children left to study in Spain, France and the United States. Her shame is clear:

> Gracias a él, me avergonzaba de los tatarabuelos porque explotaron a los indios en las plantaciones de maíz, arroz, caña de azúcar y palo de tinte mientras sus mujeres ingénues y obedientes o arrogantes y soberbias rezaban las vísperas o las novenas o el rosario en la Parroquia de San Andrés, la misma que seguía llamando a los fieles a misa: taaaaannnnn, taaaaannnnnn (p.56).

This personal history of power, domination and, as she learns later, injustice, causes a further jolt to Marcela's attempts at reconciliation with her past.[30] Her sense of complicity and contamination by this past

---

30 This sense of injustice stems from the fact that her mother worked as a maid for the Souza family, through whom she came to meet her future husband. She was initially ostracised by his wider family due to their perception of her as inferior.

is underlined in the text at various points but most forcefully in her tour of the 'real' San Lázaro during which, led by Miguel, she is accused of not wanting to see the other side, 'Es lo mismo que te pasa con tu familia. No quieres verlos como son. Te da miedo' (p.129). The link drawn here most explicitly between place and people, is the link she actively tries to disavow, and the second element in the opening passage of this section that merits further reflection. In this next section, I shall explore the relationship between self and place through a reading of discourses on tourism and modernity.

'Finding Oneself'

Marcela's emphatic, 'No era la gente lo que me daba sentido, sino el lugar' (p.163) suggests that she has distanced herself from the more shameful aspects of her Souza background. It also, however, evokes the rather clichéd notion of finding oneself through travel, which could be described as the appropriation of place for an enhanced sense of identity and which is of central concern to much of what has been written on the phenomenon of tourism in the modern era. While Marcela's travel narrative is not unaffected by the colonial discourse which has long infused travel writing, the novel is also a thoroughly modern tale of the quest for personal identity and fulfilment. Mac-Cannell's work on the modern tourist notes that the increase in leisure time accorded to the middle classes from the 1950s onwards was a major factor. Kaplan points out:

> The tourist confirms and legitimates the social reality of constructions such as 'First' and 'Third' Worlds, 'development' and 'underdevelopment', or 'metropolitan' and 'rural'. Created out of increasing leisure time in industrialised nations and driven by a need to ascertain identity and location in

a world that undermines the certainty of those categories, the tourist acts as an agent of modernity.[31]

While *El amor que me juraste* clearly works as domestic travelogue, it certainly derives much of its rationale from the idea that Marcela escapes the metropolitan, heart-breaking existence to find solace and peace of mind in the rural idyll of her ancestors. Kaplan's assertion that the tourist acts as an agent of modernity is an interesting notion when applied to Marcela, who frequently crosses boundaries between past/present, metropolitan/rural, lover/husband on a soul-searching journey for the self. Not only does she negotiate the fraught divisions between private and public, past and present, but in the process, becomes intricately enmeshed in the process of *modernización* in Mexico, in which tourism played such a crucial role. Alicia del Campo attests to the importance of tourism as a principal source of income in Mexico citing President Díaz Ordaz's contribution to a book on the theme: 'Todos los estados progresistas del mundo están interesados en el turismo. Líderes políticos e industriales, han casi universalmente reconocido las ventajas económicas (si no sociales) del turismo'.[32] Like Beatriz in *Demasiado amor*, she is deeply involved in processes she actively tries to undermine in other ways and thus her position is one of profound ambivalence.

But before examining that ambivalent positioning, it might further shed light on the complexity of her subject position to examine the ways in which Marcela conforms to certain assertions about the modern tourist made by Dean MacCannell and Donald Horne. Horne argues that tourists look for new meanings in locations, landscapes, cities and social customs other than their own, and that as part of this process they all search for markers of 'authenticity'. MacCannell describes the search for authenticity as a response to the generalised anxiety of modernity, an anxiety that is palpable throughout this text. MacCannell, in his fascinating characterisation of how this authenticity is staged in travel discourse, describes a series of six stages that

31   *Questions of Travel*, p.58.
32   'Reterritorializando lo mexicano', p.70.

the traveller attempts to 'get behind' and isolates stage six as the 'ideal, uncontaminated back region'.[33] MacCannell argues that tourists long to enter this sixth space, what he describes as a glorious location of 'authenticity'. I would contend that it is precisely the entrance into this sixth 'authentic' space that enables Marcela to acquire the sense of peace and tranquillity that has eluded her.

In the closing stages of the novel, just like Beatriz before her, Marcela is forced to confront the rot of modern Mexico. Led by the hand by Miguel as he declares authoritatively, 'Te voy a llevar al malecón para que se te baje la borrachera, y luego vas a conocer el San Lázaro de noche' (p.136), she witnesses the other side of life in San Lázaro, far removed from the colonial mansions of her forebears:

> Del cerro de San Marcos, me llevó al San Lázaro exclusivo, el que rodea la ciudad, donde vive la gente adinerada en casas con vista al mar. Fraccionamientos de lujo con nombres pretenciosos: Residencial Náutico, Fraccionamiento Bellavista, Rinconada del Mar, y después recorrimos un San Lázaro al que la luna alumbraba distinto, uno que yo no sospechaba y me sorprendió por la miseria. El contraste entre las colonias de lujo y las populares era grosero. Pasábamos por una serie de barrios sin servicios, allá donde ningún turista podría descubrirlos. Como había llovido tanto, las veredas estaban inundadas y a muchos lugares no pudimos ni siquiera acercarnos.
>
> El verdadero San Lázaro está escondido tras las lomas que rodean la ciudad amurallada. Allá vive la gente que tiene otros rostros, otra mirada, otra manera de vestir y de caminar, la que huele a maíz y a sudor, la que llega del interior del estado en busca de trabajo. Por los charcos y el calor, las calles despedían un tufo a podrido, a descomposición: eran ciénagas, fangales, pantanos (p.128).

The start of Marcela's descent into the underworld of San Marcos and her exposure to the other side of life there, constitutes a section of the novel that rather strikingly corresponds to MacCannell's notion of the ultimate stage of authenticity, the emotional high of the traveller. The new vista she contemplates, far removed from the picturesque beauty

33   See Dean MacCannell, *The Tourist: A New Theory of the Leisure Class* (Berkeley: University of California Press, 1999), pp.91–107. Also, Donald Horne, *The Great Museum: The Re-Presentation of History* (London: Pluto Press, 1984).

of the earlier descriptions, like in *Demasiado amor*, is a vision of rot and decay:

> Aunque tuvieran distintos nombres, los asentamientos se parecían: casuchas hacinadas, *llenas de lloridos de niño*, amontonadas en los ceros calcáreos, construidas con malos materiales, a los lados de unos senderos estrechos y en pendiente por los que iban y venían perros famélicos. ¿Dónde la alfombra de pasto, las palmeras, los aguacates, los mangos, los almendros, los jabines de las fincas, de las haciendas, de las mansiones de los fraccionamientos elegantes que acabábamos de ver? – Ya vámonos de aquí – le pedí (p.129, my emphasis).

Like Beatriz, Marcela poses a series of questions about the beauty of the previous visions, a beauty that has now been irrevocably destroyed. Unlike Beatriz, who wriggles from the grasp of the male representer of Mexico to confront the rotten landscape of modernity herself, Marcela is dependent on Miguel to reveal the 'real' San Lázaro to her. On one level this is symptomatic of the more conventional nature of Molina's narrative vis-à-vis the experimental nature of the Sefchovich text. In the case of Marcela, it is the 'rural' teacher who must educate her as to the authentic and genuine state of her people and her place, a relationship that replicates the active-passive, male-female dichotomies that were so shaken in Sefchovich's text. However, they are shaken here too, just in a different way. As the reader begins to comprehend the expanse of life on view in San Lázaro, the views behind the tourist lens, Marcela's ambivalent subject position is thrown into sharp focus.

The nature of this ambivalent position is illustrated by a series of dichotomies that structure Molina's text from start to finish. The 'Metropolitan/rural' binary opposition is filtered through Marcela's relationship with San Lázaro and the men in her life, both of whom are deeply attached to rural concerns in different ways. Eduardo cherishes his relationship with his rural background and Rafael is deeply involved in political events in Chiapas. The second binary relationship involves the opposition between public and private and is seen through her illict private life as Eduardo's lover as against her very public life of wife to Rafael. Third, the past is established in constant opposition to the present, where it ruptures the harmonious contemplation of contemporary reality. This duality is signalled in the text by Marcela's simple admission, 'No sabía que hubiera otro San Lázaro' (p.131), having witnessed the degradation and misery of many of its citizens' lives. The opposition between contrasting poles serves as a structural framework that defines Marcela's interstitial positioning between so many opposing worlds. Her precarious balancing on the boundaries between past and present, metropolitan and rural, public and private, render her unstable and unreliable both as a mediator of her own reality and as a narrator of the text. This ambivalence about her positioning is directly underscored in the text by the narrator's continual disavowal of her tourist status. Consider the opening lines in which she describes the scene in a passage utterly typical of travel writing of this nature, but establishes critical distance between herself and the 'tourists':

> Los graznidos de los tordos anunciaban la caída de la tarde, cuando miré el Puerto desde la terraza. Allá estaban, cercando el Parque Principal, la iglesia de San Andrés, el ayuntamiento y los hoteles: el San Carlos, el Soledad y el San Francisco. Bajo la arquería de los portales, en los restaurantes al aire libre, los turistas bebían cerveza o merendaban antojitos de pescado o tamales de hoja de plátano mientras los vendedores de artesanías les mostraban con insistencia sombreros de jipi y vestidos y blusas bordados con punto de cruz. *Las extranjeras sucumbían como yo* ante el colorido de las flores azules, anaranjadas o rojas o amarillas en los ribetes del cuello y las mangas (p.11, my emphasis).

This ability to slip from one enunciatory position to another, illustrated first, by her observation of the tourists from afar, adopting a supposedly more authentic subject position, and second by her admission that she has been seduced, as they are, quite literally by the 'local colour', suggests her fluid textual mobility. This textual mobility is connoted literally in the text by her real ability to travel about the country unhindered and unmolested, a freedom few women, even those from the privileged ranks of the upper middle classes, enjoy uninhibitedly today in Mexico. This disavowal is present at a later point too: 'No me dio ningún detalle histórico del lugar *ni me tomó como una turista* con la que debía lucirse, y se lo agradecí' (p.128, my emphasis). And yet this is exactly how she consumes San Lázaro, as a tourist, eagerly seduced by the vibrancy and energy of the local, and then gradually lured to the back rooms, to those hidden from view initially, to be exposed to the total performance of authenticity as choreographed by Miguel. This strategy of disavowal, temporary alignment and then estrangement operates as an apt metaphor for the protagonist's ambivalent, fluid and ultimately unfixed relationship with the realities of modernity that she confronts in San Lázaro.

1994: The Past/Present Collision

Further evidence of this ambivalent positioning is to be found in the persistent eruptions into her life of a modern Mexico of which she is undoubtedly a part but with which she cannot be reconciled. Her complicity in what she witnesses cannot be denied, her poignant question, 'También me he preguntado si no fue el ejemplo de mi papá lo que se me metió en el cuerpo sin que me diera cuenta' (p.145), shows that she is not oblivious to her own role in the creation of the inequalities she witnesses on her trip. Her vain attempt to divorce the people from the place simply serves to underline the inextricable links between the hidden horrors of the San Lázaro she now confronts and her family's direct role in creating them. The haunting image of the children screaming eloquently underlines the sense of pain involved in her search for a self with which she can be at peace.

Aside from the stark confrontation with the dark side of the tourist industry in San Lázaro, exemplified by the extremes of poverty she witnesses, the text is also punctured with other 'encounters' with modern Mexico. The first occurs by way of background information at the start of Chapter Two:

> Conocí a Eduardo en su consultorio, en 1994, cuando la situación política del país era un caos y la violencia y la inseguridad surgían en todas partes. Cada día, a partir del primero del año, nos despertamos con acontecimientos insólitos: el conflicto armado en Chiapas; la muerte del candidato del PRI, Luis Donaldo Colosio; el suspenso de la lucha por el poder entre los priístas; la movilidad de Manuel Camacho Solís, que un día era regente, otro secretario de Estado, otro más comisionado para la paz en Chiapas, y otro más dejaba entrever que se lanzaría como candidato a la presidencia de la República; la apar-

ición del subcomandante Marcos, el guerrillero poeta que estaba en todos los medios de comunicación; el destape de Ernesto Sedillo, sucesor de Colosio; la lucha por la reforma electoral; el debate en la televisión de los candidatos del PRD, del PAN y del PRI a la presidencia; el nombramiento de José Francisco Ruiz Massieu como secretario general del PRI; el asesinato de José Francisco Ruiz Massieu; el desfile de comisiones y fiscales especiales para esclarecer los asesinatos de Colosio y Ruiz Massieu, y de procuradores para dar seguimiento a la procuración de justicia en torno de esos asesinatos; el secuestro del banquero Alfredo Harp Helú; la desaparición del diputado Muñóz Rocha (p.21).

I quote this passage in its entirety in order to properly pose the question – what function can a passage like this possibly have in this narrative, other than, to quote the promotional paragraph again, 'parallel the emotional vicissitudes in Marcela's own life'? Given that even the most tumultuous love-life ever could hardly be said to parallel kidnappings, disappearances, assassination and armed rebellions, are they simply there to remind the reader of the Mexicanness of the narrative, serving only to stamp the local on a text that mostly reads as a quintessential liberal middle-class feminist quest for empowerment and understanding? What this passage clearly does, as in *Demasiado amor* before it, is to anchor the narrative to a particular historical moment (in this case a most specific year) in Mexican history. And yet, many of the subsequent digressions about the current political situation, while they happen at pivotal moments of the narrative are staged almost ironically:

Llegué a Nueva York por la mañana, al Hotel Beacon en Broadway y la Calle 75, cerca del Parque Central, el día que terminaba el congreso al que había ido Eduardo. Eso fue dos semanas antes del primer intento de ruptura y tres del segundo, y un poco después de que encarcelaran a Raúl Salinas de Gortari como presunto asesino intelectual de José Francisco Ruiz Massieu, por lo que había un gran revuelo en la política del país (p.121).

In this passage, her break-ups with Eduardo are almost comically aligned with the political assassination of Massieu, a parodic interlinking of the public life of the nation and the emotional upheavals of her own life.[34]

The series of dialectic relationships, mentioned earlier between public-private, past-present, and urban-rural is further explored through the eruption into the text of the armed uprising in Chiapas, an event of momentous significance for Mexico in that it marked the first formal rebellion against the previously unopposed forces of neo-liberalism espoused by the technocratic governments led by Miguel de la Madrid and Carlos Salinas de Gortari.[35] In many ways, the *zapatista* uprising did more to unsettle the onslaught of *modernización* in Mexico than any other event since the Tlatelolco massacre of 1968. Chiapas thus is integrated into the text as though an essential element of any narrative about Mexico in 1994. Integration is achieved by way of the character of Marcela's husband, Rafael, who is originally from Tuxtla Gutiérrez, the capital of Chiapas, and who represents many *chiapanecos* through his law offices in the city. As Marcela baldly states, 'El despacho y Chiapas eran por esos días las obsesiones de Rafael' (p.139):

> Los Chiapanecos buscaban a Rafael para pedirle sus consejos o sus servicios por las demandas interpuestas a los campesinos por invasión de tierras; o a los caciques de siempre por ocupar las posesiones de los indios desplazados de sus comunidades. Lo llamaban cuando había alguna detención ilegal o un des-aparecido, porque tiene buenas relaciones y puede no sólo investigar sino mediar (p.139).

She goes on to outline his total immersion in the standoff:

> Cuando Rafael regresaba de Chiapas, venía cansado y deprimido y discutía con sus paisanos sobre sus teorías de la Guerra: la lucha de la Iglesia de derecha,

---

34 This echoes Angeles Mastretta's novel, *Arráncame la vida*, in which she adopts the same kind of strategy: 'Ese año pasaron muchas cosas en mi país. Entre otras, Andrés y yo nos casamos' (Barcelona: Bolsillo, 1990), p.7.

35 See Roger Bartra's discussion of technocracy, 'The Crisis of Nationalism', in *Blood, Ink and Culture*, pp.104–32. See also, Aguilar Camín and Meyer on the aggressive neo-liberalisation of the economy from López de Portillo onwards. *In the Shadow of the Mexican Revolution*, pp.251–69.

muy conservadora, y la de izquierda, a la que llamaba el sector progresista, el que trabajaba en las comunidades. Hablaba del sincretismo religioso que sostenía el espíritu de lucha en las comunidades por las influencias espirituales de su idiosincrasia. Deliberaba sobre el desarrollo desigual de los chiapanecos, y decía que los campesinos que se habían unido a la guerrilla ya eran indígenas con cierta educación autodidacta y que habían aprendido mucho con las políticas rurales de autogestión; reflexionaba sobre los grupos maoístas que no prendieron ni fueron aceptados por los indígenas, y sobre los guerrilleros de la generación de Marcos, según él, marxistas creativos (p.138).

Again I quote this passage at length to draw attention to how much the narrative itself digresses into this 'other' Mexican story and also to highlight the debate it generated about the left in Mexico, a debate that continues today. What is perhaps more interesting from our discussion's point of view, however, is Marcela's response to these treatises. She chooses to respond to his theories about the crisis by repeating the religious retorts of her mother:

Oíd: salió el sembrador a sembrar, y al arrojar la semilla, parte de ella cayó a lo largo del camino y vinieron las aves del cielo y se la comieron; otra parte cayó en pedregales, donde no encontraron tierra [...]

– Las semillas de este Marcos – le decía un poco en broma y otro tanto en serio a Rafael – cayeron en tierra de pobres y se desarrollaron (p.139).

The quoting of her mother, along with her own interpretation of Marcos as 'alguien religioso' (p.139), points to the almost old-fashioned recourse to religion as a way of 'explaining' what was happening. Her commentary on the omnipresent, 'Todos somos Marcos' slogan to state that, 'Yo no, yo no era Marcos, ni me sentía Marcos: él era un luchador: "Deja todo y sígueme"; y yo, a pesar de mi nombre, no era una guerrera' (p.140) is also significant.[36] On one level this is

36 Latin America's tradition of liberation theology, of course, saw an explicit alignment between religious salvation and social progress. Latin American revolutionary discourse is suffused with religious imagery and iconography. For a useful overview of the connectedness of the concepts, see 'Religion, Ideology and Revolution in Latin America', a special issue of the journal, *Latin American Perspectives*. Issue 50, Vol.13, No.3 (Summer 1986). I am indebted to Lorna Shaughnessy for emphasising these links.

explained, again, by her guilt at her colonial roots ('Cuando sepa que eres finquera, no te va a aceptar en sus filas' p.140), but her recourse to religion indicates her retreat into the past, into the old answers and the old solutions where logical, rational opposition is absent. Just as in Sefchovich's text, Marcela's eye and thus her world-view is aligned with the irrational, the sensual, the telluric. This escape into religion confuses the modernity of the text by affirming the mythical power of the grand narratives and constructing a new narrative in which the power relations are remarkably unchanged.

Rafael's subsequent disillusion with the situation in Chiapas underscores the sense of political failure in the region:

> Había dejado de ir a Chiapas. Estaba harto y desilusionado de la situación. Enojado por tanta intolerancia de ambas partes, por tanta invasión de tierras, por tanta violencia por abajo del agua. Se enojaba contra la Iglesia, contra los líderes zapatistas y no zapatistas que envalentonaban a los indígenas no sólo a invadir las tierras, sino contra los desplazados de sus comunidades por haber abrazado otra religion, contra todo. Era un drama tocar el tema de Chiapas.
> – Por prender el cohete, m'hijo, saliste chamuscado – le decía su mamá.
> No es invadiendo las pinches tierras – así decía: 'pinches tierras' como se puede lograr la justicia. No van a recuperar las tierras invadiéndolas [...] Tienen que firmar los acuerdos, sentarse a la mesa a negociar (p.168).

The intrusions of Chiapas into the text and into Marcela and Rafael's narrative of frustrated love, point to concerns about the current problems in Mexico that somehow make their presence felt, despite their seeming irrelevance to the actual plot. What is clear, however, is that, contrary to the promotional paragraph already cited, Chiapas is not a simple backdrop that parallels the emotional vicissitudes in her life but an emotionally charged issue in which she becomes immersed to debate its relevance and question its role.

The insertion of the female subject into the debate about national identity is, it should be pointed out, in itself important, but the debate also functions as yet another vehicle through which she tries to find 'herself'. This is reflected on a wider level in contemporary society as the *zapatista* struggle becomes almost a playground within which the various fighting factions of the Mexican middle classes set up camp and pit their strengths. In this way it functions as an almost too convenient mechanism for the liberal middle classes to explore their own individual quests for empowerment. Allegorically, the eruption of Chiapas into their narrative of frustrated love parallels the eruption of Chiapas, the disappeared and forgotton south, into the metropolitan consciousness of modern Mexico. Chiapas is figured as the central axis around which the dilemmas and frustrations of modern Mexico – the position of the Church, the situation of the left, the vexed indigenous question – attach themselves and are endlessly debated. In the text, these debates are referenced explicitly and Marcela's ambivalent positioning offers an effective example of the dilemmas created by the increasingly intractable 'problem' in Chiapas. She rejects her husband's rational dissections of the problem, preferring instead to quote her mother's favourite passages from the bible. She sees the problem (and Marcos) as an almost biblical situation (a rich versus poor argument), in which religion emerges as solution and comfort. She also refuses to fight, thus again creating distance between herself and the people she encounters – tourists, *Zapatistas* and her relatives. Indeed the discussion about Chiapas is filtered through her husband and the long passage, quoted earlier, about the tumultuous political events of 1994 is recounted from New York at some distance from Mexico. Her insertion into the debate is clear but her subject is both distanced and yet immersed, irrational and yet strangely removed, a telling reminder perhaps of how too often women have been one step removed from political debate. The recourse to religion and the escape into the old solutions, the old explanations, offer further evidence of the complexity of her subject positioning – involved and yet distanced, engaged and yet removed.

And so the narrative concludes and yet, unlike *Demasiado amor,* there is no lofty utopia and no escape from a modernity that envelops the nation, the text and the protagonist. After her meeting with Eduardo's daughter, Elizabeth, she says:

> No quiero hacer obvio lo que siguió a aquella tarde. Una vez, hace tantos años que no me acuerdo cuándo, le llevé una pieza de piano, cortita, a la maestra María González, la mejor que tuve en la escuela de música. Le di el papel pautado y lo leyó con paciencia delante de mí, luego me hizo tocarla varias veces.
> – Otra vez.

– ¿Otra?

– ¿Qué, hablo en chino?

– Al cabo de varias repeticiones me preguntó:

– ¿No le notas nada?

– No.

– Le sobra algo– me dio la pista.

…

–Algo muy obvio, muy muy obvio.

…

A ver, otra vez.

No lo noté hasta que ella tocó la pieza, y yo la oí como si fuera de alguien más:

– El final, ¿verdad?

Si le quitas todo esto – me señaló las notas donde volvía a repetir la melodía –, si acaba aquí – hizo el ademán que hace un director de orquesta cuando indica fin, punto, se acabó –, no arrastras el final, lo haces rotundo. Mira.

Repitió el ultimo acorde y oí la diferencia.

Creo que aprendí la lección; por eso, las páginas que siguen están en blanco, llenas de silencio y de intimidad (pp.169–70).

It could be argued that it is through Molina's refusal to close the narrative that Marcela's resistance to the distinct forms of domination that have structured her life may be located. In this invitation to silence (a time-honoured trope of feminist literature)[37] and intimacy, the reader is invited to recognise the limitations of language in evoking the lived realities of the novel's protagonists. Unlike the disappearance of the fluid subject in *Demasiado amor* and the sub-

---

37 This emphasis on the silences, the so-called blank pages of feminist literary tradition, have been explored in various ways but particularly by female authors to show how women have been defined symbolically as lack, negation or absence. 'The Blank Page' refers to Isak Dinesen's eponymous story that tells of the displaying in a public museum of the matrimonial sheets of princesses complete with bloodstains offering visible proof of their virginity. That one of the canvases is blank provokes particular fascination in its spectators. Interpreted as an act of radical subversion because it suggests an alternative form of story, 'The Blank Page' is, in turn, no story but every story. Rosario Castellanos was interested in the concept and wrote an essay entitled, '"Por sus máscaras los conoceréis..." Karen Blixen – Isak Dinesen' in her final essay collection, *Mujer que sabe latín...* (Mexico: Fondo de Cultura Económica, 1973), pp.51–6. The original story can be found in *Last Tales* (New York: Random House, 1957), pp.95–105.

sequent escape into utopia, here the refusal to be fixed at the novel's end constitutes an open challenge to go beyond the limits of narrative and fiction and it is here that the political charge of the text can be realised. As with *Demasiado amor*, it should hardly surprise us that this solution is problematic. The invitation to the reader to create, the text's inability to fix or to close remains the quintessential trope of high modernist literature, a project that while often uniquely male, was also inextricably bound up with the forces of economic and political *apertura* that the text so critiques. It should come as no surprise thus, that the text cannot escape its own limitations, while it does, at least attempt to offer a way out for the reader. As with *Demasiado amor*, even with an ambivalently positioned fluid subject like the narrator in this case, it is difficult to find a space outside of modernity, when modernity is so much a part of what she has become.

Conclusion

Could it be possible to assert that both *Demasiado amor* and *El amor que me* juraste constitute 'counter-narratives of the nation' in the way that Bhabha imagines when he talks of a narrative that, 'evokes and erases the totalising boundaries of the nation disturbing those intellectual manoeuvres through which "imagined communities" are given essentialist identities?'[38] It is certainly clear that the texts stage an attack on the totalising narrative of modernity and thus contest the limits of the modernising project in ways that enlighten, entertain and resist. One could argue, of course, that as powerful masculinist discourses, travel writing even when undertaken by women, can only be instrumental in the construction of yet another rationale for power and control. In this way, these women writers' adoption of travel writing bear testimony to Audre Lourde's famous formulation, 'For the mas-

---

38   *Nation and Narration*, p.302.

ter's tools will never dismantle the master's house',[39] and the narratives inexorably lead to the creation of yet another oppressive set of hierarchies. Roger Bartra defines modernisation as 'a proposal for making the system functional again'.[40] In this way, it is a profoundly conservative strategy designed to reinscribe the system, albeit modernised, in a way that enables power relations to function in ways remarkably similar to the mechanisms of political power in place beforehand. In texts like these, the tourist/traveller becomes not just an agent of modernity, but a witness to its breakdown and reconstitution. 'In a country like this', therefore, to return to Mastretta, women writers play the unhappy role of witness, but they also participate in reconstruction. In these final reflections, I would like to invoke Roger Bartra's notion of modernisation – 'dismothernity' – as a way of conceptualising these texts' approaches to the totalising boundaries of the nation that structure them.

According to Bartra's formulation:

> we can no longer critique Mexican culture in the name of modernity, of a liberal-inspired modernity that raises up the banner of 'progress'. We have to critique modernity from the standpoint I call dismodernity, or better yet – taking a cue from *desmadre*, Mexican slang for disorder – dismothernity.[41]

In this fascinating passage, the blocks used to fashion a critique of modernity in Mexico are already feminised – disordered (in a state of *desmadre*), dismothered, dismoderned. This coding of resistance as feminine has extraordinary potential for the development of feminist critical tools with which to attack the modernising forces of Mexican political, economic and civil life. In this way the 'dismothernity' that emerges from these pages; the chaotic encounter between the ambivalent female subject and the forces of *modernidad* points to the

---

39   *Sister/Outsider: Essays and Speeches* (Trumansburg, New York: The Crossing Press, 1984), p.121.
40   'The Crisis of Nationalism', in *Blood, Ink and Culture*, p.107.
41   Bartra, 'The Mexican Office: Miseries and Splendors of Culture', in *Blood, Ink and Culture*, p.9.

pivotal role played by women (acting as agents, travellers, tourists, writers and readers) in opposition to the neo-liberalising techno-cratising forces of modern Mexico. Taking my cue from Bartra, thus, I choose to read these texts not just as a critique of male power – though they are that too – but a vicious attempt to narrate the tortuous processes of *modernización* and to bear testimony to its many casualties, primarily the poor, but which include others also on the margins, such as prostitutes and the indigenous communities of Chiapas. In this way, the texts strike at the heart of Mexican *modernización* and the very forces of 'progress' that so limit the lives of its people.

Chapter Two
The Disintegrating Self: Narrative and Survival in Susana Págano and Brianda Domecq

Susana Págano's remarkable debut novel, *Y si yo fuera Susana San Juan* (1995) and Brianda Domecq's recreation of her personal experience of kidnapping in *Once días y algo más* (1979) both feature their central female subjects in a slow process of disintegration and decay. Págano's troubled protagonist, Susana, takes refuge in an alter ego named after the character Susana San Juan of Juan Rulfo's novel *Pedro Páramo*, in order to escape the background of sadism and cruelty experienced at the hands of her unloving mother, disappeared father and abusive grandfather. Domecq's central character, Leo, is kidnapped by a gang looking to capitalise on her family's fortune.[1] Her incarceration is conceptualised as an annihilation of her former identity and a 'new beginning' in which she reinvents herself as a modern day Sheherezade, spinning tales that will ensure her survival.[2]

---

1 The experience recounted in *Once días y algo más* is based on Domecq's own experience of kidnapping at the hands of an armed gang in 1978. As daughter of the Domecq wine and sherry dynasty, she was, in many ways, an obvious target for the kidnappers. See Kay S. García, *Broken Bars: New Perspectives From Mexican Women Writers*, pp.157–203. Technically, of course, the year 1979 falls just outside the time-frame of this study. Domecq is central however, to any discussion of the *boom* as most of her texts are published in the 1980s and 1990s. I include this text in my discussion because of the crucial issues it raises with regard to narrative authority.

2 The tale of Sheherezade, as is well known, is from *Arabian Nights*, a series of anonymous stories in Arabic, considered to be among the classics of world literature. The cohesive plot device concerns the efforts of Scheherezade, or Sheherazade, to keep her husband, King Shahryar (or Schriyar), from killing her by entertaining him with a tale a night for one thousand and one nights. The best known of these stories are those of Ali Baba, Sinbad the Sailor, and Aladdin. Within the vast body of literature on the *Thousand and One Nights* and the figure of Scheherezade, there are different spellings. I will adopt the

This chapter takes as its central focus the idea of the self in crisis, in order to explore the notion of narrative as a form of survival, an argument that is common to both texts and significant for a number of reasons. First, both novels follow the trajectory of the female self from the centre of the crisis towards rehabilitation (in the case of Domecq) and towards self-destruction (in the case of Págano). Second, by foregrounding the importance of narrative in such a self-conscious way, the books inscribe the importance of the written word in the attainment of the literal and figurative liberation of their female protagonists. Finally, both novels engage critically with the idea of the literary canon. In Págano's case, this happens through the self-conscious employment of Rulfo's 'foundational'[3] text and the re-appropriation of its only major female figure. In this way, Rulfo's text is positioned as the master from which the narrative is spun. In Domecq's novel, the main protagonist Leo is studying for a doctorate in Hispanic Letters and displays a deep attachment to her books at various points in the narrative. The novels' homage to the written word and indeed the anxiety generally displayed towards the idea of the canon, illustrate the uncertain contexts in which the authors published their respective stories. In this chapter I will document the disintegration of the female selves in both texts, paying close attention to the persistent attempts to stave off annihilation through the appropriation of various narrative forms. In Págano's novel, this takes the form of immersion in the unfinished story of Susana San Juan and in Domecq's novel, it is the appropriation of the Scheherezade figure that ensures her survival, as she successfully weaves her tales forging connections with her captors through their shared experiences.

Sheherezade spelling employed by Roland Barthes, given my reliance on his views on intertextuality in this chapter.

3   The term 'foundational' is taken from Doris Sommers' ground-breaking study of what she terms the 'foundational fictions' of Latin America. See *Foundational Fictions: The National Romances of Latin America* (Berkeley: University of California Press, 1991).

The Self in Crisis

Y si yo fuera Susana San Juan narrates a heart-breaking story of personal betrayal and alienation of three female members of the same family. The grandmother, Anastasia, is released from a mental asylum after twenty five years of incarceration. She had been locked away as a result of a love affair with her brother-in-law, Beto, whom she had continued to see after being cruelly forced into an arranged marriage with Beto's elder brother, Ceferino. She is released after years of treatment including a frontal lobotomy, graphically described, and is represented as a stereotypically 'crazy' old woman. Locked in the past and hating her present, Anastasia is the embodiment of the cruelty and abuse suffered by Susana, her grand-daughter, during her childhood. Aurelia is the deeply troubled daughter born to Anastasia during her loveless marriage to Ceferino. As Ceferino's daughter, Aurelia is rejected by her mother and, traumatised by this rejection, she too becomes a mother incapable of loving her daughter. Though Aurelia is presented as relatively sane – hers is the only voice of 'normality' during much of the narrative – she loses all sense of reason towards the end of the novel, attempts suicide and, in a bitterly ironic gesture, is taken from the family home and placed in a mental asylum by her daughter. Aurelia's daughter, Susana, is also presented as 'crazy' and in need of professional treatment. Indeed much of the novel is devoted to her frequent sessions with a psychiatrist. During these sessions, it emerges that she has repressed most of the unspeakable cruelty of her childhood in which she is mentally abused by her grandfather. As a result, she becomes the archetypal 'body in revolt' as described by Julia Kristeva, lapsing into fits of hysteria that are triggered by sudden piercing realisations of her past.[4] These fits serve to remind her of a

---

4   Kristeva describes the 'body in revolt' as, 'a body disavowed by consciousness which it is yet unable to ignore'. She outlines its many manifestations: 'The subject's reactions to these abjects is visceral: it is usually expressed in retching, vomiting, spasms, choking – in brief, in disgust. These reactions signal bodily functions which a "rational consciousness" cannot accept; yet the subject cannot adequately deny them either'. See Elizabeth Gross, 'The Body

reality she is simply unable to function in. As an escape, she turns to her alter ego, Susana San Juan, named after Juan Rulfo's famous character in his universally acclaimed novel, *Pedro Páramo* (1955). In the anecdotes recounted to the psychiatrist, the reader gains a glimpse of the sadistic past that has so scarred the three women. The novel ends with Anastasia's death, Aurelia is left incarcerated in a mental asylum, and Susana's body and mind is completely taken over by her alter ego, Susana San Juan. In the final scenes, Susana acts out an alternative ending to her grandmother's life alongside her half-brother, Pedro, with whom she professes to be in love. In this first section, I outline Susana's transgressions of the 'clean and proper' body as designated by Kristeva, to then contemplate its significance within the novel's overall structures of meaning.[5]

Susana: The Abject Body

Kristeva's conceptualisation of the abject in her long essay, *The Powers of Horror: An Essay on Abjection*, is well known and remains compelling in the way that it accounts for the policing of bodily boundaries in societies both ancient and modern. To be specific, she defines the abject as the 'place where meaning collapses'[6] where the body's borders are blurred by its leaking, seeping fluids and substances that threaten and endanger the integrity of the subject. Excrement, semen, sweat, menstrual blood and maternal milk are common examples of the abject's manifestation in an unstable and dangerous body. As Kristeva points out, societies have always rigidly controlled

of Signification', in *Abjection, Melancholia and Love: the Work of Julia Kristeva*, John Fletcher and Andrew Benjamin (eds) (London: Routledge, 1990), pp. 80–103, p.89.

5   Kristeva writes, 'The body must bear no trace of its debt to nature; it must be clean and proper in order to be fully symbolic'. *Powers of Horror: An Essay on Abjection*, trans. by Leon S. Roudiez (New York: Columbia University Press 1982), p.102.

6   *Powers of Horror*, p.2.

notions of the acceptable body, and transgressions of one kind or another are always punished. Bearing this in mind, the character of Susana is a perfect embodiment of the abject body at many points of the narrative:

> Tengo frío, un frío espantoso que me retumba en los huesos. Las mantas no son suficientes para calentarme, porque el frío lo llevo dentro, adherido a las vísceras, brotando de mí como un manantial para volverse parte de mí misma. Tiemblo mucho, de pies a cabeza. El cuerpo se me agita con violencia, enrrabiado (p.42).[7]

In this early passage in the novel, the shaking of the body and the visceral cold that permeates her are ominous portents of the agony her body will undergo to exorcise the demons of her past. One of the novel's first references to her is when Anastasia, the grandmother says, 'Esa niña tiene el demonio por dentro' (p.14), a claim repeated later in the text.[8] Indeed, the concept of exorcism is explicitly invoked in the case of the grandmother at a later stage. This parallelism between the lives of Susana and Anastasia[9] which culminates in Susana's complete immersion in Anastasia's dream at the end, is signalled at various points in the narrative. At this point, however, she is unable to contemplate her grandmother's stories which she dismisses as lies:

> Yo siento mareos y la cabeza va a reventarme. Esta maldita enfermedad quizá no termine nunca, quizá termine conmigo y me lleve lejos, para no volver a ver a la abuela que dice mentiras y a mi madre que me está volviendo loca (p.61).

---

7   All quotations are from *Y si yo fuera Susana San Juan* (Mexico City: Fondo Editorial Tierra Adentro: Conaculta, 1998). Page numbers refer to this edition and will appear after the quotations in parentheses.

8   '–¿Qué hace aquí esta niña? – Le preguntó a mi madre –, te dije que trae el demonio por dentro' (p.19) and again, a page later, 'Esta niña trae el demonio por dentro, Aurelia' (p.20).

9   In the love letters exchanged between Anastasia and Beto, Anastasia's story is fully revealed. In her poignant account of the episode in which she and Beto are apprehended by Ceferino who is later shot as a result, she makes direct reference to the idea of the devil inside her, 'Yo no lo disparé, fue ese demonio que traigo dentro' (p.61).

The refusal to hear the grandmother's story and indeed the outright rejection of her grandmother are palpable throughout the novel:

> La abuela habla como loro y ni siquiera entiende sus propias palabras. Puedo escuchar lo que dice, está preocupada, algo la angustia. Es como si hubiera salido de su mundo interno para entrar a otro que tampoco es éste. Dice cosas, no me gusta lo que dice (p.60).

The continual negative attitude towards the grandmother is an overdetermined gesture in the text, illustrated by the gradual breaking down of the young protagonist's barriers and her eventual collapse when she quite literally lets Anastasia's story become part of her own narrative of disintegration. At this point in the narrative, however, she is immersed in an horrific world in which she cannot transcend the injustices inflicted on her by her family. This inability to go beyond an unbearable reality is signalled textually, by her literal inability to breathe which, in turn, forms part of many of the body's outbursts, fits and fevers. Consider the following passage:

> Siento que me muero, no puedo respirar. El aire en esta habitación está viciado y me ahogo. Todo está en semipenumbras. Huele a incienso, Aurelia lo ha puesto por toda la habitación en un esfuerzo por invocar antiguos fantasmas. Me quiere asfixiar, me está matando poco a poco. La abuela parece querer ayudarla con su eterna pipa humeante haciendo este ambiente más pesado aún. [...] Estoy sudando. Esta cama es demasiado angosta. Hay veladoras en la cómoda y una Virgen de Guadalupe. Aurelia le dice a la abuela que se calle, la casa debe permanecer en silencio, en una tranquilidad que me hace sentir sumida en el infierno (pp.60–1).

Later the difficulty with breathing arises again, as in the following passage in which Susana fantasises that she was once Anne Boleyn:

> En mi otra vida seguramente fui Ana Bolena, porque todas las mañanas despierto con una extraña sensación en el cuello, como si la sangre corriera por mi garganta hasta mojarme el pecho, y la cintura y todo el cuerpo. Siento un horrible escozor en la nuca y a veces me falta el aire (p.63).[10]

10 Ana Cruz García makes an interesting point in relation to the connection drawn between Susana and Ann Boleyn: 'Hay ciertas características interesantes sobre el personaje de Ana Bolena, aristócrata del siglo XVI, por las que la narradora

Here it is blood that she imagines running down her body, an explicit evocation of the pain endured by Susana throughout. As the text progresses, it becomes clear that each fit or convulsion is triggered by either a memory of the past and/or a sharp physical reminder of her painful reality. In the following passage, Susana San Juan describes Susana's violent outbreak of vomiting and fever to the psychiatrist:

> Hace un par de días tuvo una fuerte recaída. Gritaba horriblemente y se golpeaba la cabeza contra la pared. Me costó mucho trabajo tranquilizarla. Aurelia quería amarrarla a los barrotes de su cama, pero yo logré calmarla a tiempo. Todo fue por culpa del idiota de su padre. Ahora resulta que el hombre tiene un hijo con otra mujer, un medio hermano de Susana. ¿No le parece ridículo, doctor? A mí me parece abominable. Lo peor de todo es que se llama Pedro. Esa noche Susana tuvo fiebre y vómitos. Lo insultó y le escupió a la cara; le dijo que no quería volver a verlo y mucho menos conocer al mentado Pedro. [...] La mamá de Susana la agarró a cintarazos. Pero Susana ni los sentía y se ponía más violenta cada vez, luego empezó a echar espumarajos por la boca y Aurelia se asustó. Entonces llegué yo y la empecé a tranquilizar con caricias y palabras suavecitas para hacerle sentir un poquito de cariño, pues nadie podrá dárselo (pp.69–70).

Several elements in this passage are worthy of discussion. First, the lapse into fever and convulsion is set in train by the reappearance of her father after many years, along with a half-brother about whom Susana knew nothing. Second, the fever reaches a new level of violent intensity requiring her to be restrained. Finally, the passage presents Susana San Juan who has assumed control of the narrative in the form of the first person, and who consoles and pacifies the young girl. Indeed, the passage signals the start of Susana's demise as a character

Susana se podría haber sentido identificada. Formó parte de las damas de honor de la primera esposa de Enrique VIII, Catalina de Aragón y, tras el divorcio de ambos, se convirtió en su segunda esposa. Igualmente, Susan ansía ser la segunda esposa de Juan aunque sabe que no es posible. Ana Bolena fue un ser grandioso y pasional. Fue considerada como una mujer bella y astuta que despertó pasiones, incluso después de su muerte trágica por decapitación al haber sido acusada de adulterio e incesto'. Ana Cruz García, 'Locura y feminidad: representaciones de la loca en la obra de Elena Garro, Susana Págano, Ana Castillo y María Amparo Escandón', Ph.D, University College Cork, 2007, p.66.

who throughout the final part of the novel can only function as Susana San Juan. The rest of the narrative then, documents Susana's deterioration, as described by Susana San Juan, who takes care of her, 'Más de cuatro meses estuvo delirando entre sudores fríos y vómitos constantes' (p.77). Finally she loses her battle with life:

> Pasaron varios días antes de que Susana empezara a perder la esperanza. Se podían ver bajo sus ojos las ojeras del cansancio y la desilusión. En una semana había perdido tres kilos, parecía envejecer a los veinticinco años (p.79).

Susana San Juan continues her descriptions in the first-person form, narrating the story of Susana's death to the psychiatrist, 'Algunos meses después de haber llegado a Comala, cayó irremediablemente en cama. Sudaba a raudales y tenía fiebre. Su mirada ya no pertenecía a este mundo' (p.80). The final descent is noted as the body stops convulsing and accepts the inevitable:

> Los últimos meses de su enfermedad, Susana ya no me reconocía. Había cesado la fiebre, los sudores y el vómito. Parecía estar en coma, en estado vegetativo. Cuando finalmente cerró los ojos, me quedé observándola un largo rato (p.81).

These descriptions of the body in revolt eloquently illustrate the permeability of corporal limits and the precarious nature of the subject as described by Kristeva: 'the body's inside [...] shows up in order to compensate for the collapse of the border between inside and outside. It is as if the skin, a fragile container, no longer guaranteed the integrity of "one's own and clean self"'.[11] Susana's literal abjection of her 'own' self to adopt the self of an 'other,' is graphically illustrated and Susana metamorphoses into Susana San Juan to attain the physical and mental 'tranquilidad' she so desperately craves. This yearning for a tranquility that is physical, metaphysical and psychological is inscribed in the text throughout and constitutes one of its most poignant elements.[12] The tranquillity that so eludes Susana is

---

11   *Powers of Horror*, p.9.
12   Interestingly the terms 'tranquilidad' (tranquilizar; tranquila) punctuate the text and form the thread that links Susana to her alter ego: 'Mientras las cosas tranquilizan' (p.50), and 'Me sentí más tranquila' (p.18). See also other references to the same concept (p.49, p.60 and p.120).

filtered through an anguished existence, codified at an explicit level as a yearning for a loving mother figure, so clearly unavailable to her in the form of her biological mother, Aurelia.

Abject Motherhood

Maternal absence is central to Kristevan discourse on the abject. She contends that the maternal figure must be removed to enable the child to assume its identity and that, as the child's position becomes increasingly unstable in its journey towards adulthood, the mother's body becomes a site of conflicting desires. In this text, there is a conflict between the 'real' unloving mother, and Susana San Juan who functions as the absent mother in a very heartrending way. In one of the early descriptions of Susana's physical torment, she reaches out to Susana San Juan for comfort:

> ¿Sigues aquí, Susana San Juan? Cuéntame un cuento; cántame una canción, Susana San Juan; pero no me escucha porque no puedo hablar. Se sienta en la vieja mecedora, junto a mi cama, para velar mi sueño. No puedo dormir, aunque estoy muy cansada. Cierro los ojos y sólo puedo verte a ti y sentir la presencia de ella (p.42).

Here, in an eerie parallel with the earlier passage in which the grandmother is ignored, Susana is not listened to because of her inability to enunciate the pain she is suffering. There are many references to Susana San Juan's nurturing role with regard to her troubled counterpart as, for example, when she tells the psychiatrist:

> Susana está en su casa porque tiene fiebre. La he estado cuidando noche tras noche. Aurelia, su madre, no ha sido ni para llevarle un té. Pobrecita, a veces tiene pesadillas (p.43).

In this passage, an explicit comparison is set up between Aurelia the 'bad' mother and Susana, the 'good' one. Given that she is the alter ego of Susana, this insistence on Susana San Juan's motherly qualities alongside the love she demonstrates for her 'charge,' lends itself to be read psychoanalytically as Susana's desperate yearning for maternal love: 'Pero no está sola porque me tiene a mí. Yo la cuido como si fuera mi hija, podría serlo, ¿sabe? Pero yo nunca tuve hijos, por eso la quiero tanto' (p.44). The text spells out the connection on various occasions: 'Susana murió en mis brazos. Sentí tanto su pérdida como si de una hija se hubiese tratado' (p.77). The 'final' words of Susana to her 'mother' are again heartrending:

> ¿Estarás conmigo todo el tiempo, no me dejarás ni un segundo?

> – Ni un segundo, Susana. Nunca te dejaré (p.80).

Here, the 'mother' speaks words of comfort, promising to be with her forever, in stark contrast to the cold unloving mother figure embodied by Aurelia. What is more, Susana's 'death' in the text coincides exactly with Aurelia's suicide attempt, providing further testimony to the absolute gulf that exists between them.

This tension between the 'good' and 'bad' mothers in the text is interesting in the context of Kristevan theory on the abject. As stated earlier, Kristeva maintains that the ritual defilement of the mother figure in many religions helps to preserve stability in that it prevents the mother engulfing her children:

> This is precisely where we encounter the rituals of defilement and their derivatives which, based on the feeling of abjection and all converging on the maternal, attempt to symbolize the other threat to the subject: that of being swamped by the dual relationship, thereby risking the loss not of a part (castration) but of the totality of his living being. The function of these religious rituals is to ward off the subject's fear of his very own identity sinking irretrievably into the mother.[13]

The anxiety articulated here with regard to the overwhelming mother figure is also figured in the text in a particularly overt way when Susana San Juan tries to explain Susana's predicament to the psychiatrist:

13   *Powers of Horror*, p.64.

A Susana no la ha amado nadie; ni siquiera Juan, como ella se empeña en creer. No existe un hombre que se haya sentido apasionado por Susana, por su mente, por su cuerpo o su personalidad. Susana carece de todo eso. Nunca ha sido bonita, ni siquiera atractiva; no es un ser para inspirar pasiones, como yo. No tiene personalidad ni carácter; *su madre nulificó en ella cualquier cosa que pudiera superarla. Las madres son egoístas, en especial la de Susana; le aterraba que su hija pudiera superarla en cualquier sentido, por eso le prohibió cualquier actividad que pudiera convertirla en un ser pleno, autónomo, inteligente. Y Susana se dejó aplastar, hundiéndose en sus sueños, en sus fantasías inalcanzables* (p.56, my emphasis).

This explicitly lays out the potentially damaging role of mothers generally and the particularly venomous effect of Susana's own mother, Aurelia. Of course, what is far more chilling is the fact that the 'good' mother figure, represented by Susana San Juan, enacts precisely the engulfing role envisaged by Kristeva as she totally annihilates her 'child' at the end of the novel. Susana's 'death' – textually represented as the complete takeover of her body and mind by Susana San Juan – bears sinister testimony to the stark vision of maternity outlined in the novel in which all mothers consume their young and erase their subjectivity.

This is a supremely interesting view of motherhood in a novel from 1990s Mexico given that in the previous two decades the role of the mother had undergone dramatic changes at socio-economic level. It is widely acknowledged that the Mexican family structure has changed. Brígida García points to the statistically dramatic change with regard to female 'heads of household' during this time, a change underscored by the rapid economic development in the *maquiladora* sector which employs predominantly women.[14] Furthermore, much of

14   Brígida García, 'Economic Restructuring, Women's Work and Autonomy in Mexico', in Harriet Presser and Gita Sen (eds), *Women's Empowerment and Demographic Processes: Moving Beyond Cairo* (Oxford: Oxford University Press, 2003). *Maquiladoras* are foreign-owned assembly plants in Mexico. The general *modus operandi* involves the import of machinery and materials duty-free for assembly in the *maquiladora* followed by immediate export. The companies include Fisher Price, Samsung, Ericsson and Toshiba among others. *Maquiladoras* predominantly employ women: 'In the early days women made up as much as 80% of the assembly plant workforce, today they number close to 60%. While they can legally be hired at the age of 16, it is common for these

the discussion surrounding globalisation and feminisation of the labour market has promoted the idea that masculinity is undergoing a crisis and this crisis exists alongside a pronounced fear of what Nikki Craske calls the '(s)mother' figure.[15] These changes find resonances in art and most particularly in cinema, as many films of the 1990s explore the complex changing role of the sacred mother figure set against the real-life constraints of a globalising modern society.[16] In many respects, Págano's novel seems to have little sense of the sociohistorical context and yet it constitutes a bitter social commentary in its indictment of a system that leaves three female members utterly brutalised by the most extreme forms of patriarchal power.[17]

girl-women to get false documents in order to go to work at ages as young as 12, 13 or 14'. *Mexican Labour News and Analysis*, 3 February 1999, Vol.4, No.4, n.p. See also, Susan Tiano, *Patriarchy on the Line: Labor, Gender, and Ideology in the Mexican Maquila Industry* (Philadelphia: Temple University Press, 1994), and Rachael Kamel, Anya Hoffman (eds), *The Maquiladora Reader: Cross-Border Organising Since NAFTA* (American Friends Service Committee (AFSC), 1999).

15   Nikki Craske, '(S)mothering Politics: Motherhood as Political Identity', conference paper, Society of Latin American Studies, University of Liverpool, 14–16 April, 1998. In this she outlines how the centrality of the mothering role has led to a reconfiguration of roles within the traditional Mexican family. See also Sylvia Chant, 'Urban livelihoods, employment and gender', in Robert N. Gwynne and Cristóbal Kay (eds), *Latin America Transformed: Globalization and Modernity* (London: Edward Arnold, 2004), pp.210–31.

16   This anxiety over gender roles has been played out on the big screen in the films of María Novaro, particularly *Lola* (1989) in which the role of motherhood is depicted as both complex and contradictory. For an analysis of motherhood in Mexican cinema, see Márgara Millán Moncaya, *Derivas de un cine en femenino* (Mexico: UNAM y Miguel Angel Porrúa, 1999), and Miriam Haddu, *Contemporary Mexican Cinema (1989–1999): History, Space, Identity* (Lewiston: Edwin Mellen Press, 2007), pp.81–114.

17   The main body of the narrative in Págano's text is concerned, as is documented here, with the psychic disintegration of its main protagonist. However, the novel as a whole constitutes a damning critique of gender politics. Neither is it devoid of direct social commentary when certain aspects of the modernising process in Mexico are gently criticised: 'La ciudad es hermosa, a pesar del aire sucio, de los microbuses como elefantes que estorban en todos lados, de la gente olvidada de su propia persona' (p.72). There are also direct historical

The 'Lost Father'

In tandem with this bleak portrait of toxic mothering, is an equally powerful father-longing which is figured in the text by Susana's affectionate memories of her grandfather and which are juxtaposed with Susana San Juan's longing for 'Juan'. The choice of 'Juan', the author of the character Susana San Juan, as opposed to 'Pedro', her husband in the Rulfo text, raises certain questions about creativity and the canon that will be addressed in the next section. At this point, what is of primary interest is the way in which the 'Juan' figure is inserted into the text. In many cases he is invoked erotically, as a love interest in physical descriptions:

> Sus manos son como de algodón, tan suavecitas. Te acaricia con demasiada delicadeza; a veces lo quisieras sentir más brusco, un poco salvaje quizá. Pero te gusta su ternura. Es el primer hombre en tu vida, y te agrada pensar que será el último. Por eso es tan cauteloso, tranquilo y a veces inseguro. Tal vez sea mejor así, si fuera más apasionado, te despedazaría como una bomba. Pero tú misma te das cuenta del calor tan inmenso que te abrasa el vientre. Sus ojos tristones, llenos de recuerdos violentos, te enternecen y hacen que lo desees. Vives de él y para él. Desde que leíste su novela, prometiste no pertenecer a nadie más, no hay más hombre para ti, sólo Juan, sus ojos, sus manos, su frente arrugada, su aire de nostalgia y pureza (pp.47–8).

In the following passage, he is also evoked as a love interest and the anxiety over possible rejection or abandonment is palpable:

> Estás recostada, sientes la cama demasiado grande para ti sola, ahora que ya se ha ido. Quisieras olvidar la huella de su cuerpo en tu memoria; es como un castigo por haber gozado de un ser que no te corresponde. Sin embargo, es

references, 'Mucha gente ha perdido sus ranchos y haciendas; es injusto que le quiten a la gente honrada sus pertenencias. Siempre dije que ese presidente [Cárdenas] no nos traería nada bueno' (p.53). Later, there are references to the bloody extremes of the Mexican Revolution with an account of the rape of the mother's servant: '– Aquellos hombres colgados de los árboles [...] sus caras están amoratadas y sus ojos abiertos llenos de terror. Los soldados arrasan con todo, especialmente con las mujeres. A Minga la viola uno de ellos y a mi madre por poco y la matan' (p.91).

tuyo; es tu amante y tu esclavo. Sus olores se quedan contigo, así como su tímida sonrisa y sus palabras de poeta. Pero cada vez que se va sientes un enorme vacío; un vacío muy dentro de ti, *pero no le puedes pedir que se quede; tienes miedo de su respuesta.* Recorres tu cuarto con la mirada; puedes sentir su presencia en cada esquina, en cada rincón polvoriento y lleno de pesadillas. Cierras los ojos para ver los suyos, pero no los encuentras porque se han ido. ¿En dónde estás, Juan?; regresa, Juan (p. 48, my emphasis).

Here the fear of loss is inscribed in the text and the appeal for him to 'return' recalls both her actual father who abandoned her as a young child, and her grandfather – the father figure of her childhood – whom she recalls with affection in her 'conscious' state of mind. Her appeal for him to return creates here a similarity with the longing for the mother, which is articulated so precisely through the figure of Susana San Juan. The loss of both father figures in her 'real' life, therefore, is played out in parallel in her fantasy world as she shouts in frustration at her abandonment and loss:

– Por supuesto, ella me lo cuenta todo. A veces sueña que va a la Rotonda de los Hombres Ilustres a poner flores en la tumba de Juan, pero nunca lo encuentra porque Juan no está enterrado ahí. Se despierta gritándole que vuelva, a veces lo insulta en sueños porque la ha dejado sola (pp.43–4).

It is at this point that a very interesting connection is established between the textual references to Juan and those referring to her grandfather/father. References to both men are often placed alongside each other in the text. This is seen in the passage above which leads immediately to one of the saddest memories recounted about Susana's childhood suffering at the hands of her grandfather. In this section, as before, it is Susana San Juan who narrates Susana's story to the psychiatrist:

Una noche soñó que su abuelo le pegaba horriblemente por haberse comido un gusano del jardín. Se despertó muy asustada jurándome que nunca ha tenido jardín, que le busque a su abuelo para pedirle perdón. Ella quiso mucho a su abuelo, y él a ella. Su abuelo murió hace muchos años.
– ¿De que murió?
– ¿Quién?
– El abuelo de Susana.

– No lo sé [...] no lo sé, pero era muy bueno– miró al doctor con rabia, me enfurecen sus preguntas, sus ansias por saberlo todo–. Me invitaba helados a escondidas de mi madre y me llevaba a Coyoacán a pasear. Luego jugábamos a las escondidillas en el jardín.
– Pero tú le dijiste a Susana San Juan que nunca has tenido jardín (p.44).

The implications of this passage are worth observing in some detail as it illustrates clearly the mental battle raging between two different versions of the grandfather's story. On the one hand, there is the grandmother's story of incarceration and abuse by a cruel and sadistic husband and yet, on the other, there are Susana's conscious memories which recall her grandfather as the affectionate father figure missing from her life. The grandmother's version is, of course, rejected violently by Susana on one plane of reality. The emphatic nature of her rejection, however, may be interpreted as overdetermined, in that it becomes obvious that she has repressed the 'real' version, a repression that is articulated in this passage in which she has nightmares about him beating her for eating a worm from the garden. The 'conscious' Susana denies that she has a garden, thus enabling her to repress the horrible memories she has of being punished by both her grandfather and her mother for her games there. A few lines later she suddenly 'remembers' their game-playing in the garden when it becomes safe for her to do so. Her denials are thus strategic and function as mechanisms of protection against the horrific memories that threaten her being. This is a portrait, therefore, of a subconscious in absolute torment – unable to accept the brutal truth of her grandfather's behaviour towards herself and her grandmother, Susana chooses denial and repression.

The role of 'Juan' here is interesting in that he functions in this passage as the trigger for a memory about the grandfather. This establishes a textual connection between them which positions him as the 'other' *abuelo*, the 'creator'/father of Susana San Juan, positioned here as the 'mother'. He is also, however, Susana's erotic love focus and it is this dual positioning of his character that most effectively conveys the distortion of Susana's mind. This vague suggestion of incest is, of course, explicit in the Rulfo text[18] and in this novel is

18   The incestuous relationships in both texts will be examined in the next section.

hinted at in other passages recalling the grandfather. The textual connection just outlined between Juan and the grandfather also occurs at other points in the text:

> Desde que tuve fiebre, tengo pesadillas casi todas las noches. Si fuera de noche durante seis meses, tendría pesadillas constantemente y no podría ver el otoño. Durante seis meses tendría miedo de que me llegara la muerte, porque la muerte llega siempre de noche. El abuelo murió de noche. Yo no podía dormir y lo vi. Murió en los brazos de Aurelia. *¿Y a tí, Juan, ¿cuándo te agarró la muerte?* (p.45, my emphasis).

Tracing the progression of dark thoughts in this passage, it can again be seen how a parallel is evoked between Juan and the grandfather. In this nightmare, Susana writhes in anguish thinking about her own death and also about her grandfather's death in the arms of her mother. Immediately, to block out the pain of the reality, she resorts to the fantasy world and transfers the question onto Juan. The fact that many of these 'memory' passages end with Susana falling into a deep sleep, again underlines the idea of escape from a reality that is too cruel:

> Subo a mi cuarto, me siento cansada, terriblemente cansada. En ocasiones duermo demasiado. Puedo estar todo un día entero durmiendo, soñando tonterías o con la mente en blanco. Ahora es uno de esos días, cuando nada tiene sentido, mejor sería dormir profundamente hasta ya no despertar más. Me recuesto en la cama, más por costumbre que por ganas de hacerlo. Los párpados empiezan a caer pesados sobre mis ojos sin que pueda evitarlo. Y no quiero evitarlo. Duermo profundamente, sin sueños, sin prisas, sin culpas (pp.45–6).

Fantasy and oblivion become the only relief from her tormented world and Juan becomes the thread that connects the world of cruel reality with the fantasy that enables her release. In this long passage, Juan features again as erotic love object, but the anxiety of abandonment is also palpable:

> Algo ha sucedido en mi vientre desde que me tocaste. Siempre pensé que mi cuerpo nunca dejaría de ser inmaduro aunque pasaran muchos años. Me has hecho muy feliz, Juan. Ahora podré empezar a ser mujer, una mujer de verdad.
> Me gustaría ir contigo a todos lados; a esas importantes reuniones con tantos escritores famosos, como tú. Me gustaría que me llevaras de la mano y

les gritara a todos que soy tuya, tu mujer. Pero nunca me llevarás porque estás casado. No es que tenga algo en contra de Clara, debe ser una mujer hermosa; pero me da rabia no ser yo quien lleve tu nombre, no ser yo quien lleve flores a tu sepultura. Me traicionaste, Juan, me volviste esclava de tu cuerpo y de tu mente sabiendo que estabas muerto. Y por eso yo ahora desearía estar a tu lado, en el mismo féretro; como Juan Preciado en los brazos de Dorotea, los dos en el mismo ataúd, compartiendo juntos la muerte y los recuerdos. Pero te fuiste antes de que yo dejara las muñecas, por eso sigo niña aunque con cuerpo de mujer. Regresa Juan, regresa y ya no seas cruel conmigo. Pero no vendrás, sé que no podrías hacerlo por mucho que yo te lo pidiera (pp.50–1).

In what constitutes almost classic Freudian displacement,[19] the plea for her grandfather to return and its implied reproach are transferred onto Juan, when she entreats him to come back.[20] The helplessness

19 The notion of displacement in Freud's work, as is well known, refers to the way in which the primitive impulses of latent dream-thought are re-worked. According to Freud, displacement takes place when the affect (emotions) associated with threatening impulses are transferred elsewhere (displaced), so that, for example, apparently trivial elements in the manifest dream seem to cause extraordinary distress while 'what was the essence of the dream-thoughts finds only passing and indistinct representation in the dream'. For Freud, 'Displacement is the principle means used in the *dream-distortion* to which the dream-thoughts must submit under the influence of the censorship', 'New Introductory Lectures', in *The Standard Edition of the Complete Psychological Works of Sigmund Freud*, trans. by James Strachey, 24 Vols, Vol.4 (London: Hogarth, 1953–1974), p.22. Repression, which Freud sometimes called the 'dream-censor' in his discussion of dreams, is continually re-working the latent dream-thoughts, which are then forced to assume distorted or even unrecognizable forms. Freud called this translation of latent dream-thoughts into the manifest dream the 'dream work'. The two main ways in which repression re-works the primitive impulses of the latent dream-thoughts is by way of condensation (1) or displacement (2). See *The Standard Edition of the Complete Psychological Works of Sigmund Freud*, Vol. 5, pp. 339–487.
20 The very use of the word, 'regresa' here, of course, invites a Freudian reading. Susana's earnest plea for him to return in this text, thus, again aligns him with the grandfather and Freud's infamous term, the 'return of the repressed'. According to Freud, the very act of entering into civilised society entails the repression of various primitive desires. Each person's psychosexual development includes the surpassing of previous 'love-objects' that are tied to earlier sexual phases (the oral phase, the anal-sadistic phase). However, according to his research, even well-adjusted individuals betray the insistent force of those

suggested by the final line reinforces the sense of loss and abandonment that defines the character of Susana. The appeal to Juan not to leave, not to disappear, would seem to place him in the classic position of displaced father/grandfather figure: 'Estando contigo, todo es tranquilidad, todo está bien. Te quiero, Juan. *No vuelvas a desaparecer*' (p.60, my emphasis). Later in the text, this connection is made even more explicit as Juan is admired as an icon of fatherhood:

> Debes ser un gran padre, aunque quizá un poco distante y meditabundo; [...] Sin embargo, tus hijos deben adorarte; ¿cómo no idolatrar a alguien tan perfecto y completo como tú? (p.59).

This image of Juan as the good father is set up in direct contrast to the character of her real father who reappears towards the end of the text. The real Susana's reactions and responses to this man follow a typical pattern. Unable to face the reality of the father who abandoned her, she takes refuge in the fantasy identity of Susana San Juan as in when she says, '– No me acuerdo de usted y no me llame Susanita porque mi nombre es Susana San Juan' (p.46). Here, as before, the Susana San Juan persona functions as the flight from the reality that is too painful to contemplate (in this case, the abandonment by the father). Thereafter, her need for escape is more acute and she takes refuge, as before, in several classic abject gestures. This is seen at several points: she says of her father, 'Me dio lástima; pero también quisiera golpearlo, morderlo, matarlo' (p.59). Later she reveals that, 'Fuimos a ver una película en donde todos se matan por cualquier cosa. Salí con ganas de vomitar y le dije que no volvería al cine con él, ni a ningún otro lado' (p.60).

Fatherhood, therefore, in Págano's text is as toxic a construct as that of motherhood and certainly as destructive. A rapprochement of sorts is negotiated between Susana and her grandmother when Susana finally appears to accept Anastasia's history and actually relives her grandmother's dream albeit in a grotesquely, distorted manner. However, no such relief is in store for the father figure. The character of Juan disappears from the narrative once Susana 'dies' but is in turn

earlier desires through dreams, literature, or 'Freudian slips'; hence the term, 'return of the repressed'.

reincarnated in the form of Pedro (the connection with Rulfo's text is again unmistakable), and takes the form of erotic love focus for the final section of the novel. The re-writing of *Pedro Páramo* is completed as Susana San Juan and Pedro dance together in the twilight, enacting Anastasia's wedding: 'Bailan muy cerca el uno del otro, sintiendo sus cuerpos, sus alientos' (p.135). Thus in a bizarre way, the novel ends quite traditionally with a wedding and a happy union, an ironic, self-reflexive comment on the conventions of fiction and an issue that will be discussed in the next section.

Anxieties of Authorship: Ambivalence and Desire[21]

As stated at the beginning of this chapter, both texts under discussion, *Y si yo fuera Susana San Juan* and *Once días y algo más,* raise questions about the enduring importance of the canon that illustrate the profound ambivalence felt by women writers in their engagement with literary tradition generally. In this section, I return to the notion of ambivalence (present here in a very different form from its manifestation in Chapter One), and try to illuminate some of the issues highlighted by this intriguing text. First, as has been established, the character Susana San Juan is taken from the Juan Rulfo novel, *Pedro Páramo*, the story of a corrupt Mexican *cacique* in the small fictional

21   The term 'anxiety of authorship', is from Sandra Gilbert and Susan Gubar's work, *The Madwoman in the Attic: The Woman Writer and the Nineteenth Century Literary Imagination* (New Haven: Yale University Press, 1979). In this study they trace the evolution of a female literary tradition and the persistence of certain figures and images, isolating the trope of madness as central to female constructions of the self in the nineteenth century. In a play on Harold Bloom's famous term 'anxiety of influence', Gilbert and Gubar argue that the woman writer suffers from an 'anxiety of authorship', 'a radical fear that she cannot create, that because she can never become a "precursor" the act of writing will isolate and destroy her', *The Madwoman in the Attic*, p.49. In the Mexican context, see Catherine Grant, 'Authorship and Authority in the Novels of Rosario Castellanos', Ph.D, University of Leeds, 1991.

town of Comala in the aftermath of the Mexican Revolution. Published in 1955, it remains the most acclaimed novel of contemporary Mexican fiction and catapulted Juan Rulfo to international attention.[22] A blackly pessimistic exploration of the human psyche, Susana San Juan is the only notable female character. She is the eponymous hero's object of desire whom he marries only to realise that, though he may possess her physically, he can never colonise her mind. She remains thus aloof and unattainable (in the psychological sense), finally dying after much physical and mental torment. Here I quote the line that synthesises the essentially enigmatic nature of Susana San Juan:

> ¿Pero cuál era el mundo de Susana San Juan? Esa fue una de las cosas que Pedro Páramo nunca llegó a saber (p.80).[23]

A cogent outline of the difficulties involved in ever 'knowing' the human subject, this passage also captures the eternal mystery of 'woman', a Mexican interpretation of the infamous – and indeed endlessly mocked – question posed by Freud, 'what does a woman want?'[24] The similarities between the Rulfian creation, Susana San Juan, and the character of Susana in the Págano text are clearly es-

---

22 Rulfo's text is sometimes included, though problematically, as part of Latin America's *boom*, frequently defined as the arrival of novels that dealt with issues of history, identity and society and their enthusiastic reception on the international stage. The *boom* is epitomised by the novels of Gabriel García Márquez, Mario Vargas Llosa, Julio Cortázar and Carlos Fuentes among others. For a good introduction to the area, see, John King, 'The boom of the Latin American novel' in *Cambridge Companion to the Latin American Novel* (Cambridge: Cambridge University Press, 2007), pp. 59–80.

23 All references to the novel are from *Pedro Páramo y El llano en llamas* (Barcelona: Planeta, 1990) and will appear at the end of the citations in parentheses.

24 This question is posed by James Strachey, official translator of Freud into English, in a footnote to his introductory remarks to Freud's 1925 paper on female sexuality. In it, he quotes Ernest Jones as saying that Freud said: 'The great question has never been answered and which I have not yet been able to answer despite my thirty years of research into the feminine soul, is, what does a woman want?' No date is given for the remark. Ernest Jones, *The Life and Work of Sigmund Freud* (New York: Basic Books, 1955), p.421.

tablished from the outset. Both are constantly referred to as 'crazy', and yet uncertainty clouds the definition of the term in both. Indeed both texts interrogate fixed notions of madness/insanity and expose the fragile discourse as entirely dependent on point of view, a concept introduced quite explicitly in the Rulfo text:

> −¿Y quién es ella?
> −La última esposa de Pedro Páramo. Unos dicen que estaba loca. Otros, que no.
> La verdad es que ya hablaba sola desde en vida (p.66).

In this passage, madness is shown as dependent on standpoint ('unos dicen que estaba loca. Otros, que no'), a construction that seems to replicate Foucauldian discourses on madness.[25] Indeed, Foucault's argument that the historical discourse of madness has frequently been used as a brutal means of silencing and marginalising certain groups (including women), has many resonances in both texts.[26]

Further evidence of commonality between both characters can be found in the anxiety surrounding Susana's attachment to her dead mother in *Pedro Páramo* which echoes the poignant quest for maternal affection undertaken by Susana throughout the Págano novel:

> − Debe haber muerto hace mucho.
> − Uh, sí! ¿Hace mucho. ¿Qué le oíste decir?
> − Algo acerca de su madre.
> − Pero si ella ni madre tuvo…
> − Pues de eso hablaba.

---

25 Foucault's ground-breaking study which was published in 1961, firmly established 'madness' as a discourse formed out of prevailing ideologies and belief systems – an historical construct which can silence and marginalise certain forms of behaviour in any given moment, a premise that is shared in the Rulfo and Págano texts. Michel Foucault, *Madness and Civilisation: A History of Insanity in the Age of Reason* (London: Routledge, 2001).

26 For feminist analyses of Foucault and madness, see Elaine Showalter, *The Female Malady: Women, Madness and English Culture 1830–1980* (London: Virago Press, 1987). For a fascinating analysis of madness in Susana Págano, see Ana Cruz García, 'La locura femenina: representaciones de la loca en la obra de Elena Garro, Susana Págano, Ana Castillo and María Amparo Escandón', Ph.D, University College Cork, 2007, pp.129–77.

… O, al menos, no la trajo cuando vino. Pero espérate. Ahora recuerdo que ella nació aquí, y que ya de añejita desaparecieron. Y sí, su madre murió de la tisis. Era una señora muy rara que siempre estuvo enferma y no visitaba a nadie.
– Eso dice ella. Que nadie había ido a ver a su madre cuando murió.
– ¿Pero de qué tiempos hablará? Claro que nadie se paró en su casa por el puro miedo de agarrar la tisis. ¿Se acordará de eso la indina?
– De eso hablaba (pp.66–7).

In this passage we see that the quest and longing for the mother is identical in both protagonists and the similarity is further cemented by the protagonists' attachment to another mother figure. As already discussed, in *Y si yo fuera Susana San Juan*, this manifests itself as an intense attachment to the fictitious character of the Rulfo novel; in *Pedro Páramo*, the attachment is to Justina:

La había cuidado desde que nació. La había tenido en sus brazos. La había enseñado a andar. A dar aquellos pasos que a ella le parecían eternos. Había visto crecer su boca y sus ojos 'como de dulce'. El dulce de menta es azul. […] Le mordía las piernas. La entretenía dándole de mamar sus senos, que no tenían nada, que eran como de juguete. 'Juega –le decía–, juega con este juguetito tuyo' (p.75).

Furthermore, there is persistent ambiguity in both texts with regard to the possible incestuous relationships between Susana San Juan and her father Bartolomé (in *Pedro Páramo*), and between Susana and her grandfather (in *Y si yo fuera Susana San Juan)*. In Rulfo's text, this ambiguity surrounds Susana San Juan and her father from the moment of their arrival in Comala:

– ¿Han venido los dos?
– Sí, él y su mujer. ¿Pero cómo lo sabe?
– ¿No será su hija?
– Pues por el modo como la trata más bien parece su mujer.
– Vete a dormir, Fulgor (p.69).

The suggestion of incest is further evoked during a conversation between Bartolomé and Susana when they discuss the possibility of Susana marrying Pedro:

– ¿De manera que estás dispuesta a acostarte con él?

96

– Sí, Bartolomé.
– ¿No sabes que es casado y que ha tenido infinidad de mujeres?
– Sí, Bartolomé.
– No me digas Bartolomé. ¡Soy tu padre! (p.71).

This ambiguity is never resolved and Susana can never acknowledge her identity as the daughter of Bartolomé:

– ¿Y yo quién soy?
– Tú eres mi hija. Mía. Hija de Bartolomé San Juan.
En la mente de Susana San Juan comenzaron a caminar las ideas, primero lentamente, luego se detuvieron, para después echar a correr de tal modo que no alcanzó sino a decir:
– No es cierto. No es cierto.
Este mundo, que lo aprieta a uno por todos lados, que va vaciando puños de nuestro polvo aquí y allá, deshaciéndose en pedazos como si rociara la tierra con nuestra sangre. ¿Qué hemos hecho? ¿Por qué se nos ha podrido el alma? Tu madre decía que cuando menos nos queda la caridad de Dios. Y tú la niegas, Susana. ¿Por qué me niegas a mí como tu padre? ¿Estás loca?
– ¿No lo sabías?
– ¿Estás loca?
– Claro que sí, Bartolomé. ¿No lo sabías? (p.71).

This passage inscribes the 'madness' of Susana at the same time as it articulates the despair and disillusion of her father. The hellish world of Susana San Juan is a world in which she is unable to communicate with those around her, and as a result, she is cast as mad displaying many of the same abject features as her textual counterpart in Pagano's novel.[27] She is often naked and suffers from convulsions. One description describes her, 'la boca humedecida, entreabierta y las sábanas siendo recorridas por años inconscientes' (p.141). Thus, Susana San Juan is also the archetypal abject body, a 'body in revolt' against structures she can neither control nor understand. Págano, therefore, establishes multiple points of contact between the two Susanas, creating a continuum between the two texts when she posits

27   That Susana's world is hellish is explicitly outlined in the novel in the following exchange between Justina and Susana: '– ¿Tú crees en el infierno, Justina? – Sí, Susana. Y también en el cielo. – Yo sólo creo en el infierno – dijo. Y cerró los ojos' (p.91).

Susana as the textual 'daughter' of the Rulfian creation. On this level, the text may be read as a provocative attempt to 'rescue' the forgotton female character from Rulfo's text and to reinvent her for a 1990s readership.

The overdetermined intertextuality of the text, however, begs many other questions that remain unresolved in the novel itself. What is the purpose of the complex intertextual relationship established by Págano and what is the reader to make of the reinvention of Rulfo's classic text? On one level, as just stated, it may be read as a striking example of resistance in that Págano literally takes the most famous female figure of the Mexican literary tradition and reinvents her script. In this way it functions as a classic feminist gesture of agency in which power and authority is taken from the male writer and assigned to the female.[28] The father-like qualities assigned to Rulfo in the text would seem to add weight to this reading and uphold the conventional notion of author as figure of authority.[29] To re-imagine this most canonical text, therefore, involves a certain unmasking of the ideology of the author, a rewriting that unsettles the notion of an established

28   This gesture finds resonances in many cultures in the various other attempts to 'feminise' canonical texts. These include feminist responses to Shakespeare, featuring Virginia Woolf's famous speculations about 'Shakespeare's Sister' in her essay, *A Room of One's Own*, and Charlotte Brönte's *Shirley* (1849) which has been interpreted as a re-writing of *Coriolanus*. See *A Room of One's Own* (England: Hogarth Press, 1929) and *Shirley* (Oxford: Oxford University Press, 1998). The most striking example in the Hispanic context is possibly Kathy Acker's provocative and avant-garde re-writing of *Don Quixote* in her *Don Quixote: A Novel* (London: Paladin Books, 1985), which was later adapted for stage. See also Marianne Novy (ed.), *Women's Revisions of Shakespeare: On the Responses of Dickinson, Woolf, Rich, H.D., George Eliot and Others* (Urbana: University of Illinois Press, 1990).

29   It is precisely this idea of the author as father that Págano explores in her text. See Michel Foucault, 'What is an Author', in David Lodge (ed.), *Modern Criticism and Theory: A Reader* (London and New York: Longman, 1988), pp.196–210. Graham Allen writes, 'notions of paternity, of authority, of filiation – fathership, ownership, giving birth, familial power – all attach themselves to the name of the author in order to endorse it at the same moment as they express through it dominant social structures of power'. *Intertextuality* (London and New York: Routledge, 2000), p.71.

classic.[30] According to this logic it would seem to follow that Susana San Juan would be revitalised and rewritten in a more sympathetic manner, one that would question her status as ultimate enigma and her construction as insane. And yet the text refuses this route, and takes the character on a bizarre journey in which she is positioned as a fantasy mother figure who engulfs her young (the protagonist, Susana). What is more, she appropriates Susana's body and mind in a grotesque denouement that sees her re-united with her textual counterpart Pedro, as they dance closely together during their supposed 'marriage'. To complicate matters further, Pedro's identity as half-brother to the 'real' Susana reinstates the incestuous subtext of both novels.

The refusal to allow Susana's character to end in the way that Rulfo envisaged suggests further evidence of feminist resistance to the plot of the famous novel. Roland Barthes's fascinating analysis of Balzac's short story, *Sarrasine* has a particular resonance here. In Balzac's tale, the narrator tells the story of Sarrasine to a woman as part of a contract; 'the truth I exchange for a night of love'.[31] It transpires however, that the story horrifies the listener so much that she cancels the contract.[32] For Barthes, the woman's refusal to take part in the denouement the man has in mind for her – his plot – is akin to a refusal to let herself be narrativised, to 'allow anyone to make a story of her'.[33] Various critics have pointed to the significance of the woman's final words: 'No one will have known me. I am proud of that'.[34] These may be interpreted in the biblical sense as sexual

30   Barthes's celebrated text, 'The Death of the Author' along with Foucault's essay, 'What is an Author', from the same year (1968), examine this author ideology (in Foucault's terms, the 'author-function'). Both essays are reproduced in David Lodge (ed.), *Modern Criticism and Theory: A Reader* (London and New York, 1988), pp.166–72 and pp.196–211.

31   Roland Barthes, *S/Z*, trans. by Richard Miller (London: Jonathan Cape 1975), p.xx.

32   *S/Z*, p.33.

33   Jeremy Tambling, *Narrative and Ideology* (Milton Keynes and Philadelphia, Open University Press, 1991), pp.94–6. See also, Graham Allen, *Intertexuality*, pp.79–86. I shall return to this view of narrative as a contract between writer and reader in the next section.

34   *S/Z*, p.254.

knowledge but they also relate to the sense of knowledge as 'narrativising' or organising of content. Jeremy Tambling points to the etymology of the verb 'to narrate' (from the Latin, *gnarus*), which comes in turn from *cognoscere* meaning 'knowing', establishing the sense of narrative as a means of knowing the world.[35] Taking my cue from Barthes here, it would seem that Págano too refuses to accept the narrativisation assigned to Susana San Juan by Rulfo, and instead posits her first as the target of fantasy and finally as the devouring mother figure. She thus rejects Rulfo's denouement in which death in madness is the only result for Susana San Juan and instead immerses her in a different, completely feminised tale in which all the drama is played out through the central female characters and from which the male characters are definitively sidelined. The rejection of the Rulfian plotline here, thus, is paralleled in *Sarrasine* in which Clotilde, the young protagonist also rejects the path outlined for her and refuses the narrator's promise of love. In this way Págano's ending also functions as an incisive and ironic critique of traditional narrative (in the sense of the realist novel) and its insistence on a *desenlace feliz* or happy ending.

If this line of argument is continued, it becomes possible to advance an emancipatory reading of the text in that the re-enactment of the marriage ceremony of the wronged grandmother, Anastasia, is designed to bring alive her dream of marriage to Beto, even if only after her death. In this regard, it must be remembered that the supposed insanity of Anastasia is revealed as the result of her brutal incarceration as a punishment for infidelity.[36] In this way, the novel illustrates in graphic manner the cultural misogyny of a societal system that punished all transgressions and was particularly vicious with regard to women. Indeed, the *locura* of the young Susana herself may be interpreted as a logical response to a miserable childhood at

35   See *Narrative and Ideology*, p.94.
36   Incarceration of women who transgressed was commonplace in Mexico (and, of course in many parts of the world). Angeles Mastretta makes reference to these *manicomios* in her acclaimed novel, *Arráncame la vida* (Madrid: Alfaguara, 1986), p.63. Alcoholism, disputes over inheritance, and unwanted pregnancies, were all considered valid reasons for the incarceration of women (sometimes for life) in institutions.

the hands of an abusive grandfather and a mother incapable of love. The 'madness', thus, is explained as a rational and inevitable response to unspeakable cruelty, following again Foucauldian concepts of madness – already seen in the Rulfo text – as circumscribed by very real networks of power. Indeed Anastasia's fate may be read as the product of a collision between two vicious extremes: patriarchy (which denies her any right to choose a partner) and capitalism (which precipitates the arranged marriage in the first place as a mechanism of increasing the landholding of both 'interested' families). In this scenario, the acquisition of land is isolated as the driving force in the lives of the unfortunate protagonists. This is social commentary in the sense that it narrates the total disintegration of Susana's psyche as a way of coping with the brutal events of her family, the utter disregard for the feelings of her grandmother and the subsequent brutalisation of the whole family – Jaime and Aurelia. In this way, the novel does indeed connect to a wider context though in a muted, understated way. The ending, thus, provides a restorative justice of sorts for Anastasia who has been so cruelly abused by a system that sacrificed her feelings of love for the commercial and economic interests of her family. In this way, a feminist envisioning of Susana San Juan is indeed possible, if rather problematic, couched as it is in a language of ambivalence and uncertainty.

Perhaps, however, the novel's textual content is not the ultimate key to the meanings inherent within it. Indeed, it is in the curious ending of the novel that the political charge of the novel rests. To return again to the etymological origins of the word, 'narrative', the only possible relief afforded to the disintegrating self of the protagonist is the constant and, probably, infinite escape into other narratives. The panorama of narrative possibilities envisioned in the text function as the escape valves for the anguished female self. They include the story of Susana's imagined relationship with the author figure, the re-invention of the Susana San Juan character as engulfing mother, the tale of Anastasia and her tortured disintegrated psyche, and finally, the denouement which details another narrative in which multiple figures converge to modify and reinvent earlier versions. It is no accident that the novel ends in a grotesque parody in which, as already outlined, the protagonist, metamorphosed into her textual idol, seeks love in the arms of Pedro, her half-brother, thereby reuniting the 'lovers' of the intertext in a ritual of love. This enactment of the marriage of Anastasia and Beto, acted out by the characters of Susana and Pedro, is described as the only 'real' moment of their lives: 'Deseas que no termine este momento, el más feliz de tu vida, el más real, quizá el único que de verdad ha existido' (p.135). In this final scene, there is a union of sorts between the two texts: the Rulfian and Págano creations merge as they act out yet another narrative, that of Beto and Anastasia. Here, thus, is the Rulfian story of Pedro and Susana.[37] Here too is Págano's version of Rulfo's story of Pedro and Susana. Narrative begets narrative which in turn begets even more narrative. What is more, narrative becomes the only way for the self to survive – it is, in fact, through narrative and through the fantasies that derive from the 'already written', to use Barthes's term, that the self is saved from itself.[38] As Barthes maintained, each *lexia* (segment of meaning) is a signifying point which 'leads us out into the infinity of the social text, demonstrating the manner in which intertextuality [...] explodes and disperses within the text and shatters the illusion that narrative can provide an ultimate meaning'.[39] In the intertextual universe, an infinite number of meanings are possible and so Págano inscribes Barthes's vision of the boundless nature of intertextuality in the novel's rejection of linear and non-totalizing form. The ending,

37   The coupling of Pedro and Susana in the Rulfo text was, itself, grotesque, a rape of sorts in which Pedro possessed Susana's body but was never able to access her mind. It functions, therefore, as a necrophiliac gesture in which she is represented as a kind of corpse (a shell of a human from which the self has been abstracted). This omnipresent concept of death permeates the novel explicitly: all its protagonists are dead, a fact revealed a few pages into the novel. The corpse is, also, a classically abject incarnation, as Kristeva writes, 'Corpses show me what I permanently thrust aside in order to live. These body fluids, this defilement, this shit are what life withstands, hardly and with difficulty, on the part of death [...] My body extricates itself, as being alive, from that border. Such wastes drop so that I might live, until, from loss to loss, nothing remains in me and and my entire body falls beyond the limit – *cadere*, cadaver'. *Powers of Horror*, p.3.

38   It is in Barthes' concept of *déjà* that we find this notion of the always 'already written or read'. See *S/Z*, pp.72–4. See also *Intertextuality*, p.73.

39   *Intertexuality*, p.83.

thus, may be read as ironic, in the way it functions as incisive critique of the traditional novelistic denouement of the happy marriage. It is also, however, grotesque in its parodic representation of a simulated marriage between half-brother and sister, of whom one is clinically insane. This ending also provides evidence of the novel's painstaking dismantling of ideology and functions as poignant testimony to the plight of women under patriarchy. In the Págano world, as in that of Barthes, plurality is the final condition of any text, the only 'truth' available. Unlike Barthes, however, this plurality does not lead to *jouissance* but to confusion and decay.[40] Meaning, thus, is something always under construction in Págano's nightmare world, never quite finished and therefore, ultimately beyond reach.

Once días y algo más

A similarly crisis-ridden self – engaged in a dramatic struggle for survival – is also at the centre of Brianda Domecq's interesting fictionalised account of her ordeal as a kidnap victim during an eleven-day period in 1978. Domecq, the daughter of the Domecq wine and sherry dynasty, constituted a clear kidnapping risk in many ways, though the text is at pains to point out that Domecq and her husband live a fairly typical upper middle-class existence in Mexico City and have little access to the vast financial resources of the company. In a text almost twice as long as Págano's, Domecq describes in detail the sensations, desires and relationships that unfold over the period in captivity before she is rescued by the police. In many ways, this is

---

40   Views of intertextuality which celebrate the way in which the single subject is abandoned are styled by both Julia Kristeva and Roland Barthes as *jouissance*. As Robert Young states: '"Jouissance" means enjoyment in the sense of enjoyment of a right, of a pleasure, and, most of all, of sexual climax. "Jouissance" and "significance" invoke the sense of an ecstatic loss of the subject in a sexual or textual coming – a textasy'. *Untying the Text: A Poststructuralist Reader* (London: Routledge and Kegan Paul, 1981), p.31.

another example of the infamous 'Stockholm syndrome', a term coined by criminologist, Nils Bejerot in reference to the experience of the bank robbery at Norrmalmstorg, Stockholm during which the bank robbers held bank employees hostage for five days in 1973.[41] In this novel, Domecq starts to form a bond with each of the kidnappers in turn, formulating imaginary identities for them all (Cantinero, Santa Claus, el Indeciso/Oreja Parada, el Pícaro and el jefe) according to their different personalities. With Cantinero and el Pícaro in particular, she forms a close connection. She is rescued in a dramatic police operation and all the kidnappers except for one (it is inferred from the information disclosed that the one who escapes was her closest confidant, el Pícaro) are arrested and brought to justice. What is of primary interest in my analysis of the story is just how much it also narrates the story of a subject in crisis, precipitated, of course, by very different events than the ones involved in Págano's tale. This crisis manifests itself first as a return to the womb and a rebirth of sorts, in which Leo, the protagonist/narrator, must redefine herself and her existence. It is interesting that in this reconceptualisation of the subject much abject imagery is also employed, though not quite as extensively as in the Págano novel. What is also interesting is the role played by narrative itself in the text. As an aid to this process of self-discovery, Leo enters into a Faustian pact in which she very consciously decides to 'win over' her captors and thus ensure her survival should things turn ugly. This 'Scheherezade' strategy sees Leo manically 'narrating herself', revealing to her captors her thoughts, desires, histories and political opinions one after the other as a

41 'Stockholm syndrome' is the term applied to the emotional bond that sometimes develops between captives and captors. It is perhaps most famously associated with Patricia Hearst, the daughter of the newspaper publisher Randolph Hearst, who was kidnapped in 1974 by the Symbionese Liberation Army. She assumed a new name and identity and began to participate in some of the illegal activities of her captors, including a bank robbery. She and her kidnappers were captured by the police and she served three years in prison. Her case was later to become the subject of a feature film, *Guerrilla: The Taking of Patty Hearst* (2004) starring Joely Richardson in the title role. See 'Interview with Brianda Domecq' in Kay S. García, *Broken Bars: New Perspectives from Mexican Women Writers*, pp.170–1.

desperate mechanism of survival. Finally, in this section, I turn my attention to the importance assigned to books – Leo's lifeblood – and their role in the narrative. As with Págano's text, there is a striking anxiety around notions of 'literature', books and women's role as intellectual that manifests itself in various ways in the text. In the last part of this analysis, therefore, I return to the category 'Anxieties of Authorship', to examine this ambivalence about narrative and women's place in an evolving literary tradition.

The Disintegrating Self: The Child Returns

The story opens as the protagonist, Leo, is kidnapped at knife point and taken away in her Datsun car. The novel outlines the events surrounding the capture with striking clarity: 'Veo el brillo amenazante de una navaja y me hundo. Caigo en el vacío, en un miedo totalizador. Son las dos cuarenta. Han comenzado los once días' (p.18).[42] In the descriptions of the days that follow, much emphasis is placed on the representation of fear:

> El miedo carece de límites, se desborda de la pantalla, de la hoja del libro, de la orilla de la voz. [...] Pero el miedo, esa enorme corpulencia amorfa que ocupa el cuerpo tragándose hasta el aire, engullendo la realidad, bloqueando la vista, inmovilizando los miembros, untando los sentidos... eso nunca lo había sentido hasta hoy, hasta ese momento de parálisis en el callejón empedrado cuando dejé de existir y en mi lugar sólo palpitaba el terror (p.21).

The notion that she has ceased to exist leads to her rebirth, a process which happens physically (in the sense that she is blindfolded and utterly dependent), but also mentally in that she takes the decision to narrate her way out of the situation as a way of resuscitating her existence. The assessment of her predicament is at times hysterical, but often, rational and calculated too – a mode she adopts increasingly

42 *Once días y algo más* (Xalapa: Universidad Veracruzana, 1979). All references are to this edition and will appear after quotations in parentheses.

as she adapts to her new situation: 'Bueno, las cosas no están tan mal. Aún soy capaz de pensar en mi propia comodidad; sigo existiendo' (p.29). This calm response to the unusual circumstances explains, perhaps, her later formulation of a plan to escape annihilation at their hands: 'Respiro hondo. Debo calmarme, aplacar las olas del miedo, pensar claramente. Tranquila: por el momento no pasa nada' (p.32). The concept of 'tranquilidad', the inner peace and calm that so eluded the protagonist in Págano's novel, is invoked in Leo's case too and here it is also thwarted. The sudden uncertainty of her situation prompts Leo to have extreme physiological reactions, feeling in turn, too cold and too hot. During this period and her deliberation on the nature of fear, the threat of death is ever-present: 'El frío es cruel, no me deja dormir. Mi cuerpo ha renunciado al calor, tomando actitudes de cadáver' (p.35). This death of sorts is described as the entry into a new world, one that is womb-like and strangely reassuring: 'Es irónico: sólo la estrechez casi *uterino* del *Datsun* parecía segura' (p.33, my emphasis). This idea of going back to the beginning is reinforced as she describes the sensations evoked by the capture:

> Ingresaba a un mundo nuevo, a un país extraño en el que no comprendo el idioma; es un lenguaje nuevo de sonidos y sensaciones, de roces, de órdenes verbales, de movimiento codificados que aún no logro descrifrar. País del miedo, extraño, pequeño e ilimitado, amenazante y uterino, misterioso, recién nacido, sin historia ni futuro, país de terror presente, eterno, paralizado. Lugar del ¿que será? del ¿dónde estoy? del ¿cuándo, y cómo y quién? País de sombras breves, susurros y silencio, absurdo, espanto, sobresalto. Yo yo, Leo-miedo, Leo-cosa, Leo-objeto ... pregunta tras pregunta, tras el miedo (p.36).

This passage is fascinating on a number of levels. First, there is the uterine imagery, again repeated from before, simultaneously evoking ideas of hope and security as well as fear and uncertainty. This notion of rebirth, of course, of entering a world with neither future nor past may be read psychoanalytically[43] as the world of the semiotic, in

---

43   The psychoanalytical undercurrent is strong and persistent in both novels – Págano's protagonist Susana is forced to attend a psychiatrist by her mother and the novel recreates their dialogues in much detail. In Domecq's tale, the constant references to the protagonist's memories of psychotherapy also point to the centrality of this discourse in the role of self-formation. In this way, the

Kristevan terms, the world in which the 'Law of the Father', to use Lacan's phrase, has yet to be implemented.[44] The semiotic is often represented in feminist psychoanalytical writing, therefore, as a world of infinite (creative) possibility, though here it also connotes fear, shadow, terror and paralysis.[45] The space is threatening and also hellish: 'no sé si daba vueltas o era mi propio mareo que me hacía ingresar a una región desconocida, un mundo de espacio y tiempo diferentes [...] hacía el nivel onírico, hacia el peor de los infiernos, hacia el miedo y lo desconocido' (p.44). On a literary level, it is interesting that this is often the space posited as liberatory, empowering and creative, a space in which a new language is envisaged. Here, the new language is indeed creative but the self is violently torn in two ('yo-yo, Leo-miedo, Leo-cosa'), a linguistic embodiment of the splitting process that occurs at the moment of extreme trauma signalled by the kidnapping. This split persona is then thrust back into a very dark space, the darkness enforced by a blindfold (the Kristevan *chora* par excellence)[46] and from which she must literally re-imagine herself, re-learn the language of her surroundings:

stories also privilege the 'feminised' narrative of psychoanalysis – one that is rooted in personal experience – as the most effective weapon for the female subject in her struggle for self-realisation.

44   Julia Kristeva, along with many other feminist critics, broadly follows Lacanian ideas on self-formation in which he draws a fundamental distinction between the Imaginary and the Symbolic. According to Lacan, the former involves a pre-linguistic universe inhabited by the child in which they do not see any bodily distinction between themselves and those around them. The Symbolic, then, represents the stage after the acquisition of language in which the subject enters into a society characterised by rules and regulations that are rigidly policed. For Lacan, this stage is associated with the 'Law of the Father'. See Julia Kristeva, *Desire in Language: A Semiotic Approach to Literature and Art* trans. by Thomas Gora, Alice Jardine and Leon S. Roudiez (eds), (New York: Columbia University Press, 1980), and Jacques Lacan, *Ecrits: A Selection* (New York: Routledge, 2001).

45   See, for example, Hélène Cixous's famous exploration of female creativity in 'The Laugh of the Medusa', trans. by Keith Cohen and Paula Cohen, *Signs* (Summer 1976), pp.875–93.

46   Kristeva employs this term (taken from Plato's *Timaeus*) to refer to that space, at the heart of the Kristevan semiotic, in which the fluidity of the self is registered and in which the fixing of identity and subject position is constantly

Sentí nadar o más bien hundirme en un pantano espeso de preguntas y dudas. De alguna manera aquella realidad perdida debía sustituirse por otra, inmediata, sólida, en la que pudiera anclarme y sobrevivir. Había que comenzar de nuevo, ponerle nombre a las cosas, darles una dimensión táctil, redescubrir sus reglas y límites (p.54).

The urgency of survival is posited from the beginning and the notion of the new beginning and the new language is explicitly articulated. She reiterates this position a few lines later when she states that her psychic state absolutely depends on her ability to survive in her new-born reality, 'una recién nacida realidad en la que yo ponía nombres a las cosas para anclar mi psique perdida' (p.55).

In this new state there is an inextricable link between language and the naming of the self, a link that is dealt with in detail throughout the text. Questions of representation are therefore posed and explored. How to represent death, fear, the self: these are all issues that Domecq seeks to address from the confines of her darkness, and she starts to imagine the space in which she can begin the process of re-construction:

Desconozco la lengua de los ciegos y mis oídos novatos registran sonidos intraducibles, el golpe de una puerta metálica, el rechinido de un piso de madera, el roce de una manga con la pared. *Comienzo a construirme una casa imaginaria para tener donde habitar:* tiene una cochera, una escalera, un corredor largo, un cuarto pequeño al que entro girando ligeramente a la derecha; ¡extraña casa! (p.45, my emphasis).

Here it is notable how the idea of a new language is raised, positing again the intimate link between selfhood and representation. Here the space is strange, like the 'strange country' of the earlier description but it is starting to become familiar and has lost the sinister threatening air. That air of menace, however, returns intermittently as Leo hovers between nihilistic despair, fear and calm acceptance of the situation. The sense of insecurity is palpable and the idea of the lost self resonates in many passages, 'Perdí toda noción de mí misma en

disturbed. The *chora*, thus, according to Kristeva, is the space in which stable meaning may be resisted and dismantled. *Desire in Language: A Semiotic Approach to Literature and Art*, p.133.

un temblor epicéntrico' (p.43). The inability to breathe, also apparent in Págano's novel, is present here too, as are descriptions of drowning and paralysis:

> Algo, un grito, el llanto, la desesperación me ahoga. No podía respirar. Me sumí en el asiento, paralizada. Abrieron la puerta; una mano me tomó firmemente del brazo. Temí no poder caminar al sentir el mareo subir desde los pies (p.43).

Her actions become helpless and childlike:

> Manoteé absurdamente (¿por qué todo me parece tan absurdo, tan vergonzoso, ahora que recuerdo?) en el aire y traté de apartar la prenda de mi boca. [...] Tragué aire contra el pánico. Otra mano me tomó del otro brazo y no supe si me puse o me pusieron de pie. Traté de colocar un pie enfrente del otro y me tambaleé. Me sujetaron (pp.42–3).

In these descriptions of her utterly dependent state, Domecq also has recourse to the abject, 'tenía la boca pastosa, llena de una pegajosa saliva aterrorizada' (p.47). Elsewhere she invokes death viscerally but also sensually as smell, horrifying and insistent: '*La* muerte es grandiosa; pero *mi* muerte es pequeña, íntima, vergonzosa, como ensuciarse las pantaletas o tener mal olor en las axilas. El olor de la muerte es un olor especial' (p.38). This trace of the abject gives way, however, to several monstrous evocations of her in which she struggles to regain those fundamental physical movements she had painfully learned over time as a child:

> Soy una cobarde; me castañeteaban los dientes, se me doblaban las rodillas, caminaba borrachita [...] Gelatina, masa tambaleante, estúpida, horrenda de mieda. Siento vergüenza, ¿por qué? ¿Por qué soy tan dura conmigo misma? ¿No me sobrepuse al miedo? ¿No subí las escaleras? ¿Subí? ¡Me subieron! Creo que si me sueltan me desmorono. Otra vez era niña pequeña, sola, sin amor (p.43).

So horrified is she by this reduction to a child-like state that she does not recognise herself, 'No era persona, no era gente, era cosa, miedo sin fin, objeto absurdo e inútil' (p.43). In this passage the self and fear become one, there is no longer any separation between the two, and her meditation on fear, therefore, becomes a meditation on the self itself:

> Pero no tengo más imágenes, no tengo nada que llene el horror y lo concreto; sólo películas, novelas, ficciones de terror. Y esto no es ficción, sólo es terror, miedo puro, sin límites, sin letras anunciando FIN, sin pies llevando el cuerpo agotado a la calle, al coche, a la casa, a la cama, ya tranquilo y seguro en la realidad cotidiana. Esto no termina nunca, no tiene bordes ni forma; nada más *es*, para siempre (p.45).

This fascinating passage perfectly encapsulates the way in which the text grapples with the difficulties inherent in representation. Here it articulates what is often seen as the classically postmodern dilemma relating to representation and originality in that postmodernism is frequently conceptualised as the 'death of representation'.[47] Thus fear cannot be represented itself without its familiar recourse to its previous incarnations. As Barthes writes of beauty, it 'cannot really be explained [...] it can only say: I am what I am. The discourse, then, can do no more than assert the perfection of each detail and refer 'the remainder' to the code underlying all beauty'. Elsewhere he asserts, 'every body is a citation: of the "already written"'.[48] In this text fear, like beauty, may only be accessed by recourse to its historical citations. In this way it is indelibly constructed through historical and cultural discourses. On the other hand, its endless, infinite nature inscribes it forever as a 'permanent' fixture, a notion lent further weight by the Spanish sense of the verb 'ser' meaning intrinsic and enduring.

47   The crisis of representation is neatly summed up by Umberto Eco in his now infamous definition of postmodernism: 'a man who loves a very cultivated woman and knows he cannot say to her, "I love you madly" because he knows that she knows (and that she knows that he knows) that these words have already been written by Barbara Cartland. Still there is a solution. He can say, "As Barbara Cartland would put it, I love you madly" [...] He will have said [...] that he loves her, but he loves her in an age of lost innocence'. *Reflections on the Name of the Rose* (London: Secker and Warburg, 1986), p.67. This notion of an 'age of lost innocence' connects directly to Baudrillard's ideas about the crisis of representation. See, Jean Baudrillard, 'Simulacra and Simulations', in Mark Poster (ed.), *Selected Writings* (Oxford: Polity and Blackwell, 2001), pp.169–87.

48   *S/Z*, p.33.

In this way, it is posited as 'essence', a notion surely at odds with the first statements that clearly locate 'fear' as a product of language, both filmic and literary. It is a concept that defies its limits and overspills all boundaries of definition. As Domecq states earlier in the text, 'El miedo carece de límites, se desborda de la pantalla, de la hoja del libro, de la orilla de la voz' (p.21). This tension between the oscillating views on fear and its effects is evidence of the internal battle raging within Leo, between the intellectual subject and the embodied subject, a battle that I shall address at a later stage in the chapter.

Scheherezade, Survival and the Narrated Subject

Key to an understanding of Págano's ambivalent reworking of Rulfo's famous female character is an appreciation of the plurality of narrative itself. As Barthes demonstrated in his excavation of Balzac's text, each *lexia* may be likened to a minor earthquake in its myriad interpretative possibilities. A cornerstone of his work on *Sarrasine* is the idea of narrative as contract, as commercial and intellectual exchange, an idea that is absolutely central to any understanding of Domecq's text. Barthes writes:

> At the origin of narrative, desire. To produce narrative, however, desire must vary, must enter into a system of equivalents and metonymies; or: in order to be produced, narrative must be susceptible of change, must subject itself to an economic sytem. The theory that *Sarrasine* offers as a fable is that narrative is a legal tender, subject to contract, in short, merchandise [...] In *Sarrasine* the narrative is exchanged for a body (a contract of prostitution), in Scheherezade, The *Thousand and One Nights* can purchase life itself.[49]

49   He later clarifies: 'By a dizzying device, narrative becomes the representation of the contract upon which it is based: in these exemplary fictions, narrating is the (economic) theory of narration: one does not narrate to "amuse", to "instruct", or to satisfy a certain anthropological function of meaning; one narrates in order to obtain by exchanging; and it is this exchange that is represented in the narrative itself: narrative is both product and production, merchandise and

Here Barthes invokes the legend of Scheherezade who, captured and imprisoned to be executed, begins to tell stories as way of prolonging the moment of execution. This she manages to do for the fabled thousand and one nights before the king finally relents and saves her life. The story has inspired writers from all cultures and traditions with its emphasis on the seductive power of the narrative act. In the Latin American tradition, there are references to the legend by Jorge Luis Borges, and Isabel Allende to name just a few.[50] Feminist critics have been wary of too reductive a reading of the story while they acknowledge that Sheherezade does showcase the ability of women to 'talk' their way out of a situation.[51] Here Barthes eschews any gen-

commerce, a stake and the bearer of that stake: a dialectic even more explicit in *Sarrasine* since the very "contents" of the Narrative-as-Merchandise (a story of Castration) will prevent the bargain from being completed'. *S/Z*, p.89.

50   In Borges's story, 'Sur', the protagonist is reading his copy of the *Thousand and One Nights* as he travels towards his fatal destiny in the south of the country. See *Ficciones* (Argentina: Emecé Editores, 2004). Isabel Allende draws a direct connection between Scheherezade and her female protagonist or narrator, 'The main idea within *Eva Luna* and *Stories of Eva Luna* is based on the woman narrator like Scheherazade who exchanges her stories for what she needs', John Rodden (ed.), *Conversations with Isabel Allende* (Austin: University of Texas Press, 1999), p.205. See also Helena Araujo, *La scheherezada criolla: Ensayos sobre escritura femenina latinoamericana* (Colombia: Universidad Nacional de Colombia, 1989).

51   The tale of Scheherezade is summarised as follows: 'once upon a time there lived a malicious and cruel King Shahryar. He used to take himself a new wife every day, only to kill her the next morning. Soon there was only one girl left in the whole city – Scheherezade. Her father brought her to the palace of the King and said goodbye to her, pouring tears as he thought that he would never see her alive again. But, fortunately, he was mistaken. As King Shahryar could not sleep at night, Scheherezade offered to the King to listen to a fairy tale she would tell him, so that the night would not seem to him so long and boring. Scheherezade started to tell a fairy tale, and it was so interesting, that the King did not notice the coming dawn. The King got so curious about how the fairy tale would end, that he did not execute Scheherezade and soon as it darkened, again he called her to him so that she would continue telling the story. So it repeated for the second and for the third night. One thousand nights, almost three years did Scheherezade tell the magic fairy tales and when the one thousand and first night came and Scheherezade finally finished with the last story, the King told her that he would not execute her even if she knew no more fairy

dered angle on the Scheherezade debate and instead invokes her as an example *par excellence* of narrative as contract.

In Domecq's novel, this trope is also explicitly present, with similar stakes involved. For Leo to escape possible death at the hands of her captors, she makes a very conscious decision to try and 'win them over'. Furthermore, the idea of 'contract' is unequivocally defined in one of the first conversations held between Leo and el Jefe:

> – ... pero le debo advertir. Está bien que hable usted con los muchachos, platíqueles todo lo que quiera si eso la divierte, pero no les vaya a hacer preguntas, ninguna pregunta. Si usted llega a saber algo sobre nosotros que pueda ponernos en peligro, no podré cumplir con lo pactado (pp.60–1).

Here, thus, a contract is established whereby she can talk to her captors but never ask questions on fear of death. This emphasis on 'lo pactado' is central to all el Jefe's conversations with his kidnap victim. It is a term she vociferously objects to and he obliges her by changing it towards the end of the narrative to 'convenido'. Her immediate response to the warning is one of reassurance and determination to unburden herself to her kidnappers: '– No tenga usted cuidado. Procuraré no enterarme de nada. Les platicaré sobre mi vida; ¡pobrecitos! Se van a aburrir de lo lindo' (p.61). The agreement she enters into (to never ask questions) is broken immediately in order to facilitate her rapidly elaborated game plan – to establish a bond, a sense of intimacy between the kidnappers and herself as a way of escaping physical harm or death. This calm and determined approach is signalled from the beginning, but she becomes more forthright as time progresses and slowly begins to appreciate how her behaviour

tales'. http://middeast.com/archives/30 (last accessed 24 July 2006). There is, in particular, emphasis on the figure of Scheherezade as feminist icon within a Middle Eastern context. See *Scheherezade Goes West: Different Cultures, Different Harems*, by leading feminist, Fatema Mernissi (New York: Washington Square Press, 2001). See also, Djebar Assia, *A Sister to Scheherezade*, trans. by Dorothy S. Blair (New Hampshire: Heinemann, 1993), and Charlotte Weber, 'Unveiling Scheherezade: Feminist Orientalism in the International Alliance of Women, 1911–1950', *Feminist Studies*, Vol.27, No.1 (2001), pp.125–57 as examples of how the figure continues to have contemporary relevance.

might actually affect the outcome of her ordeal. When she snaps at Santa Claus, she corrects herself, and so establishes rules for a complex game that will be played for the rest of her captivity:

> – No quise ser brusca, pero usted me asustó – digo, tomándole firmemente la mano. Confianza crea confianza. Mi gesto no es insincero sino calculado para producir un efecto. Hasta ahora este tipo me ha parecido tierno y casi inofensivo, pero también puede resultarme útil (p.73).

The awareness of her power to influence her surroundings becomes more finely attuned with powerful effects:

> Revisé mi situacion. [...] Los secuestradores no mostraban agresividad hacia mí, sino todo lo contrario; por lo tanto, mi primer plan intuitivo seguía siendo el más coherente; *había que ganármelos*. El problema principal sería ocupar el tiempo para evitar la desesperación. Anoche, por órdenes del jefe, me trajeron un radio [...] Por otra parte, podía hablar con mis guardias, lo cual no sólo encajaba perfectamente bien con mi plan, sino tambien aliviaba la tensión de la soledad y la monotonía del silencio (p.82, my emphasis).

The game plan thus is established, and from this point onwards the objective is to build up a rapport with her captors and create a sense of affection and intimacy through the one tool at her disposal, her ability with words. She begins therefore to tackle them in turn. When Santa Claus tells her the story of how he has followed her for weeks at university, at home, and at the shops, she plays along:

> Comenzaban a confirmárseme las sospechas. ¡Con razón me había producido desconfianza! Se sentía muy importante con su trabajo, pero al mismo tiempo era vanidoso, necesitaba reconocimiento; se regocijaba revelándome el intricado proceso de mi cacería. Como presa, había que mostrarme debidamente impresionada por la astucia del cazador (p.94).

In this revealing passage Leo shows herself to be shrewd, and the pleasure with which Santa Claus relates the story of his hunting down of Leo is now, ironically, of course, transferred to her as she embarks on another hunt. With Indeciso next, she initiates a similar mission:

> Pasé el día contándole de mi vida a grandes rasgos, desde la llegada de mi padre a América hasta mi matrimonio; quise hacerle entender que si bien puede parecer un lecho de rosas, nadie se ocupó de quitarles las espinas. Les entrego

114

mi existencia a cambio de convertirme en persona otra vez. Me recompensan con su sorpresa cuando hablo de la soledad de mi infancia en los Estados Unidos (p.99).

Here it becomes apparent that the verbal hunting game is also paying dividends for Leo personally, in that she is now slowly recovering her lost humanity, the 'psique perdida' of the first few days in captivity. She also derives pleasure from their reactions to her stories, a signal that the game, so simply conceived, will not be as simple to execute. She elaborates:

El Indeciso escucha, comenta y pregunta. Si el Jefe me dijo la verdad anoche, éste repetirá todo lo que hemos comentado. Paulatinamente me convertiré en ser humano para ellos. Lo extraordinario es que también yo misma me redescubro al recordar épocas pasadas, reintegrarlas al presente y recuperar sucesos olvidados, sensaciones desechadas, verdades que habían dejado de ser conscientes. Como si ayer me hubiera desmoronado por completo y ahora comenzará una lenta reconstrucción. No solo respecto a ellos siento curiosidad, sino también respecto a mí misma. ¿Comó enfrentaré ésto, qué haré, hasta dónde soy capaz de manejarlo, hasta dónde me hundiré? Por un momento en la mañana sentí que dominaba la situación, pero había olvidado los subes y bajas, esta especie de montaña rusa por la que se desliza mi conciencia, la aterrorizadora inestablidad, la incertidumbre. Todo es tratar de echar bases y encontrarse en medio de un pantano, aferrarse a algo y descubrir que es paja, se rompe, no existe (p.100).

Here the precarious nature of her new-found power is unambiguously exposed. While she is achieving her stated objective and drawing her interlocutors into her narrative game, she is becoming aware of its effects on her and is more than a little wary. In this way she hovers uncertainly on the boundary between control and submission, a state she likens to a swamp. Narrative, therefore, as Leo quickly discovered, is a two-way process and, once immersed in its enactment, there is little she can do to escape. To return to Barthes, 'narrative is determined not by a desire to narrate but by a desire to exchange: it is a medium of exchange, an agent, a currency, a gold standard'.[52] The supposed exchange that will deliver her sane and safe from her ordeal is already complicated by the exchange that also comes with com-

---

52   *S/Z*, p.90.

panionship, with reactions and shared feelings. This element of the exchange is one that surprises her and from which it is particularly difficult to escape.

Not only is she drawn into their lives, then, but she starts to painstakingly reconstruct her own life through the telling of events in her new surroundings. She becomes more confident and extends the range of topics:

> También hablamos de política, o más bien, hablé. Dirigí la conversación cuidadosamente hacia temas sociales, los problemas del campo, la angustiante realidad de los cinturones de pobreza alrededor de los centros urbanos, el peso de la explosión demográfica, la necesidad de redirigir la economía hacia áreas de infraestructura. Quería saber si el Indeciso tenía alguna preparación ideológica. Averigüé lo que deseaba. No sólo carecía de ella sino además parecía ser la primera vez que oía hablar de estos problemas (p.101).[53]

In passages such as this one, she showcases her 'intelligence' and 'knowledge' about Mexican society, in a way that positions her as superior to her kidnappers and that cements their feelings of insecurity in relation to her. Through these manipulations she literally 'gets what she wants' as this passage attests and starts to arm herself with valuable information to ensure the outcome of the contract is favourable. The days, therefore, become filled with interminable conversations about herself:

---

53   There are several moments like this throughout the novel in which Domecq pauses to consider the social problems of Mexico, ironically never alighting on the causes of 'delincuencia', one of the most talked about topics of Mexico City and obviously the reason why she is in captivity. Kidnapping remains a major crime in Mexico – indeed it has been classified as the second country in the world after Colombia for its kidnapping rate which is on the increase. Among the different types of kidnapping, one of the most common is *secuestro exprés*, or 'express kidnapping'. In this type of kidnapping, an unwitting victim is taken by car to a bank machine and instructed to empty his/her account. It is only very recently that the penal code has been changed so that citizens accused of express kidnapping can receive prison sentences of between seven and twenty years if not more when mutilation or homicide are involved. It is also the subject of a recent Venezuelan feature film, *Secuestro exprés* (2006), testimony to its increased presence in the popular imagination.

Se me están agotando los temas. He estado hablando con ellos casi sin parar, entregando pedazos de mi vida, construyendo un personaje con una realidad llena de alegrías y sufrimientos, aciertos y errores, valor y cobardía. Les regalo poco a poco recuerdos que una vez contados parecen pertenecer más a ellos que a mí. Voy desprendiéndome de mi vida, entregándola para que me la cuiden, no la dañen, me la guarden hasta que pueda usarla de nuevo; trozos enteros a-lineados como partes de mi propio rompecabezas que voy dejando aquí (p.156).

Here, the narrative contract, the exchange, which starts as a calculated attempt to literally win them over ('ganármeselas'), soon becomes a cathartic journey towards the self. Inherent in passages like these is the way in which words, once released from the body, become public property and no longer belong to their owner, a concept that Domecq has tackled elsewhere in her work.[54]

It is clear then, that the process of exchange has become emotionally complicated for Leo. The first note of unease with her strategy was signalled in the earlier passage when she derived pleasure from the interaction with Indeciso. Her interaction with her captors further intensifies, and results in an immensely complex emotional relationship between them all. She continues with the tactic of 'winning them over' with certain subtle performances of anxiety and upset:

– ¿Está usted my ocupado? – pregunto –. Pensé que me podía acompañar un rato. He estado sola casi toda la mañana y cuando me encuentro sola tengo la triste tendencia a remojarme la venda (p.118).

In these passages she appears almost petulant, demanding their attention like a spoilt child. In the exchange that follows, however, she reaches a deeper understanding of their situation and humorously betrays her own as that of intellectual bourgeois snob:

Intercambiamos unos comentarios al azar y entre ellos me dice que parezco ser una mujer muy segura de mí misma. Me río: ya tengo tema. Comienzo a hablar de mi crisis, la idea del suicidio, el proceso de psicoanálisis y la lenta recuperación. No entro en detalles por que supongo que no entenderá mucho de eso; en gran parte hablo para mí misma, para distraerme y escuchar un rato mi propia voz. Él sigue arreglando los radios, a veces dudo que me escuche, pienso

54   See her provocatively entitled collection, *Mujer que publica...Mujer pública: Ensayos sobre literatura femenina* (Mexico City: Diana, 1994).

que quizá le sorprenda mi experiencia, pero al final la que se sorprende soy yo (pp.118–19).

Here she benefits again from revealing intimate episodes from her life such as her nervous breakdown and subsequent psychoanalysis. It is clear that she speaks almost wholly for her own benefit since the words seem to function in part as a second therapeutic treatment. The contention that he would not really understand the finer points of her treatment, belies, as already stated, her intellectual snobbery and her class prejudices. The surprise referred to at the end of the passage comes when he counters her story with the news that he is a recovering alcoholic. At this revelation, at least, she has the capacity to laugh at her own pretensions, '¡Ándale señora burguesa, supera eso con tus pláticas y tonterías!' (p.119).

The one-sided narrative, therefore, is turned on its head and her interlocutors' experiences, stories and personalities become integrated as factors into the equation, further complicating the result. At times the exchange is playful, at others, more menacing and uncomfortable for Leo. During this war of words, Santa Claus starts to taunt her with details of everything they have learnt about her during her surveillance. She interjects: 'Trato de cambiar el tema, pero él está fascinado con su éxito e insiste. Por fin lo corto en seco. Mejor hablamos de otra cosa' (p.120). Cut short by her brusque tone, he exits the room leaving his tool box behind him. She reflects: 'Tengo la sensación de estar jugando al gato y al ratón, y yo soy el ratón' (p.121). She takes a conscious decision: 'Voy a voltearle el juego' (p.121) and calls him back to tell him that his tools are there. Coquettishly she says:

Deben estar todavía por ahí y si me levanto puedo tropezarme. Además – digo, adoptando una expresión traviesa – imagínese que me quisiera escapar. Me deja usted tentaciones a la mano (p.121).

In these exchanges it is clear that power is a fluid concept that moves between captor and captive, elusive and ever-changing.[55] The game

---

55   Indeed the nature and concept of power in Domecq's work is essentially a Foucauldian view that defines power as fluid and subject to exchange and also retains the Foudauldian emphasis on circulation. For more on the Foucauldian

which she imagines herself to be controlling, is constantly under threat and can be thwarted at any given moment by any one of her captors who exercise real power over her being and frequently like to assert it. Furthermore, they also enter into verbal games, taunting her with their superior knowledge about her daily life, tempting her with notions of escape, and generally undermining any sense of security she manages to establish while imagining herself in control. It is no surprise that Leo's descriptions of herself are often expressed in terms of animal images like the cat and mouse analogy invoked above. Elsewhere she asks, '¿Sabe lo que es estar enjaulada como un animal, ciega, día tras día, pensando en la angustia de mis hijos, la enfermedad de mi padre, la soledad de mi esposo' (p.222). She later likens herself to a 'perro casero' (p.187) when she pathetically describes her desire to make herself necessary to them. To a certain extent, of course, she is successful, even el Jefe acknowledges her cunning, 'Usted se los ha ganado con su plática, sus bromas; según parece bromea usted mucho con ellos' (p.169), confirming that her objective in part has been realised.

vision in Domecq's work, see Lorraine Kelly, 'Fenced In: The Limits of the Female Self in the Work of Brianda Domecq', Ph.D, University College Cork, 2007.

The Stockholm Syndrome: Narrative Complexities

This tumultuous and complex network of narrative relations is further problematised by Leo's increased sense of closeness and dependence on her captors, and leads to a rather classic case of what is often referred to as the Stockholm Syndrome. This syndrome, as already mentioned, was coined by Swedish criminologist, Nils Bejerot and has its origins in the robbery at a bank in Norrmalstormberg in Stockholm. It is applied to situations in which the kidnap victim displays feelings of affection and dependence towards his/her captors. In extreme cases, as with the infamous example of Patty Hearst, this can have major implications regarding the victim's personal life as well as complicating issues concerning the release and ransom of the victim. The first signs that Leo is beginning to succumb to this syndrome appear shortly after her attempts to connect with them through her narrative:

> Siento agradecimiento. Se esfuerzan por hacer esto lo más agradable posible, aun Santa Claus con todo su profesionalismo y seriedad muestra cada vez mayor confianza hacia mí y, extrañamente, yo hacia él. Debe ser efecto de la intimidad, de la total dependencia. Poco a poco se me olvidan los primeros momentos, la sensación de terror, el frío, la tristeza y comienzo a sentir que esto es la realidad, la única realidad. Una vida pequeña, encerrada y muy extraña, pero no del todo desagradable, algo aburrida, quizá absurda, pero también tranquila. Una diminuta existencia nueva, conmigo en el centro; todo viven hacia mí, sin que me mueva (p.138).

Researchers of the syndrome point to the victim's increased sense of helplessness and dependence on the captors that can lead to feelings of affection and trust (*confianza*). Furthermore, the enforced enclosure of the victim ensures that, as Leo describes, the kidnap victim remains always at the centre of attention in this strange new world. This is further compounded by Leo's captors' dancing attendance on her:

> – Apuesto que en su casa no la atienden así – dijo Santa Claus.
> – No, en mi casa no me atienden así. Ustedes me van a mal acostumbrar.
> [...] Es tan poco lo que puedo hacer aquí y con la dependencia total empiezo a apreciar los pequeños gestos, las palabras comprensivas, los silencios

gratos, los favores inesperados... Es un nuevo lenguaje, difícil de entender (p.139).

She later confesses to feeling jealous when she hears them joking in another room without her, 'Me hubiera gustado tenerlos aquí para charlar, bromear, compartir el festejo. ¡Qué absurdo!' (p.139). The fact that she is aware of how absurd the situation is makes it no less real or easy to resist. In fact she makes little attempt to resist any of her feelings as she begins to experience a genuine sense of companionship and affection for them. In this passage she describes the relationship between herself and the captor she names el Cantinero:

> Cada uno de ellos se distingue por una multitud de señales nuevas, como si la ceguera hubiera abierto compuertas inesperadas del conocimiento. Manos nuevas en un mundo nuevo: las del Cantinero, tan callado, tan necesitado de cariño; no puede resistir el anhelo de tocarme cuando me da algo o me guía al baño con su brazo alrededor de mi cintura. Hay un calor humano ahí que me produce ternura, no puedo evitarlo. Somos tan torpes los dos: no sé si siento lástima por él o por mí misma. [...] Cuatro hombres en mi mundo nuevo, comienzan a tener una realidad, una personalidad, una relación específica conmigo (p.148).

Her immersion in this new world begins to come full-circle and she starts to acquire a sense of security and comfort:

> Mis guardias me acompañaron con sus quesadillas y me sentí casi en familia. A mi alrededor, y no exactamente a pesar mío, comienza a crearse un ambiente habitable, casi acogedor, de convivencia (p.161).

Perhaps the best summary of the situation, however, is made by Leo right at the end of the ordeal in which she, rather dispassionately, synthesises the appeal of her new world and describes its daily routine:

> Mientras tanto, este pequeño mundo funciona: al rato vendrá el Cantinero con el café caliente y sus tímidos 'Buenos Días'; un poco después llegará el Pícaro y transcurrirá la mañana con tonterías; Santa me traerá el desayuno contento de verme con apetito de vuelta; el Jefe vendrá con las noticias. Pediré pescado frito con ensalada, para medio día; Oreja Parada tendrá que dar su vuelta para dejar los cigarros y las cervezas que ayer se acabaron y se quedará en la puerta un momento queriendo incorporarse al pequeño grupo del que se ha excluido por

chismoso; comeré a gusto; me bañaré en la tarde, el Pícaro me cambiará la venda, llegará el cantinero con mis sangrías y buscaré una nueva queja para la gerencia, cenaré tacos al pastor otra vez y me dormiré. Es un mundo muy sencillo: no hay problemas, no hay complicaciones, todo es directo y fundamental. Hay que esperar, eso es todo (pp.268–9).

Here it is clear that simplicity and the inability to do anything about her situation is what has proved to be most appealing to her. Waiting becomes the only option available. Her final words on the subject attest to a utopian world full of shared humanity in which the convivial relationship shared by them all is one replete with humour, intimacies and (at times) sexual tension:

> Esta noche hemos olvidado ser secuestradores y secuestrada, y descubierto una humanidad compartida, una extraña hermandad como la que sentí desde el primer día con esa mano en el hombro, un sentimiento que corre silencioso por debajo de las situaciones y las clases sociales (p.161).

Mind/Body Dichotomies

It is to the subject of sexual tension that I would like to turn now, as a way of teasing out the rather confused depictions of femininity and sexuality in the novel. Indeed, Leo's capture documents a struggle between the two Leos, the fragmented self referred to in the earlier section of this chapter. On the one hand, there is the embodied Leo, sexualised, wife to Ariel and therefore both feminine and desirable:

> Recordé con una añoranza infinita las manos de Ariel, manos compañeras que envejecerían junto con las mías, fuertes y tiernas, capaces de aceptar mis pechos o mis lágrimas, mis peticiones o mis ternuras, mi pasión o mi locura (p.29).

On the other, there is the 'intelligent' Leo, strangely disconnected from her body, who can manipulate her way out of her unusual situation using her verbal and mental skills. This Leo is an asexual, sister-like figure. Indeed the text in general charts the gradual

122

disappearance of Leo's body to make way for a strangely asexual body that is supportive of her fellow kidnappers. The struggle between the two elements (body/mind) is directly explored at the start of the narrative:

> Termino de pintarme los ojos, me arreglo el cabello y vuelvo a revisar mi imagen en el espejo: definitivamente señora de *Satélite*. Cada día está peor la cosa. Comenzó hace como seis años cuando decidí cortarme el pelo, hacerme permanente y maquillarme más los ojos. A Ariel le gustó y me hizo sentirme más bella y joven. [...] Ahora, me gusta cómo me veo, me agrada mi imagen pero en algún lado existe una contradicción y siempre tengo la ligera sospecha de que, vestida así, debería ir a jugar cartas o asistir a un té-canasta, y no a *El Colegio de Mexico* a perseguir empecinadamente un doctorado en letras hispánicas (p.11).

This incompatibility between desirable body and estimable mind is therefore established very early on, and the text itself narrates the gradual takeover of the body by the mind through its ability to narrate or name the self. Leo's contemplation of herself in the mirror in the opening pages of the novel expresses a sense of awareness of her image:

> Aprovecho la parada para revisarme en el espejo. Cara brillosa. Me espolvoreo la nariz haciendo caso omiso de las pequeñas arrugas alrededor de los ojos, suficientes ya para contar mis años y algunos más. No me molestan los años, me molestan las arrugas. Es injusto que mientras la cara de Ariel desarrolla interesantes y profundas líneas de carácter, la mía se convierte en una especie de papel crepé inservible. Debe ser la herencia de mi madre o tener algo que ver con las hormonas femeninas (pp.15–16).

This passage with its emphasis on self-reflection is reminiscent of Rosario Castellanos's famous musing on the self-image of the Latin American woman writer:

> Cuando una mujer latinoamericana toma entre sus manos la literatura lo hace con el mismo gesto y con la misma intención con la que toma un espejo: para contemplar su imagen. Aparece primero el rostro: bello, en la nitidez del perfil,

en la profundidad de los ojos, en la longitud de las pestañas, en la boca expresiva, en los pómulos firmes, en la barbilla graciosa.[56]

This mind/body dichotomy is of course central to much philosophical thinking and indeed is key to much feminist discourse on the nature of self formation.[57] According to this formulation, systems of meaning are predicated on the basis of a series of binary divisions such as Sun /Moon, Nature/Culture, Male/Female, Mind/Body, Activity/Passivity, Day/Night among others. Hélène Cixous, in her essay, 'Sorties', maintains that culture depends upon a 'violent hierarchy' of binary codes, each replicating a fundamental divison between man and woman.[58] Man is largely associated with the mind and with rationality; woman, on the other hand, is associated with the body and with madness. What happens in this text is that Leo/the narrator is concerned to present herself as 'intelligent' or 'intellectual' – a view of herself that is simply untenable alongside any vision of herself as feminine or attractive. In the next section, I will explore how these overdetermined references to 'intelligence' and 'astucia' form part of a wider anxiety around the domain of knowledge and books and which may be linked in turn to the author's position within the realm of Mexican letters. Here I will confine my analysis to the body discourse as it is presented in the text and, in particular, to the way in which Leo as 'attractive body' gradually disappears to be overtaken by her mind.

Leo's awareness of her 'womanly powers' is clear from the beginning. Indeed in comparing herself directly to el Jefe, she displays an acute sense of her authority and power as woman, as kidnap victim and as a member of the upper middle class. She outlines this aware-ness, 'Él tiene muchas ventajas, pero yo tengo una muy importante: soy mujer' (p.118). From this it can be seen how gender and fem-

---

56   'María Luisa Bombal y los arquetipos femeninos', in *Mujer que sabe latín...* (Mexico City: Fondo de Cultura Económica, 1984), p.144.
57   See for example, Simone de Beauvoir, *The Second Sex* (New York: Vintage Books, 1973).
58   Hélène Cixous, 'Sorties: Out and Out: Attacks/Ways Out/Forays', in Catherine Belsey and Jane Moore (eds), *The Feminist Reader: Essays in Gender and the Politics of Literary Criticism* (New York: Blackwell, 1997), pp.91–104.

ininity in particular will play an important part in the 'guerra de personalidades' (p.118) raging between all the male characters. This acute sense of power that relates directly to her feminine attractiveness is expressed on more than one occasion. In reference to Santa Claus:

> Quisiera ignorarme, pero como la mariposa alrededor del foco, no puede alejarse durante mucho tiempo. No entiende mi juego. En vez de desprecio y rechazo, aceptación y admiración; en vez de rabia y resistencia; acomodo y bromas. Siento su confusión. Sabe que estoy jugando pero duda, porque no es el juego esperado (p.150).

She soon declares herself disillusioned by how little her supposed feminine wiles are affecting her captors. She humorously describes her impotence:

> Una cosa es cierta sin lugar a dudas: las mujeres somos muy poco gratas en este extraño mundo de hombres. Con excepción del Cantinero que tiembla como el Ángel de la Independencia cada vez que se me acerca, los demás parecen inmunes a mis encantos femeninos. En fin, aunque el deseo del Cantinero no es el máximo halago del mundo, es el único que recibo a lo largo del día. Quizá por eso me cae bien. Con el Jefe y Santa Claus son inútiles mis poderes de seducción. Al Jefe le gustaría verme rendida a sus pies, pero no físicamente (pp.148–9).

Furthermore, when el Pícaro enters into the network, later on in the text, he constantly undermines her attractiveness with various unkind remarks:

> – ¿Qué tanto se cubre? – agredió – ¿Qué cree que le voy a hacer? A mí no me interesan sus piernas, ni me interesa usted. Si quiero una mujer, puedo tener la que quiera. Y si usted se me antojara, la tomaría y no podría hacer nada (pp.189–90).

> – Es usted una tonta. A mí no me interesa estarla viendo; ni que estuviera 'tan buena'. Además, ya la vi cuando se bañaba, como Dios la trajo al mundo (p.207).

> Si cree que me gusta debería verse en un espejo. Tengo todas las mujeres que quiero allá afuera y a usted no la necesito para nada (p.235).

This final remark brings Leo back to the mirror in which she contemplated herself before the kidnap ordeal. Ironically perhaps, his remarks simply serve to reinforce her already negative assessment of her body. In the perpetual darkness of the blindfold, she struggles to cling on to any former sense of vanity (personal cleanliness is of the utmost importance to her as is the combing of her hair). The remarks by Pícaro must also be taken in the context of his clear admiration and affection for her, and to a certain extent are playful. His constant denials of her attractiveness attest to the confusion of his feelings for her and his often dramatic mood changes towards Leo, from tender to cruel and back again, further reinforce this. What is clear is that Leo is increasingly valued for her mind as opposed to her body which is (also increasingly) conceived of as ageing and unattractive. This process, in turn, allows for Leo the mind, the intellect, to take over and attempt to win the war. It is the subject of Leo's textual formation as an intellectual, therefore that will form the basis of analysis in the next section in an attempt to explore the processes through which Leo (and by extension, Domecq) is established as a 'serious' writer.

Anxieties of Authorship

In this section I return to the notion first applied to Págano's novel which focused specifically on that text's intricate intertextual network. Here I contend that the anxiety of authorship is dispersed in a different way, attaching itself to an overdetermined attention to books and their importance, alongside a concerted attempt to emphasise the 'intellectual' nature of the book's protagonist, Leo. As already noted, the protagonist perceives a certain contradiction in the way in which her appearance, which connotes wealth and upper middle-class status, might be aligned with an image of academic study such as the one in which she is immersed in El Colegio de México.

> Ahora, me gusta como me veo, me agrada mi imagen pero en algún lado existe una contradicción y siempre tengo la ligera sospecha de que, vestida así,

debería ir a jugar cartas o asistir a un té-canasta, y no a *El Colegio de México* a perseguir empecinadamente un doctorado en letras hispánicas (p.11).

The knowledge that the protagonist has embarked on a course of study in Hispanic literature leads to many references to various esteemed authors from that tradition. When kidnapped, one of her first reactions is: 'Vi la mano cortar cartucho, oí el chasquido y me senté sin más en la mirada azul y existencialista de Onetti y sus *Cuentos completos*' (p.22). There are references too to authors from outside the Latin American tradition like Shakespeare and Faulkner, as well as multiple references to Latin American male writers. In a revealing anecdote, she recounts how she eagerly consumed the discount offers on books from the local supermarket, purchasing an eclectic collection of established 'classics':

> – *En el supermercado han puesto en oferta todas las publicaciones de la Universidad y del Fondo de Cultura Económica; hay ediciones increíbles que podrían agregarse a la biblioteca, si es que tenemos algo extra...*
> – *Compra lo que quieras; ya veremos como lo compensamos.*
> – *¡Eres hermoso! Ya lo hice. Me hubieras visto llegando a la caja: dos lechugas y los tres volúmenes de* La Capital, *un paquete de bistek y las* Obras completas *de Villaurrutia, dos kilos de toronja y las* Poesías *de Carlos Pellicer, y entre los cacahuates, el atún, el queso y la sardina, Ruben Darío, Hegel,* La civilización maya *y* Economía y sociedad *de Max Weber* (pp.40–1).

The references are overwhelmingly to established canonical authors and seem to form part of a determined attempt to locate herself as an 'intellectual' immersed in the 'serious' study of literature. There are multiple references to her attachment to books revealed in part through her anxiety that her books and notes have been lost during the kidnapping:

> Le quiero pedir un favor – me dirigí al que conducía; él era el peligroso, el importante –. Por favor cuídeme los libros. No me interesa lo que hagan con el auto, ni con mi bolsa, con nada, pero los libros no tienen valor alguno excepto para mí; no los vayan a destruir. Estoy haciendo un trabajo, tengo todos mis apuntes... Por favor, a usted le encargo que cuide mis libros (p.39).
> ¿Dónde están mis libros ahora? No me los dieron. Los pedí y no me los trajeron. ¿Qué hicieron con ellos? (p.41).

– Usted tiene mi carpeta y dentro de mi bolsa traigo plumas a montones y de paso, me puede traer mis libros. Sé que no los puedo leer, pero si los tuviera conmigo me sentiría mejor. Así me aseguro de que no se pierdan. [...]
¿Dónde estaban mis libros, la carpeta de apuntes, la bolsa? (pp.84–5).

The incessant questioning as to the whereabouts of the books can be explained, on one level, as the heightened sense of anxiety of the kidnap victim. There are also several anecdotes that reinforce the protagonist's affection for and devotion to books and reading. Recalling a conversation with her mother about her birthday, she remembers asking for books:

– ¿Qué quieres para tu cumpleaños, Leo?
– Libros.
– ¿Qué libros quieres? No sé que te gusta.
– Ay, mamá, entonces dame un crédito en la librería y yo escojo (p.41).

Later, in response to a question by her daughter as to whether she has ever stolen anything, she confesses to having stolen books:

– ¿Mami, alguna vez has robado algo? [...]
– Robé unos libros cuando tenía más o menos tu edad, un poco más. [...]
– Es que me gustaba mucho leer y sólo dejaban sacar un libro a la vez de la biblioteca. Había cuatro que quería; los metí en la mochila y salí como si nada. Durante mucho tiempo los tuve escondidos debajo de la cama, pensando que alguien me descubriría. Luego los leí muchas veces; ya eran míos.
– ¿Y no te sientes mal por haberlos robado?
– No sé. Es raro con los libros. Claro, ahora entiendo que hice mal, porque ya nadie más pudo leerlos. Algún día donaré mi biblioteca y así compensaré mi robo (p.41).

In addition to these anecdotes and the bewildering number of references to books and reading, the text also contains multiple assertions of the protagonist's intelligence:

Sólo en una cosa estuvimos totalmente de acuerdo, por lo menos en ese momento.
– Es usted una mujer muy inteligente – me dijo.
Por un instante, me permití sentirme segura de mí misma (p.101).

She is labelled 'inteligente' elsewhere (p.154) by her captors. In other places she is referred to as different to other women (p.169) and el Jefe attests to the fact that, 'Los muchachos la admiran mucho' (p.169). On various occasions she compliments herself on her wit, and el Pícaro, in a vain attempt to outwit her, states, 'Ya ve, usted no es tan inteligente' (p.180). As will be recalled from the earlier section, these images of Leo as intelligent and shrewd become more predominant as the body images either disappear or are negatively invoked. In this way, 'Leo de afuera' paves the way for the compelling figure of Leo, the intellectual, devoted to her books and lauded for her intelligence. This careful positioning of Leo serves various purposes. On the one hand, multiple references to books and reading are to be expected from a doctoral student of literature. On the other, the overdetermined nature of their presence begs many questions given that it is also clear that the references function as a marker of class position and status, illustrated by her ambition to donate her library at a future date. This difference is first asserted as a way of distinguishing between herself and other women of a similar class position:

> Sentí los libros con mi pie. ¡Mis libros! Mi trabajo de Onetti, los apuntes... Me sentí valiente; ellos debían darse cuenta de cuán valiente era en ese momento. […] No era una señora rica cualquiera. Era una intelectual, una rebelde, una revolucionaria. Las señoras ricas no se preocupan por sus libros, ¡no tienen libros!, se preocupan por sus joyas, por su coche, por su dinero... no por sus libros (p.40).

The denomination of herself as intellectual rebel, even revolutionary, seems risible in the context of her family's vast wealth and yet the inner conflict between her leftist leanings and her situation as an immensely privileged upper-class member of society manifests itself frequently in the text. In this sense, the presence of the books functions in a way that is reminiscent of Bourdieu's notion of 'cultural capital' in that her cultural knowledge marks her out as, 'different to other women'.[59] This difference is also to her distinct advantage in the

---

59   In Pierre Bourdieu's, 'The Social Definition of Photography', Bourdieu discusses what he terms, 'the hierarchy of legitimacy' that surrounds the

battle with her captors. Indeed, her excessive attachment to the books strikingly establishes the vast chasm that exists between herself and her kidnappers, a weapon she quickly realises she can use to her advantage: 'Que era yo una señora loca por preocuparme por mis libros, o, ¿habrán sentido una incipiente admiración? Debió haberles extrañado por lo menos; era un comienzo' (p.39). This difference is established at various points in the narrative:

> – ¡Es usted muy cruel! Si destruyó esos libros es imperdonable. Han destruido un trabajo de seis meses. ¡No me hable más. Si hay una cosa que no soporto es una persona que no respeta los libros (p.248).

She enters into various conversations with them about literature (and indeed 'high' art generally):

> Hoy me preguntó sobre literatura y le recomendé unos autores. Es el único que se ha interesado en mi profesión. Confesó ser autodidacta y aficionado a la lectura, pero pienso que se debe a otra cosa: su ambición máxima es superar el Jefe (p.150).

In another exchange, she quotes Rulfo:

> – Rulfo dice que con cada suspiro se va un poquito de vida.
> – ¿Quién?
> – Rulfo: es un escritor mexicano (p.106).

classification of art in the modern period. He delineates three spheres of cultural legitimacy within this hierarchy; the 'Sphere of Legitimacy', the 'Sphere of the Legitimizable', and the 'Sphere of the Arbitrary'. The first sphere claims universal value for its art and includes such activities as music, painting and literature. These practices, as Andrea Noble explains, are designated as 'highbrow', are culturally perceived as fixed and therefore representative of 'eternal' values. These activites also have strong associations with the signature and originality. *Tina Modotti: Image, Texture, Photography* (Albuquerque: University of New Mexico, 2000), p.74. See also Pierre Bourdieu, 'The Production of Belief: Contribution to an Economy of Symbolic Goods', trans. by Richard Nice, in Richard Collins et al (eds), *Media, Culture, and Society: A Critical Reader* (London: Sage, 1986), pp.131–63. According to Bourdieu, thus, Leo's attachment to such 'high-brow' works of literature places her comfortably within the 'Sphere of Legitimacy', a position that will be of immense use.

These exchanges are characterised, as is often the case in the narrative, by a strange ambivalence. On the one hand, the protagonist uses her academic advantage and knowledge as a way of clearly establishing superiority. On the other hand, she shows herself to be remarkably aware of the myths surrounding this crude marking of class and social difference. As already documented, she is often surprised by their responses to her stories: in a conversation with Pícaro about music during which she expounds on the virtues of various classical composers, he demonstrates his vast knowledge on the subject of jazz music. A similar experience occurs with Cantinero with whom the protagonist shares a love of cooking and culinary traditions and about which he is surprisingly knowledgeable. She also demonstrates an acute awareness of the precarious nature of her status and is frequently depicted as unsure of herself, as this description of her first experience of the Colegio de México illustrates:

> *El Colegio de México* es un mastodonto de concreto que parece aun más frío e inhóspito bajo el horizonte interminable de nubes. [...]
> Recuerdo el primer día que llegué aquí, temblando insegura de mí misma, temerosa de no dar la medida. ¡Los mitos! ¿Cuántas veces las decisiones importantes de la vida están tomadas por la existencia de un mito engañador? (p.14).

The acknowledgement of the deceptive power of myth is interesting here, as she frequently endorses those very myths that posit academic, and often literary acumen, as arbiters of cultural and social standing, seen in her attachment to the literary tradition. Here, then, there is an ambivalence inherent in the protagonist's engagement with academic tradition that is never resolved. I shall now examine this in the wider context of Domecq's relationship with the Mexican literary tradition.

As mentioned at the beginning of this chapter, there is an uncertainty surrounding the contexts of publication of these texts, both of which are first novels by the authors. Domecq writes *Once días y algo más* in 1979 and it is published by the Universidad Veracruzana in their 'ficción' series, conceived by their Dirección Editorial, as they explain to, 'estimular y presentar nuevos valores literarios'.[60] It re-

---

60   Publicity material on back of the text.

ceives a lukewarm critical response and it is not until the publication of her second novel, *La insólita historia de la Santa de Cabora*, in 1990, that Domecq receives any critical acclaim.[61] Is it any wonder, therefore, that this novel displays many signs of 'first novel anxiety' and makes multiple references to other authors who are canonical and replete with authorial status? The overanxious nod to 'important' texts in the Latin American tradition present in the text must be seen in the context of a protagonist at pains to establish herself as serious and credible and may, in turn, be interpreted convincingly as a bid for acceptance in the competitive world of serious literary publishing. The obvious connections between the protagonist/narrator and the author (kidnapped for a similar length of time), further cement this reading. What is more, the uneasy introduction to the text on the back of the novel illustrates an anxiety on the part of the publisher keen to signal that the 'nuevos valores literarios' present within the novel may not be to everyone's taste. Defining the text primarily as a 'testimonio de primera mano', the publisher then goes on to reassure the reader that 'no obstante la fidelidad de su versión de los hechos, la narración no está carente de valores literarios'. Notwithstanding the ludicrous nature of this supposed 'endorsement' of Domecq's text, this assessment raises the spectre of testimonial literature, and the ongoing and controversial debate regarding its status as literature. It is not my intention to rehearse that debate here,[62] but Domecq's 'novel' exhibits the multiple anxieties inherent in that genre in its confused and confusing exploration of the 'real' kidnapping of the author herself. The inevitable tension between the woman writer and the received canon is laid bare, therefore, and it is left to the publishers to hope that the perceptive reader will somehow 'get', or appreciate the 'nuevos valores literarios' present in the text. Desperately trying to establish the protagonist as a person with serious academic credentials, the text

---

61   Domecq discusses the successes and failures of her work in a frank interview with Gabriella de Beer in *Contemporary Mexican Women Writers: Five Voices*, pp.124–42.

62   See Georg M. Gugelberger (ed.), *The Real Thing: Testimonial Discourse and Latin America* (Durham: Duke University Press, 1997) for an excellent synthesis of the debate.

strives to go beyond the testimonial genre by craving similar authorial status as that accorded to the multiple authors listed in the text. It must be remembered that the very mechanism of survival is ensured by the protagonist/narrator's 'way with words', thus showcasing authorial flair in a very direct manner. In this way, Domecq stakes a claim for herself as a player in the Mexican literary game, a game she continues to play but with more critical and commercial success in years to come.

Conclusions

The homage paid by both novels discussed here to the written word, indeed the anxiety displayed towards the idea of the canon in general, illustrates the uncertain contexts in which the authors published their respective stories. Págano's novel, as already seen, has a different trajectory to Domecq's, but is similar too in its overdetermined invocation of the canon – in this case, the major canonical work in the history of Mexican fiction. *Y si yo fuera Susana San Juan*, despite winning the Premio Nacional de Novela José Rubén Romero in 1995, struggled to find a publisher and Págano speaks of the ongoing struggles of women writers to be published in Mexico.[63] Again, there is ambivalence here – on the one hand, the desire and the need for acceptance as signalled by the invocation of the major canonical figures in both works (Rulfi, Onetti etc). On the other hand, there is also subversion – the desire to take the Susana San Juan character in a totally different direction in Págano, and in Domecq, the use of the testimonial genre to display the protagonist's ability with words and her 'writerly' talent. This attachment to a canonical tradition within which women writers struggle to be accepted, and in which they rather problematically locate themselves, is effectively signalled through the

---

63   See interview with Ana Cruz García, 'Locura y feminidad: Representaciones de la loca en la obra de Elena Garro, Susana Págano, Ana Castillo y María Amparo Escandón', Ph.D, University College Cork, 2007, p.139.

self-conscious status of the narratives themselves. As well as being compelling stories in their own right, they also perform stories about the act of narration itself, thereby questioning a system that has historically undermined women writers and staking a claim for both Págano and Domecq's inclusion. Leaving aside for the moment the troubling image of women writers desperately knocking at a forbidding canonical door for admittance, these texts dramatically illustrate the continuing practical, literary and sociocultural difficulties experienced by women writing in Mexico during this time period, and it is on these difficulties that I will now focus in the next chapter with reference to one of Mexico's most successful women writers to date, Angeles Mastretta.

Chapter Three
Angeles Mastretta and the Curse of the Popular

Of all the women writers publishing as part of the so-called *boom femenino* in Mexico, no one has attracted more media or critical attention than Angeles Mastretta. Indeed, it could be argued that Mastretta is the emblematic mother of the *boom*, a phenomenon which might be said to date from 1985 when her best-selling novel, *Arráncame la vida* was published. Her work has ignited an 'encendida aunque no muy luminosa polémica',[1] regarding the merits and values encoded in her fiction and the spawning of a new phrase 'literatura light'. She raises challenging questions regarding the changing role of women as both consumers and producers in the cultural market-place, the shifting contours of publishing world-wide and the very nature and definition of literature itself. In this chapter, I would like to explore the ramifications of this debate as Mastretta is centrally important to the conceptualisation of its terms of reference. As the first best-selling woman writer in Mexico, she incarnates what might be labelled the spirit of the *boom* and her trajectory as writer and literary celebrity demarcates its very limits. There is no question but that Mastretta is Mexico's most 'popular' woman writer from this period and that her two major novels – *Arráncame la vida* (1985) and *Mal de amores* (1996) – remain pivotal to any discussion of the *boom* and its effects. I focus exclusively on the debate surrounding the works of Mastretta and, unlike the other chapters in this book, will avoid discussion of the texts themselves.[2] My objective is to illuminate the terms of reference governing the debate thus far and to examine Danny Anderson's intriguing assertion that there is a 'competition for legitimacy being

---

1   Gustavo Guerrero, 'Angeles Mastretta y el triunfo del *best-seller*' *Reforma*, 28 September 1997, p.3.
2   There is already a large volume of criticism on the fiction itself – published primarily in Spanish and English – but there are studies also in German. For a selection of this criticism, please consult the bibliography.

conducted in the field of Mexican literary production, in which publishers, writers, and readers as book buyers are all taking positions'.[3] I aim to look at these stakeholders in turn including the writer, the reader, the critics and the politics of prize-giving as well as the crucial role of the publisher as a way of examining various questions regarding the legitimacy of cultural production by women and its continuous and ongoing struggle for critical acceptance.

Mastretta's background is well-known: born in Puebla, the daughter of an Italian diplomat, she studied journalism at the Universidad Nacional Autónoma de México (UNAM) and received a place at the Centro Mexicano de Escritores in 1974 under the tutelage of various well known literary figures, including Juan Rulfo and Salvador Elizondo. Her first novel, *Arráncame la vida*, was an overnight success and firmly launched Mastretta's career as masterful story-teller. *Mujeres de ojos grandes* (1994), a collection of short stories or vignettes was also a success but it was with the publication of *Mal de amores* in 1996 that her status as controversial literary icon was copperfastened.[4] Since then, she has published the short novel, *Ninguna eternidad como la mía* (2003), and several other volumes of work. It is, however, on the reception of and reaction to her two novels that attention is focused in this chapter.[5]

---

3   Danny Anderson, 'Creating Cultural Prestige: Editorial Joaquín Mortiz', *Latin American Research Review*, Vol.31, No.2 (1996), p.31.

4   For a selection of critical work on Mastretta, please consult bibliography.

5   A full list of Mastretta's published works is available in the bibliography.

Arráncame la vida: Tearing the Critics Apart

To date this novel has sold more than half a million copies in Mexico and over one million copies world-wide.[6] It has also figured on the best-selling lists in Germany, Italy and Spain. It was selected for translation into no less than fourteen languages including German, English, Italian, French, Danish, Turkish, Norwegian, Portuguese, Hebrew and Dutch.[7] Moreover, it won the Premio Mazatlán in Mexico in 1985 and propelled Mastretta overnight into a literary celebrity *par excellence*. Meg Brown attests to its overnight success in Germany where it capitalised on the extraordinary appeal of Isabel Allende and was marketed in a similar way to her book, *La casa de los espíritus*: 'Many reviews compare Mastretta to Allende, and so the "Allende phenomenon" is the first factor in acquainting the Germans with Mastretta'.[8] She cites a typical review in this vein: 'Like Allende, Mastretta is a masterful story-teller who takes her readers away into the fascinating and suspense-loaded world of Latin America'.[9] It was also a best-seller in Spain and prefigures the extraordinary turnaround in sales of Latin American titles in Spain. This, in turn, is largely due to the reconfiguration of the Spanish-speaking publishing industry, a phenomenon that will be examined in a later section. It was the first time a woman writer had been this commercially successful in Mexico: four years later, Laura Esquivel was to beat all Mastretta's records with *Como agua para chocolate*, which was another extraordinary

---

6   Mauricio Carrera, 'Mastretta y sus ángeles, Mujeres poderosas, barcos a la deriva', *Uno más uno* (suplemento sábado), 11 April 1998, p.3 and http: //www.amazon.com/gp/product/product-description/1573226556/ref=dp_ proddes (last accessed 2 April 2007).

7   Arturo García Hernández, 'El premio no me hace ni mejor ni peor escritora: Angeles Mastretta', *La jornada* (Cultura), 5 July 1997, p.25.

8   Meg H. Brown, 'The Allende/Mastretta Phenomenon in West Germany: When Opposite Cultures Attract', *Confluencia: Revista Hispánica de Cultura* (1994), Vol.10, No.1, p.93.

9   Marion Rathmann, 'Catalina tanzt den mexikanischen Tango', *Wetzlarer Neue Zeitung*, 13 August 1988, cited in Meg Brown, 'The Allende/Mastretta Phenomenon in West Germany', p.94.

success at home and abroad and was later made into a phenomenally popular film.[10]

Arráncame la vida tells the story of Catalina Guzmán, the wife of corrupt politician Andrés Ascencio, and their turbulent years of marriage. Publicly she plays the role of loyal wife while conducting a number of affairs, most notably, a passionate relationship with orchestra conductor and composer, Carlos Vives. A brief glance at audience responses in both Spanish and English from Amazon.com serves to illuminate the appeal of the novel for its many readers: 'This book is read-it-again and tell-all-your friends fabulous' (anonymous, 26 September 1997) and:

> I loved this book! Anyone who has preconceived notions of the female in Mexican society should read this book. The protagonist is gorgeous, lusty, feisty, sympathetic and a survivor. Interestingly the egomaniacal general is not one-dimensional and has moments of pathos. Fabulous […] can't wait to read Mastretta's earlier work, *Lovesick* [sic] (Ilka A. Olsen, 6 March 2002).

Reactions in Spanish are in a similar vein: 'Es una obra de literatura impactante y encantadora que no le permitirá dejar de leerla hasta el final' (Rodríguez de Mizrahi, 11 July 2002), 'Incredible, gorgeous […] Everybody has to read it', and one anonymous reviewer entitles her critique, 'Passionate Women... Beware!':

> This book gives the reader an insight into what it's like to be a woman from the heart, the mind and the belly. Just as it makes you laugh on one page and cry on another, it will also make you so angry you'll stay up at night […] angry at her, angry at her husband and angry with yourself because you find something likeable in the horrible husband of this likeable woman. I loved it! (3 September 1999).[11]

---

10 As well as achieving unprecedented domestic success with *Como agua para chocolate*, Laura Esquivel is one of the most popular Spanish-language authors in the United States: '*Como agua para chocolate* (*Like Water for Chocolate*) has sold approximately 250,000 copies since it was released in 1989 making it one of the top selling, if not the top selling Spanish-language books in North America', Jim Milliot, 'How Big is the Market', *Library Journal*, 1 November 2001, p.3.

11 All reader reviews come from Amazon.com.

However, it is also interesting to note that in the reader responses recorded by Amazon, although there is widespread evidence of the overwhelming likeability of the novel, there is also ambivalence and an awareness of the generic conventions employed: 'Highly recommended if you want something lite, relaxing and that makes you laugh and become more cynical about politicians and society'(Liliana Rodriguez, 1 February 2005). Sergio, from Chicago, cautions:

> Recomiendo leer con mucho cuidado ya que es fácil perderse con tantos acontecimientos y todo el fervor de haber leído todo el libro para el tan 'simple' final de la novela fue algo decepcionante (6 July 2004).

The telling appearance of the words, 'simple', and 'lite' in these reviews, finds resonance in the more vituperative criticism received by the novel in certain sectors of the Mexican critical community and aptly outlines the polarised nature of the reactions to the novel in general. In brief, *Arráncame la vida* unleashed a storm of hostile and often highly personalised critical attacks and firmly relegated the text to the realm of 'literatura light'. Martha Robles, for example, derisively labels Mastretta's work as 'un puente que enlaza a las medias letras con la tentativa literaria'.[12] It is clear, then, that amidst ecstatic reader reaction and the media frenzy over the novel and its author, large elements of the critical community were appalled at the idea that 'readability' could hijack the pretensions of 'high' literature in Mexico in this way.

http://www.amazon.com/Arrancane-Vida-Tear-Up-Life/dp8432216399/ref=pd_bbs_sr_2/104-1846106-3028762?ie=UTF8&S=BOOKS&QID=1175590240%SI=1-2 (first accessed 17 August 2005).

12   Mauricio Carrera, 'Mujeres poderosas, barcos a la deriva', *Uno más uno* (suplemento sábado), 11 April 1998, p.3. See also Fabienne Bradu's review of *Arráncame la vida*, 'Crónica de narrativa', *Vuelta*, Vol.129 (August 1987), pp.59–62.

Mal de amores: Making the Critics Sick

While the supposed intellectual conflict between 'literatura light' and 'literatura difícil' was well established by the 1990s, it reached a completely different plane of bitterness with the awarding of the Premio Rómulo Gallegos in 1997 to Mastretta's second best-selling novel, *Mal de amores*. Mastretta remains the only woman to receive the prize since its inception. Set during the Mexican revolution, the novel tells the story of Emilia Sauri and the two loves of her life, Daniel Cuenca and Antonio Zavalza and was dismissed by many critics, as another abysmal example of 'lite' literature.

The Rómulo Gallegos prize is considered among the most prestigious in Latin American Letters. It was established in 1964 in honour of Venezuelan writer, Rómulo Gallegos, acclaimed author of *Doña Bárbara*, one of the 'foundational fictions' of Latin American narrative.[13] Its list of acclaimed winners is long but includes the 'great' *boom* writers: Mario Vargas Llosa, winner in 1967 for *La casa verde*, Gabriel García Márquez, winner in 1972 for *Cien años de soledad*, and Carlos Fuentes, winner in 1979 for *Terra Nostra*.[14] Other literary luminaries associated with the prize include Fernando del Paso (*Palinuro de México*, winner in 1982) and Abel Poss (*Los perros del paraíso*, winner in 1987). Awarded every two years since 1987 (and every five years previous to that), it seeks to recognise the 'best' work of fiction in the Spanish language. In 1995, acclaimed Spanish novelist, Javier Marías won for *Mañana en la batalla piensa en mí*,

---

13 The term, 'foundational fiction' is from Doris Sommer's study, as mentioned in Chapter Two.

14 As already mentioned in Chapter Two, the term, *boom*, is, of course, used here in reference to what Philip Swanson defines as a 'phenomenon of publishing, consumption and reception. It marks the period when Latin American, or more particularly Spanish American, fiction became internationally visible on some scale for the first time'. *Latin American Fiction: A Short Introduction* (Oxford: Blackwell Publishing, 2005), p.60. He dates the *boom* from 1962 when the Biblioteca Breve prize was awarded to Mario Vargas Llosa for *La ciudad y los perros*, the first time it had been awarded to a non-Spaniard.

praised by critics for its unashamed 'literariness' and its perceived preoccupation with form and style.[15]

Mastretta, as already mentioned, was the first woman writer to ever win the prize, a notable feat in itself and for which she received tremendous publicity and increasing visibility in the Mexican press. There was extraordinary coverage of the prize, including many interviews with the author along with reports about the awarding of the prize, reactions to the prize and the prize ceremony itself in the Mexican press.[16] Furthermore, the Minister of Tourism accompanied Mastretta to the awards ceremony in Caracas a fitting reminder of the 'cultural capital' (to return to Bourdieu's term) embedded in literary prizes. As explained in Chapter Two, cultural capital designates the ways in which cultural events accrue 'capital' in the same way as material goods. Prize-giving ceremonies, according to Bourdieu's theory would have a high capital measurement.[17] Moreover, Mas-

---

15   The editorial reviews from Amazon.com, confirm this. Liam Callanan of *The New York Times Book Review*, writes, 'The [...] construction, intricate and delicate, is occasionally breathtaking [...] he assembles layers of meaning that, at their best, are dazzling'. It should be noted, too, however, that many of the editorial reviews are also critical of Marías's overblown style. For further reaction to his work, see Amazon.com
http://www.amazon.com/s/ref=nb_ss_b/104-1846106-3028762?url=search-alias%3Dstripbooks&field-keywords=javier+marias (last accessed 3 March 2007) See also, Alexis Grohmann, *Coming Into One's Own: The Novelistic Development of Javier Marías* (Amsterdam: Rodopi, 2002).

16   A brief glance at the numerous titles is suffice to appreciate the extensive presence: 'Recibió Mastretta el Rómulo Gallegos por *Mal de amores*', *El nacional* 3 August 1997, p.11, 'Recibe Angeles Mastretta el Premio Rómulo Gallegos', *Reforma* 13 August 1997, p.5C, 'Galardonan en Venezuela a la escritora Angeles Mastretta', *Excélsior*, 2 August 1997, p.4,19ª, 'Mastretta recibira mañana el Premio Gallegos' *Excélsior*, 1 August 1997, p.6B, Arturo García Hernández, '*Mal de amores,* es la primera mujer en obtener el Rómulo Gallegos', and 'El premio no me hace ni mejor ni peor escritora; Angeles Mastretta', *La jornada* (Cultura), 5 July 1997, p.25. I shall return to Mastretta's interviews with press and critics at a later stage.

17   Bourdieu's term, derived from his work on the educational system in France in the 1960s, is now in widespread use across various disciplines including cultural and literary studies, sociology and philosophy. First articulated with Claude Passeron in *Reproduction in Education, Society, Culture* (Beverly Hills, California: Sage, 1977), it was developed and elaborated in many subsequent

tretta's pleasant personality and attractiveness has always made her a popular cultural ambassador for Mexico and she has charmed audiences at home and abroad with her witty, pleasing interviews.[18] However, the backlash engendered by the awarding of the prize was vicious and severe. As well as the laudatory and, at times, sycophantic reception of the new novel, there were also many reviews that lamented the awarding of the prize to *Mal de amores* denouncing the text and regarding its recognition by the Rómulo Gallegos committee as a debasement of literature:

En verdad, resulta sencillamente incomprensible que un certamen como el Rómulo Gallegos acabe coronando a un *best-seller* – que, en sus mejores momentos, es una mala película mexicana – lo sé – también las hay muy buenas – y, en sus peores, la simple transcripción de una almibarada telenovela.[19]

This critique, expressing a commonly held perception in Venezuela (at least according to its author), was re-published in the Mexican press in 1997. In a similar attack, Alberto Farfán writes in sarcastic terms of the similarity between Angeles Mastretta and Yolanda Vargas Dulché (the director responsible for the phenomenally successful, *historieta semanal, Lágrimas, risas y amor*):

Vargas Dulché y Mastretta se ubicarían en 'lo que se ha dado en llamar literatura femenina' género en el que 'no se requiere de un vocabulario vasto, ni de ideas o voluntad estética', elementos que propiciarían un amplio número de lectores.[20]

works. See, for example, *Distinction: A Social Critique of Taste*, trans. by Richard Nice (Cambridge, Massachussetts, Harvard University Press, 1984).

18   See, for example, Arturo García Hernández, 'La charla sin poses, nítida, ya tenía embelesada a la audiencia' and '"¿Éxito Mastretta? Éxito el de *La Tigresa*", dice Angeles', *La jornada* 17 May 1986 (n.p.).

19   Gustavo Guerrero, 'Angeles Mastretta y el triunfo del *best-seller*' *Reforma*, 28 September 1997, p.3.

20   Alberto Farfán, '¿La Vargas Dulché de intelectuales? Ignorancia y enajenación en los *fans* de Mastretta', *Uno más uno* (suplemento cultural), 21 September 1997, p.26.

He cites Martha Robles, who states:

> Su lenguaje se desprende de la emoción primaria para crear enredos amorosos o de clase entre protagonistas vulgares y un tanto impostados, pero dispuestos a vencer la adversidad anticipada desde las primeras líneas del relato.[21]

The vitriol reached ever new extremes, as demonstrated by the following piece from satirical column, 'El búho' in the Mexican newspaper, *Excélsior*:

> Un par de días antes de las elecciones se anunció uno de los fenómenos más sospechosos y dudosos de los últimos tiempos: la escritora Angeles Mastretta, la gran resucitadora del folletón, heredera de las glorias de Caridad Bravo Adams y admiradora de Barbara Cartland – como puede comprobarse leyendo sus libros–, obtuvo el prestigiado premio Rómulo Gallegos, que por consiguiente ya no lo es tanto, gracias a su novela *Mal de amores*. [...] ¿Qué estará pensando el viejo maestro Rómulo Gallegos, cuyo quehacer literario es musculoso y exuberante, plagado de pasiones y vigor narrativo, ahora que sabe en el mas allá que el premio que lleva su nombre, el que han ganado Carlos Fuentes, GGM y Arturo Uslar Pietri, fue otorgado a la Mastretta, una mujer que no va más allá del riguroso oficio en su empeño de darle cierto nivel literario al telenovelón? Rómulo Gallegos, autor de robustas y ejemplares novelas como *Canaima* y *Doña Bárbara*, debe estar revolcándose en su tumba.[22]

Thus, Mastretta and her award-winning novel, *Mal de amores,* suffered the backlash of a disgruntled critical establishment who perceived it as the last straw in a long-running ideological battle with the market-place:

> La prensa repite que se trata de un reconocimiento a la literatura femenina y no dudo que habría que celebrarlo si así fuera. [...] Pero me temo que, en el caso de *Mal de amores* y de Angeles Mastretta, se trata menos de una victoria de la literatura femenina que de una derrota de la crítica, neutralizada una vez más

---

21 Alberto Farfán, '¿La Vargas Dulché de intelectuales? Ignorancia y enajenación en los *fans* de Mastretta', *Uno más uno* (suplemento cultural), 21 September 1997, p.26. See also Martha Robles, *La sombra fugitiva: escritoras en la cultural nacional* (Mexico: UNAM, 1985).
22 'El búho', 'Premio light', *Excélsior*, 20 July 1997, p.1.

por la lógica del mercado que la obliga con tanta frecuencia a inclinar la cerviz y la fuerza a admitir que un buen producto es una buena obra.[23]

It is worthwhile, perhaps, deliberating further on the ideological agenda so clearly embedded in these passages, some of it explicit, some of it less so. What is evident, in so many of these critiques, is that some clearly understood definition of 'literature', never categorically outlined, is being debased and insulted by the appearance of these preposterous texts. The existence of such texts invokes repuganance, according to this extreme viewpoint. That they should be held in such high esteem by cultural/literary barometers such as the Premio Rómulo Gallegos, is beyond acceptance. Furthermore, the enemy lines in this great battle are clearly and firmly delineated from the outset as publishers, readers and also feminist and postmodern critics:

> *Mal de amores* representa más bien un 'best-seller de género', una obra que, siguiendo las reglas de la mercadotecnia editorial, ha sido concebida y ejecutada con vistas a explotar un provechoso filón. De ahí que no sea difícil describir sus características: es un producto que se destina a un público mayoritario (¿quién ignora hoy que las lectoras son más numerosas que los lectores?), tiene un modelo ya reconocido (*La casa de los espíritus, Como agua para chocolate*, etcétera, etcétera), introduce algunas variantes temáticas (por ejemplo recetas de yerbero en lugar de recetas de cocina), se elabora en un estilo llano y simplificado (muy 'visual', dicen los manuales), y respeta las normas del realismo foletinesco decimonónico (muchas narraciones, mucho diálogo y pocas descripciones). Añadase una simpática escritora identificada con una buena causa y prepárese una exhaustiva campaña de lanzamiento en los medios de comunicación. *Tout le reste*, claro está, *n'est que littérature.*[24]

There are many elements worthy of extrapolation in this passage. First, disparaging references to the 'market-place' and the 'market' abound in these critiques, including this one, with few critics bothering to explore the nuances of the changing market-place or the indisputable fact that other texts, deemed worthy of inclusion in the

23   Gustavo Guerrero, 'Angeles Mastretta y el triunfo del *best-seller*', *Reforma*, 28 September 1997, p.3.
24   'Angeles Mastretta y el triunfo del *best-seller*', p.3.

great panorama of fiction written in the Spanish language, are also best-sellers.[25] Notwithstanding the obvious holes in the argument here, it is clear that the market is being set up as a redoubtable enemy of 'literature' and that it should be faced down in every possible way. Second, according to this logic, there are certain generic formulae which guarantee commercial success in a work of this kind, as enumerated by Guerrero above.[26] Again the gaps in the logic are clear and his assertion that the 'visual' style results in a lot of story, a lot of dialogue and little description is very much open to question. *La casa de los espíritus* and *Como agua para chocolate*, singled out by him for particular censure, are particularly given to long descriptive passages. Indeed, this technique of 'loading' and in many cases, 'overloading' the narrative with hyperbolic, ultra-long descriptions is central to a certain kind of magical realist narrative, made famous by Gabriel García Márquez.[27] Fourth, Guerrero considers the figure of Mastretta herself, acknowledging the importance of her character ('simpática') in the vital relationship with the press and the media in general. Again, this argument hardly holds up to scrutiny given the exhaustive media

25   Gabriel García Márquez's novel, *Cien años de soledad*, constitutes the most glaring evidence of this. One million copies of the forty year commemorative edition were published by Alfaguara in 2007. El universal.com, 28 March 2007 (last accessed 2 July 2007). Telling evidence of its enduring popularity was its selection for Oprah's Book Club in 1998 and its re-issue in Harper's Perennial Classics Series in 2004.

26   See also, Antonio Márquet, '¿Cómo escribir un best-seller?: La receta de Laura Esquivel', *Plural: Revista Cultural de Excélsio*, Vol.237 (June 1991), pp.58–67.

27   While it is important to acknowledge that magical realism does not begin or end with Gabriel García Márquez, he remains the figure most clearly associated with the trend. The tendency to loaded, hyperbolic descriptions is clearly ascertainable in his work and is also a feature of Allende and Esquivel's fiction in general. Indeed, as is well documented, Allende was accused of plagiarising Gabriel García Márquez's style. The accusation of plagiarism is interesting in the context of the discussion here in its assumption that writers like Allende must resort to emulating the narrative masters of the real *boom*. See, Lloyd Davies, *Allende: La casa de los espíritus* (London: Tamesis, 2000). For a good collection of key essays on magical realism, see Lois Parkinson Zamora and Wendy B. Faris (eds), *Magical Realism, Theory, History, Community* (Durham, North Carolina: Duke University Press, 1995).

treatment of many other writers, male and female, who do not produce the kind of genre-driven material so reviled by Guerrero and his ilk.

Finally, and most tellingly, Guerrero acknowledges the feminisation of the market-place (equated in his view with its debasement) but which, in fact, is a crucial element worthy of further examination. Negative insinuations about the 'readers' of these texts also appear in other critiques:

> ¿Habrán sabido los jurados que con esta decisión le daban a la novela rosa, a la literatura light en el lenguaje de la globalización, su pase automático 'a las grandes ligas de la literatura?' Un género que no había pasado *de los libreros de las señoras cursis*, hoy se instala en los escenarios más respetados de la escritura. Y habíamos visto a Juanga y a Lola Beltrán cantar en Bellas Artes y a Carlos Monsiváis ganar la beca Guggenheim; ya nada más nos faltaba esto (my emphasis).[28]

It is acknowledged that the dramatic economic and social changes evinced in Mexican society from the 1970s onwards, have led to the creation of a female consumer eager and, for the first time, in a position, to buy literature.[29] In short, these changes have been brought about by a very rapid process of *modernización* which has led to much greater employment opportunities for women from the working and lower middle classes. The most dramatic examples of this rise in employment, is found in the spread of the *maquiladoras* or assembly plants along the border in Northern Mexico (and indeed elsewhere in Mexico) from the 1970s onwards and this trend has been much documented.[30] The textile plants that make up many of these *maquilas*, as they are popularly referred to, are largely manned by female workers. This has led, in turn, to a pronounced increase in the number of female-headed households and to the situation that currently exists, namely that women have disposable income. That many of them

28 'El búho', 'Premio light', *Excélsior*, 20 July 1997, p.1.
29 It is often difficult to obtain hard data on reader statistics, for an analysis of the problems, see, Jesús Anaya Rosique, 'Estadísticas del sector editorial: problemas y perspectivas – I', *Libros de México*, Vol.19 (April–June 1996), pp.63–70.
30 This trend was noted in Chapter Two in relation to the rapidly changing role of motherhood in Mexico.

choose to spend this on books is now indisputable. As Juan Villoro attests, 'Un dato clave es que el público lector en su mayoría está integrado por mujeres: la literatura es uno de los pocos oficios donde se requebraja el machismo mexicano'.[31] While the latter assertion is clearly open to question given the misogynistic nature of much of the criticism of Mastretta and other female writers, it does bear testimony to the extreme change in market-place values over a relatively short space of time. In Guerrero's eyes, of course, this can only lead to a further dilution of high literary values as the demand by the 'señoras cursis' for 'woman-centred' narrative increases. This profound societal change is absolutely essential in explaining the emergence of the *boom femenino* and is, perhaps, the single most important factor in accounting for its time-scale.

The dichotomy of views reflected in some of the reader responses to *Arráncame la vida*, seen earlier, encapsulates the polarising effect of Mastretta's fiction. This stark division is even more apparent with regard to the prize-winning *Mal de amores*. A brief glance at some of the reader reviews on Amazon.com confirms this:

> If you're looking for literature, forget it. This is barely at summer beachtime reading level. On the other hand, if you like romance novels set in 'mysterious exotic locations' this may be just for you [...] How sad that fiction from this area of the world is now coming to this. And Borges wept ('Yeah, I know, re-reading what I wrote it sounds snobbish, but I'm still angry that I spent the money for this tripe') (Dr. Jon Heaton, 2 October 2001).

Others wax lyrical: 'este libro lo he leído como 5 veces y cada vez me gusta más' (A Reader, 10 July 1999). Cynthia Herber writes:

> Everytime I read anything by her (and I always do it in Spanish) I marvel at the exquisitness [sic] of her carefully chosen language and at the perfect way she tells the story of life in Mexico. This book comes to remind us of what it is to transform everyday life into literary masterpieces (29 December 1999).

---

31   Juan Villoro, 'Escribir, en México', *Libros de México*, Vol.30 (January–March 1993), p.48.

An anonymous reviewer affirms:

> *Lovesick* is a great work written in the Mexican form of historical fiction that will thrill readers who enjoy a novel written from a different perspective and writing style. Angeles Mastretta writes like an angel as she brings a unique, refreshing style to the genre (22 March 1997).[32]

Thus the ambivalence registered about her work, critically, is also inscribed in the reader responses to the text.

Literatura Light

Even this brief examination of the controversy generated by Mastretta's winning of the Rómulo Gallegos serves to underline the highly polarised nature of the Mexican literary scene in the 1980s and 1990s. Perhaps the best evidence available to illustrate the parameters of the debate around *literatura light* comes from the widely publicised feud between literary magazines, *Macrópolis* and *Vuelta*. While this debate happens in 1992 and thus predates the publication of *Mal de amores*, it clearly indicates the depth of feeling around the issue and the entrenched positions of contributors on both sides. *Macrópolis*, which titled its issue, 'Por una literatura fácil',[33] made a valiant attempt to widen the terms of the debate as they saw it and to argue for greater flexibility with regard to the definition of key terms, like 'novel', or 'literature'. This was, however, dismissed out of hand by the acerbic editorial of *Vuelta*, entitled, 'En defensa de una literatura difícil':

---

32   All reader responses are taken from Amazon.com,
      http://www.amazon.com/Lovesick-Angeles-
      Mastretta/dp/1573226556/ref=sr_1_1/104-1846106-
      3028762?ie=UTF8&s=books&qid=1175523977&sr=8-1 (last accessed 3 April
      2007).
33   The *Macrópolis* editorial was also published in 1992. See Debra Castillo, *Easy Women: Sex and Gender in Modern Mexican Fiction* (Minneapolis: University of Minnesota Press, 1998), p.11.

En nuestro país, un grupo de periodistas doblados de escritores – y metidos con buena fortuna, a editores – se pronuncia, desde hace años por una 'literatura democrática' que, definida plebiscitariamente, encuentra su legitimidad en su naturaleza política antes que en sus virtudes literarias. Con el loable propósito de fomentar el desarrollo del mercado literario nacional mediante la introducción de baratijas, las obras "democráticas" defienden como su mayor virtud su ligereza y propagan el gusto por lo pintoresco y lo anecdótico. No es extraño que estas bodas de la ideología y el mercado reciban el padrinazgo de nuestros educadores, cuya visión instrumental no percibe en la literatura sino un instrumento didáctico, un documento útil para la historia, una herramienta para la formación del sentimiento nacional y un elemento de la cohesión social de las mayorías. De la literatura light al libro de texto hay sólo un paso [...] pero una literatura se muere y una sociedad se degrada si el propósito central es la publicación de best-sellers y de obras de entretenimiento y de consumo popular.[34]

Vuelta's editorial here, constitutes a barely-disguised attack on Angeles Mastretta and, indeed must be taken in the context of the politics of legitimacy and authority of the major cultural voices in Mexico. This has often been explained in terms of the well-publicised rivalry between the intellectual followers of *Vuelta* (led, until his death, by Paz) and those supporters of Héctor Aguilar Camín's *Nexos*. It is, therefore, no small coincidence that much of the wrath of *Vuelta*'s editorial is directed at Aguilar Camín's wife, Angeles Mastretta. Furthermore, the accusation that journalists are simply masquerading as writers and 'in' with publishers, may again be taken as a reference to Mastretta who is well-established as a journalist in Mexico. Moreover it obliquely mocks the close association between *Nexos* and the publishing house, 'Cal y arena' which emerged during the 1980s, dedicated to storytelling and reader accessibility, and became a major promoter of commercially successful writers like Mastretta, Aguilar Camín himself and satirical journalist, Guadalupe Loaeza.[35] In the

---

34 'En defensa de la literatura difícil', *Vuelta*, Vol.16, No.188 (July 1992), pp.11, 14.

35 See Danny Anderson, 'Creating Cultural Prestige: Editorial Joaquín Mortiz', *Latin American Research Review*, Vol.31, No.2 (1996), pp.3–41. For other contributions to the debate on *literatura light* versus *literatura difícil*, aside from the aforementioned issues of *Vuelta* and *Macrópolis*, see Enrique Serna, 'Vejamen de la narrativa difícil', *Sábado*, 18 December 1993, pp.1–3 and María

heady atmosphere of the 1980s and 1990s, thus, with the configuration of publishing dramatically altered, it is of little surprise that a pronounced backlash to a supposed market take-over by women writers and readers occurs with such intensity.[36] While this satisfactorily accounts for the backlash perhaps, it hardly indicates a way out of the impasse created – in the concluding section of this chapter, I hope to explore ways in which this might be achieved. Before then, however, it is necessary to continue my examination of the various figures involved in literary production in Mexico.

Mastretta – la superescritora[37]

In this section, I examine another central player in the field of literary production – the writer – in order to explore the specific ways in which Mastretta responds to this critical pigeon-holing and, more generally, how she is presented and represented in the Mexican press and media. It is fair to say that Angeles Mastretta has an extra-ordinarily high profile in Mexico: innumerable press interviews, book tours, question-and-answer sessions, television and radio appearances

Zimena and Alejandra Toledo, 'Por una literatura fácil', *Macrópolis*, 26 March 1992, pp.32–7.

36   It is perhaps, worthwhile remembering here the long-standing tradition of hostility and resistance to women writers in general in Latin America. As Debra Castillo reminds us, 'What is curious and ideologically significant is that the existence of such women [she refers to writers in general] in pre-1980s literary history is both categorically denied and fiercely repressed'. 'Finding Feminisms', in Sara Castro-Klarén (ed.), *Narrativa Femenina en América Latina; Prácticas y Perspectivas Teóricas/ Latin American Women's Narrative: Practices and Theoretical Perspectives* (Vervuert: Iberomamericana, 2003), pp.351–71, p.353.

37   In an interview with Mauricio Carrera during a book tour of the US, Mastretta's daughter uses the term, 'superescritora' in relation to her mother. Carrera also cites another phrase in use by the publishers to describe Mastretta when he calls her, 'la nueva estrella de la literatura latinoamericana'. See 'Mujeres poderosas, barcos a la deriva', *Uno más uno* (suplemento sábado), 11 April 1998, p.3.

all contribute to a definite sense of her public persona. Indeed, judging from her extensive presence, it is clear that she is central to the Mexican cultural scene, as journalist and commentator, as novelist and as feminist. As market concerns channel publishers towards the courting of more publicity, the book itself plays an increasingly minor role in a scene that privileges the extra-literary backdrop made up of television appearances, readings, book-signings and so on. As Aralia López González points out:

> la literatura, sin duda, tiene un valor de cambio y sus manifestaciones se han convertido no sólo en mercancías concretas, sino también en espectáculos y eventos sociales, [lo cual es bastante difícil de valorar actualmente].[38]

In the many interviews with Mastretta published in the Mexican press, her amusing and stimulating answers provide interesting reading as she outlines her views on feminism, narrative, characterisation and the act of writing itself. It is also the case, however, that the sustained critical backlash against her work also figures dominantly in her own perceptions of herself as a writer. Interestingly, the critical rejection hovers uneasily behind the questions of even the most sycophantic of interviewers as in the following example, from a report on an early public appearance after the publication of *Arráncame la vida*:

> La charla sin poses, nítida, ya tenía embelesada a la audiencia, aún a los de la mirada cargada de erudición que hubieran esperado la menor provocación para entablar una polémica sobre teoría literaria.[39]

The same interviewer in a different, again largely positive piece, gently hints at a possible critique of the author's work, '¿El que sólo te guste contar historias, implica el rechazo a experimentar formal-

---

38 'Quebrantos, búsquedas y azares de una pasión nacional (dos décadas de narrativa mexicana: 1970–1980)', *Revista Iberoamericana*, Vol.59, Nos.164– 165 (July – December 1993), p.680.
39 Arturo García Hernández, '"¿Éxito Mastretta? Éxito el de *La Tigresa*", dice Angeles' *La jornada* 17 May 1986 (n.p.).

mente?'[40] This awareness of critical hostility means that it is now commonplace for almost all interviews to make reference to the extra-literary controversy that surrounds her. An interview I participated in with BBC World after the announcement of the Premio Rómulo Gallegos further underlined this tendency, when the interviewer asked if the awarding of the prize might be considered controversial, given the disapproving voices from the Mexican critical academy.[41]

Alongside this heightened awareness of the critical sensitivity with regard to her work, is a clearly discernible ambivalence in much of the reporting on Mastretta in Mexico that while on one end of the scale is caustic in its rejection of her style of writing, is accompanied on the other by a sense of national delight in her success overseas. Many newspaper reports make reference to the extraordinary achievement of the Rómulo Gallegos, while others report in glowing terms the success of Mastretta in foreign markets such as Chile, Germany and Vene-zuela.[42] In this kind of reporting there is an evident sense of cultural pride as a result of her popularity:

> Como para reafirmar la popularidad de los escritores latinomamericanos aquí, la mexicana Angeles Mastretta transita entre los peldaños 10 y 11 con su libro *Tango mexicano*. Por cierto, que el propio semanario *Der Spiegel*, de gran prestigio en el RFA, dedicó algo más de una página a la obra de Angeles Mastretta, con comentarios muy favorables.[43]

This is evident throughout many newspaper publications including *La jornada*, *Excélsior*, *El día* and *La reforma* as the novels begin to conquer world markets:

---

40   Arturo García Hernández, 'El premio no me hace ni mejor ni peor escritora: Angeles Mastretta', *La jornada* (Cultura), 5 July 1997, p.25.

41   This interview was conducted with BBC World in August 1997.

42   See, for example, articles reporting the success of *Mal de amores*, at number three on the best-selling list for 1996. 'Éxito de Libros de Angeles Mastretta en Chile', *Excélsior*, 28 December 1996, p.7B, and 'Destaca Mastretta en librerías chilenas', *Reforma* (Cultura) 27 December 1996, p.16C.

43   'Novela de Angeles Maestreta[sic] entre los libros más vendidos en Alemania', *El día*, 25 August 1988 (n.p.).

> *Arráncame la vida* de Angeles Mastretta acaba de ser publicada en España; la editorial Gallimard la editará en Francia el año entrante y la Ferdirelli en Italia. También se publicará en Alemania, Inglaterra y Estados Unidos.[44]

It is not the case, therefore, that all coverage of Mastretta is negative, indeed quite the contrary. Much of the reporting around Mastretta's success and indeed the more serious articles on the content of her work are generally admiring and at pains to point out her achievements. That the minority negative view, therefore, has been so widely reported is, in itself worthy of investigation and in particular, on how it has impacted upon the writer's perception of herself and her work.

Mastretta, herself, makes numerous references to her rejection by the critics and is acutely aware of the debate engendered by her work. In answer to the question, '¿Vives este premio con reivindicación ante la crítica que te ha sido aversa?, she says:

> No estoy segura de tener reivindicación frente a esa crítica. La única re-ivindicación sería que esa crítica me pudiera leer sin prejuicio y simplemente dijera este libro me gusta o no. Lo que uno no puede hacer es cambiarle el gusto a la crítica. Los críticos son lectores y tienen su modo de descifrar la literatura y todo el derecho del mundo a decir que no les gustan unas cosas y que sí les gustan otras. Si yo he tenido la inmensa fortuna de tener tantos lectores, bueno, no puedo tener tantas fortunas. A veces duele que digan: 'esta señora es simple, hace literatura *light*, es fácil, no le cuesta trabajo, escribe deliberadamente para vender'. ¡No es cierto! ¡Eso no se puede! Hay muchos que no han leído mis

---

44   Javier Aranda Luna, 'El periodismo esclaviza más que la literatura: Mastretta', *La jornada*, 10 April 1987. Other articles include Patricia Vega, 'Angeles Mastretta, Premio Mazatlán de Literatura 1985 por su novela *Arráncame la vida*', *La jornada*, 6 January 1986 (n.p.). Braulio Peralta writes, 'La primera novela de Angeles Mastretta, *Arráncame la vida*, editada en febrero de este año por Océano, ya va en su segunda edición y, hasta el momento, ha sido en-tusiastamente aceptada por los lectores y la crítica literaria, en lo general', 'Mi novela es una historia, no un ensayo feminista: Angeles Mastretta', *La jornada*, 11 June 1985 (n.p.). See also, 'Adela Palacios [wife of celebrated thinker Samuel Ramos] dedica su novela a la premiada Angeles Mastretta', *Excélsior*, 5 March 1988, pp.1–3B, 'De su obra *Arráncame la vida*: Mastretta vendió derechos a la TV Venezolana', *Excélsior*, 14 August 1997, p.7B and the innumerable articles and announcements in the press and on radio about her Rómulo Gallegos win.

libros porque son libros que se venden mucho y para ellos eso es suficiente: 'Se entienden y se venden mucho, deben ser una porquería'.[45]

The admission that it hurts, at times, to be the subject of such vicious critical attack is an endearing trait and typical of the frankness of her style. In a later interview on receiving the Rómulo Gallegos, she states:

> Yo había asumido que en la vida tenía el premio de los lectores y había a-ceptado que el premio de la crítica no lo tendría nunca; por eso para mí es importante este premio, pues me lo otorgan mis pares, otros escritores, y los críticos. Hay gente que escribe con la certeza de que está acompañada de la crítica, yo siempre lo escribí con la certeza de que yo no lo estaba, lo cual no me hacía pensar que haría una novela mala o mal escrita.[46]

During a typically forthright interview, conducted whilst on an exhausting book tour of the US, she talks wistfully of how she would like to break into the American market and of how satisfying it is to discard the 'extraliterario' that surrounds her in her home country:

> Quiero pensar que puedo vivir feliz sin tener éxito en Estados Unidos, pero eso no quiere decir que no me importe en absoluto. Más tarde, en los muelles, la vista fija en el transbordador que se aleja, dice: Una de las cosas buenas de estar aquí es que quien te conoce, te conoce por tu obra, y no por lo extraliterario que te rodea. Aquí soy Angeles Mastretta y no me salen conque si *Nexos* o que si *Vuelta*; se interesa en leerme y no en si mi literatura es light (o una versión rosa del *realismo mágico*, como recuerda el reportero), o 'un puente que enlaza a las medias letras con la tentativa literaria', como escribió Martha Robles.[47]

The wish to be 'big' in the US is understandable and it remains a curious fact that it is in non-English-speaking countries that Mastretta has had the most commercial success. *Lovesick* does actually break through the US market alongside healthy sales of *Women with Big Eyes* and *Tear This Heart Out*, the latter, having been reissued there to

45 'El premio no me hace ni mejor ni peor escritora: Angeles Mastretta', *La jornada*, 5 July 1997, p.25.
46 Humberto Isidro Bruno, 'Amar a dos hombres y ser feliz: Angeles Mastretta', *Uno más uno*, 27 December 1997, p.16.
47 Mauricio Carrera, 'Mujeres poderosas, barcos a la deriva', *Uno más uno* (suplemento sábado), 11 April 1998, p.3.

maximise interest in *Lovesick*.[48] It is also clear from the above passage, that Mastretta is acutely aware of the negative reactions to her work, to the extent of being able to quote Martha Robles, one of her staunchest critics. Elsewhere, she incisively defends her work as 'light', citing Italo Calvino in support of her stance. Furthermore, there is a pronounced emphasis in almost all of her interviews on her concern for her readers, her desire for accessibility and the immense gratitude she feels for her 'success':

> A mí el calificativo de ligero no vayas a creer que me hace tan infeliz porque me adscribo a la ligereza que a mí me conviene. Hay un libro maravilloso de Italo Calvino en el que dio seis entrevistas que se llama *Seis propuestas para el próximo milenio*. Son las entrevistas que dio en Harvard y habla de cómo debería de ser la literatura y uno de los atributos que debería de tener es ligereza. Habla de las múltiples cualidades que tienen las cosas que no nos pesan pero es de una gran sabiduría ese texto sobre la ligereza. Yo estoy completamente adscrita a él. Me digo. ¡Qué maravilla, ojalá que yo tuviera esta ligereza! Cuando me dicen que lo que yo escribo es ligero, digo, bueno pues yo me adscribo a Calvino y me autodisculpo. Es muy bonita teoría y yo me la debería de aprender además para poder hacerla mía y darte justificación basada en ella. Yo creo también que no tengo buena fortuna con los críticos pero no se puede tener tanta buena fortuna. Pero yo tengo muy buena fortuna con la gente, la mayoría de las veces con mujeres.[49]

This passage contains many interesting observations not least the fact that it showcases Mastretta's desire to answer the criticism that has haunted her throughout her career. That she invokes an intellectual of the stature of Italo Calvino is telling in that it inscribes her yearning to be taken seriously.[50] Calvino staunchly defends the notion of 'lightness':

48 Carrera attests to the major difficulties experienced by Mastretta initially breaking into the US market, a fact attributed to the less than satisfactory translation of *Arráncame la vida* (*Mexican Bolero*), 'Mujeres poderosas, barcos a la deriva', pp.3–6.

49 Jane Lavery, 'Entrevista a Angeles Mastretta: La escritura como juego erótico y multiplicidad textual', *Anales de literatura hispanoamericana*, Vol.30 (2001), p.294.

50 Mastretta was recently nominated to serve as President of the jury for the IX Premio Alfaguara de Novela in 2006 when it was awarded to Peruvian novelist, Santiago Roncagliolo. Alfaguara have published Mastretta's work since 1994.

My working method has more often than not involved the subtraction of weight. I have tried to remove weight, sometimes from people, sometimes from heavenly bodies, sometimes from cities; above all I have tried to remove weight from the structure of stories and from language.[51]

In this way, she attaches herself to Calvino's ideas as a way of entering the debate directly. She finishes the passage, however, as in so many of her interviews, with a frank acknowledgement of her relationship with certain critics and an affirmation of her interest in 'the people', especially women, a clear indication of her market awareness. This populist strain is found in many of her interviews, 'Mastretta afirmó que su compromiso como autora es recuperar al público para ofrecerle una obra que le resulte entrañable y cercana, "escribir bien y con sencillez para presentar algo que la gente comprenda"'.[52] In interviews like these, she seems almost to pander to the criticisms, to the extent of stating that 'simplicity' is one of her goals, again in direct response to the two most commonly used words employed to attack her. Thus, the polarised views of Mastretta's works that range from fawning adulation and delight to disgust and disapproval at their supposed simplicity and *ligereza,* is subsumed into Mastretta's own conceptualisation of her work and encoded through innumerable interviews.

Seix Barral, a subsidiary of Planeta, have published Angeles Mastretta's most recent work, *El cielo de los leones* (Barcelona: Seix Barral, 2006) and, also, various editions of much of her earlier work.

51   *Six Memos for the next Millenium* (New York: Vintage Books, 1993), p.330.
52   'Mastretta Tiene el Bosquejo de Nueva Obra', *Excélsior,* 2 October 1997, p.6B. See also, 'Braulio Peralta, 'Mi novela es una historia, no un ensayo feminista, Angeles Mastretta', *La jornada,* 11 June 1985 (n.p.) and Humbero Isidro Bruno, 'Amar a dos hombres y ser feliz', *Uno más uno* (Sábado), 27 December 1997, p.16.

Pescador', 'El oso hormiguero', 'Cuadernos de estraza', among others, dedicated to bringing out various more 'marginal' works of literature. These were to flourish particularly in the 1970s before they came to a resounding end with the oil crisis and the devaluation of the *peso* in 1982.[61] It was this, above all else, that precipitated the crisis in publishing and which led to quite drastic changes in the industry's configuration. As Danny Anderson attests:

> In 1982, amidst devaluation, disruptions in the international oil market and nationalisation of the Mexican banking system, the publishing industry experienced a major crisis. Devaluations radically affected the already precarious Mexican publishing industry because it depends on imported paper. Moreover, dramatic increases in production costs immediately raised the cost to potential buyers, a small group of consumers who were themselves suffering the effects of the devaluation in all aspects of their daily lives.[62]

Such was the extent of the crisis that prominent intellectuals such as Carlos Monsiváis, José Emilio Pacheco and Elena Poniatowska published 'El derecho a la lectura' in a bid to stave off the crisis and to reinstate the central importance of reading to Mexican society.[63] These

61   Francisco Hinojosa, 'Las editoriales marginales en México (1975–1978)', *Revista de la Universidad de México*, pp.62–4. Other presses discussed here include 'Ediciones El mendrugo', 'Cuadernos del caballo verde' and 'Editorial Hyperión'.

62   'Creating Cultural Prestige: Editorial Joaquín Mortiz', p.27. He further adds: 'The dynamics of this crisis were widely discussed throughout the Mexican press in the last quarter of 1982 and throughout 1983. The publishing industry in this period owed its visibility and viability to the concerted efforts of the 'grupo de las 10', publishers who united to propose restructurings necessary for the economic survival of the Mexican publishing industry. These publishers were Siglo Veintiuno, Nueva Imagen, Era, Joaquín Mortiz, Prensa Médica, Martín Casillas, Nuestro Tiempo, Centro de Investigación y Docencia Económicas (CIDE), El Colegio de México and the Fondo de Cultura Económica. Special issues of *Diálogo* (1983) and *Casa del Tiempo* (1983b) provided overviews of the publishing crisis', p.27.

63   Jean Franco, *The Decline and Fall of the Lettered City: Latin America After the Cold War* (Cambridge, Massachussetts and London, England: Harvard University Press, 2002), p.11. She draws attention to the publication in 1984 by all the major Mexican publishing houses of Carlos Monsiváis, José Emilio

writers felt that the crisis was so acute as to call for civic action on behalf of the right to read.[64] Mastretta's phenomenal success is aptly illustrated within this context: in the first two years since *Arráncame la vida*, had been published, it had been issued in ten editions and had sold 50,000 copies.[65]

In the wake of the oil crisis, many publishers curtailed their output drastically. Others folded or reorganised but the most striking trend was the merging of many presses with large multinational publishing corporations. Grijalbo, for example, was bought by Italian publishing house, Mondadori (now part of the Random House/Mondadori group). Joaquín Mortiz – since its inception, a source of 'quality' literature often publishing formally experimental work – was bought by the Spanish transnational giant, Planeta. The third of the three 'big' players in Mexican literary publishing is also of Spanish origin; the Grupo Santillana, which boasts Alfaguara (1980), Alfaguara infantil juvenil, Altea, Taurus (1974), Aguilar (1986), Ediciones El País and Alamah amongst its subsidiaries. Alongside the clearly defined business objectives of these various global publishing giants, are clearly articulated missions that evoke their evangelical nature with regard to their role in the dissemination of civilisation. Planeta and Santillana share in common a missionary zeal that seeks to promote culture in the Spanish language and they both own countless smaller presses as well as shares in television and radio companies (Antena 3; Onda Cero and Radio España) and large newspaper publications (*El país* in

Pacheco, Elena Poniatowska's call for action, *El derecho a la lectura*, cited in *Decline and Fall of the Lettered City*, p.281.

64 Of course, the crisis in publishing needs to be placed in perspective. As Juan Villoro reminds us, approximately 1% of the literate community actually buys books (a figure he estimates at around 500,000). He also points out that the traditionally popular sub-genres, like the *historieta semanal* will often sell up to 10 million copies a month but a best-selling novel may only sell 10,000 in total. He further adds that there are 10 million Indians in Mexico, who between them speak a total of 56 different languages and who are totally excluded from any reading community. Moreover, almost all the book shops in Mexico are located within a circle of 20 streets in the south of the capital. Juan Villoro, 'Escribir en México', pp.45–6.

65 'Javier Aranda Luna, 'El periodismo esclaviza más que la literatura: Mastretta', *La jornada*, 10 April 1987 (n.p.).

Spain). Of course, this zeal must be reconciled with the *raison d'etre* of their existence (the desire to make money) and it is between these two ideological poles that the directors of the presses, as well as their writers in Mexico and elsewhere in Latin America, struggle to position themselves. Thus Alfaguara's stated objective, 'de llegar al mayor número posible de lectores',[66] is accompanied by an acknowledgement that the company actively seeks to create and consolidate a 'panhispanic' perspective:

> Alfaguara ha desarrollado estrategias de comunicación que permiten que la información fluya entre todos los lectores, escritores y críticos de habla española. Lo que se propone conseguir es que un buen escritor argentino, mexicano, chileno, uruguayo o colombiano sea tan conocido en Venezuela o en España como en sus países de origen.[67]

Planeta is equally interesting to scrutinise from this point of view. Similar in concept to the Santillana group, Planeta Internacional was established in Spain and from the outset, 'se dedicó a trabajar los mercados extranjeros, prestando una atención especial a América Latina'.[68] Planeta owns a bewildering number of smaller publishing houses including Joaquín Mortiz, Seix Barral (Mastretta's most recent publisher), Editorial Espasa, Ediciones Temas de Hoy, Ediciones del Bronce, Editorial Planeta Mexico, Venezuela, Uruguay and the Grupo Editorial Planeta (Argentina) among many others.

The fact that the three big publishing groups operating today in Mexico are Italian (Mondadori) and Spanish (Planeta and Santillana) in origin is interesting and stems from the general unease in the publishing climate in Europe in the 1980s. With only sluggish growth, European publishers turned their eyes to new markets and saw in the Spanish-speaking market in Latin America new opportunities for growth and expansion:

> Evidentemente entre los editores franceses, italianos, alemanes, etcétera, existe una inquietud por tener acceso a nuevos mercados, pero debido al lento

---

66   http://www.santillana.com/co/quienes_somos.htm (accessed 17 August 2005).
67   http://www.santillana.com/co/quienes_somos.htm (accessed 17 August 2005).
68   José Angel Leyva, 'Por la órbita editorial de Planeta', *Libros de México*, Vol.18 (January – March 1990), pp.5–6.

crecimiento de los mercados europeos, volvieron los ojos hacia él de habla hispana, de América Latina concretamente.[69]

In addition to the lucrative market beckoning from Latin America, was the evident increase in the Spanish-speaking market in the US, again marked out as a target by both Planeta and Santillana:

> El creciente interés por la lengua española, tanto en Brasil y Estados Unidos de América como en los países de la Unión Europea, ha impulsado al Grupo Santillana a diseñar nuevos proyectos que verán la luz en los próximos años y que reforzarán nuestra oferta de español como lengua extranjera.[70]

Online retailers also carry Spanish-language titles. Amazon.com, for example, has a substantial Spanish-language section bearing testimony to the rapid growth in that sector. As Jim Milliot writes:

> Everyone in the publishing industry agrees the demand for Spanish-language books is growing and that it promises to be an even more important market in the years ahead. The signs of growth can be found throughout the industry: Baker and Taylor reports that sales of Spanish-language books are up 40% in the year to date; Borders Group has increased the number of Spanish titles it carries from 5,000 to 30,000 over the course of the last year; and Scholastic reported that its Lectorum subsidiary, which includes publishing, distributing, and bookselling, had sales of $10 million in fiscal 2001.[71]

So while it is clear that major multinationals have almost complete control of publishing in the Spanish-speaking world, it is not quite so clear what impact this has had on the kind of literatures being published and, in particular, on the work of women writers such as Mastretta. However, one of the major changes evinced by the take-over of these publishing giants has been the specialisation of several different press lines that develop best-selling series. 'Colección Fábula' by Planeta is the obvious example in this category. This is the collection that launched Laura Esquivel's internationally successful *Como agua para chocolate* and which has followed up the interest in 'story-telling' by Mexican women writers, publishing Rosamaría

69   José Angel Leyva, 'Por la órbita editorial de Planeta', p.8.
70   http://www.santillana.com/co/quienes_somos.htm (accessed 17 August 2005).
71   'How Big is the Market', *Library Journal*, 1 November 2001, p.1.

Roffiel (*Amora*, 1989), Brianda Domecq (*La insólita historia de la Santa de Cabora*, 1990) and Sara Sefchovich (*Demasiado amor* in 1990, *La señora de los sueños* in 1993 and *Vivir la vida* in 2000). These novels exemplify the emphasis on readability, accessibility (code words for 'simplicity' and *ligereza* to the 'enemies' in the critical community), as well as realism. 'Cal y arena', as mentioned previously, which publishes both Mastretta and the hugely popular Guadalupe Loaeza, also opts for this emphasis. This concentration of women writers in a single publication line is interesting in that it suggests a publishing strategy of market visibility for women writers in a very particular way.[72]

Literary prizes, accruing ever more commercial capital (if losing somewhat in the traditional cultural capital stakes), also bear testimony to a certain kind of visibility of women writers. Meg Brown attests to the 'female factor' as central to the success of Isabel Allende and Angeles Mastretta in Germany: 'Mastretta's photograph, which often appeared with reviews of the novel and in advertising, portrays her as a self-confident, beautiful, and feminine Latin American lady'.[73] Jean Franco likens the Premio Planeta to a Miss Universe contest,[74] and the prizes themselves are extraordinarily lucrative – the Premio Alfaguara is worth some $175,000 in prize money alone, while the Premio Planeta is worth a staggering 600,000 euros. The prize money, of course, represents only a fraction of the commercial gain of the prizes as their announcement is inevitably accompanied by a rocketing in sales. Women writers figure prominently in these prize-winning stakes (former winners of the Alfaguara include *Últimas noches del paraíso* by Clara Sánchez, *La piel del cielo* by Elena Poniatowska, *Delirio* by Laura Restrepo and *El turno del escriba* by Graciela Montes and Ema Wolf). Female prize-winners of the Premio Planeta include Carmen Posadas (Uruguay) for *Pequeñas infamias*, and the Spanish writers, Soledad Puértolas, Rosa Regás, Maruja

72   Danny Anderson, 'Creating Cultural Prestige: Editorial Joaquín Mortiz', p.30.
73   'The Allende/Mastretta phenomenon', p.94.
74   Jean Franco writes, 'It is little wonder that prize ceremonies organised by the Planeta publishing house resemble the Miss Universe contest and are designed to promote best-sellers', 'What's Left of the Intelligentsia: The Uncertain Future of the Printed Word', in *Critical Passions*, p.203.

Torres and Lucía Etxebarria. Other recent winners of both prizes include Tomás Eloy Martínez from Argentina, Eliseo Alberto from Cuba, Sergio Ramírez of Nicaragua, Antonio Skármeta of Chile. The diverse origin of these writers provides ample evidence of Alfaguara and Planeta's objective to reach out to the entire Spanish-language world and thus it seems that the global reach of these Spanish-language giants is bearing fruit.

So while it is clear that a certain kind of 'readable' woman writer is being marketed in a particular way by these publishing conglomerates, it remains difficult to assess the precise impact it has had on the smaller presses subsumed. In an interesting interview, the founder of Grijalbo remarks on the transformations that have occurred since the take-over by Mondadori:

> En México y en España padecemos un complejo. Cuando se le da participación a una compañía extranjera la gente cree que la empresa fundadora pierde su personalidad. No es cierto tal cosa. Mondadori respeta el nombre de las colecciones y de las empresas originales. El que desaparezca determinado porcentaje de Grijalbo no significa que los nuevos accionistas vayan a perjudicar el libro; a ellos también les interesa que se sostengan y cumplan las ventas. Publicarán los que consideren vendibles, independientemente de ideologías. Lo que ocurre es que antes la mayoría de los intelectuales, autores de libros, eran de izquierda, pero hoy no lo son tan de izquierda, no son mayoría.[75]

Interestingly, this overdetermined emphasis on the independence maintained by the smaller presses upon their takeover, is discernible too in the interview with Joaquín Diez-Canedo on the changes at Joaquín Mortiz:

> Originalmente, Mortiz conserva su plena autonomía editorial y ganó cobertura y penetración comercial, y un mejor manejo de los recursos. De entonces acá, se ha procurado converger con los proyectos del grupo. Encaminados a una proyección internacional, tanto por la venta de derechos y la distribución en el

---

75   José Angel Leyva, 'El nuevo mundo de Grijalbo', *Libros de México*, Vol.17 (October–December 1989), p.12.

extranjero de los fondos con autores nacionales como por la adquisición de títulos de interés para el mercado mexicano.[76]

Here again, the emphasis on editorial independence is acknowledged only for it to be admitted that it has given way to compromise and a commitment to converge with Planeta's larger objectives. It is crystal clear, then, that publishing houses like the left-wing Grijalbo and Joaquín Mortiz with its traditional emphasis on young, experimental writers are now subsumed into global publishing giants. It is also clear that these publishers' desire for profit through massively increased sales (both these passages make reference to 'ventas') has diluted, certainly, if not exorcised completely, the original visions of these companies.

To return to Mastretta, and her position within this industry in perpetual flux, it is perhaps opportune to enquire where she stands amidst the shifting contours of publishing in Mexico. The origins of her 'coming to writing'[77] are well-known:

Un día un editor que yo conocía me dijo que necesitaba una persona joven que se dedicara a buscar escritores a los que publicarles libros en la editorial que estaba fundando. Yo, que tenía treinta años y llevaba diez trabajando como periodista, le dije que lo que yo necesitaba era que alguien me publicara a mí y no buscar a nadie. Entonces él me preguntó: ¿Pero tú tienes un libro escrito? Le dije que no pero que no se preocupara porque lo quería escribir y se lo escribiría. Y así fue. Un verdadero acto de magia, una cosa muy loca. El pensaba que yo iba a vender dos ejemplares, y yo trabajé dos años pensando que iba a vender dos ejemplares. Y después, el libro *Arráncame la vida* (Premio Mazatlán de Literatura, 1985 y traducido a catorce idiomas), resultó una buena fortuna.[78]

76 José Angel Leyva, 'Joaquín Mortiz, las grandes transfiguaciones editoriales', *Libros de México*, Vol.31 (April–June 1993), p.12.
77 This phrase is taken from Hélène Cixous's book, *'Coming to Writing' and Other Essays*, trans. by Deborah Jensen (Cambridge, Massachussetts: Harvard University Press, 1992). It is frequently invoked in a feminist critical context to account for the arduous journey undertaken by many women writers to arrive at the point of writing.
78 Ana Anabitarte, 'Angeles Mastretta: Sólo los besos son más placenteros que las palabras' (Entrevista con la escritora mexicana, autora de *Arráncame la vida*).

With the resounding success of her first novel (published initially by Editorial Océano), she opted to be published by Alfaguara for several editions but *Mujeres de ojos grandes* (1990), *Puerto libre* (1994), *El mundo iluminado* (1998) and *Mal de amores* (1996) were all published by Cal y arena, the publishing house closely associated with the magazine, *Nexos*, edited by her husband. Her latest three books, however, *Ninguna eternidad como la mía* (1999), *El cielo de los leones* (2006) and *La vida te despeina/Life Messes Up Your Hair: Mujeres en busca de la felicidad* (2006) have all been published by Seix Barral, a subsidiary of Planeta.[79] By jumping between editors and publishers in this way, she exhibits the easy confidence of a best-selling author who has choices and who is, in all likelihood, being courted by various presses because of her sales value. In the cases of Alfaguara and Seix Barral however, she has been taken on by presses newly acquired by multinational giants (Santillana and Planeta) with a proven interest in developing series of readable authors for marketing throughout the Spanish-speaking world. In the case of 'Cal y arena', its emergence on the scene in the 1980s, as previously mentioned, was again to capitalise on the new kind of reader accessibility exemplified by the work of writers like Mastretta, Aguilar Camín and Guadalupe Loaeza.

Back to the Backlash

It is hardly surprising, therefore, that writers traditionally associated with these presses feel 'edged out' by the more specialised lines and Planeta, Grijalbo/Mondadori and Santillana's preoccupation with readability. Even this brief foray into the complex world of publishing in Mexico suffices to demonstrate how the industry has been completely reconfigured since the economic crisis in the early 1980s. It is,

http://www.babab.com/no01/angeles_mastretta.htm, pp.1–2 (first accessed 17 August 2005).

79   She is currently working on her latest book, *maridos*, which is due to be published in 2008. Personal contact, Angeles Mastretta, 16 April 2007.

perhaps, easier to understand the vociferous critical outcry at the unprecedented increase in readability when the stakes are so high for all concerned, but particularly, for the writers. It is important also to remember that this kind of caustic bickering in the closed literary circles of Mexico is not new. The 'high' literary scene of the 1960s and 1970s, 'a community of producers creating for an audience of other producers'[80] led to the imposition of the derisive label, 'la mafia'. During this time Fernando Benítez controlled a large sector of the writing commmunity through his direction of *México en la cultura* (suplemento dominical de *Novedades*) until 1961 and his subsequent move to *¡Siempre!*. Vicente Leñero, among others, attests to the damaging legacy left by Benítez's policies and cultural agenda during this era.[81] He is also blistering in his critique of Emmanuel Carballo's personal interference in his own career and, in an intriguing prefiguring of Mastretta's fate at the hands of certain Mexican critics, launches an outspoken diatribe on the awarding of the Biblioteca Breve prize for *Los albañiles* to Leñero (several years before it was awarded to Fuentes).[82] Recalling the era, he says:

Carballo publicó una crítica que a mí me dolió muchísimo y que me hizo entender mucho del fenómeno cultural en México. Dijo [Carballo] que con el

80 Danny Anderson, 'Creating Cultural Prestige: Editorial Joaquín Mortiz', p.31.
81 'Durante mucho tiempo lo vivimos en México cuando Fernando Benítez controlaba, por así decirlo, a un sector muy amplio de los escritores, los mejores escritores que había entonces en México en los años sesenta; pero creo que se cometieron injusticias terribles en ese tiempo con los que no participaban de esa política cultural. Yo señalo dos injusticias que a mí me parecieron garrafales y que luego el tiempo ha hecho más notorias, a Jaime Sabines en poesía ('¡Jaime Sabines no existía en la poesía mexicana!'), y a José Revueltas que se le ninguneaba en una forma espantosa', 'No, a los párrafos que enjuician libros: Entrevista con Vicente Leñero', *Revista de la universidad de México* (October–November 1978), p.13.
82 Danny Anderson, 'Creating Cultural Prestige', Javier Prada, 'Las decisiones editoriales', *La Gaceta del Fondo de Cultura Económica*, No.245, pp.56–7. See also, Aralia López González, 'Quebrantos, búsquedas y azares de una pasión nacional (dos décadas de narrativa mexicana: 1970–1980)', *Revista iberoamericana*, Vol.59, Nos.164–5 (July–December 1993), pp.659–85.

premio que me habían dado en España, este premio antes tan prestigiado había perdido todo su valor.[83]

He goes on to severely criticise the general community of critics in Mexico in a telling series of comments:

> Yo pienso que tal como se hace la crítica en México no le sirve al escritor porque no le da argumento, no le da una visión más amplia y normalmente, así como las buenas críticas están muy adjetivadas, muy llenas de elogios, las malas críticas están llenas de adjetivos hirientes, son muy peyorativas. No le sirven ni al escritor ni al lector.[84]

Therefore, it hardly requires stating that this kind of atmosphere has often if not always existed – an inevitable consequence perhaps of a literary elite controlling the methods of production, publishing and distribution. In the highly charged attacks against Mastretta, there is a discernible nostalgia for a golden era of Latin American letters, symbolised most forcefully by the 1960s period in Mexico. Aralia López González gives a compelling account of this era saying that from the 1950s onwards:

> Los escritores se profesionalizan, las instituciones literarias adoptan una fisonomía más formal, surge un espacio crítico consistente [...] Es ya por entonces, cuando el trabajo intelectual y artístico comienza a especializarse, al mismo tiempo que surge un mercado para sus obras. Esto es lo que permite una cierta autonomía de la actividad creadora manifestada, en principio, por una mayor preocupación por los aspectos estéticos más que por los históricos, sociales o políticos.[85]

This era witnesses the 'great' writers of Mexican literature so closely associated with the cycle of revolutionary literature – Juan Rulfo, Agustín Yañez, Juan José Arreola and José Revueltas. Alongside these eminent figures, there is a very large group of authors, led, perhaps by Carlos Fuentes and heavily influenced by Gabriel García Márquez (who arrived in Mexico in 1961) and Julio Cortázar. The aesthetic preoccupations of these groups, mentioned by López Gon-

83   'No a los párrafos que enjuician libros', pp.13–14.
84   'No a los párrafos que enjuician libros', p.14.
85   'Quebrantos, búsquedas y azares de una pasión nacional', p.660.

zález in this passage, are transformed in the 1970s leading to a more politically charged atmosphere in the wake of the Tlatelolco massacre. This era's symbolic figurehead is Elena Poniatowska, in turn connected closely with the publishing house, Era which specialised in *testimonio* literature from this period onwards.[86]

The nostalgia for a golden era also needs to be understood in the wider context of a public yearning for the next big writer in Mexico. This kind of hankering can be seen in the furore surrounding the publication of Jorge Volpi's *En busca de Klingsor*,[87] and is encapsulated by Jorge Aguilar Mora when he speaks of:

> a huge confusion in the Mexican novel, a lost sense of direction. It's like a crisis of narration in Mexico (among current narrators, myself included). There is no one with that grand sense of security to write a first sentence like Pedro Páramo's: 'I came to Comala because they told me my father lived here'. There is no writer currently capable of anything like this.[88]

These kind of absurd sentiments are echoed elsewhere as when Joaquín Diez-Canedo says:

> what is certain is that the future Pazes, the Fuentes, the Leñeros and the Poniatowskas are nowhere to be seen, the Pachecos, Sabines, Arreolas, Pitols, Elizondos, Galindos, Monterrosos, Garibays, López Páezes, and García Ponces, the Arredondos, Castellanos and Vicenses of the 21st century. Perhaps their reincarnations are no longer possible today, nor necessary.[89]

86   See Danny Anderson, 'Creating Cultural Prestige: Editorial Joaquín Mortiz', pp.30–1. See also Aralia López González, 'Quebrantos, búsquedas y azares de una pasión nacional', p.675.

87   Jorge Volpi's novel won the Biblioteca Breve award by Seix Barral in 1999 causing a sensation in the literary world: this was the first of his works to be published in Spain. Luis Fonseca cites Guillermo Cabrera Infante's opinion of the novel, 'es una muestra ejemplar del arte que quiero llamar ciencia-fusión. Fusión de la ciencia con la historia, la política y la literatura para conformar eso que llamamos cultura'. *El país*, 28 November 1999.

88   Mora, cited in Mariana Pérez de Mendiola, *Gender and Identity Formation in Contemporary Mexican Literature* (New York and London: Garland Publishing Inc., 1998), p.7.

89   Cited in Pérez de Mendiola, *Gender and Identity Formation in Contemporary Mexican Literature*, p.8.

Perhaps, as Mariana Pérez de Mendiola asserts, this kind of longing for a bygone era is simply a disillusionment, characteristic of fin-de-siècle eras.[90] What is beyond doubt, is that the literary scene in Mexico has diversified to such an extent that one group of writers, the aforementioned 'mafia' will never again be allowed to dominate as they once did.

Diez-Canedo's assertion, however, that reincarnations of past geniuses are no longer possible nor necessary does provide, perhaps, a mechanism with which to widen the parameters of the debate around *literatura light* and *literatura difícil*. It is clear that literature itself is flourishing.[91] It is also clear that there is an ongoing proliferation of genres including the urban chronicle, the travel text, autobiographies and biographies,[92] the detective novel,[93] 'la historia novelada', and *testimonio*, to name just a few. All of these genres to some extent or other contest traditional definitions of the novel and undermine its

90 *Gender and Identity Formation in Contemporary Mexican Literature*, p.7.

91 'What's Left of the Intelligentsia?: The Uncertain future of the Printed Word', in *Critical Passions*, p.203.

92 The biography of iconic film star, María Félix, by Enrique Krauze, *María Félix: Todas mis guerras*, (Mexico: Debolsillo, 2003) has, to date sold 200,000 copies. See 'Escritoras: Publicaciones femeninas', *La jornada*, 7 July 1997, p.29.

93 Paco Ignacio Taibo II is Mexico's most popular writer of detective fiction. He has won numerous prizes and has written nine novels featuring Héctor Belascoarán Shayne, his one-eyed, half-Irish, half-Basque anti-hero. An upsurge in production of what might best be termed, 'urban chronicle' or *crónica* has been notable since the 1970s. Aralia López González confirms, 'Quizá sea en la crónica donde se han estado dando, consistentemente, las mejores páginas de la historia literaria de estas décadas', 'Quebrantos y azares de una pasión nacional', p.674. From Emilio Pérez Cruz, *Borracho no vale* (Mexico: Plaza y Janes, 1988) to the prolific output of Carlos Monsiváis, Mexico boasts numerous writers of this genre. See Rubén Gallo (ed.), *The Mexico City Reader* (Madison: University of Wisconsin Press, 2004) for a good selection of these authors including Alma Guillermoprieto, Juan Villoro, Carlos Monsiváis, Ricardo Garibay, José Joaquín Blanco among others. With the awarding of the Premio Juan Rulfo to Carlos Monsiváis in September 2006, it would appear that the *crónica* is finally moving into the mainstream. See Esperanza López Parada, 'Un escritor ubícuo', *El País*, 6 September 2006.

stature. Arguably, therefore, the emergence of these genres bears testimony to the demise of the once supreme generic form. Indeed it is often stated that the novel itself is in crisis and it is certain, given the diffuse nature of publishing lines operating today, that it will never again recover the hallowed status it enjoyed during the international *boom*.[94] This crisis can also be explained in postmodern terms as a wider disillusionment with traditional 'truth' forms and the collapse of the grand narratives, commonly cited definitions of postmodernism. Added to this is the emergence of mass culture and particularly the influence of the visual on the literary. The derisory comments about film-scripts and *telenovelas* in the comments cited earlier on Mastretta's work lend weight to this view. Jean Franco asserts:

> the effects of mass culture disseminated by the media had a considerable impact on the intelligentsia, for whom the printed book was no long the emblem of cultural literacy [...] The printed book, once the instrument for acquiring cultural capital, now encountered powerful rivals in radio and television. This was especially true in times of economis crisis, as in Mexico in the mid-1980s.[95]

This dilemma might be conceptualised in a number of different ways but perhaps most obviously by the notion that 'story-telling' has taken precedence over form or genre. This return to 'story-telling' has been noted by many critics who insist on a category of writing called the *post-boom*.[96] That stories, therefore, continue to be of paramount importance is not in doubt. What has changed is that those stories are now being expressed or communicated in myriad forms, through

---

94   López González writes: 'Muchos textos desbordan el género. En este sentido es que se puede hablar hoy de la crisis de la novel: su mutación e hibridación, que coincide con la crisis del concepto de verdad en otros espacios del conocimiento en particular con relación a la historia', 'Quebrantos, búsquedas y azares de una pasión nacional', pp.678–9.

95   *The Decline and Fall of the Lettered City: Latin America After the Cold War*, p.11.

96   See, for example, work by Philip Swanson, *Latin American Fiction: A Short Introduction* and Donald Leslie Shaw, *The Post-Boom in Spanish-American Fiction* (New York: SUNY Press, 1998).

telenovelas, performance art,[97] cinema, detective fiction, urban chronicle, biography, autobiography and *testimonio* as previously mentioned. It is hardly surprising that the traditional novelistic forms – whether realist or modernist in conception – hold little appeal for the many writers and authors grappling with the mass-mediatised world. Moreover, these forms posed particular problems for women writers given the novel's close alignment with the foundational fictions of nation formation in Latin America which so clearly excluded women. Thus much work by women writers is involved, as Jean Franco points out, in 'the project of displacing the male-centered national allegory and exposes the dubious stereotyping that was always inherent in the epics of nationhood that constitute the Latin American canon'.[98] Furthermore, the genres at the disposal of women – poetry and narrative for the most part, 'come to them loaded with the freight of history'.[99] It is hardly surprising thus, that the chosen narrative forms of women writers have become more and more diffuse.

What is so interesting about the intense backlash and 'the free expression of misogyny' (the assertion is Kristine Ibsen's)[100] articulated so precisely by the critical panning of Mastretta's work is the fact that her texts have also provoked enthusiastic critical responses, often (though not exclusively) outside Mexico.[101] Many of these responses come from academic circles, predominantly influenced by feminist literary theory, and which seek to valorise and reinstate 'literatura light' as worthy of critical examination.[102] Thus it is not the

97 Rubén Gallo explores some of the very innovative ways of telling stories including photography, video installation and performance in contemporary Mexico. See *New Tendencies in Mexican Art: The 1990s* (New York: Palgrave Macmillan, 2004).

98 'Going Public: Reinhabiting the Private', in *Critical Passions*, p.57.

99 'Going Public: Reinhabiting the Private', p.59.

100 *The Other Mirror: Women's Narrative in Mexico, 1980–1995* (Westport, Connecticut and London: Greenwood Press, 1997), p.1.

101 Aralia López González makes reference to the attempts by the Programa Interdisciplinario de Estudios de la Mujer, El Colegio de Mexico, to expose the generalised misogyny behind these attacks on 'literatura Light'. 'Quebrantos, búsquedas y azares de una pasión nacional', p.665.

102 Examples of this criticism with regard to Mastretta include Jane Lavery, *Angeles Mastretta: Textual Multiplicity* (London: Tamesis, 2005), Kay S.

fact that either side of the *literatura light* versus *literatura difícil* is necessarily more 'right' than the other. Indeed both positions, are in many ways, depressingly predictable. A critic, like Guerrero to take just one example, is horrified at what he sees as 'high' literature being contaminated by the popular.[103] Clearly a feminist critic (like myself) could argue cogently and in a persuasive manner for an amplification of the terms of the debate. I could point to the many instances of literary innovation or profound insights into the human condition to be found in Mastretta's novels. I could argue that readability does not necessarily equate with *ligereza* or simplicity and plead that age-old prejudices concerning literature be put aside, as Mastretta herself does. None of this, however, seems to work. As I argue elsewhere, however, whatever the merits of feminist literary criticism in this regard (and there are many), 'it must be acknowledged that almost [sic] twenty years after the publication of many of these texts in Mexico, none of these critical analyses seem to be 'getting anywhere' in terms of changing the perception of the texts in Mexico'.[104] It remains to be seen, thus, whether the ultimate effect will be to simply reinforce dichotomies and not widen the options for the reception of these writers in their own domestic spheres. It is perhaps time, there-

García, *Broken Bars: New Perspectives from Mexican Women Writers*, Gabriella de Beer, *Contemporary Mexican Women Writers: Five Voices*. In addition, numerous essays have appeared that examine this aspect of Mastretta's work. *Mal de amores* has not attracted the same critical attention as *Arráncame la vida* but there are, nevertheless, several critical studies that focus on the gender dimensions of the work. See, for example, Carlos M. Coria-Sánchez, 'El discurso feminista de Angeles Mastretta en *Mal de amores*', *South Carolina Modern Language Review*, Vol.3, No.1 (Spring 2004), (n.p).

103   It is interesting to note how this discourse is often couched in a kind of medical discourse and, once again, into old polarities between 'clean' and 'dirty'. A colleague at a conference once remarked to me that you couldn't even use Esquivel's 'literature' as 'papel de water' (toilet paper).

104   Nuala Finnegan, '"Light" women/ "Light" Literature: Women and Popular Fiction in Mexico since 1980, *Donaire*, No.15 (November 2000), p.19. In the passage quoted above, 'these writers' refers in general to those women writers categorised as 'light' in Mexico and includes Angeles Mastretta, Laura Esquivel and Sara Sefchovich. This particular article examines María Luisa Puga and Sara Sefchovich.

fore, for critics to, in the words of Jane Lavery, 'move beyond that sort of lexicon and to look for a "new" language' which would embrace the entire range of writing emerging from the *boom*'.[105]

Conclusions

So where does the trawl through the 'literary apparatus' surrounding acclaimed writer, Angeles Mastretta really leave us in terms of understanding the positionality of the various players in the literary process? Aralia López Gonález, in the evocatively titled final section, 'Conclusiones sin conclusión', to her masterful overview of Mexican fiction in the 1970s and 1980s, outlines a total of nine separate strands that all contribute to the diverse cultural make-up of 1990s Mexico. Taking my cue from López González, in the sense that my final section is also a conclusion without a conclusion, I would tentatively suggest that the dilemmas encountered by the many stakeholders in the cultural arena in Mexico are linked to the inexorable process of *modernización*. As José Joaquín Blanco points out:

> El asunto fundamental de la literatura mexicana en la segunda mitad del siglo XX es la modernización del país, la brusca y forzada transformación de una nación preindustrial, rural, campesina, con poderosas atmósferas indígenas, aparentemente aislada de la vida occidental y arraigada en modos tradicionales, en un país industrial y urbano [...] Los novelistas cierran el mundo mexicanista, indígena y rural, y se pierden en las vistas y caóticas dimensiones urbanas; [...] descubren estéticas modernas y se proponen ahondar en los destinos irrepetibles de personajes que aspiran a ser considerados ciudadanos del siglo XX.[106]

105 Jane Lavery, personal correspondence, April 2007.
106 He adds, 'Los hechos sociales e históricos desgarrados se asumen frecuentemente como centros del debate, encarnando así – en los mejores casos – el inicio de una cultura civil donde una literatura se moderniza para alcanzar los grandes perfiles de un país que se expande [...] En tal sentido podría hablarse de la literatura de estas tres últimas décadas (1950–1980) sólo como el principio de una nueva cultura mexicana cuyo posterior trayecto resulta

According to Blanco, therefore, the writing trajectory (and with it that of publishing) is following a path of modernisation that has seen immense changes in the make-up of industrial and civil society in Mexico. The modernising process begun with Miguel Alemán in 1946, intensified particularly during the 1980s during the *sexenios* of Miguel de la Madrid (1982–1988), and most infamously, Carlos Salinas de Gortari (1988–1994). The Salinas *sexenio* realigned national priorities along clearly defined neo-liberal lines and it is no surprise that many of the dramatic changes in culture occur during his time in office. Indeed Salinas's presidency heralds a complete restructuring of cultural politics as the Instituto Nacional de Bellas Artes and its Departamento de Literatura, responsible in the 1970s for the literary workshops and 'Casas de la Cultura' built throughout Mexico gave way to the creation of CONACULTA or the Consejo Nacional para la Cultura y las Artes which becomes the major body responsible for literary promotion in the country.[107]

As already discussed, the process of modernisation propels women into the official workforce for the first time, creating, again for the first time, the novel concept of the female consumer. The new-found economic freedom of women had its impact too in the cultural sphere in that a space opened up for woman-centred stories to be heard, a space that was very quickly filled to bursting point with diverse and successful literary endeavours by women writers. Journalists like Guadalupe Loaeza and Cristina Pacheco, novelists like Brianda Domecq, Carmen Boullosa, Laura Esquivel, Angeles Mastretta, Silvia Molina, María Luisa Puga, Sara Sefchovich and many others, some of whom had been successful before the 1980s, now found themselves at the centre of an explosion in publishing opportunities. Thus, women writers in their turn, are also propelled into the writing 'workforce' for almost the first time, and are able to make a living from their writing. Even in the earlier generation of writers, Rosario Castellanos worked

impredecible; y del que apenas se podrá apuntar que estará unido cercanamente a la vida y a la civilización industrial y urbanas de occidente, con conflictos económicos y sociales propios de ese marco', 'Aguafuertes de narrativa mexicana, 1950–1980', *Nexos*, Vol.56 (1982), p.24.

107 'Quebrantos, búsquedas y azares de una pasión nacional' pp.679–80.

as both an academic and diplomat, as well as a writer, and Elena Garro died in utter penury. Elena Poniatowska, on the other hand, technically their contemporary, is exceptional in that she has always lived from her journalistic output. In this category of professional writers there are many writers including Sara Sefchovich, Laura Esquivel, Angeles Mastretta, Guadalupe Loaeza and Carmen Boullosa.

Thus the development of a female readership, is in turn inextricably linked to the project of *modernización* in Mexico, which has seen women's disposable income rise dramatically. Moreover, the economic crisis of the 1980s which ironically led to the turnaround in women's economic status in Mexico provoked a publishing crisis that led, for the most part, to the takeover of smaller presses by large multinational conglomerates. Within this flurry of change, it is often difficult to ascertain which comes first – promotion of readability by the publishers or the readable texts. It might be more properly understood as a fluid and ever-evolving dynamic in which writers move to fill spaces created by publishers and the market, their texts in turn generating new demand that comes to be filled again. What is absolutely irrefutable is that new publication lines have now opened up publishing possibilities for writers that previously simply did not exist.[108] Thus the globalisation of publishing and the marketability of certain kinds of stories written by certain kinds of women seem to explain the dramatic rise of the 'readable' novel. It is also worth pointing out that this is by no means exclusive to the Spanish-speaking market and that debates over 'chick lit' bear remarkable similarity to the ones happening over *literatura light* in the Hispanic

---

108 In the 1950s–1960s the *Letras Mexicanas* series in FCE was the highest aspiration of any Mexican writer as Vicente Leñero attests: 'En aquel entonces publicar en Letras Mexicanas era lo máximo a lo que podía aspirar un escritor', 'No, a los párrafos que enjuician libros', p.13. See also, Ana Domenella, 'Territorio de leonas: Narradoras mexicanas en los noventa', in Ana Domenella, Luzelena Gutiérrez de Velasco, Nora Pasternac, Gloria Prado y Graciela Martínez-Zalce (eds), *Territorio de leonas: cartografía de narradoras mexicanas en los noventa,* (Mexico City: Universidad Autónoma Metropolitana, 2001), pp.19–44, pp.36–41.

world.[109] It is also the case, however, that the backlash against 'chick-lit' in the English-speaking world at least, has not been infused with the same bitterness as that witnessed in Mexico.

Taking this explosion of possibilities into consideration, it would be unwise to ignore the writers' own stake in popularity (and indeed translatability), recalling again Mastretta's hopeful desire to break into the North American market. Jean Franco makes this point and laments that intellectuals do not:

> begin the process of dismantling their own position of privilege. And a good place to begin might well be with questioning their stake in the 'the popular' especially when the popular, in their representation, inhabits those places where they themselves are privileged visitors.[110]

Perhaps it is this final assertion that holds the key to reconceptualising debates around literary worth and value. Until such time as all the players in the immensely important game of literature are fully evaluated and recognised, the situation where defenders of 'high' literature fend off encroachment into their territory by writers of popular fiction will continue. As women writers themselves are immersed in a system of globalised culture, they are powerless to escape its clutches as they compete for publisher and reader attention along with critical respectability. At the same time they accrue enormous benefits – both cultural and commercial – that see them propelled into positions of relative power for the first time in Mexican history. Thus, we return, once again, to the notion of ambivalence as the only way of satisfactorily accounting for the almost impossible situation of women writers positioned at a cross-roads, with so many competing and at

109 'Chick lit' is now widely understood as a term to denote genre fiction aimed almost exclusively at young women. The term has generated considerable controversy in the way that it seems to denigrate a certain kind of women-authored, women-centred narrative. Rachel Donadio points to the differing meanings that accrue with the term when it proliferates outside the Western metropolitan centres, as is increasingly the case with 'chick lit' in both India and Eastern Europe. Italy also boasts its own burgeoning 'chick lit' genre with new work by Camilla Vittorini. See, 'The Chick Lit Pandemic', *New York Times*, 19 March 2006.

110 'Globalisation and the Crisis of the Popular', in *Critical Passions*, p.218.

times converging interests including market forces and reader interest, critical horror, and publisher expansion. So women writers of popular texts remain, in many ways, in a no-win situation and until such time as the rigid boundaries policing definitions of literature are re-drawn and expanded, they will continue to struggle against a largely male-dominated literary institution that will clamour loudly for their exclusion.

Chapter Four
Class, Gender and Questions of Feminism in Guadalupe Loaeza and Rosamaría Roffiel

This chapter examines the work of pioneering writers, Guadalupe Loaeza and Rosamaría Roffiel. I choose to label them pioneers, Loaeza because of the unprecedented success of her political and social satire that has made her a household name, and Roffiel because of her work's unabashed celebration of lesbian love and the feminist community. In this sense, their voices are new and unique in the panorama of Mexican writing. Both come to prominence during the 1980s with Loaeza's *Las niñas bien* (1987) selling more than 50,000 copies in its first year alone.[1] Roffiel's novel, *Amora* was the first lesbian novel in Mexico published in the same year as Laura Esquivel's best-selling *Como agua para chocolate*.[2] According to the author herself, the first print-run (3,000 copies) ran out and for ten years it circulated in photocopy form. It has since been re-edited.[3]

[1] Julia Van Loan Aguilar, 'Humor in Crisis: Guadalupe Loaeza's Caricature of the Mexican Bourgeoisie', *Journal of American Culture*, Vol.20, No.2 (Summer 1997), p.2. See Roselyn Costantino, 'Resistant Creativity: Interpretative Strategies and Gender Representation in Contemporary Women's Writing in Mexico', p.6. Cherie Meacham points out that Loaeza had sold more than 500,000 books by 2000. See 'A Woman's Testimony on the Mexican Crisis', *Letras femeninas*, Vol.26, Nos.1–2 (2000), p.111.

[2] Deborah Shaw writes, 'Laura Esquivel's novel [...] was a long-running bestseller in Mexico, and it spent over a year on the best-seller list of the *New York Times*. By 1994, 780,000 copies had been sold in the United States in English. It was translated into twenty-nine languages'. *Contemporary Cinema of Latin America: 10 Key Films* (New York and London: Continuum, 2003), p.37.

[3] Roffiel writes, 'Cuando edité *Amora* con Planeta, en septiembre de 1989, la edición se agotó a los tres meses. La segunda edición salió en enero de 1990 y jamás la sacaron de la bodega. Diez meses después la editorial me dio una disculpa porque no sabía que había pasado'.

Loaeza and Roffiel are linked too through their preoccupation with women and in particular, women from the Mexican middle classes. As Cherie Meacham notes of Loaeza, 'Her position is unabashedly bourgeois, female, and middle-aged'.[4] Roffiel's work too, focuses exclusively on the politically aware, middle-class educated urban woman.[5] It is this connection that in turn aligns them with the greatest pioneering force in Mexican feminist literature of the twentieth century, Rosario Castellanos. As is well known, Castellanos wrote prose, poetry, drama, essays and worked as journalist, academic and diplomat. She died in 1974, in Tel Aviv, Israel as a result of a tragic accident.[6] Castellanos's later work, the collection of short stories, *Ál-*

http://www.planeta.apc.org/pipermail/boletina/2004-December/000010.html. She also attests to its circulation underground: 'se agotó esa primera edición y por diez años siguió circulando fotocopiada'. See Silvia Lailson, 'Aún con resistencias y prejuicios, las editoriales empiezan a publicar literatura lésbica', http://www.jornada.unam.mx/2000/10/02/lesbianismo3.htm.

4   'A Woman's Testimony on the Mexican Crisis: Guadalupe Loaeza's *Sin cuenta*', p.111.

5   As well as *Amora*, Roffiel has published poetry and a collection of short stories/chronicles, *El para siempre dura una noche* which also feature prominently the struggles of middle-class women in Mexico City and which are all partly autobiographical. Roffiel writes in *Amora* of the close autobiographical content of the work, 'Sí, en efecto, ésta es una novela muy autobiográfica. Casi todas las personajas existen. Casi todos los nombres fueron cambiados. Y casi todo ocurrió realmente', from the 'Dedicatoria', *Amora* (Mexico City: Planeta, Colección Fábula, 1989). See also, *El para siempre dura una noche* (Mexico City: Sentido Contrario, 2003).

6   Castellanos died in 1974 from an electric shock in a freak accident while serving as Mexican ambassador to Israel. It was rumoured for some time that her death was the result of suicide but no evidence was ever uncovered to support this theory. The unusual circumstances of her death are evoked in the poem, 'Recado a Rosario Castellanos' written by her friend Jaime Sabines after her death. See Oscar Bonifaz's biographical account of Castellanos's life. *Rosario* (Mexico City: Presencia Latinoamericana, 1984), pp.7–8. For criticism and biography on Castellanos, see Maureen Ahern, *The Rosario Castellanos Reader: An Anthology of her Poetry, Short Fiction, Essays and Drama* (Austin: University of Texas Press, 1988), Nuala Finnegan, *Monstrous Projections of Femininity in Rosario Castellanos's Prose* (Lampeter: Edwin Mellen Press, 2000), Joanna O'Connell, *Prospero's Daughter: The Prose of Rosario Castellanos* (Austin: University of Texas Press, 1995), Aralia López González, *La*

bum de familia (1971) and the play, *El eterno femenino* (1973), move
away from the concerns of her earlier fiction – provincial Mexico and
the tensions inherent between communities of *ladinos, indígenas* and
state powers.[7] Instead, this later work showcases the plight of the
middle-class Mexican woman, trapped in patriarchal structures that
are both debilitating and destructive. There are many reasons why the
work of Loaeza and Roffiel invites comparisons with Castellanos.
Both writers profess admiration of Castellanos and cite her at various
points throughout their work. Their fiction attempts to excavate the
minutiae of women's lives and reveal destructive patriarchal patterns
in ways strikingly similar to Castellanos. What is more, the commitment to writing as a mechanism for social change permeates the
work of all three. The debt to Castellanos, thus, is palpable in both
Loaeza and Roffiel and is articulated explicitly.

It is, therefore, through the filter of Rosario Castellanos that I
focalise my discussion of both Loaeza and Roffiel, concentrating on
the ways in which they continue the Castellanos trajectory, re-writing
aspects of Castellanos's work and forging paths for self-exploration of
the Mexican female subject in the late twentieth century. The iconic
status of Castellanos within the often tortuous field of Mexican letters
has deeply penetrated the work of younger women writers in various
ways. Indeed, Castellanos exerts a particular fascination for women
writers in Mexico and remains enduringly popular as a subject of
study. As Costantino attests, 'many Mexican and Latin American women look to Castellanos as a foremother in her role as woman and as

      espiral parece un círculo (Mexico: Universidad Autónoma Metropolitana,
      1992), Elena Poniatowska, *¡Ay vida no me mereces!: Carlos Fuentes, Rosario*
      Castellanos, Juan Rulfo. La literatura de la onda (Mexico: Joaquín Mortiz,
      1985), and Beatriz Reyes Nevares, *Rosario Castellanos* (Mexico City:
      Departamento Editorial Secretaría de la Presidencia, 1976).
7   Castellanos's work, *Balún-Canán* (1957), *Ciudad Real* (1960), *Oficio de*
      tinieblas (1962) and *Los convidados de agosto* (1964) are all concerned with
      life in Chiapas where Castellanos herself was born and raised. The earlier three
      collections in particular, foreground the concerns of women but also explore the
      stark inequalities existing between *ladinas, indígenas* and *mestizas* in Southern
      Mexico during the various time periods. See Joanna O'Connell, *Prospero's*
      Daughter: The Prose of Rosario Castellanos for an excellent discussion of the
      indigenista discourses present in Castellanos's early work.

writer in Mexico'.[8] This notion of 'foremother' is interesting: I should point out that my focus steers away from the rather contentious notion of Castellanos's 'influence' on the younger writers. This approach is theoretically fraught with problems and, in a feminist context, has been well rehearsed elsewhere.[9] Rather, my examination explores the ways in which Loaeza and Roffiel (in their work published at the end of the 1980s and the beginning of the 1990s) invoke the Castellanos legacy, how they tease out the challenges posed by her later work and frequently suggest new ones. In Loaeza's case, this is most evident through her subversive use of the genre of satire. Castellanos experimented with satire, most notably in her final work of drama, *El eterno femenino*. Loaeza's often savage world of upper class Mexico in which there is little solidarity or human warmth but rather intense competition between the female protagonists, clearly echoes the equally vicious world evoked by Castellanos in her later work and

8   'Resistant Creativity', p.99. Fabienne Bradu reports that 61% of registered articles at the Instituto de Investigaciones Filológicas were written after her death. Aurora Ocampo indicates that this interest has not diminished and that there are currently fifteen theses a year written on Castellanos. She further notes that Castellanos's books sell at a rate of three thousand a month as opposed to the two or three copies which circulated during her lifetime. See Elena Poniatowska, *¡Ay vida no me mereces!*, p.58. Angeles Mastretta's essay, 'Guiso feminista' explicitly echoes Castellanos's celebrated story, 'Lección de cocina' and Brianda Domecq's re-writing of the Adam and Eve myth in *Bestiario doméstico* parallels Castellanos's attempts to do the same in *El eterno femenino*. In sum, as well as Loaeza and Roffiel, parallels and connections may be drawn between Castellanos and many of the major writers associated with the *boom*.

9   Discussions about literary influence inevitably centre on Harold Bloom's *The Anxiety of Influence: A Theory of Poetry* (Oxford: Oxford University Press, 1973) in which he addresses, among other things, the anxiety of influence that pervades (male) writers' desire for recognition and transcendence in their literary endeavour. Susan Gilbert and Sandra Gubar's response to Bloom critiques the patriarchal nature of his approach and argues that 'influence' for women writers occurs more in the form of the polarised archetypes available to them from literary tradition (for example, the 'angel in the house', the 'mad-woman in the attic'). *The Madwoman in the Attic: The Woman Writer and the Nineteeth Century Literary Imagination* (New Haven and London: Yale University Press, 1979).

perhaps, most forcefully, in the story, 'Álbum de familia'. With regard to Roffiel, it is the rather overdetermined presence of a certain kind of Second Wave feminist discourse that closely aligns the two writers. Indeed both Castellanos and Roffiel are deeply indebted to Second Wave feminist discourses in their emphasis on the middle classes. Roffiel clearly experiments with more radical material in the case of lesbianism and homosexuality generally, but it remains firmly fixed within the urban world of educated women in Mexico City. While Castellanos's world view posits women as isolated solitary creatures waging battles with misogynistic societal structures over which they have no control, Roffiel's protagonists take solace from the wider community of women and the redemptive nature of solidarity is much in evidence. In this way, her work presents an optimistic and often utopian view of women, which is in stark contrast to the bleak world inhabited by the female characters of *Álbum de familia*, Castellanos's final work of fiction published before her death.[10] In this chapter, therefore, I focus on the ways in which both writers re-affirm the feminist agenda of Castellanos's work in their eloquent exposure of destructive patriarchal power structures that control and limit the lives of the women in their texts.

10   Castellanos's novel, *Rito de iniciación* was published posthumously in 1995. Her final works, the short story collection, *Álbum de familia* (Mexico City: Joaquín Mortiz, 1971), the play, *El eterno femenino* (Mexico City: Fondo de Cultura Económica, 1975), and the collection of essays, *Mujer que sabe latín...* (Mexico City: Sepsetentas Secretaria de Educación Pública, 1973) clearly signal the new direction of her work in their concern with the plight of the middle-class Mexican woman and the position of the female intellectual in Mexico at that time.

Guadalupe Loaeza and the Satiric Mode

Guadalupe Loaeza's work is most often described by fans and critics as political and social satire.[11] She began her career as columnist in the left-leaning newspaper, *Unomásuno*, in 1982. Her column was first published as *Las niñas bien* in 1987 and was an immediate success. This was closely followed by a similar collection entitled, *Las reinas de Polanco* (1988). Loaeza's output has since been both prolific and diverse. She has published novels, historical studies and collections of interviews and stories. Loaeza began her writing career in Elena Poniatowska's literary workshop and, according to her own account, offered herself to the left-wing *Unomásuno* in 1982. In 1983, she and a number of her colleagues were successful in starting another daily newspaper, *La jornada*, which has become the most popular liberal newspaper in Mexico City today. She continues to write for *La jornada* as well as *Punto y Obelisco* and has a column in *La Reforma*. She has also worked for radio (Radio Red) and is known to writers through her own magazine, *Polanco* and her frequent television appearances (Canal 40).[12] Critics tend to focus on the humour in her work, her skill for sarcasm, irony and biting criticism. Julia Van Loan Aguilar writes:

> What is most striking about Loaeza's work is her ability to systematically direct her sarcastic humour at what is wrong in Mexican society and politics in a

---

11   Loaeza is beginning to attract substantial critical attention though there is still much ground to be covered in this regard. See Mary K. Long, Cherie Meacham, Claudia Schaefer Rodriguez, Deborah Shaw, Julia Van Loan Aguilar and others for their contribution to Loaeza scholarship. Most of the studies focus to some extent or other on the satirical nature of her work. *Las niñas bien* (Mexico City: Cal y Arena, 1987) has received the most critical attention though there is also some interesting study on *Compro, luego existo* (Mexico: Alianza Editorial, 1992), *Sin cuenta* (Barcelona: Plaza y Janés, 1996), and *Las reinas de polanco* (Mexico City: Cal y Arena, 1988).

12   Julia Van Loan, 'Humor in Crisis', p.2 and Cherie Meacham, 'A Woman's Testimony on the Mexican Crisis', p.111. See also Guadalupe Loaeza, *Detrás del espejo* (Mexico City: Editorial Patria, Nueva Imagen, 1999), pp.15–22 and pp.289–92 for an account of Loaeza's entry into the world of writing.

184

personalised, chatty tone. She manages to weave sharp, biting criticism of high society, of politicians, even of the president into the imagined small talk of an elegant cocktail party.[13]

Loaeza's name, therefore, has been forged on the basis of her sharp powers of observation and her ability to wittily present the hypocrisies of bourgeois Mexico to the reading public. My examination focuses on two specific works – *Las reinas de Polanco* and *Compro, luego existo*. The former is a collection of columns from the newspapers, *La jornada*, *El obelisco* and the magazines, *Karma*, *El norte* and *Vogue*, spanning the years 1986–1988. *Compro, luego existo* was published in 1992 and chronicles the lives of several members of the Mexican rich. Each chapter focuses on a different character and the multiple perspectives offer interesting insights into their lives of privilege. In my analysis of Loaeza's work, I will focus on her use of satire in a traditional way to expose hypcocrisy and mock bourgeois conventionality. I will also consider the ways in which her use of satire exemplifies her ambivalent positioning with regard to her subjects focusing on the ways in which Loaeza critiques patriarchal power structures and allows space for compassion and understanding of the characters she denigrates.

Satire, Irony, Humour

Satire has been defined in numerous ways; William Thrall summarises it as, 'a literary manner which blends a critical attitude with humor and wit to the end that human institutions or humanity may be improved'.[14] The corrective purpose of satire is thus immediately identified as well as its mission to entertain, and it is the tension

---

13   'Humor in Crisis', p.2.
14   William Thrall, Addison Hibbard and C. Hugh Holman (eds), *A Handbook to Literature* (New York: Odyssey Press, 1960), p.436. See also, Leonard Feinberg, 'Satire: The Inadequacy of Recent Definitions', *Genre*, Vol.1 (1968), pp.31–7.

caused by this dynamic that is central to the evolution of satire and satiric discourse.[15] Critics note that the application of the satiric method can be quite broad, as satire itself is more of an attitude or stance than a genre or type of literature. As William Haas explains, 'it is not bounded by form and structure but exists as an approach to a situation which can be present in any of the many literary forms'.[16] From its very origins, satire has occupied a central place in literary discourse.[17] Indeed Loaeza follows in a line of distinguished satirical writers from the Mexican tradition including the writing of Sor Juana Inés de la Cruz in which the author attacks certain social types of her day, and Fernando de Lizardi's nineteenth century work, *El periquillo sarniento*, which similarly mocked the Mexican bourgeoisie.[18] Van Loan Aguilar writes:

> While in colonial times satire appeared in poetry and narrative, in the twentieth century it has found its vehicle in the newspaper. In Mexico, there is a distinct tradition of a journalistic vein of satire – chronicles and witty commentaries that often couple the visual caricature of a politician or lady of society somewhat disguised with some searing verses of criticism. From Guadalupe Posada's *calaveras* (satirical poems on the imagined death of a person) in celebration of the Day of the Dead to Rius' comic strip series *Los agachados*,

15   In the English tradition, Alexander Pope, Jonathan Swift, Geofrey Chaucer among many others.

16   William Haas, 'Some Characteristics of Satire', *Satire Newsletter*, Vol.3 (Fall 1965), p.1.

17   Research shows that satire was present in one form or another in most so-called primitive societies and cultures: 'Imprecations, threats of reprisal, and invective were believed to be imbued with the "magical power" of "word-slaying." Alex Preminger and T.V.F. Brogan (eds), *The New Princeton Encyclopedia of Poetry and Poetics* (New Jersey: Princeton University Press, 1993), p.1114. See also R.C. Elliott, *The Power of Satire: Magic, Ritual, Art* (Princeton Univeristy, 1960).

18   Lizardi's *El periquillo sarniento* (Mexico City: Porrúa, 1949), first published in 1816, is frequently considered to be the first Mexican novel. Much of Sor Juana Inés de la Cruz's work also belongs to the satiric tradition. See, for example, her secular satirical play, *Los empeños de una casa*, *Obras Completas*, Vol.4 (Mexico City: Fondo de Cultura Económica, 1951), pp.3–184.

the combination of graphic and verbal caricature are directed at the same social pretense and hypocrisy Loaeza lampoons.[19]

As already stated, central to satire is a tension created by the need to criticise and thus provoke change, as well as the need to keep the intended audience on board. Wit and humour are thus of paramount importance. The satirical tools employed to create this effect are many and various but they include the use of irony, hyperbole, exaggeration, distortion, understatement, innuendo, parable, and allegory. Irony is often considered the primary satirical weapon and other techniques like syllepsis (a combination of grammatical parallelism and semantic incongruity) are also hallmarks of the genre.[20] Loaeza's work is best located in the realm of social satire with a heavy political charge. In many ways, her work constitutes classic satire in that she uses irony, hyperbole, absurdity, exaggeration and distortion to comic effect. The humour is often produced through the faithful reproduction of a typical dialogue between members of the elite class. In 'Una misa chic', Loaeza recounts the exchanges heard outside the church when mass is over:

> '¡Hola! ¿Cómo están? ¿Van a ir a comer a casa de los Luján?' [...] '¡Me encanta tu sombrero!' 'Te lo trajeron de París?' 'Oye, qué bueno que te veo. Necesito una cocinera que sea una *cordon blue*. Allí te la encargo.' 'No sabes qué estupendo resultado me ha dado la crema de Madame Simonne.' [...] '¿Cuándo regresan a París?' 'Acabamos de estar en el rancho de los Sánchez Navarro. ¿A ustedes nunca los han invitado?' Tu *ensemble* está muy *chic*. ¿Lo copiasta [sic] de algún figurín francés? (*Polanco*, p.126).[21]

Irony is also produced through witty narrative observations:

19   'Humor in Crisis', p.4.
20   Pope's classic piece of satire, *The Rape of the Lock* presents some good examples of the sylleptic technique: 'or stain her Honour, or her new Brocade [...] Or lose her Heart, or Necklace, at a Ball' from *Rape of the Lock*, Canto II, lines 105–10. See, Alexander Pope, *The Rape of the Lock* (London and New York: Routledge, 1971).
21   *Las reinas de Polanco* (Mexico City: Cal y Arena, 1989). All page references will appear in parentheses after the quotations in the text.

Yo gasto, tú gastas, ella gasta, nosotros gastamos, vosotros gastáis, ellas gastan. El verbo gastar es, sin duda, el más conjugado de todos, dentro de un sector de mujeres que trabajan sin necesitarlo, o bien que en sus chequeras personales aparece, además de una cuantiosa suma, el *milagroso* 'Y/O' entre el nombre de su marido y del suyo propio (*Polanco*, p.85).

Loaeza also uses hyperbole to illustrate the obscene consumerism rampant among this sector of society. There are examples of ironic satirical technique in the creation of incongruity, as well as comic send-ups of their exaggerated consumerist tendencies, 'y yo, gaste y gaste; come y come; compre y compre' (*Compro*, p.122).

The emphasis on consumerism found in Loaeza's work, and indeed the attention to language used by this sector is also present in Rosario Castellanos's satirical play, *El eterno femenino*, which was published in 1973 but never performed.[22] *El eterno femenino* narrates the arrival of a salesman to the salon who has a miraculous new invention, a micro-chip that can be implanted in a woman's head which will prevent her from thinking. The assistants choose a customer, Lupita, to be the recipient and there are various scenes of graphic hallucination and nightmare. At the end of Act I, in one of the first of such scenes, Lupita is catapulted into a nightmarish consumer frenzy when she is visited by a quiz show host having murdered her husband for committing adultery with his secretary:

Se ha ganado usted un premio cedido por la Perfumería París, cuyos productos huelen...y huelen bien. He aquí un maravilloso, un estupendo frasco de brillantina para el pelo. Un frasco de brillantina que limpia, fija y da esplendor. Lupita ¿querría usted agradecer este regalo de la Perfumería París, cuyos

---

22   It is interesting to note in this regard that the story, 'Álbum de familia', mentioned earlier, from the eponymous collection, also began as a drama, entitled *Tablero de damas*. Its theatrical context remains very much in evidence in its reliance on dialogue and its 'staged' quality. Castellanos herself was disappointed by her foray into theatre, declaring that 'Después del fracaso absoluto de la pieza "Tablero de damas" [...] me convencí de que mi forma de expresión no era el teatro'. *Los narradores ante el público* (Mexico City: Joaquín Mortiz, 1966), p.96. See Kathleen O'Quinn, '"Tablero de damas" and "Álbum de familia": Farces on Women Writers', in Maureen Ahern and Mary Seale Vásquez, *Homenaje a Rosario Castellanos* (Valencia: Albatros Hispanófila, 1980), pp.99–105.

productos huelen... y huelen bien, al público que tiene la bondad de escucharnos?

Lupita: Agradezco mucho... (Se atora)

Animador: ...a la Perfumería París, cuyos productos huelen... y huelen bien...

Lupita: ... y huelen bien...[...]

Animador: [...] 'Latex, la casa que acaba con las latas porque tiene un surtido completo de latas', le regala a usted estas sopitas, estas salsitas, estas mermeladitas... Señora, déjese de latas, abra una lata. Latex le proporciona a usted todo lo que su cocina necesita. ¿Latas? No. Latex.

Lupita (*que empieza a estar rodeada de los objetos que se acumulan en torno suyo, embobada por lo que ocurre.*) ¡Qué bonito! Pero realmente, no sé... Es demasiado.[23]

In passages such as this one, Castellanos effectively captures the vacuous and inane consumer scene in Mexico in the early 1970s. She also inserts interminable lists to emphasise consumerist obsession, lists which are also found in Loaeza's work. The following passage illustrates the point:

Animador: [...] Este evento ha sido organizado por la cadena de tiendas A.B.C. A: adquiera. B: buenas. C: cosas. Usted resultó vencedora del concurso A.B.C. Adquiera buenas cosas. [...]

Mientras Pedrito se desgañita y el animador explica y Lupita insiste, se descargan encima de ella licuadoras, lavadoras, estufas, pasteles que forman una pirámide que la sepulta. Encima de la cúspide hay un pastel con una velita. Lupita, sintiendo que se asfixia, clama desde lo profundo del abismo.

Lupita: ¡Auxilio! ¡Socorro! Sáquenme de aquí! ¡Me ahogo! Me ahogo... Auxilio... Socorro... [24]

Both Castellanos and Loaeza, then, expose the shallowness inherent in much consumerist discourse. Both also emphasise the superficial nature of many women's conversations, and it is interesting to note that both often pause to dwell on the penchant for foreign words and phrases. Loaeza points to the ludicrous insertion of French and English words into the women's speech. In this way she exposes the pretentious nature of the upper middle classes as they establish their superiority in the social pecking order by bickering over the use of English in certain contexts. Ana Paula, the protagonist of the chapter

---

23 *El eterno femenino*, pp.66–7.
24 *El eterno femenino*, pp.68–9.

'La cena', in *Compro, luego existo*, commits several *faux pas* in relation to the misplaced use of certain words and phrases. Indeed she is the constant butt of her friends' sneers:

> A los ojos de estas señoras, Ana Paula tenía dos defectos im-per-do-na-bles: no sabía hablar inglés y se vestía ¡pé-si-mo! [...] Cuando ocasionalmente dejaba caer alguna expresión coloquial de las más socorridas por sus amigas – por ejemplo: 'Give me a break'–, nadie le entendía. Para colmo, cada vez que se refería a Nueva York, invariablemente decía 'Nueva Yor' (*Compro*, p.56).

These cruel jibes serve to highlight the shallow nature of the interaction amongst this sector of Mexican society, which is mercilessly revealed by Loaeza's writing. Castellanos too points out the increasing use of English among the Mexican upper classes and its function as a subtle marker of social acceptability. *El eterno femenino* features an exchange on the same subject between some of the beauty salon's clients:

> Señora 1: (*Dubitativa*): No sé si quedarme o irme. Tengo una cita en el Club de Golf.
> Señora 2: ¿Cómo pronuncias *Club*? A la inglesa, a la francesa o a la española?
> Señora 3: Ay, tú, ni que fuera chocolate.[25]

In the short story, 'Domingo' from the short story collection, *Álbum de familia*, there is also pretentious use made of certain English expressions, like 'un whiskey en las rocas'; 'open house' and 'self-made man'.[26] Both writers, then, are firmly located within a satirical tradition that has as its target the vacuous consumer-driven world of modern Mexico city.

---

25 *El eterno femenino*, p.179.
26 See 'Domingo', *Álbum de familia*, pp.23–46.

It should be clear, therefore, that Loaeza's satirical send-up of modern consumer society finds resonance with Castellanos's earlier exploration of the same subject. It should be noted too that *El eterno femenino* is situated in a beauty salon – forming an immediate parallel with the chapter, 'Un week-end en el D.F'. from *Compro, luego existo*, in which Ana Paula visits her local beauty salon. Loaeza, like Castellanos, has isolated the beauty salon as an important site in which her privileged protagonists play out their desires and negotiate their anxieties. In choosing the salon, Loaeza continues Castellanos's quest to examine the middle-class psyche of Mexican women in ways that provoke, stimulate and entertain. By taking the beauty salon as a setting, Castellanos draws attention not only to the growing consumer culture in Mexico but also to her frustration at the importance assigned by society to 'adorno' or decoration in all of its forms. This, she notes, is particularly pernicious with regard to the adornment of the female body but is also relevant with regard to the decoration of their homes, increasingly the focus of Mexican women's energy, and which, according to Castellanos, might be more satisfactorily directed elsewhere. This frustration finds expression at various points throughout *El eterno femenino*:

> Oscuro. La luz va a iluminar ahora una de esas mezclas de sala de recibir y de aula, tan frecuentes entre las señoras de la burguesía Mexicana que acaban de descubrir que la cultura es un adorno y dedican a ella, si no su más arduo esfuerzo, sí sus mejores horas. En esta ocasión, el grupo es muy selecto, lo que quiere decir, muy poco numeroso. Cotorrean que es un gusto durante el intervalo que separa una clase de otra.[27]

Castellanos wrote at length about the detrimental influence of female fashion. In an article entitled 'La participación de la mujer mexicana en la educación formal', she says:

---

27 *El eterno femenino*, p.179.

Pasivamente acepta convertirse en musa para lo que es preciso permanecer a distancia y guardar silencio. Y ser bella. Esto es, sujetarse a todos los caprichos de la moda que unas veces la quiere obesa, hasta el punto de no acertar a moverse y otras esbelta hasta el punto de no poder ejecutar el más mínimo movimiento sin sufrir un desmayo, producido por su plausible debilidad y por la asfixia que le produce el corsé que la ciñe con ballenas de acero y el pie oprimido por el calzado minúsculo y la cabeza agobiada por el peso de la peluca que, en ocasiones, requiere un ayudante para ser sostenida.[28]

The use of the beauty salon in both bodies of work, then highlights Castellanos's concern, articulated here, about the continued existence of these limiting myths in the shaping of female identity.

As we have seen, Loaeza's work is located within a rich satiric tradition and employs many classical satirical techniques. Of particular interest here is the way in which Loaeza borrows one of the more popular modes of satirical expression – the beast fable – which proliferated during medieval times and was employed particularly as a way of disseminating anticlerical satire.[29] The beast fable enjoyed wide popularity, particularly the anonymous Roman de Renard, in which the fox in his traditional cunning mode, speaks alongside a lion, wolf, bear, cat, and cockerel, all of whom comment on a roster of human infirmities and abuses: 'From the perspective of animals, the social, political, and religious peccadilloes of humanity have been depicted by such major poets as Chaucer, LaFontaine, Dryden, and Swift'.[30] In the chapter set in the beauty salon, Loaeza introduces the character of Oscar, Ana Paula's treasured dog, into the narrative. His function is, like Roman de Renard before him, to act as satirical voice-over. Indeed much of the really bitter criticism comes from the dog and not from the omniscient narrator present elsewhere in the chapter. It is Oscar who announces disgust for the beauty salon: 'De todos los

---

28   *Mujer que sabe latín*, pp.23–4.
29   Often composed in Latin, they drew upon the legacy of Aesop. The beast epic of Reynard the Fox is the best known and survives in various forms, the earliest version probably being the Latin poem, *Ysingrimus* by Nivard of Ghent (*c*.1152). See Wm. A Nitze, 'Review of *Le Roman de Renard* by Lucien Foulet', *Modern Language Notes*, Vol.30, No.5 (May 1915), pp.145–9.
30   Alex Preminger and T.V.F. Brogan (eds), *The New Princeton Encylopaedia of Poetry and Poetics*, p.1115.

lugares a los que su ama lo llevaba, el que más odiaba era el salón de belleza. ¿Por qué, entonces, insistía en hacerlo? ¿Por qué mejor no lo paseaba por la barranca de Alpes para que sus pulmoncitos pudieran respirar aire puro' (*Compro*, p.139). The reader is informed that the dog, 'odiaba el ambiente que se respiraba allí. Cada vez que su ama lo llevaba, salía indignado por todo lo que había visto' (*Compro*, p.138). As well as his disdain for the place, he is utterly repulsed by the behaviour he witnesses there:

> No soportaba a esas señoras autoritarias que llegaban dando órdenes: 'Te me apuras, porque tengo que salir en quince minutos. A ver tú, tráeme un vaso de agua. Y tú, dile al chófer que vaya a la tintorería por mi vestido rojo y que me lo traiga aquí para cambiarme. Tú, veme a buscar el último *¡Hola!* Y tú, que no estás haciendo nada, ve a avisarle a Lety que ya venga a secarme.' Desde el regazo de su ama, observaba las miradas duras, los rictus de satisfacción y la actitud prepotente (*Compro*, p.138).

At first the clients's words are repeated (as though directly overheard by the dog) creating an effective exposé of their arrogant, overbearing behaviour:

> En una ocasión, escuchó a una clienta que llevaba una batita strapless, decirle a Anita, que estaba pintando las uñas de su ama: 'Pues fíjate que ya me hice la operación de las bubis ($22,000 en el Hospital Angeles, con el doctor García Naranjo). No sabes cómo me quedaron. Te juro que me siento Raquel Welch. Desde entonces, mi marido está loco conmigo' (*Compro*, p.138).

This relatively gentle depiction of their arrogant behaviour gives way to more incisive criticism, however, as Oscar becomes the vehicle through which the text's condemnation and moral revulsion are articulated. This censure is communicated effectively through the strategic repetion of certain verbs that intensify the critique:

> No Óscar no *las aguantaba*. Menos *toleraba* a aquellas que, después de hacerse quién sabe cuantas cosas, prácticamente no dejaban propina. No *toleraba* a aquellas que les contaban, ya fuera a la peinadora o a la manicurista, con todo lujo de detalle, sus viajes a Nueva York: 'Pues fíjate que en el hotel Pierre, los desayunos son ma-ra-vi-llo-sos. No sabes todo lo que me compré.' *No toleraba* a aquellas que llegaban con la nana de sus hijos, la que durante horas y horas esperaba a que terminara la señora. [...] *No toleraba* a las que no dejaban de

hablar acerca de las sirvientas: '¿Te acuerdas de la recamarera que te platiqué que acababa de entrar a la casa? Pues fíjate que resultó ser bruja. Después descubrí que a mis hijos les contaba cuentos de fantasmas y cosas horribles que habían pasado en su pueblo. Además, fíjate que me salió ratera. Se robó mi anillo de compromiso y el Cartier de la nena.' *No toleraba* a aquéllas que, a las seis de la tarde, de pronto exclamaban: 'Ay, no le he dicho al chófer que se vaya a comer', siendo que dos horas antes, ellas, las patronas, tuvieron el privilegio de pedir ensaladas y sandwiches (hechos con pan de La Baguette) de jamón y queso gruyère (my emphasis, *Compro*, pp.138–9).

In this telling passage, the careful repetition of the verb 'tolerar' reinforces the absolute unacceptability of the women's behaviour. Moreover, unlike much of Loaeza's work, the narrative voice passes moral judgement on their behaviour. In this case, the dog departs from the humorous and gentle send-up in evidence elsewhere to reinforce the destructive aspects of these ladies' existence. It underlines the actual consequences of their complete dependence on the service industries (maids, beauticians and chauffeurs), and reveals the 'real' effects of their lives on these other strata of society.

The emphasis on the verb 'tolerar' in the passages spoken by Oscar is interesting to evaluate in the context of the traditional moral stance adopted by the satirist. James Sutherland maintains that it is 'the mark of the satirist that he cannot accept and refuses to tolerate'.[31] According to Maynard Mack, 'Satire asserts the validity and necessity of norms, systematic values, and meanings that are contained by recognizable codes'.[32] Robert Harris adds:

Satire is inescapably moral and didactic [...] even when no definite, positive values are stated in the work as alternatives to the gross corruptions depicted by the attack. The satirist does not need to state specific moral alternatives to replace the villainy he attacks because the morality is either already present in the lip service his target pays to virtue, or it is apparent by implication. The satirist presupposes an educated readership which will easily be able to

---

31 *English Satire* (Cambridge: Cambridge University Press), p.4.
32 Maynard Mack, 'The Muse of Satire', *Yale Review*, Vol. 41 (1951), p.85.

discover the implicit morality without any help other than a few ironic hints from the writer.[33]

Satire is indeed so thoroughly concerned with justice, morality, and virtue, that it bears a number of striking resemblances to the basic ethical viewpoint of Christianity: 'Both satire and Christianity believe strongly in the fallen nature of man, believe that proper conduct is not possible for a man without a guide'.[34] The notion of satire is frequently aligned, therefore, with timeless, traditional concepts of virtue and morality, and is frequently conservative in its conception as the satirist rails against the hypocrisies of modern society. Much of Loaeza's wrath is directed at the follies of modern society, indeed it is precisely in this way that she conforms most closely to the classical ideals of the satirist. Claudia Shaefer-Rodriguez, in her study on Loaeza, agrees with this view of the satirist and argues that, despite good intentions on the part of Loaeza, that her writing actually has an 'an ideologically conservative function in Mexican society, along with most literary journalism'.[35] She further states that, 'The so-called entertainment value' added to reportage by literary journalism permits a public display of criticism (critique) while relying on its very stance of ambiguity, personalisation, and the implicit concept of 'soft news' to diffuse its potential power of resistance. Consequently, she believes that the texts have a cathartic function 'for the social body to be able to continue on its way without "real" interruption'.[36] This is, of course, fascinating in the context of Loaeza's work which, though it combines anger, mockery and scathing sarcasm, is complicated by its function as entertainment. It is often argued that satire, by its very nature, rarely offers a constructive view. Instead, while it clearly works in part as a form of dissent, it also tends to simply establish the

---

33   'The Purpose and Method of Satire', www.virtualsalt.comsatire.htm (accessed 29 August 2006).
34   Robert Harris, 'The Purpose and Method of Satire', www.virtualsalt.comsatire. htm (accessed 29 August 2006).
35   'Embedded Agendas: The Literary Journalism of Cristina Pacheco and Guadalupe Loaeza', *Latin American Literary Review*, Vol.19, No.38 (July–December 1991), p.72.
36   'Embedded Agendas', p.73.

error of matters rather than provide solutions. I would argue, however, that Guadalupe Loaeza's satire does indeed have an explicitly corrective nature and is oppositional in very effective ways. It is to these aspects that I would now like to turn in an effort tease out further the complexities of her positioning as satirist.

Narrative Position: The Absent Narrator

It has been clear that Loaeza adheres closely to many traditional conceptualisations of satire through her extensive use of hyperbole, irony, sarcasm, caricature and other satirical techniques. It is also clear that the moral stance traditionally adopted by the satirist is present too. However, I would strongly argue that this moral stance wavers continually and that it is through the wavering narrative position that much of the political charge of Loaeza's work lies. Indeed, what is absent in much of Loaeza's output is any sense of a coherent moral voice. Instead there is an ambivalent narrator, who is at times complicit, at times compassionate, at times antagonistic, at others, vicious. While ambiguity of narratorial position is frequently characteristic of satirical work, what is of most interest here is the way in which that ambiguity allows for alternative interpretations to emerge from her work, interpretations that go beyond mere witty condemnation of the women she critiques.

We have seen how much of the comical effect of her writing is derived from the use of irony, most often employed by a narrator in an omniscient position. The absence of any narratorial interference in her work, however, is also an effective satirical tool and one that allows the subjects access to textual space that is not complicated by authorial intrusion. Examples of this abound in *Las reinas de Polanco* in which harsh social critique appears alongside the humorous lampooning of the eponymous protagonists. In her article on the McDonalds' opening she concludes:

196

Por eso es que desde el martes 29, día en que el delegado de la Miguel Hidalgo, Manuel Díaz Infante, inauguró este sensacional *McDonald's*, apenas a unos cien metros, en el entronque de Palmas y Periférico, los vendedores ambulantes, los niños pordioseros, las Marías y los lanzafuegos dicen a los conductores: 'No me acompleta para mi Big Mac?' (*Polanco*, p.33).

Into her ironic observation of the arrival of McDonalds, she inserts several very marginalised voices, now also competing within this aggressive neo-liberal world.

Many of the pieces in *Las reinas de Polanco* are portraits of the forgotton sectors of Mexican society and are presented with little narrative comment. In 'Una esquina muy Mexicana', she writes about the life of the windscreen cleaners that can be found on all the main thoroughfares of Mexico City. Narrative interference is kept to a minimum and they are accorded almost all the available space. The essay opens with a description of the insults hurled at them by the drivers in the cars whose windscreens they try to clean. Thereafter, the text is wholly given over to them (in the form of direct speech) until the end, when the omnisicient narrator returns for one simple sentence: 'De regreso a mi casa, subiendo por Reforma, me limpiaron el parabrisas, cuatro veces en diferentes esquinas. Sin embargo, nunca me pareció mi visión más oscura...' (*Polanco*, p.78). In 'Payasos mexicanos', Loaeza interviews the youngest clown, Amado, who is only three years old. In this essay, the narrator is absent completely and again all textual space is assigned to Amado and his family. In this way, her stance is made clearer by her absence from the text and the silenced voices of the marginalised are able to shine through. It is in these pieces, therefore, when the narrative voice is absent or strangely muted that the critical edge to her work is at its most effective.

Narrative Position: The *niña bien* Speaks

As well as absenting herself completely from the micro-narratives of Mexico's poor, Loaeza also experiments with narrative voice. It is clear that much of her work relies on the traditional use of omniscient narrative. It is also the case that many of her columns utilise the traditional use of the first-person narrator as a way of personalising the material. We saw, however, that the insertion of the dog character into 'Un week-end en el D.F'., which was perfectly in keeping with the satirical tradition, expanded on the critique offered up to that point in the text and that in fact, much of the really sharp criticism emanated from his point of view. In the same text, Loaeza experiments with the use of a first person narrative voice in the chapter, 'Un week-end en N.Y'., allowing the *niña bien* to enter into her text *en primera persona* for the first time. The results of this are interesting, not least because the character-type, such a focus of mockery in most of her work, emerges as a complex construction and demonstrates an acute social awareness. Furthermore, by assigning her *niña bien* a voice, a much more profound and poignant criticism is enabled as the fragility of her societal positioning is laid bare.

Initially, Alejandra, the character seems familiar, cemented into the reader's consciousness from its humorous treatment in Loaeza's extensive writing:

> La verdad es que yo sí creo que como te ven, te tratan. Si llegas superbien vestida, con un supertraje sastre, una supermascada de seda y con una superbolsa, te tratan ¡super! (*Compro*, p.113).

It becomes immediately apparent, however, that this *niña bien* is very socially aware: 'Me he fijado que en los buenos hoteles, los doormen y las mucamas también son muy snob. A leguas identifican qué tipo de turista eres y si vienes del primer o tercer mundo' (*Compro*, p.113). The inclusion of 'también' here indicates her own highly tuned sense of snobbery and indeed it is this sense of nuance that reveals that she herself is not immune to social criticism:

> Ya en el restaurant, me doy cuenta que yo me arreglé tipo México. Las señoras están mucho más informales y por un momento me siento como las que critico que viajan en Turista: superemperifolladas (*Compro*, p.114).

As well as an acute sense of social awareness, Sofía also perceives the farcical nature of much of her social behaviour and interaction. On one occasion in a restaurant, she comments:

> Se me hace muy chistoso que el mesero, que se ve a leguas que es mexicano, nos hable sin embargo en inglés. Luego va y le pasa la orden obviamente en español a otro, también mexicano. Pero ambos, él y nosotros, seguimos la farsa y nos negamos a reconocernos. No sé ya quién esnobea a quién (*Compro*, pp.115–16).

Here, unlike in much traditional satire, the object of derision is also a perceptive chronicler of her own folly:

> Pero mañana nos vemos para cenar. Comentamos el shopping, la comida, y les recomiendo ampliamente la visita de la New American Wing y la galería de arte asirio en el Met (¡hipócrita, con lo que me aburrí!) (*Compro*, p.118).

As well as perceptive social commentary, the narrator also reveals a more sensitive side, one that is rarely exposed:

> Al día siguiente me pongo un supertraje de los que me compré en Europa para ir a Saks, porque quiero que me vean superelegante. Siempre que paso por la catedral de Saint Patrick me dan ganas de ir a ver a la Virgen de Guadalupe que dicen que está allí. Pero me da pena. ¿Qué tal si me encuentro a alguien conocido? Y yo como mensa pidiendo perdón por mis pecados y por ser tan consumista, ¿no? (*Compro*, p.118).

What emerges most palpably, however, from the first-person narration of the trip to New York is a sense of vulnerability that has, in Loaeza's other work, remained undisclosed due to her control of the narrative through the omniscient voice:

> En la tarde nos fuimos a cenar con los Parada a La Grenouille. Según yo, iba guapísima y elegantísima con mi saquito rojo de piel tipo Chanel, con unas mallas negras opacas y unos zapatos de gamuza del mismo color que el saco. Y la verdad, ya que llegas ahí, te ves (por lo menos yo) como el periférico junto a un free-way. Todo lo que creías que se veía bien se te empieza a hacer gacho,

gacho. Como que te comienzas a sentir fake. Como que hay algo que te falla. Como que a pesar de que tienes puesto un supervestido carísimo, con un chal in-cre-í-ble, te ves como local de los setenta. La verdad es que no logro entender qué nos pasa a las mexicanas cuando viajamos. Incluso las que son guapísimas y millonarias como Ana y Sofía, cuando me las he encontrado aquí, se ven fatales. Parecen como esas venezolanas nuevas ricas. Como que siempre hay algo que nos traiciona, pero no sé qué es. Será que hablamos mucho con las manos, o gesticulamos demasiado. Será que no hablamos quedito o que nos reímos muy fuerte. Será que somos demasiado espontáneas y vehementes. Afortunadamente le hablo al mesero en francés y como que nos trata mejor (*Compro*, p.121).

In this fascinating passage, the precarious sense of self-worth of Loaeza's female subjects is exposed once and for all. As in earlier passages, however, its impact is much more striking coming as it does directly from Alejandra herself. To have assigned these observations to the omniscient narrator would have simply copperfastened that authorial stance, one which the reader is more than familiar with. Instead, by allowing Alejandra to articulate the sense of dislocation, insecurity and anxiety, she reveals the subjects to be themselves fragile and, above all, human – an element difficult to extrapolate from the omniscient narrator.

Narrative Position: The Empathetic Narrator

This emphasis on the humanity of the *niña bien* is a new departure in Loaeza's work, and it is perhaps no surprise that it is in the novel, *Compro, luego existo*, that this new vision is given the space to develop. It is also in this novel that a more empathetic omniscient narrator emerges, to allow identification and sympathy for the character of Ana Paula in the chapter entitled, 'La Cena'. Ana Paula is presented as a typical *nouveau riche* caricature with no 'class' or 'taste'. She is an object of ridicule amongst her friends because she dresses badly and speaks no English. In her desperate attempts to integrate her husband Beto and herself into their group, she spends an

200

obscene amount of money on a lavish banquet that goes disastrously wrong because of a number of embarrassing *faux pas*. What is of primary interest here, is the degree to which Ana Paula is presented as worthy of our compassion. The authorial intrusions in parentheses, take the form of societal admonishment but in a very ironic way. They signal the absurdity of many of the social conventions in operation and expose the ludicrous artificial 'rules' that police the behaviour of this section of Mexican society. In this example, Ana Paula is castigated by the nameless narrator for her use of 'cabello' instead of 'pelo':

> – Ay, Sofía, me encanta como traes el cabello – la elogió Ana Paula. Al oirla, Sofía se quiso morir. (Ay, Ana Paula, cero y van cuatro. Bien sabes que no se dice 'cabello', sino pe-lo. Y luego te quejas porque te rechazan. Pon un poquito de atención, por favor) (*Compro*, p.79).

Here the narrator calmly points out the dreadful linguistic error that has elicited the disdain of Ana Paula's guests. The biting irony of the words nonetheless underlines the cruelty of this world in which people are rejected for saying the wrong word. Moreover, by admonishing her to pay attention, the arbitrary nature of the laws that govern their behaviour is highlighted (who, for example, decided that 'cabello' was unacceptable?). In another example, Ana Paula is humiliated by her friends when they all ask for tequila and she has to admit she has none. In desperation she turns to her husband:

> – Rey, ¿por qué no vas a comprar una botella de tequila en una carrera a esas tiendas que abren las veinticuatro horas? Es que ya se fue el chofer – dijo Ana Paula con un nudo en la garganta (Ay, Ana Paula, cero y van cinco. No tiene la menor importancia. Entre más vulnerable te sientan estas personas, más desagradables serán) (*Compro*, p.80).

Here, Ana Paula is a pitiful figure and the narrator emphasises her vulnerability openly. Ana Paula, therefore, while presented as a typical overbearing *niña bien* in many ways, is also shown to be vulnerable, pathetic and worthy of compassion. In this exchange with her maid, Celia, the reader feels some empathy for her as her lack of self-worth is openly articulated:

– Oye, ¿y no me veo demasiado gorda con esta falda tan cortita?
– No, señora, se le ve bien.
– ¿No se me ha bajado la pintura de los ojos?
– No, señora.
– No se les vaya a olvidar calentar las tazas de consomé antes de que pasemos a la mesa.
– No, señora.
– Oye, ¿no me maquillé demasiado?
– No, señora, se ve bien.
– Ay, es que estas personas son de lo más fijado del mundo. Bueno, ya me voy. Sírvame por favor una copita de Bailey's con hielo frappé, porfa, ¿sí?
Ana Paula salió más contenta con su copa en la mano [...]
Gracias a Celia, Ana Paula había recibido un poquito de calor humano. La había escuchado decir que no se veía tan mal y hasta había percibido en sus ojos una mirada de admiración hacia su patrona (*Compro*, p.78).

The text emphasises the vulnerability of Ana Paula which is exposed at the same time as her self-satisfied and imperious nature. The ability to present both angles of the character attests to Loaeza's skill as a writer, but also reveals the complexity of her narratorial configuration.

Maids, Mothers and Entrepreneurs

Thus far it has been clear the extent to which Loaeza plays with the narrative voice in her work so as to evoke multivocal nuanced portraits of the society with which she engages critically. This section looks at the way in which Loaeza treats the figures of mothers, maids and what I term the 'entrepreneurs' in her work, returning again to the rich prose of Rosario Castellanos to further tease out the implications of her stance on these subjects. In *Las reinas de Polanco*, it could be argued that most of the textual space belongs to certain marginalised sectors of Mexican society including the windscreen cleaners or the child clowns as described in an earlier section. She also devotes considerable time and space to the exploration of the maid-mistress relationship in articles that, for the most part constitute poignant exposés of societal injustice. In her essays, 'Upstairs' and 'Down-

202

stairs', Loaeza's attention is directed to the enormous difference between the circumstances of the maids and their mistresses:

> No hay nada más contrastante dentro de un típico hogar mexicano, que el cuarto de una patrona, y el de la sirvienta, criada, trabajadora del hogar, o simplemente *maid*, como las llaman las que se sienten muy *ladies*. No importa la colonia, nivel social o económico, por lo general, la diferencia entre estas dos recámaras, es apabullante (*Polanco*, p.73).

There follows a long description of the miserable room assigned to the maid, accompanied by the comments:

> A pesar de eso las patronas dicen cosas como: '¡Ay, oye, cómo viven en sus casas, aquí están como reinitas!'
> 'A veces son tan incivilizadas, uno trata de hacerlas personas, pero no entienden. Todo lo rompen, lo echan a perder. Cuando se les cae algo dicen: "se me chispó." Por eso tienen su cuarto así, son unas puercas. Si siempre está tapado su baño, es que lo llenan de papel. Que lo destapen ellas. Ni de chiste voy a pagarles un plomero. Me niego rotundamente a entrar a su cuarto. Nada más me deprimo y hago corajes. De seguro está como una pocilga. ¡Qué horror!' (*Polanco*, p.75).

The piece ends with direct speech, another example of the absence of authorial interference as noted earlier. The emphasis on the fact that the maid is dirty is interesting and returns us once more to the writing of Rosario Castellanos who was also deeply concerned with the position of the maid in Mexican society. In a previous study on Castellanos's work, I noted how the figure of the maid is conceived in bourgeois ideology that was articulated from the nineteeth century onwards. It is particularly striking that working-class (and in the Mexican case, often indigenous) maids were frequently labelled both physically and morally dirty.[37] This close association between phys-

---

37 See my discussion of the character of Modesta Gómez in Castellanos's short story collection, *Ciudad Real*, 'Feminine Dis-ease in *Ciudad Real* by Rosario Castellanos', *Hispanic Research Journal*, Vol.2, No.1 (February 2000), pp.45–60. For a good examination of the figure of the maid, see Clair Wills, 'Upsetting the Public: Carnival, Hysteria and Womens' Texts', in Ken Hirschkop and David Shepherd (eds), *Bakhtin and Cultural Theory*, (Manchester and New York: Manchester University Press, 1989), pp.130–52.

ical and moral dirt led to the common depiction of the servant girl/maid as 'whore', and therefore a threat to the stability of the family unit. In Loaeza's work the emphasis on dirt is also striking, but so too is her acute awareness of the vast gulf existing between the social classes at this point in Mexican history. The essay, 'Vivir al día' is a good example of the gulf between the *patrona* and Carmen the maid, when the *patrona* asks Carmen to justify the amount of money she has spent on food. After a long list of purchases, the text ends:

> ¿A qué se debía tanto gasto y tanta enemistad entre ellas? ¿Quién era la culpable? La inflación, esa que no respeta ni clase social ni profesión ni edad ni sexo ni mucho menos nacionalidad. La inflación, ese cáncer, era lo que las estaba separando, enfermándolas de más en más. Por culpa de esa maldita enfermedad las dos se habían vuelto desconfiadas, hostiles, deshumanizadas. Las dos se estaban amargando. A las dos se les iba el dinero como arena entre los dedos. De pronto, las dos se miraron y comprendieron que eran víctimas del mismo azote. En esos momentos, un sentimiento de impotencia las invadió. [...] Sus ojos se llenaron de lágrimas. Tuvieron ganas de abrazarse, de consolarse. Pero no pudieron. Algo que sucedió hace miles de años, se los impedía. [...] Una se fue hacía la cocina y la otra hacía su recámara.
>
> Desde ese pequeño diálogo, Carmen y su patrona se hablan de menos en menos. La primera sigue haciendo las compras en el super; y la segunda, gastando el dinero (*Polanco*, pp.56–7).

In this passage, an attempt to breach the gulf is identified, strangely, by the fact that they are both suffering (albeit in drastically different ways) by the enormous inflation caused by the 'crisis'. Loaeza, however, presents a pessimistic picture of how this further cements the abyss that extends between the two women, and firmly rejects any possibility of solidarity or mutual support. In her essay 'Lucha en Las Lomas', she again returns to the conflictual situation between a maid and her mistress when the maid informs her that she wants a raise. The mistress's reaction is predictably hostile:

> La señora no puede dejar de sentirse chatajeada, presionada y dependiente de estas 'horribles *maids*', como las llama ella, criadas encajosas, que no hacen más que pedir, mal encaradas, pero sobre todo, mal agradecidas; ¿cuándo se iban a imaginar estas indias que podían vivir como gente y no como animales como tenían costumbre de vivir en sus pueblos?; muchachas irresponsables, flojas buenas para nada, les da uno la mano y se cogen el pie, ¿qué más pueden

pedir, con televisión en su cuarto, tres comidas garantizadas, agua caliente, uniformes, y encima de todo esto quieren ganar como si fueran secretarias ejecutivas, cuando ni saben contestar el teléfono? (*Polanco*, p.71).

In this essay, following Loaeza's technique of allowing marginalised or subaltern characters to 'speak', the maid is also assigned passages of direct speech:

La sirvienta la mira fijamente, de pronto se acuerda que la odia, que la detesta, que no la puede ver ni en pintura: 'vieja hipócrita, si yo tengo "defectitos", usted nació toda defectuosa, por eso el licenciado ya ni viene a cenar y llega bien tarde. [...] todo el día me trai como su burro, vieja coda'. [...] 'Ay señora, si mi compañera de Virreyes, está ganando 60 mil pesos y también es recamarera. Ella no riega el jardín, ni limpia la plata. De verdá (*sic*), que ahora el dinero no alcanza para nada. Dice Jacobo, que van a volver a subir la leche, el pan y la tortilla [...] Fíjese, una falda y un *bleser* (*sic*) que me compré en abonos, me salió en 23 mil pesos' (*Polanco*, p.72).

Again predictably, the standoff over the wages is unresolved and the piece ends, 'El silencio se hacía cada vez más difícil, más pesado y más insoportable' (*Compro*, p.73). In these interventions into the maid/mistress relationship, Loaeza again shows herself to be intensely aware of the ethnic and class divides in Mexican society. By assigning the maid's situation such ample textual exploration, she underlines the systematic exploitation of domestic servants and draws attention to their plight. Furthermore, she exposes a major unresolved issue with regard to women's liberation in Mexico, demonstrating the women's utter dependence on the exploited maids.[38]

38   By refusing to allow for the possibility of any positive outcomes in their confrontations, she perhaps leaves herself open to the accusation that her satire fulfils an expository function, as opposed to one that agitates for change. On the other hand, exposure of the situation in this way is not to be under-estimated, and, of course, the pessimistic encounters between the mistresses and this largely ignored under-class make for compelling reading. In the introduction, I noted the importance of this issue on a global scale. Rosario Castellanos, in a very personal essay, talks of her less than ideal treatment of her faithful companion and maid (*cargadora*), María Escandón. She writes, 'Yo no creo haber sido excepcionalmente caprichosa, arbitraria y cruel. Pero ninguno me había enseñado a respetar más que a mis iguales y, desde luego mucho más a mis mayores', 'Herlinda se va', in *El uso de la palabra*, p.245.

205

Loaeza is similarly empathetic with regard to the fraught status of the mother in Mexican society. While many of the subjects she mocks are mothers themselves, it is only when she discusses their mothering role directly that any human warmth is glimpsed. In an hilarious essay detailing the idiotic attempts of one of the *niñas bien* to get her child to attend his weekly session with the psychologist, the piece ends:

> Así, mientras Luisito cambiaba constantemente de canal, Clara sentía como las lágrimas le escurrían por las mejillas, rodando por su cuello, hasta llegar a empapar su hermosa blusa de seda color bugambilia (*Polanco*, p.96).

While this clearly constitutes a total send-up of the mother who does not know how to behave towards her son, it ends on a poignant note attesting again to the vulnerability of her satirical targets. In another piece on mothers entitled 'Madres históricas', she muses on the mothers of various famous men including Julio Cortázar, Emiliano Zapata, Mario Moreno (Cantinflas) and Cary Grant. She concludes:

> No en balde, la señora Creel, protagonista de la telenovela *Cuna de lobos*, mantuvo la atención de millones de televidentes durante meses. A través de su personalidad, seguramente muchas madres mexicanas intentaron exorcizar su rol de abnegada. No sería extraño que al verla tratar a Juan Carlos con tanta maldad, habrán pensado en silencio: 'Cómo me gustaría ser como ella. Si tan sólo pudiera hablarle en ese tono a mis hijos, quizá me respetarían más. Estoy harta de ser buena y abnegada' (*Polanco*, p.100).

This concern with the role of the self-sacrificing mother, along with her determination to rescue some of these women from historical oblivion, again links Loaeza to Castellanos who was famous for her demythification of the *abnegada madrecita Mexicana*.[39] Loaeza continues her exploration of the archetype in her essay, 'Y tener que festejar a las madres…', which features savage recollections from children, grannies and mothers about Mother's Day and effectively

---

39 This notion of *abnegación* receives ample treatment in Castellanos's work who uses the phrase, 'abnegada mujercita mexicana' in her celebrated story, 'Lección de cocina', *Álbum de familia*, p.9. She later revisits the subject in her essays, 'La abnegación: una virtud loca', 'La liberación del amor', and 'Un árbol crece en Tel Aviv', in *El uso de la palabra* (Mexico City: Ediciones de Excélsior-Crónicas, 1974), pp.48–53, pp.53–6 and pp.220–3, respectively.

206

continues Castellanos's firm mission to unburden the mothers of Mexico from this all-consuming role.

Another interesting strand in *Reinas de polanco* is Loaeza's emphasis on the initiative and entrepreuneurial spirit of the *niñas bien*. The narrative pays tribute to their courage in the face of adversity at the same time as it sends them up with sarcastic humour. 'La crisis en Polanco' treats the subject of the *niñas bien* and their experiences of the economic crisis of the early 1980s. In this piece she notes their entrepreneurial skills in selling *pepinos dulces* or *pays de manzana* out of the backs of their cars (*Polanco*, p.69). There is considerable attention paid to the women's astute understanding of the economic situation and their desire to see the banks reprivatised. Indeed, at no point are they portrayed as individually stupid. Instead there is a sense of their lack of fulfilment and a frustration that so many of their skills go unemployed. In another piece on the infamous pyramid money-making schemes, the enthusiasm shown by the *reinas* is striking:

> Las responsables de las pirámides más organizadas y serias, se procuran estudios de algunas universidades especializadas en finanzas y crean un fondo de 300 dólares por participante, para garantizar la inversión del avión. Si no se gana y – dicen – tampoco se pierde (*Polanco*, p.31).

The piece ends tellingly as Loaeza sounds a note of caution:

> Hay quienes dicen que los maridos de estas señoras están muy enojados, porque sus esposas se están haciendo todavía más millonarias que ellos, y que temen que con tanto dinero terminen por convertirse en directoras de sus propias Casas de Bolsa (*Polanco*, p.31).

In another article, Loaeza interviews Lourdes Quintana of Boutique Cabassi, a self-made woman who has created a very successful business. While the ironic tone that permeates most of the collection remains firmly in place here, there are several narratorial reflections that divulge the rather more nuanced attitude of the interviewer:

> Y pienso que ahora a las *niñas bien* todo les parece de lo más normal. Difícilmente se escandalizan, sobre todo aquellas que ya se liberaron de maridos, de familias posesivas, de prejuicios sociales. Estas, las que trabajan, poco a

poco van entendiendo que la vida no es de color de rosa todos los días, *que a veces, es gris, beige o simplemente color de hormiga* (*Polanco*, p.44, my emphasis).

This grudging admiration for many of the women that she observes, complicates the authorial distance created between the subjects particularly in the more straightforward satirical sections. In addition to these rather ambiguous portrayals of the *reinas* adapting to their new 'impoverished' circumstances, Loaeza completes the collections with some rather moving reflections on the sadness of some of the women's lives. In a very ironic piece on the horror of turning forty, Loaeza closes with a perceptive insight into the real suffering endured by the protagonist of the piece and poses the question, 'Les explicará ese martes mientras sienta por adentro que se le vienen encima todos los cumpleaños del mundo, incluso los que no ha cumplido, y que inevitablemente seguirá cumpliendo. ¿Será de verdad tan difícil para una mujer cumplir 40 años?' (*Polanco*, p.113). Here is a genuinely sympathetic portrait which seems to provide a veiled critique of society that refuses to allow women grow old. She follows this up with another piece on turning fifty:

A mi manera de ver, la naturaleza es muy injusta con las mujeres. Mientras la mujer envejece, el hombre se siente a esa edad más atractivo e interesante que nunca. Con sus canitas de hombre maduro no teme echarse una canita al aire' (*Polanco*, p.115).

Her essay, 'Crónica de una vejez anunciada' is also a meditation on old age and the arrival of a grey hair. In these essays, Loaeza unquestionably offers a sympathetic portrait of the women she so hilariously mocks. Alongside the sarcasm is admiration, sympathy and a frustration that their behaviour is so constrained by the structures within which they live. Thus while these pieces do not quite constitute feminist celebrations, it is certainly the case that there has been an irrevocable shift in the positioning of the satirical narrator that questions the conservative basis of satire generally and expands the text's interpretive possibilities.

208

Castellanos and Loaeza: The Fault of Intelligent Women

I return in this final section to Rosario Castellanos and most spe-cifically to the direct relationship between the two writers, which is articulated in Loaeza's essay from *Las Reinas de Polanco*, 'La culpa de las mujeres inteligentes'. We have already seen the many parallels between Loaeza's work and some of Castellanos's later work. The use of satire, the choice of the beauty salon as setting, the exploration of the maid system and the meditation on mothers – all point to both formal and thematic connections between the two writers. It is, how-ever, in Loaeza's essay, 'La culpa de las mujeres inteligentes', that Rosario Castellanos is invoked directly. This essay, a piece that seems to follow Castellanos in her meditations on the differing gender roles and their effects on society, opens in her usual playful style as she suggests that most women are more intelligent than their husbands: 'Pocas cosas provocan más culpa en las mujeres casadas que el saberse más inteligentes que el marido' (*Polanco*, p.105). Loaeza then introduces Castellanos by saying, 'Rosario Castellanos, poeta y escritora que tanto enseñó con su vida a las mujeres' (*Polanco*, p.105), and quotes a passage from one of her essays at length. In the passage quoted, Castellanos laments the continued labelling of women as inferior in contemporary society in her typically trenchant style: '"El mundo que para mí está cerrado tiene un nombre: se llama cultura. Sus habitantes son todos ellos del sexo masculino"' (*Polanco*, p.106). Loaeza responds to the piece by wondering, '¿Cómo es posible que una mujer tan excepcional como Rosario Castellanos insista en que es inferior?' (*Polanco*, p.106). The essay continues with a moving an-ecdote about a friend who delighted a recent dinner party with stories of her parents' first meeting. The follow-up to the tale occurs when Loaeza herself calls the friend and finds her distraught by her husband's excoriation of her behaviour that night and his verbal abuse of her:

> Al otro día, mi amiga me habló. Su voz parecía lejana y triste. Cuando le dije que hacía mucho que no la veía y sentía en tan buena forma, lo único que tuve

como respuesta fue un largo silencio. [...] Y entre sollozos me contó que había reñido horriblemente con su marido 'No te puedes imaginar todo lo que me dijo cuando salimos de tu casa. Todavía no nos subíamos al coche cuando empezó a gritarme: "Cada vez estás peor. No hablas, ¡rebuznas! Te crees muy graciosa, pero en realidad cansas con tus historias. [..] Deberías de ir con un loquero. No dejaste hablar a nadie. ¿A quién diablos le importa cómo se conocieron mis suegros? [...] Mira, no te paré, porque soy muy controlado y además no me gusta hacer escenitas en público. Hasta tenía ganas de pegarte. Cada día me recuerdas más a tu mamá. Pobrecita, me das lástima, a toda costa te quieres reafirmar. ¿Qué quieres probar, que eres una idiota?"' (*Polanco*, pp.107–8).

By ending the article with the friend's quotation, Loaeza allows the silenced woman to speak without interference, a luxury that she does not enjoy in real life. Indeed the theme of 'silenced women' generally permeates the essay. In this way, Loaeza also refuses to re-enter the text herself, thereby wholeheartedly endorsing the woman's story as her own point of view. It is here that a feminist sensibility becomes discernible even while it confines itself largely to the periphery. In invoking Castellanos so directly, she further emphasises the feminist concerns of the text. It becomes obvious to the reader that while she is savagely critical of the society that has created the *niñas bien*, she is also aware of the reality of patriarchal structures and the continuous nature of the struggle against them.

Complicity and Ambivalence

It is clear, therefore, that the apparent contradictions, ambiguities and complexity of narrative positioning in Loaeza's work raise many tantalising questions. On the one hand there is a vicious (if very witty) critique of a whole community of women many of whom are portrayed as shallow, cruel, exploitative and stupid. On the other hand, they are also portrayed as fragile, often vulnerable and exploited in turn by a patriarchal system that continues to see them as inferior. They are enterprising and frequently more in tune with the economic and social realities of their lives than their male counterparts. They are

210

also often on the receiving end of cruel treatment from both their peers and their partners. What emerges thus is what Loaeza herself terms a 'visión oscura', a murky and ambivalent exploration of a world in crisis.

The ambivalence of the narratorial position may be explained at various levels, but crucial to its understanding is a sense of Loaeza's own position, which Deborah Shaw has described as her status as both insider and outsider:

> As a literary journalist, Loaeza needs to cultivate a sense of authenticity in order to claim the right to represent discourses, and claim identification with the narrative voice. She does this by harnessing her own social position. She gives herself the authority to comment upon the *niñas bien* and represent reactionary discourses because she inhabits the same spaces that they do: she lives in the same neighbourhood as they do, and goes to the same shops and to the same parties as they do.[40]

This insinuation of herself into the framework she so comprehensively demolishes with her satire, is significant with regard to the question of subject positioning. In her book, *Los grillos y otras grillas*, she opens with the disclaimer: 'Estas páginas fueron escritas para hacer reflexionar (y sonreír). Sin embargo, si alguien se ofende al leerlas, piense *que la autora es quizá también una grilla*. Es que todos llevamos un grillo dentro' (my emphasis).[41] The aligning of herself alongside the subjects to be ridiculed, is again complicated by the playful insertion of the word 'quizá' (perhaps). Her account of how she came to write for the newspaper, *Unomásuno* paints her in many ways as a typical *niña bien*:

> Recuerdo que cuando empecé a leer el periódico de la 'oposición' de los primeros ochentas, *Unomásuno*, los domingos no me podía dormir sin antes leer el texto de Cristina Pacheco. Así sucedió un 21 de agosto de 1982. Al terminarlo me dije, con la cara cubierta de crema hidratante que usaba en ese entonces que creo que era Estée Lauder: 'Así como ella escribe sobre los pobres, yo podría hacerlo sobre los ricos', me dije en tanto cerraba mis ojitos, cuyas pestañas estaban cubiertas de pomada 'Talika', según la cual hacía crecer

40   'The Literary Journalism of Guadalupe Loaeza and Cristina Pacheco', *Bulletin of Latin American Research*, Vol.18, No.4 (1999), p.439.
41   *Los grillos y otras grillas* (Mexico City: Cal y Arena, 1991) (n.p.).

las pestañas mientras una dormía. Al otro día, tuve que ir a buscar unos cojines que había mandado a hacer con un tapicero que tenía su tallercito sobre la avenida Patriotismo. Al verme llegar, exclamó con la misma calidez con la que lo hubiera hecho Pepe el Toro: '¿Que pasó, güerita? Fíjese que sus cojines todavía no están. ¿Por qué no se da una vuelta y regresa en dos horas?' Todavía con la cara de interrogación en mi rostro, le pregunté: '¿Una vuelta que dure dos horas? Ay, maestro, ¿qué voy a hacer en todo ese tiempo.' 'Pusss váyase a tomar un cafecito aquí a Vip's, el que está a tres cuadras.'[42]

This reflection is interesting on a number of levels. First, she identifies her writing as a political project in that she sets herself up as a direct counterpart to Cristina Pacheco, who is another household name in Mexico because of her stark portraits of the poor and marginalised sectors of society. She declares herself to be Pacheco's counterpart for the rich and yet Pacheco is the archetypal committed writer, a voice for the marginalised. Loaeza, on the other hand, speaks for, through, and against the rich at one and the same time. Also, by stressing her overt political awareness alongside the portrait of herself wearing a face mask, she suggests that the superficiality so brilliantly exposed in relation to the subjects of her work is something she also shares. Furthermore, the tale of how she came to work in the newspaper office reads again like a typical morning in the life of a *niña bien*, as the sales assistant sends her to have a coffee to kill time until her cushions are ready.

Loaeza directly addresses the question of her own complicity in one of her earliest pieces: '¿A cuál de estas categorías perteneceré yo, que ya no soy ni tan niña, ni tan bien? ¿Y usted, lectora, a cuál? ¿Y a cuál pertenecerá la que me lo preguntó?'[43] In this passage she evades the answer to her own question but crucially asks the same question of her reader. Indeed, her readership constitutes another vital component of any consideration of the meaning of her work. Many of the stories and articles are written for *Unomásuno* and *La Jornada*, long considered to be liberal, left-wing publications. Her public pronunciations similarly align her with a readership firmly on the left.[44] This

42   *Detrás del espejo* (Mexico: Editorial Patria, 1999), pp.289–90.
43   *Las niñas bien*, p.12.
44   Her recent support for the now defeated candidate, Andrés Manuel López Obrador (AMLO), leaves no doubt as to her political affiliations. She has

212

of course ensures a readership sympathetic to her criticisms of Mexican high society which is central to the success of her writing as a whole. Loaeza writes:

> Siento una profunda responsabilidad de poder colaborar en *Unomásuno*... Allí apareció como una denuncia, una crítica social. En cambio si este mismo texto se publica en un diario de derecha, su intención se diluye y hubiera quedado exclusivamente en un nivel anecdótico.[45]

Here, she insists that her work is read as social critique and not just as entertainment. The ambiguity in the narratorial position exemplifies the problematic position of the middle-class woman and in particular the elite, intellectual woman. She occupies the position of the traditional satirist, critiquing modernity and the ills of modern society. In her riposte of the various factions doing battle in the media during the Salinas years, she writes, '*Salinista modernista:* Están naturalmente por la continuidad, pero sobre todo, por hacer más política, mucha política y más moderna'.[46] Modernity here is conceptualised as continuity, the status quo, and yet it is modernity (the widening of economic parameters and the courting of women writers for niche publishing lines, seen already in Chapter Three) that has enabled Loaeza to write professionally as a broadcaster and journalist. She is more than aware of this contradiction and of the deep complicity of her position with regard to other women in her class. Indeed, as has been noted, she has a sneaking admiration for many of these women and her work can sometimes read as a feminist celebration of the very lives she denigrates. The way in which Loaeza invokes Castellanos's views on gender roles further cements this interpretation. It is clear,

---

campaigned ceaselessly on his behalf throughout: '"nos guste o no, es el personaje de esta campaña. En todos los espacios radiofónicos y de análisis está presente y así estará también en el próximo debate donde brillará por su ausencia"'. El universal.com, 20 April 2006. Similar sentiments were frequently repeated by Guadalupe Loaeza throughout the bitter political campaign. See http://www.eluniversal.com.mx/notas/344050.html (last accessed 3 April 07).

45   'Literary Journalism of Guadalupe Loaeza and Cristina Pacheco', p.440.
46   *Los grillos y otras grillas* (Mexico City: Cal y Arena, 1991), p.83.

then that she does, to a certain extent, display the feminist critique inherent and explicit in Castellanos's final works.

We have seen, therefore, how the extreme censure offered by Loaeza's satire frequently comes, not from the omniscient narrator, but rather from those 'other' narrative voices – the dog in *Compro, luego existo* and the first-person narrator in 'Un week-end en N.Y'. Moreover, unlike her first collection, *Las niñas bien*, she starts to distinguish between the caricatures. Indeed much humanity and compassion is reserved for the character of Ana Paula in *Compro, luego, existo* who is seen, in many cases, as a classic victim.[47] Thus the narrative position is ultimately complex and ambivalent, exemplifying perfectly the position of this actual writer vis-à-vis her subjects and vis-à-vis the writing tradition that has assigned her a voice. The fact that her readership ensures the effect is always comical and that change is never an outcome – they are all readers of *Unomásuno* and *La jornada* after all – returns us to Schaefer's argument about literary journalism and indeed much of the study on satire that points to its inherently conservative properties. The criticism of satire, perfectly encapsulated in Tynan's description of George Bernard Shaw as no more than a 'demolition expert' involved in 'intellectual slum clearance' is apt too in the case of Loaeza.[48] While she effectively demolishes much of the world she lampoons, it is certainly not clear what alternative solutions might exist. The effect, whilst comical, is also ultimately conservative. This should come as no surprise given the complicity of the author herself in the world she

47   R. Ferrnández-Levin also makes this point, 'Although the women who populate these narratives are far from being downtrodden, they are clearly victims, if not of appalling poverty and labor injustice, of monolithic male paradigms that deny them the right to control their social and personal destinies'. 'Trapped in a Gilded Cage: Guadalupe Loaeza's Unhappy Women', in Juan Cruz Mendizábal and Juan Fernández Jiménez (eds), *Visión de la narrativa hispánica: Ensayos* (Indiana: Pennsylvania, 1999), pp.81–96, p.83. Fernández-Levin writes of Loaeza's later work, *Mujeres maravillosas* (1997) and similar criticism can be found on *Sin Cuenta* (1996) in which the protagonists figure more obviously as victims.

48   Cited in James Sutherland, *English Satire* (Cambridge University Press, 1958), p.3.

surveys. These notions of complicity and ambivalence connect Loaeza to all the other writers examined thus far, and will be further examined in the next section of the chapter.

Rosamaría Roffiel: 'Un otro modo de ser'

In this section of the chapter, I turn my attention to Rosamaría Roffiel, writer of the best-selling lesbian novel, *Amora*. Roffiel began her career as a journalist in *Excélsior* when its director Julio Scherer was dismissed by then president Luis Echeverría over political differences. Many of the journalists who had worked alongside Scherer left with him to found the progressive newspaper, *Proceso*. In 1979, after the victory of Daniel Ortega in Nicaragua, she left Mexico and worked for three years co-ordinating the Sandinista publication, *El Trabajador*. Returning to Mexico in 1982, she founded *Fem*, Latin America's first feminist journal and worked for this publication for several years.[49] Like Loaeza, therefore, Roffiel is most at home in the journalistic world and her foray into 'fiction' comes at a relatively late stage in her career. Since *Amora* she has published *El para siempre dura una noche*, a collection of personal anecdotes structured as a series of essays/stories/chronicles. Both Loaeza and Roffiel, therefore, fall firmly into the category of chronicler, arguably the most innovative and exciting genre currently being explored in Mexico.[50] Roffiel's work is also largely preoccupied with gender roles and in particular the lives of middle-class women in Mexico City. The personal experiences of the protagonists detailed in her work are derived, in part, from their engagement with the feminist movements that swept the

---

49   See Elena M. Martínez, 'Entrevista con Rosamaría Roffiel', *Confluencia*, Vols.8–9, Nos.1–2 (Spring–Fall 1993), pp.179–80.

50   Reference has already been made in Chapter Three to the importance of the chronicle in the contemporary literary tradition. Other female chroniclers include Alma Guillermoprieto, Julieta García González and Elena Poniatowska.

Western world and, to a much lesser extent, the developing world in the 1960s and 1970s.[51] References to Second Wave Feminism and the struggle for women's rights in Mexico abound in her work. Like Castellanos's work from the 1970s onwards, the protagonists occupy a world in which these struggles are a constant, as they grapple with the persistent societal stereotyping that renders them paralysed in roles such as *la divorciada, la soltera, la casada* and *la lesbiana*.[52] In this way, the connections between Roffiel and Castellanos are also marked and Roffiel's work might perhaps best be summed up as yet another search for Castellanos's oft-quoted 'otro modo de ser humano y libre. Otro modo de ser'.[53] Unlike Castellanos, however, and in spite of the

---

51   The term, 'Second Wave' is attributed to Marsha Lear. See, Maggie Humm, *The Dictionary of Feminist Theory* (Columbus: Ohio State University Press, 1995), p.251. It is generally acknowledged that Second Wave Feminism or the Women's Liberation Movement emerged from the New Left in the 1960s. While there is debate over the usefulness of numbering the different historical phases of feminism (into first, second and third), it is clear that the Second Wave refers to the activism of the 1960s and 1970s that focused on civil rights and equality. Amber E. Kinser writes: 'These terms gave activist women of the late '60s the double-rhetorical advantage of cultivating new ideas while simultaneously rooting them in older, more established ground. Identifying itself as the second wave revived the movement for the public after seeming to lie dormant for some time. [...] The second-wave attention to *women's* rights, and more importantly, to women's *liberation*, emerged seemingly out of nowhere and needed to re-establish itself as neither particularly new nor fleeting. The labeling that linked the two periods of feminist movement was a rhetorical strategy that helped give clout to '60s women's activism and positioned it as a further evolution of earlier and larger movement'. 'Negotiating Spaces For-Through Third Wave Feminism', *NWSA Journal*, Vol.13, No.3 (2004), p.129. For a good overview of the Second Wave, see Linda Nicholson (ed.), *The Second Wave: A Reader in Feminist Theory*.

52   Rosario Castellanos's poem, 'Kinsey Report', dedicates a section to each of these 'types' of women in a parody of the infamous Alfred Kinsey reports. See A.C. Kinsey, W.B. Pomeroy, E.E. Martin, Sexual Behavior in the Human Male (Philadelphia: W.B. Saunders, 1948) and Sexual Behavior in the Human Female (Philadelphia: W.B. Saunders, 1953). These reports impacted hugely on the general public because of their bold challenge to prevailing beliefs about the nature of sexuality.

53   'Meditación en el umbral', *Poesía no eres tú: Obra poética 1948–1971* (Mexico City: Fondo de Cultura Económica, 1972), p.316.

emphasis on the most brutal abuses of patriarchal power witnessed by the book's characters on a daily basis, Roffiel's world view is highly optimistic and often utopian in outlook. In this, she eclipses Castellanos and forges a path forward that is ultimately very rewarding for the women who tread it.

Amora

Roffiel wrote *Amora* in 1982:

> como ejercicio catártico para liberarme de una relación amorosa que había terminado dolorosamente. Abandoné el manuscrito durante cinco años. Lo retomé en 1988 y lo concluí en menos de un año. Fue la primera novela lesbiana que se publicó en Mexico (ahora hay otra, *Dos Mujeres*, de Sara Levi Calderón). *Amora* es mi humilde contribución a la visibilidad de las feministas y las lesbianas en la historia de mi país.[54]

The novel charts the story of the narrator, Lupe, and her passion for Claudia, a typical *niña bien* who struggles to accept her sexuality. The tale of their burgeoning love affair is interspersed with episodes recounted from the narrator's work with the Grupo de Ayuda a Personas Violadas (GRAPAV). Other chapters recount conversations with Lupe's many friends and Roffiel also explores Lupe's relationship with her niece, Mercedes. *Amora* received mixed critical reviews when it was published with many of its critics relegating it to the status of feminist pamphlet.[55] It is certainly true that *Amora*

---

54   Elena M. Martínez, 'Entrevista con Rosamaría Roffiel', p.180.
55   In an interview with Elena M. Martínez, Roffiel talks about the reception of the novel: 'La noche de la presentación, en septiembre de 1989, hubo una gran fiesta en el Bar Bugambilia. Más de quinientas personas llegaron a celebrar conmigo'. 'Entrevista con Rosamaría Roffiel', p.180. On the critical reception of the novel, she explains, 'La crítica ha estado muy dividida. Paradójicamente, los periódicos supuestamente más liberales y progresistas (*La jornada* y *UnoMásUno*) le hicieron reseñas poco favorables. Algunos críticos trataron a la novela como un "mero panfleto feminista." Por otro lado, la mayoría de los

mounts an attack on patriarchal power hierarchies in both subtle and obvious ways. Through its frank exploration of the love that blossoms between Claudia and Lupe (along with the many references to other lesbian couples), the book represents a major breakthrough in Mexican letters.[56] My discussion of the novel centres on the ways in which it continues the Castellanos quest to create 'un otro modo de ser'. I maintain that it does this in various ways: first, it enacts a ferocious critique of heterosexual relations – very similar to Castellanos's famous musings on this topic; second, it exposes the brutality of male violence and its shocking consequences for women in Mexico; third, it showcases feminism as a way of living – not just a political doctrine – most particularly through its utopian vision of a community of women living in harmony; finally, in allowing the lesbian love story to triumph in the book, it suggests a definite way forward and refuses to contemplate negative solutions. In this way, the book continues the Castellanos quest but most unusually provides answers that, for the protagonist, at least, offer hope and fulfilment. However, in keeping with the work of all the women writers explored in this study, Roffiel's novel too is scarred by an ambivalence. The ambivalence in this text is diffused through the exclusive nature of the feminist vision that emerges, one that is anchored solely in middle-class concerns. It is further compounded by the juxtaposition of images of harmonious lesbian existence and of extreme male violence. In the gulf that exists between both realities, Roffiel lays bare the contradictions and ambivalences at the heart of Mexico's radical transformation of gender roles.

periódicos y revistas en la ciudad publicaron reseñas muy positivas'. 'Entrevista con Rosamaría Roffiel', p.180.

56   It is not, of course, the only Mexican work of fiction to focus on lesbian relationships. Sara Levi Calderón's novel, *Dos mujeres*, was published in 1990. For a comparison of the two novels, see Deborah Shaw, 'Erotic or Political: Literary Representations of Mexican Lesbians', *Travesía: The Journal of Latin American Cultural Studies*, Vol.5, No.1 (June 1996), pp.51–63. Work by Sabina Berman and Nancy Calderón, among others, continues to foreground the issues surrounding lesbian identity in contemporary Mexico. See Claudia Schaefer, *Danger Zones: Homosexuality, National Identity and Mexican Culture* (Tucson: University of Arizona Press, 1996).

Heterosexual Relations: 'No puedo cambiar de amo'

From the wealth of feminist research on the topic, it is clear that heterosexual relations as they have been constructed in modern societies, often limit and constrain women into roles that are at best less than satisfying and at worst, destructive.[57] The initial aims of the feminist civil rights movements focused, in particular, on the figure of the wife in the middle-class West as the archetypal oppressed victim. Betty Friedan's *The Feminine Mystique* exploded for once and for all the myth of the contented housewife in suburban North America. Through the work of NOW (National Organisation of Women), Friedan and her contemporaries tried to provide alternative solutions to the 'problem that has no name', so poignantly exposed by her research.[58] Rosario Castellanos is deeply indebted to Friedan and indeed much of Friedan's liberal-reformist feminist critique makes its way into her essay writing.[59] Castellanos, it must be remembered, was well acquainted with the drive for women's rights in North America. She

---

57 See Adrienne Rich's essay, 'Compulsory Heterosexuality Compulsory Heterosexuality and Lesbian Existence'. First published in 1980, it is still vitally important in its searing criticism of the institution of heterosexuality and its elaboration of the 'lesbian continuum' as a way of describing woman-identified experience. According to Leila J. Rupp, the essay 'has shaped our understanding of lesbian history and the history of sexuality in the most momentous ways' as witnessed by its (still) central status in queer theory'. See the special issue on her essay, 'Women's History in the New Millenium: Adrienne Rich's Compulsory Heterosexuality and Lesbian Existence: A Retrospective', *Journal of Women's History,* Vol.15, No.3 (2003). For the original essay, see *Blood, Bread and Poetry: Selected Prose 1979–1985* (New York: W.W. Norton and Company, 1994), pp.23–75.
58 *The Feminine Mystique,* 1963. See also Marilyn French's acclaimed novel, *The Woman's Room,* published in 1977 for a classic literary exploration of the same phenomenon.
59 Castellanos wrote an essay paying homage to Friedan's achievements. See, 'Betty Friedan: análisis y praxis', in *Mujer que sabe latín...* (Mexico City: Fondo de Cultura Económica, 1973), pp.120–4. Lita Paniagua also attests to Friedan's influence on the emerging feminist movement in Mexico, 'La lucha por la superación femenina', *Kena* (September 1972), p.4.

spent the years 1966–1967 teaching in the US at Indiana and Wisconsin. She was thus exposed to the movement at the height of its historical influence and when she returned to Mexico, wrote many essays berating Mexican women for their apathy and passivity in the struggle for civil rights.[60] It is this same liberal-reformist doctrine that appears forcefully in Roffiel's work and which stages an eloquent attack on the oppressive force of compulsory heterosexuality. *Amora*, in particular, invokes Adrienne Rich's notion of the 'lesbian continuum' outlined in her essay, 'Compulsory Heterosexuality and Lesbian Experience'. She defines the continuum as the range of woman-identified experiences, a connection shared by all women across time and space.[61] According to Rich's argument, women can find strength, personal fulfillment, and, ultimately, liberation by reconnecting with other women. She maintains, however, that this goal is constantly undermined by men's demands. Roffiel's celebration of women-identified experience through her positive evocation of the community of friends in *Amora*, provides convincing evidence of a 'lesbian continuum'.

There are many references in the text to the unsatisfactory nature of heterosexual relations and her book pokes fun at men in general: 'A ellos los han educado para que sean unos cabrones y a nosotras para que seamos las pendejas gracias a las cuales ellos pueden seguir siendo cabrones' (p.43).[62] Much of the vitriol directed at men in general comes from Norma, a friend of Lupe's, who is presented as utterly disillusioned with men and heterosexuality:

60   See 'Las indias caciques', 'La liberación de la mujer, aquí', and 'La liberación del amor', in *El uso de la palabra* (Mexico City: Ediciones de Excélsior-Crónicas, 1974), pp.24–7, pp.48–52 and pp.53–6 respectively. She refers to a march organised in 1970 by women to commemorate their attainment of the right to vote and she criticises certain establishments in Mexico for still refusing to admit women. See 'La liberación de la mujer aquí', pp.48–9.

61   'Compulsory Heterosexuality and Lesbian Existence', in *Blood, Bread and Poetry: Selected Prose 1979–1985*, pp.23–75. Although she later clarified her position in light of the critical response, Rich's continuum was widely interpreted as suggesting that all women who had emotionally intimate relationships with other women could be considered 'lesbian'.

62   All page references to *Amora* (Mexico City: Planeta, Colección Fábula, 1989) will appear in parentheses after citations in the text.

Tengo amigas superchingonas que se dejan joder por tipos que ni se entregan ni son extraordinarios en la cama, ni siquiera son ricos y, a veces, son a- burridísimos y, bueno, para colmo, hasta les ponen los cuernos. [...]

Lo que quiero decir es que así es como la mayoría de las mujeres vive a los hombres, como el único y más importante objetivo de su existencia. Les conceden todavía más valor que el que se dan ellas mismas (p.42).

Her diatribes are similar in nature to the outburst of the narrator in Castellanos's short story, 'Lección de cocina'. In this passage from Castellanos's story, the narrator reflects on her status as housewife:

Yo rumiaré en silencio mi rencor. Se me atribuyen las responsabilidades y las tareas de una criada para todo. He de mantener la casa impecable, la ropa lista, el ritmo de la alimentación infalible. Pero no se me paga ningún sueldo, no se me concede un día libre a la semana, no puedo cambiar de amo.[63]

'Lección de cocina' is at its most powerful in passages such as this one in which women's roles are interrogated incisively and in which the institution of marriage is emphatically denounced. Roffiel also addresses the question of marriage, stating clearly her antipathy to it as an institution. Declaring herself, 'no creyente en el matrimonio' (p.39), she elaborates, 'me parece antinatural, tramposo, por lo menos así como está instituido' (p.39) in a way that aligns her very firmly with Castellanos's views on the subject. Roffiel expands her criticism:

– Cuando dos personas se unen en un momento determinado de su vida es porque ambas ven hacia el mismo punto, pero como somos seres evolutivos – los que lo somos, desde luego – pues empezamos a caminar, y generalmente una pareja camina hacia direcciones distintas, a ritmos diferentes y entonces viene el rompimiento. Es cuando hay que saber que llegó el momento de transformar la relación amorosa en una amistad que tendría que durar, esa sí, para siempre (p.39).

Castellanos is much more forceful in her criticism of the institution of marriage:

El matrimonio es el ayuntamiento de dos bestias carnívoras de especie diferente que de pronto se hallan encerradas en la misma jaula. Se rasguñan, se mordisquean, se devoran, por conquistar un milímetro más de la ración

63   *Álbum de familia*, p.15.

destinada a cada uno. Y no porque importe ni la cama ni la ración. Lo que importa es reducir al otro a esclavitud. Aniquilarlo. [64]

The bitterness apparent in passages such as this one from her short story, 'Álbum de familia', is unparalleled in any of her other work. Roffile is less forceful in her critiques but the myth of heterosexual coupledom is effectively dismantled nevertheless. Lupe's friend, Vica, speaks passionately about her experience:

> Por un lado quieren una mujer independiente y por el otro se mueren porque seas sumisa. Son unos inmaduros. Eso es lo chistoso. Nos la pasamos buscando a nuestro padre y encontramos puro hijito. Te deshaces por tener un hombre que te dé seguridad, protección, fuerza, y encuentras cuates que quieren que seas su mamá. Yo he sido la terapeuta de todos mis amantes y, además, una extraordinaria terapeuta. Los ayudo a crecer, a madurar, para que después disfruten de esa madurez con otras mujeres. Fíjate que ya no (p.122).

Here, Vica criticises what she sees as the perpetual immaturity of men and the impossible situation of women who find themselves expected to be both submissive and independent. Other sections of Roffiel's text focus more specifically on the sexual act and on the negative experiences of the female protagonists:

> – Sí, y después te sigues muriendo de frustración por que mientras ellos en un dos por tres, ¡zas!, se vienen, tú por más que te frotas, brincas, fantaseas, te paras de cabeza, ¡nada! Apenas estás conectando la palanca de *on* y ellos ya acabaron, y encima te preguntan, '¿Qué tal, te gustó?' […] Sí, qué pena, son tan pocos los hombres que se toman la molestia de conocer a fondo la sexualidad femenina (p.58).

Castellanos also pauses to reflect on the nature of sexual relations in 'Lección de cocina'. Here she sharply criticises the role of mythology in the perpetuation of damaging and limiting archetypes:

> Pero yo, abnegada mujercita mexicana que nació como la paloma para el nido, sonreía a semejanza de Cuauhtémoc en el suplicio cuando dijo 'mi lecho no es de rosas y se volvió a callar.' Boca arriba soportaba no sólo mi propio peso sin

---

64   'Álbum de familia' from the collection, *Álbum de familia*, p.132.

el de él encima del mío. La postura clásica para hacer el amor. Y gemía, de desgarramiento, de placer. El gemido clásico. Mitos, mitos.[65]

Roffiel's ruminations on the subject echo those of Castellanos:

> – ¿Quién nos enseña cómo se hace el amor, o nos explica cómo se sienten los orgasmos? Ellos van con putas y, además, son mucho más elementales para satisfacerse. Nosotras aprendemos en las películas y en los libros, que fueron hechas por hombres. Aprendemos a gemir, gritar, jadear y revolcarnos, y creemos que eso es hacer el amor y tener un orgasmo (pp.57–8).

Both writers seem to isolate culture, and in particular the myths propagated by history (in the case of Castellanos) and male-authored films and books (in the case of Roffiel) as the reason they are led to their misapprehensions about sex and their sexual disappointment. The emphasis on 'learning' in the above passage connects directly to Castellanos's vision of gender which firmly endorses liberal feminism's insistence on its constructed nature. She reminds us in 'Lección de cocina' that cooking is not something she just 'knows', 'Me supone una intuición que según mi sexo, debo poseer pero que no poseo, un sentido *sin el que nací* que me permitiera advertir el momento preciso en que la carne está a punto' (my emphasis).[66] This notion of gender as a cultural construct, famously advocated by Simone de Beauvoir in 1949 in *The Second Sex* has remained a pivotal belief of feminism world-wide.[67] The process of learning gender, therefore, is foregrounded in both texts. In 'Lección de cocina' it is filtered through the unfortunate sexual experience of Castellanos's narrator as she adopts the 'classic posture' to moan her way through her performance. This experience is replicated in *Amora* through Lupe who laments the lack of female-centred teaching on sexuality:

---

65   *Álbum de familia*, p.9.
66   *Álbum de familia*, p.13.
67   Encapsulated by her famous phrase, 'One is not born, but rather becomes, a woman', *The Second Sex* (New York: Vintage Books, 1973), p.301. De Beauvoir developed at length the idea that gender was constructed rather than natural. This notion of learned gender behaviour exerted a tremendous influence on the Women's Movements of the 1960s and 1970s.

– Mira, generalmente, con los cuates todo empieza por lo físico. Te conoces, te gustas y casi enseguida te vas a la cama. Es raro el tipo que primero quiere conocerte y amarte y luego cogerte. Ya si después del sexo se da la comunicación, pues qué suertuda (p.64).

In this passage the familiar accusations that men are too enthralled by the physical to pay much attention to emotional connection or intimacy, are voiced by way of instruction to the young (still heterosexual) Claudia. From an early point in the text, it would seem that love between women is posited as the answer to heterosexual angst, an assertion I shall return to in a later section. What is absolutely signalled, however, is the abject failure of heterosexual relations for the characters in the text.

It is important to point out that Lupe's views are presented as the 'reasoned' and 'rational' stance within a broad spectrum of feminist views that includes a much more radical vision articulated by her friend, Norma. Norma's impassioned speeches against patriarchy explicitly endorse a radical feminist vision of the kind espoused by the late Andrea Dworkin and fellow campaigner, Catherine MacKinnon:

Desde que entré al Grupo me han caído varios veintes como ése de que existen otras formas de violación: cómo nos miran, cómo nos manosean, cómo nos infunden temor. Y estoy de acuerdo con lo que dijeron las dos psicólogas que dieron la plática en la universidad: todos los hombres son violadores en potencia (p.44).[68]

It is clear that *Amora* articulates views that share much with Dworkin's viewpoint. In this way, Roffiel explores the possibility that while gender may be a construct, male violence and rape are per-

68 Andrea Dworkin and Catherine MacKinnon's work has centred on the destructive effects of pornography. Together, they helped draft an ordinance that allowed victims of rape and sexual crime to sue pornographers on the basis that the culture created by pornography supported violence against women. See, Andrea Dworkin, *Woman Hating: A Radical Look at Sexuality* (Boston: Dutton, 1974) and *Pornography: Men Possessing Women* (London: Women's Press, 1981). First published in 1979, her thesis ignited controversy as she insisted on the causal link between pornography and rape by incorporating violent domination of women as a key element of sexual fantasy. Until her death in 2005, Dworkin campaigned ceaselessly against pornography.

manent fixtures that render the liberal feminist struggle for 'equal rights' redundant. In putting forward this point of view, Roffiel echoes many voices from within the women's liberation movement, most famously associated with Andrea Dworkin but others too, like Susan Brownmiller.[69] Indeed, the words uttered in *Amora* in relation to rape bear striking resemblance to the passage from Marilyn French's famous novel, *The Women's Room*:

> Whatever they may be in public life, whatever their relationships with men, in their relationships with women, all men are rapists, and that's all they are. They rape us with their eyes, their laws, and their codes.[70]

Roffiel, then, takes Castellanos's critique of patriarchal extremes much further. This critique is expressed through the careful insertion of various narratives of male violence into the text which undercut the harmonious stories of friendship between the female characters. It is on this aspect that I will focus in the next section.

Male Violence

Alongside Roffiel's strident critique of heterosexuality as oppressive and damaging to women, is a more disturbing narrative that relates the protagonist's experiences in her work with the Grupo de Ayuda para Personas Violadas (GRAPAV). In what might be seen as typically

---

69 In another key text from the radical feminist tradition, Susan Brownmiller, published *Against our Will: Men, Women and Rape* (New York: Simon and Schuster, 1975) in which she examines what she describes as men's structural capacity to rape and women's corresponding structural vulnerability.

70 *The Women's Room*, p.462. It is worth pointing out here that this statement is uttered by one of the characters of French's novel, not the narrator. In this way, distance is established between the more radical voice of the fictional character and the omniscient narrator whose position is much more moderate. A similar process happens in *Amora* in that the narrator, Lupe, adopts a more moderate stance in relation to violence, leaving the more extreme viewpoint to her friend, Norma.

feminist fashion, Lupe works at a refuge that aims to provide medical, psychological and legal help to rape victims. It is not entirely clear what her specific role is within GRAPAV but various cases make their way onto the pages and break the continuity of the narrative about her love with Claudia. Lupe attests to the difficult nature of the work she does: 'Cada caso me aniquila. En las audiencias me dan ganas de patear a los violadores hasta reventarlos' (p.15). Later, in a conversation with Claudia, she becomes angry about the legal system that enables these crimes to happen on a daily basis:

> – En este país, el delito de violación es el único donde la víctima tiene que demostrar que es víctima. [...] En el caso de violación, cuando una mujer llega a poner su denuncia, es ella la que debe probar que, en efecto, fue violada. [...] Y no es el único colmo nacional. Hay miles.
> – ¿Apoco no hay violadores en la cárcel?
> Poquitérrimos. Todos pagan fianzas ridículas, o mordidas, y salen libres como el viento. En el Grupo tuvimos un caso en el que la sentencia fue pagarle dos mil pesos a la víctima porque su blusa se rasgó durante el ataque y la juez – ¡imagínate, una juez mujer! – decidió que ése era el precio de la prenda y que con su pago era suficiente (pp.29–30).

As well as anger at the system, there is a deep sadness expressed at some of the individual cases, most notably that of their friend and colleague, Rosa María, who is raped, and who then becomes the victim Lupe has helped so many times at the centre. In a moving encounter between the two, Lupe confesses that the rape of her friend, 'nos enfrenta a la posibilidad de nuestra propia violación' (p.70). Roffiel develops this incident into another story which she includes in *El para siempre dura una noche*. However, it is for the story of the unnamed victim early on in the text, in the chapter entitled, 'la vida es una ensalada agridulce', that the most vivid details are reserved and in which the horror of rape explodes into the reader's consciousness in a profoundly disturbing way.

Up until this point in the narrative, great attention has been paid to the loving and supportive world of Lupe and her friends. Suddenly, into this homely world intrudes a gruesome and brutal story of rape and suffering told through direct dialogue between the participants involved and in particular the male aggressor. The horrific account is all the more disturbing given its position in the middle of this cosy narrative envisioning of female support. It ruptures their world and triggers an angry response from Lupe, the narrator. At first, the extreme violence of the assault is horrifying: 'La penetró por delante y por atrás, le mordió los senos hasta casi arrancarle los pezones, lo mismo que las orejas. Marta gritaba' (p.27). It is, however, the extreme misogyny of the exchanges between rapist and victim later in the attack, that impacts the most on the reader. As the victim struggles to escape, she is violently pulled back:

> – ¿Qué te piensas, hija de la chingada, que ya acabamos? Pues estás muy equivocada, aquí te vas a quedar otro ratito conmigo, ¿qué no ves que la estamo pasando rico? La golpeó más. Le metió su miembro en el ano y después en la boca.
> – Toma, cómete tu propia mierda, ándale, eso es lo único que saben hacer las mujeres: comer mierda. Ándale, hija de puta, abre bien el hocico, mámamela sabroso, cabrona.
> De los insultos pasaba a una ronda de 'te quiero, hija de la chingada, perra inmunda, quiero hacerte un hijo, quiero tener un hijo tuyo, puta desgraciada, te amo te amo'. Y de nuevo a los golpes. Esta vez le eyaculó en la cara. El semen se le metió a Marta por la nariz, por los ojos, por la boca. Le escurrió por el cuello, hasta las orejas (p.28).

In this graphic account, the reader is suddenly catapulted into a real world in which the most destructive consequences of patriarchal power structures are terrifyingly in evidence. In this scenario, the male embodies the most extreme form of macho power which, at its worst, humiliates and subjugates the other sex so as to maintain superiority.

Rosario Castellanos did not treat the subject of rape *per se*. There are references to the rape of indigenous girls (Marcela in *Oficio de tinieblas*), and of working-class maids in provincial Comitán (Modesta in *Ciudad Real*), but in general these characters are peripheral rather than central and feature as indicators or symbols in her delicate sketching of societal injustice.[71] Her wrath as an intellectual was mostly directed towards the societal structures that so debilitated the role of women in Mexico in the twentieth century, and her campaign

---

71 See Castellanos's novel, *Oficio de tinieblas* (1962) and her collection of short stories, *Ciudad Real* (1960), both set in Chiapas.

was firmly focused on the social. A bitter critic of marriage and other patriarchal institutions, she largely steers away from the topic of male violence towards women. Nevertheless, Roffiel chooses to invoke Castellanos directly, like Loaeza does, in her second publication, *El para siempre dura una noche,* at the start of one of the more emotional stories in which the rape of the narrator's close friend, Celina, is outlined. What seems to be a re-working of the episode recounted in *Amora* about the friend named Rosa María, the narrator titles the story, 'El viento no se rompe aunque se parta en ráfagas', accredited to Castellanos as though to derive strength and solace from this poetic statement of endurance.[72] By following the title with the simple *dedicatoria*, 'Para todas vosotras', Roffiel seems to reinforce this interpretation, cementing the importance of solidarity and tracing an invisible thread of support from Castellanos, through to Roffiel and extended to the anonymous 'vosotras' who will, it is hoped, be comforted through this strategic act of allegiance and affirmation.

In the face of the brutal account of the rape in *Amora*, the theoretical treatises of the other chapters in the novel with their feminist speeches are suddenly displaced in the face of the actual suffering and torment of the victim. Nowhere else in the text does Roffiel discuss the extremes of violence against women in this way though, there are many other passing references to distressing cases and in the closing stages of the text, the women meet to attend a protest march on 'Día internacional en contra de la violencia hacia las mujeres' (p.135). Violence, thus, is never far from the consciousness of the novel's characters, and indeed, many of the friendships are forged against the backdrop of their work in the Group. Lupe is involved in one way or another with various civil liberty groups in Mexico including *el Movimiento de Liberación Homosexual* and *La Red Nacional de Mujeres* (p.160). Indeed, she attaches tremendous importance to the work of non-governmental organisations which continue the struggle for civil and human rights on a grass-roots

72   *El para siempre dura una noche* (Mexico City: Hoja Casa Editorial, Sentido contrario, 1999), pp.60–1.

level.[73] The deliberate positioning of the rape narrative towards the beginning of *Amora* is strategic in that it copperfastens the need in the reader's mind for the existence of the group to which Lupe belongs, and reminds the reader, in a very obvious way, of the potential for male violence in the society in which they live. It also vividly illustrates the abyss existing between the different strata of society – in this case between the lives of women like Lupe who help at the Group and those led by the female victims they treat. The pain generated by the confrontation between the groups leads to a textual ambivalence that unsettles the reader in a very disturbing way. This 'unsettling' links the text, again, most directly to radical feminist discourses in the West and their insistence on the connection between patriarchal power and brutal macho violence. It is in these sections that the text emits its powerful political charge.

Beyond Violence: Women's 'Liberation'

While it is clear from the above sections that *Amora* stages a convincing assault on the worst extremes of patriarchy in the form of rape, it resolutely refuses to remain mired in negativity and pessimism. Instead, as hinted at earlier, it chooses the path to redemption and happiness, achieved in the text at any rate, by the protagonist's devotion to the feminist cause and through her loving relationship with Claudia. There is particular emphasis in *Amora* on the feminist movement as it pertains to sexuality, so much so that, as mentioned already, some critics dismissed it as mere manifesto. There is no doubt but that much textual space is allocated to the discussion of the

---

73   She is not alone, of course, in attaching importance to this kind of civic organising. Carlos Monsiváis talks at length about the resurgence of civic groups from the 1980s onwards, a trend he attributes to the widespread disillusionment of people with the democratic process seen in the results of the 1988 elections in which Salinas de Gortari won. See *Entrada libre: crónicas de la sociedad que se organiza* (Mexico: Ediciones Era, 1987).

Women's Movement, both in relation to the evolution of the character of Lupe and in general terms. Much of this feminist education is imparted in the form of instruction to the younger, more naive Claudia. When she asks, '¿qué es de verdad el feminismo?', Lupe is given the opportunity to define it once and for all:

> – Supongo que hay tantos feminismos como mujeres en el mundo. Para mí, es un proyecto de vida que nos devuelve nuestro valor histórico. La primera que debe reconocer ese valor es una misma, y, a partir de él, exigírselo a los seres que te rodean' (p.75).

Here Lupe succinctly defines feminism as a personal and collective project that will restore a sense of self-worth to women everywhere. Unconcerned in this passage with the concrete struggles against male violence or oppressive heterosexual relations, Lupe opts for a very simple conceptualisation of feminism as a recognition of human value. Profoundly personal, therefore, this feminist vision is deeply rooted, as already stated, in the prototypical feminist discourse of the 1970s to which she later makes reference in depth:

> Mis años de soledad, sintiéndome un hongo extraño y diferente a cuanta mujer conocía. Ajena por completo a la realidad doméstica de mis ex compañeras de escuela, a las ansias matrimoniales y maternales de mis compañeras de trabajo, a las vidas mediocres de mis vecinas. Yo, la rara. [...] La que nunca entendió por qué no era como las demás. Qué lejos esa mañana de octubre de 1977 en que oí hablar a las feministas por primera vez y me dije – atontada por la sorpresa – '¡Pero si yo soy feminista, y no lo sabía!' Qué aturdidor el gozo al descubrir que había mujeres que vivían como yo, que esperaban lo que yo, que hablaban mi mismo lenguaje. Qué conmovedor alivio encontrar respuestas a preguntas que me inquietaban desde la infancia. Acudí a mi primera reunión en casa de Marta Lamas como quien acude a una ineludible cita con lo desconocido. Pavor, curiosidad, nerviosismo, ilusión. Éramos catorce mujeres. Comenzamos a hablar de abortos, amantes, virginidades perdidas. Nos pusimos íntimas, sinceras. Bebíamos vino tinto. Nos reímos como descosidas, a cada rato alguna se levantaba a hacer pipí. Nos sentíamos deliciosamente perversas y maravillosamente libres al comunicarnos cosas que no le diríamos a nadie más. Entonces supe que ya no estaba sola. Que había encontrado un nuevo significado de la palabra amistad (p.31).

In this passage, Lupe outlines the way in which feminism, in the form of the Women's Movement, changed her life irrevocably. The

230

Women's Movement has been defined in many ways but is often summarised now by reference to the struggle for equality in the workplace, reproductive rights and the right to work outside the home among others. As is well known, many feminist groups explored the use of consciousness-raising in which great priority was placed on the experiential and the belief that personal experience constitutes the starting point for change. It is from this core belief, of course, that the phrase, 'the personal is political' stemmed.[74] Indeed, activists like Friedan privileged this epistemology as the only way forward to achieve political change. Roffiel is, it would seem, also immersed in this discourse of the experiential and the personal. In many places, her musings read like a consciousness-raising session from the 1970s, in which women gathered strength from each other to face the daily inequities of patriarchy and oppression, 'la mayoría cargamos historias tremendas, que no sólo no han logrado aniquilarnos, sino de las cuales aprendimos a sacar nuestra fuerza' (p.32).

The feminist movement has had a deep impact on Lupe's life, a sense of which is derived from the long passage quoted above. What is perhaps most interesting is how little this feminist experience seems rooted in everyday Mexican reality. In fact, until the end of the text, the narrative makes virtually no reference to any culturally specific aspect of the Mexican Women's Movement. It is mostly devoid of cultural context and reads much more like the narrative of a North American 'coming of feminist age' tale than anything related to the specific realities of Mexican women.[75] It is only in the final pages that any sense of the movement's trajectory in Mexico is sensed:

74   Carol Hanisch is credited with the origins of this phrase in her essay, 'The Personal is Political', in *Notes from the Second Year: Women's Liberation in 1970* (New York: Redstockings, 1970), p.76. The essay defends consciousness-raising against the charge that it is 'therapy': 'One of the first things we discover in these groups is that personal problems are political problems. There are no personal solutions at this time'. See Hanisch's personal account of the history of the phrase, http://scholar.alexanderstreet.com/pages/viewpage.action?page Id=2259 (accessed 17 April 2007).

75   For an excellent outline of the feminist movement in Mexico, see Anna Macías, *Against All Odds: The Feminist Movement in Mexico to 1940* (Westport,

231

Año de problemas en el Grupo. Sí, ni modo, el feminismo no es esa religión pura y prístina que me ilusioné con ver al principio. Hay luchas por el poder, rivalidades, pleitos. Pero sigue siendo mi opción de vida, sobre todo en esta época de incertidumbres. La Red Nacional de Mujeres, integrada por grupos feministas de toda la república, sobrevive por segundo año consecutivo. *La Causa de las Mujeres*, delicioso e importante espacio, regalo de Radio Educación, cobra fuerza día a día. Temas relacionados con nosotras ocupan ya un lugarcito en los medios de comunicación y hasta en algunas secretarías y sindicatos. Puede decirse que el feminismo avanza en México, igual que el Movimiento de Liberación Homosexual (p.160).

Here Lupe's vision, compared with that expressed earlier in the text, seems to have matured somewhat in that she has now accepted the various problems and issues that accompany activism. Elsewhere Lupe also voices these doubts and pokes fun at certain elements. She therefore, starts to recognise the problems inherent in any 'movement' or collective action, and there are signs too that indicate an ability to laugh at herself and feminist doctrine generally. She refers at one point to 'el rollo feminista', and at another point confesses that 'Se me sale lo feminista y me enrasco en un rollito sobre la violación' (p.30). There are sarcastic references to homophobic 'compañeras feministas, solidarias, consistentes, a quienes les rascas tantito y resultan más homofóbicas que el Papa' (pp.112–13) and Lupe also humorously teases her friend, 'Resultan que las feministas de izquierda también tienen alma' (p.114). However, overall, the vision that emerges is one of gratitude and comfort, a reliance on a feminist community that is reassuring and necessary. The other way in which Roffiel indicates the indebtedness of her text to feminist discourse of the 1960s and 1970s

Connecticut: Greenwood Press, 1982). Martha Loustanau, in her study, *Mexico's Contemporary Women Novelists* (Massachussetts: Ann Arbor, 1973) discusses the importance of the popular magazine, *Kena*, in terms of its radical call for a re-definition of love, marriage and motherhood in Mexico. See, for example, Lita Paniagua, 'La lucha por la superación femenina', *Kena* (September 1972), p.4, and Esperanza Brito de Martí, 'Cambiemos la imagen de amor', *Kena* (January 1973) primera quincena, pp.12–13, 'El amor, los cielos y la mujer emancipada', *Kena* (October 1970), segunda quincena, pp.4–6, and 'Amor y sexo – liberación o subyugación', *Kena* (August 1972), primera quincena, pp.10–12, p.107. The role of feminist journals such as *Debate feminista* and *fem* should not be forgotton either.

232

is through the centrality of its evocation of female solidarity. It is on this aspect that I will focus in the next section.

Solidarity and Community

Female solidarity, as expressed through the support and love shown between the various women friends is, perhaps, the most pronounced element in the overall portrait of the feminist discourse in the novel. It is best exemplified by the scene at the party in which their friend Virginia appears dressed as the moon:

> La miramos fascinadas. Danza escalón por escalón, hasta llegar abajo. El piso de madera apenas gime con el discreto roce de sus pies descalzos. Sigue su baile, a veces suave, otras agitado, en instantes violento. A su alrededor, todas sonreímos. La mayoría estamos abrazadas, de dos, de cuatro, deveras. Los ojos nos brillan y no es por las cubas o las cervezas. Con una música de flauta como fondo, la luna continúa girando en su nuevo espacio. Como una sacerdotisa inmersa en un rito íntimo, rodeada por su secta de mujeres que buscan y crecen en un mundo ideado precisamente para impedírselos. Cuando termina la ceremonia, aplaudimos, gritamos, saltamos y rodeamos a la bailarina. Enseguida, empiezan a brotar mujeres con manchas blancas en una mejilla, una oreja o la mitad de la frente: todas quieren abrazar a la luna (p.137).

The sense of unfolding ritual here creates a dream-like scene in which the women are connected spiritually and emotionally. This sense of connection permeates the book and is visible in multiple forms. In the author's acknowledgements, it is explicit:

> Es para mis amigas, pero sobre todo para Cristina, Citlali, Mariana, Norma, Graciela, Fernanda, Adriana, Canela, Lillia, Berta y Luisa Fernanda, quienes enriquecieron estas páginas con sus comentarios, sus vivencias, su sentido del humor y, más que nada, con su amistad a prueba de todo (n.p.).

The relationship between Lupe and her flatmates, Mariana and Citlali, who are both also lesbians, is depicted as a positive and comforting alternative to the conventional relationship of a heterosexual couple:

Es mucho más rico vivir con amigas llenas de vida, de ideas, de solidaridad, que con un hombre que insiste en que él es el eje central de tu existencia, en una casa que ni siquiera es tuya y la cual tiene que girar alrededor de la magnífica presencia de tu marido (p.50).

Lupe describes their accommodation in affectionate detail, providing evidence of the conviviality of their living arrangements: 'Y nuestro comedorcito, ah nuestro comedorcito es rojo, con un trinchador de esos antiguos que venden carísimos en San Ángel y no tanto en los bazares de Puebla' (p.21). The happiness of their woman-centred community is highlighted through Lupe's evocations of their friendship as in the following example in which she reflects on Christmas spent in the company of her flatmates and other friends:

Para Navidad, mis amigas me regalaron ollas, sartenes, platos, cucharas. '¡Parece despedida de soltera!', se quejaban el veinticinco de diciembre que nos reunimos a comer en mi pequeño territorio ganado con sangre, sudor y lágrimas (p.21).

What emerges, then, is a portrait of love and affection, evoked by the recurring references to the support they offer each other. This idea of friendship is highlighted at many points in the text: 'Mariana y yo llegamos de visita a la cama de Citlali, la única que tiene colchón *king size* en esta casa. Amanecemos deprimidas las tres. Ha de ser porque es domingo y está nublado. Pero, ¡coño!, qué sincronización' (p.105). Elsewhere it is described as 'Domingo solidario. Citlali, Mariana, Graciela y yo nos vamos al campo. Decidimos airear nuestro dolor' (p.97). There are also references to solidarity, as for example when the house-mates comfort each other in times of emotional pain and crisis, 'La solidaridad no tiene horario' (p.93), and there is even mention of the sisterhood, 'Nosotras nos miramos cómplices, sonrientes, llenitas de esa hermandad que crece cada día más entre Mariana, Citlali y yo' (p.25). While at certain points, the exaggerated portrait can be irritating, it is important to point out, again, just how ground-breaking this narrative is in terms of its envisioning of independent urban women, many of whom are also lesbians. There is reference made in the text to the extremely unusual nature of the narrator's circumstances. In the following passage she describes how she came to live on her own:

> Además, resulté una pervertidora. Varias mujeres cercanas siguieron mi ejemplo, cuando ni siquiera se habían atrevido a pensar en ello. Finalizaban los sesenta. Eso no se había visto en la clase media mexicana. Esos libertinajes sólo existían en Europa y Estados Unidos. '¡Qué nos espera, Señor!' gritaban los padres de familia en aquella época (p.23).

What might in some ways appear as a clichéd representation of some kind of feminist utopian community, then, is also a sincere attempt to suggest alternative ways of living. I will return to this 'alternative way' later on in the chapter. Here, however, it leads to a problematic middle-class focus that fashions its critique in a very particular way.

Feminism, Class and Questions of Power

The feminist discourse in which Lupe is immersed is derived, almost wholly from Western and for the most part, North American, sources and permeates the text from start to finish. It is here too that Roffiel's text is particularly indebted to Castellanos's later work, which, as has been documented, is also derived from Western feminism. It is this reliance on Second Wave feminist discourse however, that proves rather problematic when attempting to claim *Amora* as a feminist manifesto for Mexico. It is widely acknowledged now that Second Wave feminism overwhelmingly privileged the voices and lives of the white middle classes to the detriment and exclusion of women from other classes or ethnic groups. Indeed it has been vociferously criticised for its overwhelming emphasis on the lives of middle-class women in the West. What is more, the recognition of the exclusive nature of early women's liberation movements has provoked a period of re-evaluation of feminism that has sought to position difference as its defining crux.[76] This text, however, is located within the earlier wave of activism that bore witness to rapid and indeed, dramatic changes for women – particularly middle-class women with a high degree of social mobility. The emphasis in *Amora* is also middle-class; the protagonists are all beneficiaries of third-level education, of independent means with many of them working as journalists, social workers and writers. In this way, they confirm, to a great extent, the limitations of Second Wave Feminist discourse while enacting a celebration of its core achievements in the form of economic autonomy and access to education.

The text opens as Claudia and Lupe meet for the first time at a gallery opening. Their dialogue confirms the cloying middle-class, quasi-intellectual tone: '– Eso suena a posgrado' (p.10). In a fascinating parallel with Loaeza, the men are categorised into types of *niño bien* in a passage that could quite easily be found in any of Loaeza's early work:

> Los primeros: traje impecable con chaleco y todo, zapatos Florsheim boleados, corte de pelo Zona Rosa o Polanco, Topaz y Rólex de oro. Los segundos: *jeans*, zapatos de gamuza o tenis, pelo largo y barba, Volkswagen o nada, y siempre con un *Proceso* bajo el brazo (p.10).

There are also references throughout the text to writers and to the importance of education. Lupe's library and her fascination with various works of fiction is noted in various places. There are jokes about the Universidad Iberoamericana, of which Claudia is a graduate,

---

76 There is much debate now on the notion of Third Wave Feminism, the roots of which are to be found in rhetoric from the 1980s. Most critics concur, however, that it is grounded in an awareness of ethnic and class differences. It is often associated with the call for a 'new subjectivity' made by various feminist of color and documented by Catherine Orr in her article, 'Charting the Currents of the Third Wave', *Hypatia*, Vol.12, No.3 (1997), pp.29–46. See also, Stacy Gillis, Gillian Howie and Rebecca Munford (eds), *Third Wave Feminism: A Critical Exploration* (Palgrave, 2004), Leslie Heywood, Jennifer Drake (eds), *Third Wave Agenda: Being Feminist, Doing Feminism* (Minneapolis: University of Minnesota Press, 1997), and Astrid Henry: *Not My Mother's Sister: Generational Conflict and Third-Wave Feminism* (Bloomington: Indiana University Press, 2004).

and which constitutes the prototypical *niña bien* 'hang out' which is parodied so effectively by Loaeza. The text, then, clearly shows the protagonists' very privileged existence as economically autonomous women with careers in which they are fulfilled. In this sense, the feminist utopian vision is confirmed, yet again, but it remains resolutely a middle-class victory to the exclusion of the very women who facilitated that victory through their employment and exploitation as maids and child-care workers. The paradoxes at the heart of feminism are thus left largely untouched in Roffiel's text as she focuses exclusively on the sexual and personal liberation of her lesbian role-models.

Here again, there are connections with Castellanos whose final work of prose is also mostly concerned with the plight, as she saw it, of the middle-class woman in Mexico city. Castellanos's vision, however, is pessimistic and negative and seems far removed from the loving harmony envisioned so effectively by Roffiel. In Castellanos's story, 'Álbum de familia', a group of women, all of them educated and middle-class, come together for a school reunion. In the story, any notion of solidarity is ironically exposed as an illusion and the women are evoked in animalistic terms as dirty and diseased. Images of monstrosity permeate the text as the women proceed to metaphorically tear each other apart. In the following description, Castellanos describes the greeting between two of the women reunited, Victoria and Josefa:

> La pulcritud del cuello y de los puños, el restiramiento de las medias, la torcedura de los tacones. En ellos precisamente fijó su atención mientras se aproximaba a la recién llegada para practicar juntas esa ritual – un breve contacto de las mejillas – *con que las mujeres pactan entre su deseo de besar y su necesidad de morder* (my emphasis).[77]

There is a savagery implicit in the relationships between the women in this story that is completely absent from Roffiel's novel. However, one of the interesting elements present in the above passage is the reference to female desire. Castellanos generally eschewed any exploration of lesbianism and yet, in this passage, and elsewhere in her

77   'Álbum de familia' in *Álbum de familia*, p.86.

prose, there is an acknowledgement of the existence of desire between women. In her poem, 'Kinsey Report', she examines a different 'type' of woman in each stanza, *la casada, la divorciada, la soltera* (the latter, a prime concern of Castellanos's work). One of the stanzas specifically deals with lesbian lifestyle:

> Mi amiga y yo nos entendemos bien.
> Y la que manda es tierna, como compensación
> Así como tambien, la que obedece,
> Es coqueta y se toma sus revanchas
>
> Vamos a muchas fiestas, viajamos a menudo
> Y en el hotel pedimos
> Un solo cuarto y una sola cama
>
> Se burlan de nosotras pero también nosotras
> Nos burlamos de ellos
> Y quedamos a mano.
>
> Cuando nos aburramos de estar solas
> Alguna de las dos irá a agenciarse un hijo.
> ¡No, no de esa manera! En el laboratorio
> De la inseminación artificial.[78]

Castellanos's envisioning of the lesbian world shares much in common with Roffiel with its references to travel, parties and staying in hotels. The emphasis on mobility further emphasises the very middle-class privileged existence enjoyed by these women, not to mention the almost fanciful reference to artificial insemination as though it were a realistic option for lesbian women in Mexico in the 1970s (or indeed anywhere).[79] What resonates, perhaps most force-

78 'Kinsey Report', *Poesía no eres tú: obra poética, 1948–1971*, pp.317–20.
79 On 6 November 2006, the Dictamen de la Ley de Sociedades de Convivencia was approved. It provided homosexuals with basic civil rights, 'derecho recíproco de proporcionarse alimentos, derecho de sucesión, derecho de tutela, derecho de pensión alimentaria para la persona que carezca de ingresos en caso de separación'. See Sylvia Chant and Nikki Craske, *Gender in Latin America* (London: Latin America Bureau/Rutgers University Press, 2003). It is legal for women in same-sex relationships in Mexico to avail of artificial insemination. It goes without saying, however, that access is limited due to social stigma and

fully from Castellanos's poem, however, is the defiance in the face of adversity, 'Se burlan de nosotras pero también nosotras nos burlamos de ellos y quedamos a mano'. It is clear, then, that Castellanos does acknowledge lesbian desire and lifestyle in ways that are similar to Roffiel's evocations. They differ considerably, however, in their envisioning of female desire. In the case of Castellanos, this takes the form of dark pessimism, underscored by graphic imagery of dirt, disease and monstrosity. Roffiel's work, on the other hand, evokes a utopian community of support and solidarity. Both bodies of work remain firmly rooted in the experiences of middle-class women, however, and foreground the tensions of feminist discourse with regard to class. *Amora*, as we have seen, replicates the class bias that permeated all Second Wave feminist discourse at literary, historical, sociological and cultural levels. Seen from the perspective of today, it may seem dated and, on occasion, elitist in its exclusive focus on such a privileged section of Mexican society, who though lesbian, are still privileged. The self-absorption of the protagonists is embedded throughout the text and is only punctured by the tales of male violence, as outlined earlier. It is in episodes like these that the gaps between the different Mexican lives are glimpsed but the text leaves them unconnected and they do not impinge on the joyful exploration of lesbian love that forms the core of the text.

financial constraints. See, International Lesbian and Gay Association, *LGBT World Legal Wrap-Up Survey* (November 2006), available online at, www.ilga-europe.org/content/download/6444/39689/file/World%20legal%20wrap%20up%20survey%20%20November2006.pdf (accessed 4 April 2007).

Lesbian Love

By far the most radical aspect of Roffiel's text is its candid and open evocation of lesbian love. As stated earlier, I interpret Roffiel's work in *Amora* as a continuation of the Castellanos quest for an other way of being, as expressed in her famous lines:

> No, no es la solución
> Tirarse bajo un tren com la Ana de Tolstoi
> [...]
> Debe haber otro modo que no se llame Safo
> Ni Mesalina ni María Egipciaca
> Ni Magdalena ni Clemencia Isaura.
>
> Otro modo de ser humano y libre
> Otro modo de ser.[80]

Roffiel's *Amora* is in many ways a direct textual response to this quest, one that is articulated forcefully on numerous occasions and most effectively signalled through the glorious celebration of eroticism, desire and love. From its title, *Amora*, with its explicit feminisation of the act of love, to the refreshing optimism of its closing pages and final line, 'Se puede ser tan feliz sin sentirse siquiera un poquito culpable?' (p.162), the book unveils the hitherto closed lesbian world of Mexico City. Whilst foregrounding the love-life of the principal character, Lupe and her passionate relationship with Claudia, it also includes reference to the romantic travails of many other lesbian characters and almost wholly immerses the reader in a lesbian world that is ruptured only by the violent intrusion of male violence, as we have seen. The negative representation of conventional relations between men and women is juxtaposed with the continuous elevation of lesbian love and is evoked as a progressive route to self-fulfillment and happiness. This points to a radical political message that, again, borrows much from earlier feminist discourses on lesbianism and heterosexuality.

---

80   'Meditación en el umbral', in *Poesía no eres tú: obra poética*, p.316.

Elena Martínez suggests that Roffiel's vision of lesbian eroticism owes much to the work of African American feminist writer, Audre Lorde, who is quoted at the beginning of Amora.[81] She reads the novel as deeply indebted to Lorde's unapologetic view that eroticism may be claimed as a source of female empowerment. Lorde writes, 'When I speak of the erotic, then, I speak of it as an assertion of the life-force of women; of that creative energy empowered, the knowledge and use of which we are now reclaiming in our language, our history, our dancing, our loving, our work, our lives'.[82] Roffiel borrows from this sense of *joie de vivre* and her unabashed portrayal of lesbian love reflects this. Much of the eroticism of the book is concentrated in the one chapter entitled, 'Seguramente así aman las diosas' approximately half-way through the text. This chapter describes in vivid terms the love-making of Lupe and Claudia:

> Tú, te ofreces como flor, como ola gigante. ¡Qué deseos de besarte! Pero sólo te veo y te veo... y no me atrevo a tocarte. Tus aromas me envuelven. Te siento, amor, te siento (p.71).

The rhythmic lyricism of passages such as this one replicates the physical act of love-making and would seem to endorse Lorde's view that the creative energy of women is released through such acts.

In other sections, the use of repetition has a similar function: 'Ven, vamos a amarnos, y amarnos y amarnos, y a no parar de amarnos' (p.71). Moreover, it is only in this section that Roffiel has recourse to imagery and where the prose departs from the more journalistic tone of earlier sections:

> Agua de luna, fresca, con puntos de plata. Sábana de encaje. Sudario de luz. Lecho de nácar. Dos mujeres. Dos. Cara a cara en este juego irrepetible que es el amor. [...] El tiempo no existe. Sólo esto. Fusión de suspiros, tormenta de ecos. Qué embriaguez. Qué júbilo. Un vuelo de tórtolas sobre tu cuerpo. Nido de alondra tu nido (p.71).

81   'Privileging Lesbian Eroticism: The Works of Rosamaría Roffiel and Nancy Cárdenas', in *Lesbian Voices from Latin America: Breaking Ground* (New York and London: Garland Publishing Inc, 1996), pp.117–18.

82   Audre Lorde, *Uses of the Erotic: The Erotic as Power* (Trumansburg, New York: Out and Out Books, 1978), pp.3–4.

These passages resemble more prose poetry than the conventional omniscient narration of the earlier sections. The sentences are truncated, in some cases to one word, and images drawn from nature are employed to evoke the cosmic dimensions of their love. Indeed, the kind of cosmic bonding envisioned by the dance ceremony in which the women swayed together in harmony and quoted earlier, returns here in the relationship between Lupe and Claudia: 'Bajo las sábanas, amor que pertenece al Cosmos, dos mujeres se aman con un lenguaje secreto, alejadas del mundo. A pesar de todo' (p.72).[83] In these concluding sentences, Roffiel suggests the coded nature of love between women, their need for a different and secret language and isolation from the rest of the world. It ends with a short but nevertheless trenchant reference to the difficulties and heartache endured to reach the love they have finally attained. Present here again, though, is that sense of abyss – the idea that it is only when 'alejadas del mundo' (p.72) that this erotic harmony can be realised, and only then in the face of extreme opposition ('a pesar de todo'). Once again, there is an ambivalence expressed here in an allusion to the opposition and hostility encountered by the novel's protagonists with regard to their sexuality. This shadow enters the text in the form of a reminder that the attainment of this glorious love takes place only when removed from society and after a long struggle. Love here is enabled through shared secret languages but it is a cosmic love, not a worldly one and is wholly fulfilled only in secret and away from the world.

The text then, describes a gloriously erotic vision that imbues women with a strength, resilience and energy that is directly derived from involvement in relationships with other women. It also goes further than this in the sense that it highlights the structural and political dimensions inherent in the active negation of a heterosexual lifestyle. In Roffiel's work, love of other women is clearly conceptualised as an alternative way of being:

83 While the debt to Audre Lorde has already been noted, Roffiel also recalls the writing of French activist, Monique Wittig, and, in particular, her celebration of lesbian sexuality in *Le Corps Lesbien* (1973). Wittig has had a powerful impact on feminist theory with her philosophy of lesbian materialism articulated throughout a large body of work. See, in particular, *Les Guérillères* (1969).

242

> Claro, habría que aprender a amar de otra manera. Cambiar las canciones rancheras y los boleros por una música propia, inventada por nosotras y nuestra compañera (p.33).

Here too there is another parallel with Castellanos and her final play *El eterno femenino* in which she appeals for reinvention: 'Hay que reinventarnos'.[84] So too does Roffiel and the desire for new definitions, for an 'other' kind of love finds expression at various points in the text:

> Existimos unas que todavía pensamos que el amor puede ser distinto, que no es necesario enamorarse apasionadamente para construir una relación de pareja, que hay otras formas además de la convivencia y la posesividad, que luchamos cotidianamente contra los celos, que damos una importancia tremenda a la libertad y la privacía de nuestra novia, que tratamos de hablar con honestidad para no dar cabida al resentimiento, en fin, que nos esforzamos para que nuestro amorcito sea un oasis adonde correr despues de un día de trabajar en el gobierno, hacer cola para tomar el Ruta 100 o respirar plomo y amibas desde las siete de la mañana (p.34).

This idea of a struggle connects the notion of lesbian love directly to feminist praxis and the desire to radically restructure sexual and familial relations. In the conversations about the unsatisfactory relationships with men endured by the female characters, relationships with women are posited as escape, as a positive choice leading to greater personal fulfilment: 'Para mí, descubrir que podía amar a las mujeres fue tan importante como para Colón descubrir América' (p.34). Sexual relations with women are posited as entirely distinct from heterosexual relationships between men and women:

> Mira, generalmente con los cuates todo empieza por lo físico. Te conoces, te gustas y casi enseguida te vas a la cama. Es raro el tipo que primero quiere conocerte y amarte y luego cogerte. Ya si después del sexo se da la comunicación, pues qué suertuda. A mí, con las mujeres me pasa al revés: primero se da la conocencia profunda, y lo sexual viene luego, como una consecuencia lógica (p.64).

---

84 *El eterno femenino*, p.194.

The idea that relations with women are diametrically opposed ('con las mujeres me pasa al revés') underlines the idea of an abyss existing between heterosexual and homosexual choices, a vision which is further enforced by the many disparaging references to *bugas* (heterosexual women) and their baiting of the different lesbian characters. The novel ends on a high note, however, as Lupe seems to have found an inner fulfilment in her work with the organisation and on a personal level through the development of her relationship with Claudia. As she explains, 'Total que, la neta, ando contentísima' (p.161). The text then has apparently located Castellanos's 'otro modo de ser' and has forged a way forward for its female protagonists that, while it confronts the brutal extremes of patriarchy on a daily basis, also allows space for the self to find sexual pleasure and a sense of fulfilment. It is in this way that the vision remains intact and uplifting.

Conclusions

Thus *Amora* presents itself as a radical deconstruction of heterosexuality, an energetic advocate of the importance of the feminist struggle, a celebration of lesbian love and a defiant testimony to the ongoing battles being waged in Mexico on the subject of gay rights. Like Loaeza, Roffiel foregrounds the concerns and everyday lives of middle-class women in the metropolis of Mexico City, highlighting the multiple contradictions and tensions of modern urban existence. At times, enthralling, at times profoundly irritating, they are texts that challenge and provoke on various levels – emotionally, intellectually and culturally. Their voices are again ambivalent – Roffiel's in the way in which the violent extremes of patriarchy explode into her text to expose the gaps that endure between the groups she depicts. The middle-class emphasis leaves no space for the consideration of more systemic problems, gendered or otherwise. In this way, this text never strays from its comfortable feminist community radiating solidarity and sisterhood. Loaeza's vision, however, is even more complicated as she attempts to resolve the complicity of her own positioning while maintaining a political relevance. Ambivalence remains, thus as a defining and persistent presence in the work of both of these women writers as they grapple for a stake in the Mexican literary arena, and as they seek to advance the causes of women who though often triumphant in their texts, face obstacles that constrain their freedom in real and painful ways. These texts are a testimony to that indomitable strength and courage, as Roffiel says, 'a pesar de todo' (p.72).

Chapter Five
Postcolonial Journeys: Transnational Spaces in Silvia Molina and Sara Sefchovich

In this final chapter I return to the work of Silvia Molina and Sara Sefchovich, completing a cycle of sorts in the book as a whole. The chapter focuses on what might be termed the authors' transnational fictions, in particular *La señora de los sueños* (1993) by Sefchovich and *Muchacha en azul* (2001) by Molina. These texts are obsessively concerned with locations and contexts outside of Mexico in dramatic contrast to the novels studied in Chapter One which, has we have seen, were fixated on Mexico. Their turn towards the transnational is an interesting choice. Mary Louise Pratt contends that many books receiving attention from the late 1980s onwards were aggressively transnational in character. She writes, 'In letters, at least in Latin America, women intellectuals over the past hundred-fifty years have operated in terms not of national patrimonies but of eclectic transnational canons'.[1] In Mexico, it would certainly seem that the appeal of the transnational to women writers appears obvious given their ambivalent status as outsiders to the nation state. The pre-occupation with the nation in Mexican literature – as witnessed so vividly by the texts discussed in Chapter One – has been widely acknowledged. Indeed, according to Victoria E. Campos, one of the most notable changes evident in post-1968 Mexican narrative is a return to the national past.[2] Silvia Molina points out that most

1   Mary Louise Pratt, 'Criticism in the Contact Zone: Decentering Community and Nation', in *Critical Theory, Cultural Politics and Latin American Narrative*, pp.83–91, p.84.
2   Victoria E. Campos, 'Toward a New History: Twentieth-Century Debates in Mexico on Narrating the National Past', in Santiago Juan-Navarro and Theodore Robert Young (eds), *A Twice-Told Tale: Reinventing the Encounter in Iberian/Iberian American Literature and Film* (Newark: University of Delaware Press, 2001), pp.47–62, p.48.

historical novels recently published in Mexico have fictionalised the country's immediate past. The rationale for doing so, she argues, has been to create a 'contemporary chronicle of Mexico'.[3] These books, along with many others written in the 1980s and 1990s that eschew Mexico completely, would seem to point to another preoccupation by writers and artists – the need to negotiate spaces outside of Mexico as a way of envisioning the present and interrogating the past. Many contemporary writers, including Elena Garro, María Luisa Puga and Carmen Boullosa write texts that are set outside Mexico.[4] In many of these cases, this concern with places other than Mexico is indeed a way of imagining the 'contemporary chronicle of Mexico' that Molina describes. In the texts examined in this chapter, the transnational locations function precisely in this manner – as an external lens through which to focalise modern Mexico. In this way, the exploration of spaces outside of Mexico becomes an important tool in the discovery of the country itself.

In this chapter, I will examine *Muchacha en azul* (2001) by Silvia Molina and *La señora de los sueños* (1994) by Sara Sefchovich with a view to exploring the ways in which they foreground transnational space as central to personal identity formation. This happens in a number of ways – literally, through the physical locations of their texts which span a diverse range of countries and continents, but also figuratively, as spaces in which their protagonists seek self-realisation. Both texts are grounded in a postcolonial dynamic that seeks to redress the position of women vis-à-vis the traditional patriarchal

3   Cited in Victoria E. Campos, 'Toward a New History: Twentieth-Century Debates in Mexico on Narrating the National Past', p.48.

4   Some notable examples include, María Luisa Puga, *Las posibilidades del odio* (1978) which is set in Africa and Elena Garro's *Inés* (1995), which is set in France. Carmen Boullosa's *Son vacas, somos puercos* (1991) combines a multiplicity of perspectives including European, African *mestizo* and Caribbean in her re-working of the adventures of the character, Jean Smeeks. Aside from its appeal to women writers, one of the best-known Mexican novels of the 1990s, Jorge Volpi's *En busca de Klingsor* (1999) is also set outside Mexico and features as its central protagonist, a North American physicist, Francis Bacon, aided by a German mathematician, Gustav Links, who go in search of Klingsor, reputed to be a scientific advisor to Hitler.

constructs of family and nation. In Molina's novel, this happens via a postcolonial unravelling of the conventional dichotomies that characterise first world/third world relations in a way that rather optimistically hints at the possibility of reconciliation between the two. These dichotomies are played out through the two principal protagonists, Hilda, the young Mexican protagonist sent to Paris to escape her violent family, and Herman Sulzer the Swiss geologist with whom she becomes infatuated.

In Sefchovich's *La señora de los sueños*, the text revolves around a nomadic female subject who 'travels' through literature to diverse locations, not just vicariously participating in the lives of her book's protagonists, but actively undergoing a process of transformation whereby she 'becomes' these women and occupies new subject positions. There are many points of connection between the two texts. First, they insist on the impossibility of family in the conventional sense, a notion that was dramatically undermined in their earlier work. Second, both texts dismantle the patriarchal family construct and tentatively offer 'travel' as a means of escape, however tenuous or unsatisfactory that may prove to be. Dreams, too, are central to both texts: in Molina's novel, the 'Parisian' dreams are placed in direct opposition to the dreams of 'Mexico' which are imagined in a completely different way. In *La señora de los sueños*, as the title suggests, the female protagonist is a dreamer who takes refuge in the other worlds of her books as a way of fleeing the dreary tedium of her housewife's life in Mexico City. In this chapter, I aim to explore the ways in which female identity is constructed through a continuous negotiation between self and place. While the journeys that take place in both texts differ considerably in many ways, what remains pivotal is the way in which identity is constituted as a fluid process which takes place in a transnational time and space marked by pluralism and heterogeneity. The texts explore two different approaches to female subjectivity: in *Muchacha en azul*, Molina exposes the limitations of a binary system of identity organisation and in *La señora de los sueños*, Sefchovich explores a nomadic or 'rhizomatic' identity as a progressive model for female subjectivity. In this section, I draw heavily on

Deleuze and Guattari's notion of the 'rhizome', as an emancipatory model for identity formation.[5]

Muchacha en azul: Unravelling Dichotomies

Published in 2001, *Muchacha en azul* marks another distinguished step in Silvia Molina's career as a writer and returns to the dialectics between subject and place that have long haunted her work.[6] It narrates the story of Hilda who is taken to Paris by her half-sister, Flora, in order to remove her from the family home, and particularly from the violent, conflict-ridden relationship between her parents. She is initially deeply antagonistic towards her sister and takes refuge in memories of her beloved home in San Juan. Hilda meets Herman Sulzer, a Swiss geologist, at an embassy reception and is fascinated by his promise to tell her the story of 'Africa'. After this meeting, the text engages in a continuous juxtaposition of their two stories, moving fluidly from Herman's journeys through Mexico and Africa as a geologist, to Hilda's personal journey through Paris, including the development of her friendship with Natipah – a Malaysian girl in her class at school – and the relationship between Flora and her Peruvian boyfriend, Enrique. Just as Hilda finally begins to acclimatise to her new life in Paris, Enrique attempts to rape her and, to escape his

5   See *A Thousand Plateaus: Capitalism and Schizophrenia* (Minneapolis: University of Minnesota Press, 1987).

6   Molina's novel, *La mañana debe seguir gris*, which won the Premio Xavier Villaurrutia in 1977, is set in London. The structure of *Muchacha en azul* is reminiscent of this novel in the way in which it juxtaposes the story of the current life of its protagonist – narrated retrospectively – with fragments from the protagonist's diary written during the formative turbulent years spent far away from home. Much of Molina's subsequent work focuses on Mexico: *La familia vino del norte* (1987), *Imagen de Héctor* (1990) and *El amor que me juraste* (2000). *Muchacha en azul* marks a return to her preoccupation with the outside world and her interest in the central importance of place in identity formation.

250

advances (the text does not make clear whether she escapes before or after she has been raped), she throws herself off the apartment balcony and breaks her leg. It is this incident that severs her connection with Paris and Flora sends her back to Mexico. On her return to Mexico, Hilda is reunited with her brother in the home of her aunt. The final sections of the text concern a chance encounter with Herman Sulzer in the airport and a burgeoning friendship between the two in Mexico City. The novel ends just as Herman is finally about to tell her the story of his life in Africa, thereby fulfilling the request she made of him many years previously.

The transnational preoccupations of the text are signalled immediately by the opening italicised section in which Hilda meets Herman in Mexico City airport many years after they first meet at the Mexican Embassy in Paris. Though the primary location of the text's protagonists is Paris, the novel meanders and criss-crosses a diverse range of locations including Mexico, Africa, New York, Pakistan and Algeria. Indeed, initially it seems to ground itself firmly in a post-colonial dynamic in which the subject, torn away from her beloved Mexico, is transplanted to a grey and forbidding Paris. While debates about postcoloniality often rather problematically include reference to Latin America,[7] I would contend that this text reproduces many of the

---

7   It is widely acknowledged that much of the emphasis in postcolonial studies is on former French and English colonies and that the term, 'postcolonial' is rather more problematically applied in relation to the colonies of the former Spanish and Portuguese empires. Steven Bell writes, 'With regard to the postcolonial, as with so many other critical/theoretical terms in current usage, the Latin American occupies an eccentric, a richly ambiguous, in-between position. These qualities, ironically, may make the Latin American case exemplary, even quintessentially postcolonial. The Latin American is not sufficiently white/European/imperial to be homogenized, nor sufficiently black/non-Western/colonial to be tokenized. It writes in Spanish, not in English – though this today is itself in question. Its formal independence came too long ago, and so it has not recently enough been "liberated", yet for this same reason, in many regards, it has always been "postcolonial", precocious rather than belated'. *Critical Theory, Cultural Politics and Latin American Narrative*, p.25. Furthermore, debates around postcoloniality are more frequently articulated in terms of notions of subalternity (described by Beverley as a subset of postcolonial studies), around which the Latin American Subaltern group

251

elements associated with the colonial/postcolonial relationship.[8] These include the intense concern with place and the emphasis on self/place relationships along with the notion of resistance in the form of the subaltern subject, Hilda. Furthermore, it features an unsettling of the stark binary divisions underlying the material reality of the colonial-postcolonial relationship (developed-underdeveloped, first-third, rich-poor, civilised-barbaric) that succeeds in destabilising those categories. This unravelling happens in a variety of ways as this chapter will aim to illustrate. Initially, the postcolonial resistance is signalled by Hilda's emphatic assertions of her hatred of Paris. These punctuate the text throughout and operate as an effective disavowal of European grandeur. In this way, she displays the exile's hostility and disgust at an environment she cannot understand.

At first, the opposition, Mexico-Paris, is established unproblematically. Hilda's plaintive refrain, 'no me gusta París', is juxtaposed with fond memories of a colourful, exoticised San Juan:

> En San Juan sábados y domingos, el calor, la humedad y el campo sembrado de caña y maíz esperaban la llegada de Hilda y su hermano. Los acogía una casa

formed. See *Subalternity and Representation: Arguments in Cultural Theory*, p.16. The debate around postcolonialism and Latin America is wide-ranging and extensive. See, for example, Rolena Adorno, 'Reconsidering Colonial Discourse for Sixteenth- and Seventeenth-Century Spanish America', *Latin American Research Review*, Vol.28, No.3 (1993), pp.120–4, Brett Levinson, 'The Limits of Postcolonial Theory After Said/Bhabha, or: Is Latin America a Postcolonial Site?', *Journal for the Psychoanalysis of Culture and Society*, Vol.1, No.2 (Fall 1996), pp.144–57, Water Mignolo, 'Colonial and Postcolonial Discourse: Cultural Critique or Academic Colonialism?', *Latin American Research Review*, Vol.28, No.3, pp.120–13, Patricia Seed, 'Colonial and Postcolonial Discourse', *Latin American Research Review*, Vol.26, No.3 (1991), pp.181–200, and Hernán Vidal, 'The Concept of Colonial and Postcolonial Discourse: A Perspective from Literary Criticism', *Latin American Research Review*, Vol.28, No.3 (1993), pp.113–19.

8   The colonial/postcolonial relationship has been typically characterised as being concerned with difference, hybridity, the dialectics of self and other or language and place, myths of authenticity and identity, preoccupation with genre, mimesis and abrogation, among many others. See Bill Ashcroft, Gareth Griffiths and Helen Tiffin, *The Empire Writes Back: Theory and Practice in Post-colonial Literatures* (London: Routledge and Kegan Paul, 1989).

de tejas rojas, llena de canarios y cenzontles, de tulipanes y buganvilias y de limoneros y naranjos, cuidada por los campesinos del lugar (p.19).[9]

In passages such as this one, the nostalgic longing for Mexico is poignantly described and Paris is invoked in 'enemy' terms, as the hostile aggressor who has taken her from her family:

> Era un desatino que no le gustara París, sí; pero en la penumbra de aquellos lugares estrechos, vetustos y sucios, sólo pensaba en escapar porque estaba allí a la fuerza, porque su madre la había entregado con todo (p.16).

It becomes clear at a much later stage in the novel, that the rupture with Mexico metaphorically signifies the separation from the mother, a trauma that is deeply embedded throughout the text and which is only clarified in the final letters exchanged between Hilda and her brother, Toni. During her early days in Paris, it is Hilda's fervent dislike of her surroundings that is emphasised:

> – No me gusta París.
> Hilda había comenzado a sentir el viento fresco del otoño parisino y deseaba el sol ardiente de San Juan, los volcanes nevados de la carretera, los campos de flores silvestres... La superficie verde de México, la que debía venderse en tiempos de lluvia, decía el abuelo sonorense, cuando sus terrones no se desmoronoaran por la sequía. Quería escuchar otra cosa distinta de los cláxones y los enfrenones y las protestas del taxista. Para consolarse, reconstruía sonidos familiares y apreciables, como el tañer de las campanas de las iglesias de San Juan Bautista llamando a misa, o el de las guitarras de los campesinos que cantaban sus corridos al anochecer, o el de las chicharras anunciando la lluvia. Incluso evocaba el balido de los borregos y las cabras y el mugido de las vacas arreadas por los pastores al filo de la carretera entre San Juan y la ciudad de México. Ése era el mundo en el que había crecido y el que le llenaba los sentidos y que no existía en París y que añoraba. [...]
> – No-me-gus-ta-Pa-rís.
> – No lo repitas – masculló Flora, enojada [...]
> – No me gusta París, aunque sea una tontería – insistió (pp.22–3).

This 'tontería' is repeated many more times in the text ('¡No me gusta París! ¡No me gusta! ¡No me gusta!', p.38)[10] and has the effect of

---

9   All page references are from *Muchacha en azul* (Mexico City: Joaquín Mortiz, 2001) and will appear after the quotations in parentheses.

inscribing resentment towards the European capital, characterising it as an impersonal, urban nightmare, in contrast with the provincial heaven that is colourful San Juan. This dichotomy is illustrated through Hilda's dreams which are divided into the Mexican dreams that belong to her past, and the Parisian dreams of her nightmarish present:

> Entonces soñaba que:
> Montaba un alazán por el campo, y luego de galopar, lo paraba de manos.
> Veía un perro atado y, compadecida de oírlo ladrar, lo soltaba.
> Volaba por encima de los árboles hasta llegar a las montañas que rodeaban San Juan.
> Su papá se rompía una pierna y no podía caminar.
> Su mamá se cortaba el pelo y se veía hermosa.
> No volvería a la escuela, que le gustaba más que su casa, porque las maestras se habían enfermado.
> Su hermano se quedaba a vivir en el norte y no volvía a verlo.
> Sus padres se daban la espalda y cada uno caminaba para su lado.
> Tenía una familia feliz (pp.14–15).

These dreams are worthy of consideration in various respects. First, they invoke images of both freedom and control and in Freudian terms represent her helplessness in the face of the family conflicts and her desire for escape.[11] Second, the wish to see the father, 'broken' and unable to walk, may be read, again in terms of a Freudian displacement of her hatred and disgust of him. The dreams of her brother (exiled far away) and her school (closed because the teachers are ill) are dreams of anxiety that demonstrate the perpetual disquiet she feels with regard to the only relationships that are presented as satisfactory and fulfilling. The passage ends with the image of the happy family, an image that is of course only possible in dreams, and represents the

---

10   'Pero, a pesar de todo y en definitiva, no vivía contenta en París. Los franceses no eran amables. La conserje siempre estaba de mal humor' (pp.96–7).
11   Freud's theories on dream formation are well known. We have already examined them in relation to the texts examined in Chapter Two. Here suffice to say, his two central concepts (displacement and desire) are woven into the dream thoughts of Hilda in the different locations.

collapse of this illusion in the text. In contrast, the dreams of Paris are confused and disorientating:

> Luego, en la época de París, soñaba que:
> Flora no era su media hermana sino la cocinera de San Juan.
> Para salir de París se subía a un autobús de la ruta 5 que la llevaba a México. Y México era una feria.
> Su hermano era director de una orquesta y
> su padre un violinista.
> No encontraba a sus papás por ningún lado.
> Su mamá no hablaba español sino chino.
> Pasaba un tren que debía llevarla a su casa, y ella lo perdía.
> Encontraba a Herman Sulzer en el súper y en el metro y en el cine, pero no podía hablar con él porque, cuando se acercaba, había cambiado de cara... (p.15).

That the dreams are completely different is perhaps the first obvious, but nevertheless significant element to highlight. Here too, there are frustrated attempts to escape: the bus that would bring her directly to Mexico and the train that would take her home but that she misses. What is underlined here, however, is a lack of communication and the problem with language, highlighted no doubt by the linguistic alienation she feels in Paris. Indeed, her mother no longer speaks Spanish, but Chinese instead, a further indication of their estrangement and separation. This inability to communicate is present explicitly in Hilda's futile attempts to make contact with her mother from Paris. It is not until much later that she learns that her mother has left San Juan and is living elsewhere with a new partner. The confusion of the other images constitute a mixture of desires and unarticulated anxieties. She dreams that Flora is not her sister (desire), that she cannot recognise Herman's face because it has changed (anxiety) and that her brother is leading her father (desire) – all clear signals of her tormented mental state. At this early stage in the text, Paris is conceptualised as hostile, aggressive and dark, whereas San Juan is invoked in lyrical terms emphasising its light and beauty. It is possible, therefore, to read the text as a postcolonial critique in which Mexico is privileged over Paris, the major European capital whose one positive feature, according to Hilda, is its *avenida Jorge V* precisely because it recalls the delights of Mexico.[12] In this way, the exilic melancholy so prominent in studies of the exile condition, is displayed explicitly.[13]

Hilda, according to this configuration, functions as postcolonial rebel, insisting on the primacy of the original location and emphatically rejecting the European original in favour of its more exotic 'other'. In this way, she embarks on a process of distancing herself from the European 'centre', asserting her difference and emphasising her dislike. Victoria E. Campos, in her interpretation of Edmundo O'Gorman, attests to the continued primary role of Europe in America's visions of itself and suggests that 'America was animated from without; in using colonialism as its means of passage to universal authority, Europe had led the Amerindian territories from historical specificity to historical and historiographical dependency'.[14] While this seems to suggest a rather simple binary distinction – Mexico (good)-Paris (bad) – it is immediately problematised in Molina's novel through her juxtaposition of the different dreams. These seem to suggest that the binary division is ultimately more complicated and subtle than would initially appear. The rather conventional configuration, good-bad, therefore, is immediately undercut and becomes

12   This sense of recall, triggered by visual stimuli such as the *avenida* in this example is explored in Uruguayan writer, Mario Benedetti's short story, 'Geografías', from the eponymous collection. In this story, the principal protagonists engage in a game in which they force themselves to recollect every minute detail of Montevideo as they remember it. Benedetti has written extensively on the psychology of exile, outlining what he calls, 'las siete plagas del exilio' in the following manner: 'el pesimismo, el derrotismo, la frustración, la indiferencia, el escepticismo, el desánimo y la inadaptación'. See 'Sudacas del mundo, unios', in *El desexilio y otras conjeturas* (Madrid: El País, 1984), pp.51–2. See also *Geografías* (Madrid: Alfaguara, 1984).

13   Melancholy has long been isolated as central to the exilic condition: 'Under various guises, exile means separation, banishment, withdrawal, expatriation, and displacement; its emotional expression is loss, usually manifested as sorrow, though sometimes as nostalgia', Robert Edwards, 'Exile, Self and Society', in María-Inés Lagos-Pope, *Exile in Literature* (Lewisburg: Bucknell University Press, 1988), pp.15–31, p.21. In many formulations it is combined with longing, nostalgia and what Mario Benedetti terms, 'derrotismo'. See also, John Glad, *Conversations in Exile* (Durham: Duke University Press, 1993).

14   'Toward a New History: Twentieth-Century Debates in Mexico on Narrating the National Past', p.52.

256

increasingly complicated as the text progresses. By the novel's end it has become completely dismantled, and in the next section I shall document how this process of dismantling occurs.

Dialogues With the 'Other'

It has been apparent from the passages already cited from the text that the novel constantly returns to Mexico through Hilda's nostalgic memories of San Juan. However, as her life changes completely through her 'encounter' with Paris, 'other' stories start to intrude and erupt into the Mexican narrative. These stories are channelled through other characters, primarily Herman Sulzer and Hilda's schoolfriend, Natipah. Their stories of Africa and Malaysia respectively, rupture the continuity of the Mexican narrative, throwing it into question and disrupting its centrality in the text. It starts with Hilda's friend, Natipah, and detailed descriptions of her homeland:

> Malasia, llena de montañas en el interior y de valles cerca de un mar azul como el cielo de Malasia, no como el de París. En Malasia había bosque y selva y monos y serpiente, y la gente cultivaba arroz, pimienta, té, piña y coco, y exportaba petróleo, hule y estaño (p.51).

As Natipah and Hilda's friendship develops, a dialogue of sorts commences in which their 'different but similar' cultural heritages are compared: 'Las dos habían crecido cerca de los plátanos y los mangos, pero Natipah no conocería el aroma de los hule de noche, ni Hilda el de la tierra bendecida por el monzón' (p.55). Both relate the histories of their respective countries in counterpoint: Natipah presents a full two-page outline of the history of Malaysia (pp.51–3), which is then countered by Hilda:

> E Hilda le contó a Natipah que ella sabía una historia parecida, porque antes de que los aztecas llegaran al valle de México (lo aprendía todo mundo en la escuela), habían peregrinado por todos lados porque nadie los quería, hasta que le pidieron al señor de Culhuacán que les concediera un lugar para establecerse,

257

y éste los envió a Tizapán con el propósito de que las víboras ponzoñosas, porque había miles allí, los mataran; pero cuando los aztecas vieron las culebras, se alegraron, las asaron para comérselas y acabaron con ellas. Y más adelante fundaron lo que después sería la ciudad de México, donde su dios les había dicho que lo hicieran: al encontrar un águila devorando una serpiente. Y la vieron sobre un nopal en un islote. Y por eso, le aclaró a Natipah, el escudo de México era un águila parada en un nopal devorando una serpiente (p.53).

There follows an interesting exchange in which both perspectives are presented one after the other:

Cuando Natipah le explicaba a Hilda la conquista de Malasia por los portugueses al mando de Alfonso d'Albuquerque, [...] ella le contaba de la de México por los españoles. Cuando describía la fusión de las culturas asiáticas en Malasia o alguno de sus mitos, Hilda le contaba las historias que repetía la gente de San Juan sobre el Señor y la Señora Dos que tuvieron cuatro hijos (pp.53–4).

Viewed from a postcolonial perspective, this constitutes the insertion of both Asia and America into the over-arching European narrative (Paris) that binds them together. On an allegorical level, of course, by competing for textual space in this way, they enact ancient power struggles. Hilda and Natipah's shared colonial pasts are emphasised and many bonds of intimacy are established that transcend the linguistic, cultural and religious barriers between them:

Natipah escuchaba atenta como si esos mitos le recordaran los suyos. Y cuando se dolía de la llegada de los holandeses y los ingleses, Hilda permanecía callada. Entonces el silencio se volvía gris y frío [...]
A veces se entendían por medio de dibujos, cuando, por ejemplo, Natipah no sabía cuál era la diferencia entre las pirámides mexicanas y las egipcias o no podía entender cómo eran las casas de San Juan, pintadas de colores vivos y brillantes con sus techos de tejas de barro y sus patios con geranios (p.55).

In this narrative, therefore, two third world female subjects, far from their homes, collide in an alienating Paris and find solace in their shared history of colonisation and conquest. Despite the vast socio-cultural and religious differences between them – Natipah is Muslim, from an immensely privileged background and enters into an arranged marriage (much to the disbelief of Hilda) – they share common ground and forge a solid friendship that is sorely missed by Hilda when Natipah returns to Malaysia and to her arranged marriage. The micro-narrative of Malaysia enters into a dialogue with Mexico in a way that would seem to challenge the centrality of Paris as the backdrop to the novel and call into question its supremacy. In this way, Hilda and Natipah form what Chandra Talpade Mohanty has called, in direct response to Benedict Anderson's study, an 'imagined community of women', with 'divergent histories and social locations, woven together by the *political* threads of opposition to forms of domination that are not only pervasive but also systemic'.[15] Not wishing to indulge in any idealised versions of 'global sisterhood',[16] the alliance between the Mexican and the Malaysian girl here does seem to uphold some notion of solidarity that is somehow old-fashioned and yet contemporary at the same time. As Gayatri Chakrovorty

15   Chandra Talpade Mohanty, Ann Russo and Lourdes Torres (eds), *Third World Women and the Politics of Feminism* (Bloomington: Indiana University Press, 1991), p.4.
16   Debates surrounding the term 'global' feminism have been contentious. Robin Morgan's anthology *Global Sisterhood*, which envisions notions of solidarity between women based on a shared experience of oppression, have been much criticised, perhaps most vocally by Chandra Talpade Mohanty. She takes issue with Morgan on a number of grounds accusing her of being ahistorical, of erasing the effects of contemporary imperialism, of denying women's agency, of rendering invisible the privilege of her own political location and for generalizing about women's experience across cultures. These two diverging viewpoints effectively encapsulate the debates within feminist theory during the 1980s and 1990s, between those arguing for the political necessity of strategic essentialism (mostly activists) and anti-essentialist critics dedicated to the politics of difference (mostly academics). For a useful overview of this debate see, Chris Weedon, *Feminism, Theory and the Politics of Difference* (Oxford: Blackwell, 1999) and Uma Narayan and Sandra Harding (eds), *Decentering the Center: Philosophy for a Multicultural, Postcolonial, and Feminist World* (Bloomington: Indiana University Press, 2000). See Chandra Talpade Mohanty, 'Sisterhood, Coalition and the Politics of Experience', in *Feminism Without Borders: Decolonizing Theory, Practicing Solidarity* (Durham: Duke University Press, 2003), pp.106–38. See also Morgan's interesting defence of the viewpoint underpinning the anthology, *Sisterhood is Global: The International Women's Movement Anthology* (New York: Anchor/Doubleday, 1984). http://www.feminist.com/resources/artspeech/inter/sisterhood.htm (last accessed 16 April 2007).

Spivak has argued, there is a need to 'negotiate between the national, the global, and the historical, as well as the contemporary diasporic'[17] if we are to imagine diverse feminist alliances across distinct material circumstances. To return to Pratt, it would seem that these subjects inhabit a contact zone that is represented by Paris but that then bypasses Paris in order to consider the contemporary histories of other nations and other subjects. Pratt defines the contact zone as:

> an optic that decenters community (and its corollary, identity) to focus on how social bonds operate across lines of difference, hierarchy, and unshared or conflicting assumptions. Such an approach would consider how differences and hierarchies are produced in and through contact across such lines.[18]

In the same way, the novel's focus on social bonds and the way in which they connect across lines of difference, interrogates the whole notion of community. There are no French protagonists in the book: Natipah is Malaysian, Flora's boyfriend is Peruvian, Flora and Hilda's great friend Doña Filotea is Catalan, Herman is Swiss-Mexican and even Hilda's teacher, Mademoiselle Anita, is Polish in origin. In this way, Paris operates as a displaced, decentered space in which diasporic characters from all over the world converge and communicate.

The cultural splendours of Paris are assiduously ignored through Hilda's consistently negative attitude towards the city and likewise, the centrality of European history is displaced by the continuous echoes of the histories of Asia, America and Africa. When Herman and Hilda meet at the embassy, he makes reference to the Second World War, an event of which she is almost completely unaware:

> – Cuando tú naciste – exclamó el geólogo –, ya se había acabado la guerra.
> – ¿La guerra?
> – La segunda (p.39).

That she is unaware of this important event in European history underlines again how Europe is displaced from the narrative, even though it is notionally set there. While the text does make reference to

17   *Outside in the Teaching Machine* (New York: Routledge, 1993), p.278.
18   'Criticism in the Contact Zone: Decentering Community and Nation', p.88.

contemporary French reality, it is significant that most of its commentary is reserved for the war in Algiers, which was raging in 1962, when the text is set:

> Tenía miedo a la Guerra de Argelia, porque los del Front de la Liberation Nationale andaban cazando *pieds noirs* y poniendo 'plásticos' que estallaban por todo París; y los de la Organization Armée Secrète habían comenzado una campaña terrorista en Francia de la que todo mundo hablaba. Habían querido matar a De Gaulle.
>
> La detenían con frecuencia para que mostrara sus papeles, y sentía que en una de ésas se los iban a quitar para llevarla presa (p.97).

This anxiety about being mistakenly taken for Algerian is expressed elsewhere in the novel (p.46) and indeed the Algerian question is developed at length. In the following passage, Hilda sees a news item on the issue on the television and discusses it with her sister:

> Una noche, mientras cenaban despues de ver el noticiario en la televisión, Hilda había interrogado a Flora:
> – ¿Qué pasa en Argelia? ¿Por qué ponen tanto plástico?
> Y Flora le explicó que, a pesar de que los argelinos se habían opuesto con las armas durante años, perdieron su territorio en 1875; y que desde entonces los franceses habían establecido en Argelia un regimen militar (p.98).

She first learns about Algeria from Flora, but later too from her teacher, Mademoiselle Thérèse:

> Hilda sabía, por las clases de Mademoiselle Thérèse, que al término de la Primera Guerra Mundial la economía de Argelia había tenido un rápido desarrollo, cuyo beneficio no llegaba a los argelinos.
> Y ahora entendía, por la explicación de Flora, que el Frente de Liberación Nacional había declarado la guerra a los franceses y que en esos momentos había un gobierno provisional de la república de Argelia en El Cairo, y que por eso en París se dejaba sentir la lucha clandestina del Ejército de Liberación Nacional.
> – ¿Y qué va a pasar? – preguntó.
> – Nada – se equivocó Flora.
> – Quiero regresar a México – aventuró Hilda (pp.98–9).

Here then is another interesting digression into yet another First-Third World encounter, but in this case it is a contemporary struggle that is both bloody and brutal. The alignment of Hilda with the Algerians, by virtue of her dark skin, further accentuates the connections and again would seem to draw parallels between the Third World locations explored in the novel. The European story, therefore, is dislodged from its traditional status as central to give way to a grid of intersecting histories from which Hilda emerges. It is through her encounter with these other histories – the teachings of Flora and Thérèse in the case of Algeria, and Natipah in the case of Malaysia – that Hilda embarks on a process of self-discovery. In this way, location is used, as Kaplan explains, to 'destabilize unexamined or stereotypical images that are vestiges of colonial discourse and other manifestations of modernity's structural inequalities'.[19] The process of unravelling, therefore occurs in this novel through the hybrid interplay of the complex relationships between women in different parts of the world. Before continuing this examination of the unravelling process, it is necessary to consider the colonial aspect of the text, embodied in the enigmatic figure of the geologist, Herman Sulzer.

Herman Sulzer and the 'Dark' Story of Africa

We have seen how Natipah, and, to a lesser extent Flora, are responsible for the transmission of some of the 'other' marginalised stories in the novel. It is Herman Sulzer, however, who is the primary vehicle through which the 'other' stories of the text are articulated. Herman becomes an object of fascination for Hilda when she meets him first at the Mexican embassy in Paris. He is characterised in many ways as the archetypal coloniser, and his attitude and comments are those that firmly uphold classical binaries of First-Third, civilised-barbaric and old-new. I would like to turn now, then, to the representation of Africa in the text as a way of further illuminating the colonial relationship present. Herman's mentality is first seen in reference to Africa, the memories of which punctuate the text and are

19   *Questions of Travel*, p.187.

juxtaposed with his stories about Mexico. Most of his accounts of Africa emphasise its 'savage' and 'unpredictable' nature. In one anecdote he recalls the time when his African companions ate a female gorilla, despite the fact that her young were nearby and depending on her for survival. In another tale, he is horrified by his companions' refusal to accompany a pregnant woman to get help because of their superstitious beliefs ('aquí nadie carga a mujeres embarazadas, sobre todo si no son de su tribu', p.116). In many parts of the novel, reference is made to Herman's deformed and scarred hand, and indeed it is the constant deferral of this story that in many ways constitutes the novel's mysterious heart. Hilda's earnest entreaty that he tell her the story of Africa and his, equally earnest, reply that the story of Africa is 'para mayores' only, successfully stimulate the reader's interest in this story which is finally divulged in the closing pages of the novel.

Herman's account of how he came to damage his hand relates how his desire for a woman from another tribe, one of the chief's favourite women, lead to his close brush with death. When trying to lead her away from the celebrations towards his tent, they fall into an elephant trap and he hurts his hand. People come to the rescue and a young man offers his hand to pull him out. Herman realises with horror, however, that the hand is leprous. He therefore takes the drastic decision to cut around the wound in order to avoid infection and is hence left with a disfigured and scarred hand. The account, like most of his accounts, is immersed in details that confirm the 'savage' and 'unpredictable' nature of the Africans. It is also, however, a moment of self-realisation:

> Ya en la cabaña se lavó la herida y se vendó la mano con otro pedazo de la camisa; y no pudo hacerle el amor a la muchacha. [...] Pensaba en la lepra, en el jefe bantú, en su reputación, en su deshonor, en que habría pasado si la chica hubiera muerto, en el precio que pondría a la joven si era descubierta, y él ya tenía una mujer, para que demonios quería otra (p.156).

Much of the language here recalls Frantz Fanon's classic treatise, *Black Skin, White Masks*,[20] and may be located within conventional colonialist dichotomies that feature Africa as 'dark' (the episode happens at night), dis-eased (the hand is leprous) and dangerous (the place is full of elephant traps). Furthermore, the descriptions of his desire for the women could hardly be more obvious. In short, all the colonial tropes are present here in this clichéd account of a coloniser's African adventure. And yet much of the novel revolves around the anticipation of this African revelation. When it actually comes, it almost disappoints in its inevitability and conventionality. Reading the story allegorically then, the kind coloniser (metonymically signifying 'First World') is actually betrayed by the young man (signifying 'Africa') in that the offer of help is proffered by an infectious diseased hand that actually endangers the coloniser's life. Here the blood of the two men is actually mixed, causing horror in Herman as, in a classic abject image, his hand is literally 'polluted' by the infectious African.[21] In addition, he goes to great lengths to rid his hand of the 'pollution' risking permanent deformity as a result. Thus Herman retreats from Africa, startled and profoundly disturbed by the dangerous collision with its forces of darkness. In the following passage,

20   Fanon's work, published in 1968 remains essential reading for any understanding of the colonial/postcolonial relationship in its exploration of the feelings of dependency and inferiority experienced by black people living in a white world. *Black Skin, White Masks* (London: Pluto Press, 1986).

21   Kristeva's account of abjection, as was discussed in Chapter Two, owes much to Mary Douglas's work. The notion of the abject as the collapse of corporeal boundaries is analysed by Douglas: 'Matter issuing from them [the orifices of the body] is marginal stuff of the most obvious kind. Spittle, blood, milk, urine, faeces or tears by simply issuing forth have traversed the boundary of the body. [...] The mistake is to treat bodily margins in isolation from all other margins. *Purity and Danger: An Analysis of the Concepts of Pollution and Taboo* (London: Routledge and Kegan Paul, 1969), p.121. In this conceptualization, the spilling and consequent mixing of blood represents a crossing of bodily boundaries that is dangerous and represents pollution. It is also important to remember that much of the ideology associated with women's confinement to the home in the Americas was directly linked to the fear of miscegenation and the desire to maintain purity of blood. See Jean Franco, *Plotting Women: Gender and Representation in Mexico* (London: Verso, 1989), pp.xiii–xvii.

264

he considers his narrow escape, thinking about his relationship with Beatriz, his African lover:

> Pensaba en Beatriz y su reacción si llegaba con aquella mujer. Tal vez no le diría nada porque estaba acostumbrada a compartir al macho, como las leonas de una manada. Ambas pertenecían a un mundo que no era el suyo, uno que no parecía real, donde no había pastel de cumpleaños, partido de futbol, medias de seda para las mujeres como ellas, hora del té, copas de Baccarat ni vajilla de Limoges (p.156).

Here the opposition (first world subject-African other) is evoked in bleak terms and the animal imagery employed in relation to the women, like lionesses in a pride, is positioned in dramatic contrast to the world characterised by birthday cake, football and silk stockings. He goes on to elaborate:

> No. Allí no había chocolate ni queso suizo ni el beso de las buenas noches. *Vivía otro mundo:* uno de abrelatas y cacerolas de cobre y latón, de platos de madera, de machetes y cuchillos, de arcos, flechas y lanzas, de botas para la selva y mangas para la lluvia, de insectos y antílopes y leones y simios, de explosivos y detonadores... donde no podían reconciliarse los dos mundos (p.156, my emphasis).

In this passage, no fusion of the two worlds is possible and they can only be envisioned in terms of opposition, contrast and irreconcilable difference. The two worlds remain separate and the abyss between them remains uncrossed. In this context, the escape to Mexico provides a respite of sorts, though it continues to be immersed once again, in colonial discourses. I shall continue my discussion of Herman's Sulzer's role by looking at his lengthy evocations of Mexico, which proves to be the most formative location in his life.

The Mexican Journey

Herman's journeys through Mexico position him in much the same way as the journey did in Africa. Hilda conjures up an image of him:

> A veces, también, lo imaginaba en una casa colonial, como solían tener los extranjeros en México, con un cigarrillo en la boca revisando unos planos en un estudio amplio y de buen gusto, donde tendría libreros de madera fina, atiborrados de libros: unos sobre Suiza, otros sobre México, algunos más sobre África (p.65).

Colonial attitudes are exhibited too by other Swiss characters in the text, including his father's teacher who, on hearing that Herman's father wants to go to Mexico, says, '– ¿De verdad, Sulzer, ¿quiere viajar a ese país de bárbaros? ¿A ese país de salvajes que se andan matando?' (p.36). With statements such as these, he unwittingly endorses modes of thought that have fixed divisions between First and Third worlds within such rigid parameters. This colonial mentality shines through in many of the accounts offered by Herman of his various stays in Mexico and his experiences with the community of people involved in geology there:

> Herman había entrado a Petróleos Mexicanos en 1953, asignado al norteño estado de Tamaulipas. Las oficinas estaban en el puerto de Tampico, una ciudad pretenciosa, sucia y desordenada, con un sofisticado barrio inglés donde habían vivido en casa estilo europeo los empleados de la Waters Pierce Oil Company, la Tampico Navigation Company y la Huasteca Petroleum Company (p.107).

In passages such as this one, Herman's position is undoubtedly that of the European whose collision with the Third World is marked by a binary filter that codifies the Third world (Mexico, Africa) as dirty and disordered, and who takes refuge in the pseudo-colonial centre of the 'English quarter' where all the foreign oil corporations are housed. Much of Herman's account of his stay in Mexico is suffused with biting criticism of the country and is delivered authoritatively. This is evident, too in his memories of Africa:

266

> Se convirtió, como los otros geólogos, en el jefe de una nueva tribu ir-
> reconciliable consigo misma: ya daba órdenes, ya organizaba las comidas de los
> trabajadores o actuaba como juez en los pleitos y las venganzas (p.40).

As in his jobs in Mexico, he assumes a control over his 'subjects' in a way that assigns him a European authority that appears absolute.

Just as Natipah and Hilda drew many parallels between Malaysia and Mexico, Herman also points, on various occasions, to the similarities between Mexico and the Congo where he worked for many years. In the following passage, his trip to Mexico is described:

> Entonces Herman tomó un greyhound y salió rumbo a México con la idea de
> dar con sus antiguos conocidos y recobrar la memoria de lugares y personas y
> de aromas como el de una tortilla recién hecha que confundía en el recuerdo
> con el maniok africano (p.85).

He outlines this connection on several occasions:

> Cuando Herman llego al Congo, tenía la impresión de haber estado ahí antes
> porque de niño había viajado a Guerrero, en la costa mexicana del Pacífico, con
> sus padres:
>   Las palmeras.
>   La vegetación exuberante.
>   El río Balsas lleno de peces y lagartos.
>   Un calor del demonio.
>   Las lagunas de Acapulco (p.39).

This exuberant evocation of the similarities between the Congo and the coast of Guerrero in Mexico, also attempts to disrupt the linearity of the text through its irregular positioning of the phrases in almost poetic fashion. In this way, he seems to indicate the impossibility of capturing the experience of these places in linear, regular form.[22] Not-

---

22 This inability of language to adequately capture the colonial/postcolonial experience figures prominently in debates on the conquest of the Americas. Raymond Dolle writes, 'Often avowing the indescribable nature of the wonders they had witnessed, the [...] written responses to the New World adapted Old World language and schema to evoke and interpret the unfamiliar scenes, and thus they heralded a new literary tradition', 'The New Canaan, the Old Canon, and the New World in American Literature Anthologies', *College Literature*, Vol.17, Nos.2–3 (June–October 1990), p.202. Edmundo O'Gorman discusses

withstanding the beauty inherent in this description, there is also a hint of menace with the reference to the 'demonio', constituting a sinister element that is present in almost all the descriptions of place attributed to Herman in the novel. The poverty and underdevelopment of both continents are continually asserted and exposed by Herman in a manner that is strikingly reminiscent of colonial accounts.[23] In this way, he reproduces systems of power that stratify the world into developed-underdeveloped, primitive-sophisticated and that are frequently aligned with First and Third worlds respectively:

> Cuando cambió de autobús en la frontera de México, aquel 26 de Julio, volvió súbitamente a instalarse en la pobreza de África, pues viajaba con hombres y mujeres indígenas que llevaban bajo los asientos gallinas y pavos amarrados de las patas, y olían a estufa de carbón, a sudor y a humanidad (p.85).

this 'invention of America', noting the linguistic imagining of a New World through a colonial lens. See *The Invention of America: An Inquiry into the Historical Nature of the New World and the Meaning of Its History* (Bloomington: Indiana University Press, 1961). See also, Tzvetan Todorov, *The Conquest of America: The Question of the Other*, trans. by Richard Howard (New York: Harper and Row, 1984).

23   Joseph Conrad's *Heart of Darkness* (1902), remains perhaps the classic 'colonial' text in the West in this regard. It has been critiqued from various perspectives, most notably by postcolonial writer, Chinua Achebe, who denounced the novel and its author as offensive and racist. 'An Image of Africa: Racism in Conrad's *Heart of Darkness*', *Massachusetts Review*, Vol.18, No.4 (Winter 1977), pp.782–94, reprinted with responses in Robert Kimbrough (ed.), *Heart of Darkness: An Authoritative Text*, Norton Critical Edition (New York: Norton, 1988), pp.251–62. For an excellent overview of the debate, see Inga Clendinnen, 'Preempting Postcolonial Critique: Europeans in the *Heart of Darkness*', *Common Knowledge*, Vol.13, No.1 (Winter 2007), pp.1–17. In the American context, there are numerous accounts of the conquest including Alvar Nuñez Cabeza de la Vaca, Bartolomé de las Casas and Bernal Díaz del Castillo. For an introduction to some of these works, see Susan Castillo and Ivy Schweitzer (eds), *The Literatures of Colonial Americas: An Anthology* (Oxford: Blackwell, 2001), and Francisco Javier Cevallos-Candau, Jeffrey A. Cole, Nina M. Scott and Nicomedes Suárez Araúz (eds), *Coded Encounters: Writing, Gender, and Ethnicity in Colonial Latin America* (Amherst: University of Massachussetts Press, 1994).

The stench of humanity testified to in this passage highlights how Herman sees little difference in terms of abject poverty between Africa and the Americas and he insists on this parallel being drawn throughout the novel, 'Herman vivía en México como había aprendido a hacerlo en África; de una manera salvaje; indomesticable' (p.70).

It is clear that Herman's account of Mexico is grounded in a colonial perspective that views it as underdeveloped, corrupt and poor. However, it is this perspective that serves as dramatic counterpoint to the glorious memories of Mexico's ancient past as recounted in Hilda's stories to Natipah. Flora too, through her work in the Consejo Nacional del Turismo (Office of Tourism) is involved in promoting the touristic delights of Mexico to the Parisians:

> La Oficina de Turismo donde su hermana promovía las ruinas y playas de México, y hablaba a los turistas de la cultura de los grupos indígenas mexicanos:
> – En la época de la conquista española, había varios pueblos indígenas importantes además de los aztecas y los mayas, sabe (p.47).[24]

24 Flora takes great pride in her family history and the story of her *bisabuelo materno* is recounted at length in the text: 'Allí estaba el bisabuelo materno de uniforme. Había nacido en un pueblito llamado Mochicahui, donde su padre se había asentado después de su llegada de España al puerto de Guaymas. Aquel bisabuelo había sido gobernador de Sonora, siempre lo presumía aunque no dijera que sólo cuatro meses, ya que la Legislatura le concedió licencia ilimitada porque el se sentía más soldado, que gobernante. Flora no ignoraba que se había sublevado en el distrito de Álamos en contra de la administración del coronel Ignacio Pesqueira, que había ocupado la población y proclamado el Plan de Álamos. Sabía que había sido senador en cuatro ocasiones, que había perseguido a los apaches echándolos del estado y que había sido el promotor del canal construido sobre la margen derecha del río Yaqui, la obra de ingeniería más importante de finales del siglo; pero callaba, cuando le contaba a Hilda, quien había sido aquel ancestro, que si por algo sería recordado en Sonora era porque fue veinte años el terror de los yaquis y su verdugo, y se había convertido en terrateniente gracias al territorio que le había quitado a los indios, cuya enorme extensión dotaba de agua el canal. Ese bisabuelo había adquirido varias propiedades, entre las que estaban el rancho del Pozo, la hacienda Garambullo con su molino harinero, a la que le cambió el nombre por Europa, y la hacienda de San Carlos, que se extendía por las vegas del río Sonora hasta las playas del golfo de California; propiedades que su abuelo, que estaba en otra fotografía, perdió en malas inversiones (p.131).

Herman's encounters with the inefficiencies and the corruptions of Mexico's public service are juxtaposed with Hilda's lyrical evocations of San Juan. They are contrasted further with Flora's idealisation of Mexico's beauty, packaged for consumption by Europe, in another example of appropriation and colonisation. What is perhaps most interesting however, is that while Herman's account anchors Mexico as one side of a limiting binary opposition with Europe, this account is being undermined elsewhere in the text by Flora and Hilda. His descriptions serve therefore as a cautionary reminder of the unreliability of the colonial account and call into question the narrative of Mexico as corrupt, backward and primitive.

Herman's lengthy descriptions offer a sharp critique of the country's limitations and problems. There is, for example, a pronounced emphasis on the despair and frustration felt by geologists, both Mexican and foreign, with regard to economic developments during the 1940s and 1950s:

> Después de la expropiación petrolera, nadie quería comprar el petróleo mexicano, hasta que comenzó la Segunda Guerra Mundial y Los Estados Unidos decidió levantar el boicot a México y el país pudo desarrollarse; pero la geología mexicana seguía en pañales.
>
> A los tres meses de haber llegado a Tampico, Herman Sulzer descubrió que los mexicanos no sabían hacer las exploraciones; a los once, algo peor; que los mexicanos eran corruptos y cínicos. Gastaban el dinero de Pemex en comidas, cenas y fiestas privadas, y hacían aparecer los gastos como si fueran de trabajo; y como estaba acostumbrado al orden germano, un domingo fue a las oficinas, tomó los expedientes de la contabilidad y la mañana del lunes se presentó ante un juzgado a levantar una demanda por robo y corrupción (p.109).

This stinging criticism of corruption and abuse of public funds resonates throughout Herman's account. Indeed, as a result of his negative experiences in Tampico during which time he attempts to legally hold the company accountable for its misdemeanours, he leaves and goes to work at the university. His father writes a note of gratitude to his old friend, Doctor Varela who facilitated the move:

> *Gracias por salvar al ingenuo de Herman de esos infames. ¡Sólo a él se le ocurre ir a los organismos oficiales a denunciar la deshonestidad! México*

sería un gran país si su gente fuera honrada, porque trabajadora sí lo es; eso lo sabemos tú y yo... (p.110).

The same sentiments are echoed later in Herman's equally negative assessment of the Mexican university system:

> Herman Sulzer renunció a la universidad cuando se dio cuenta de que era el modelo perfecto del desorden que existía en la mayor parte de las oficinas del gobierno mexicano; y porque el reducido presupuesto del Instituto de Geología no lo dejaba desarrollar sus proyectos. Además, tampoco allí trabajaba la gente:
> Los jefes y coordinadores salían a comer tomándose más de dos o tres horas, costumbre muy arraigada en la burocracia mexicana (p.133).

It is clear, therefore, that Herman Sulzer operates as a narrative filter through which this contemporary, highly critical, chronicle of Mexico is transmitted. As always, however, what seems to be a simple colonising or external perspective is complicated by Sulzer's increasing attachment to Mexico. He comments to Hilda on the positive impact Mexico has in general on the Swiss:

> – Los suizos en Suiza podrían ser fríos y parcos, pero en México se habían mexicanizado y eran alegres, solidarios y generosos – le comentaría Herman a Hilda (p.89).

By the time the text draws to a close, Herman is definitively 'mexicanised':

> 'Yo ya no me voy de aquí a ningún lado', pensé, 'ésta es mi segunda patria, aquí me quedo. Soy mexicano. Ya no me voy a ninguna parte, a ninguna puta colonia a empujar negros para que trabajen.' Y aquí estoy (p.89).

Here, the narrative echoes familiar colonial-postcolonial lines in which the coloniser becomes more attuned to the 'natives' and more estranged from his 'roots'.[25] By the time Hilda meets Herman in the

---

25   This narrative has, of course, been explored in multiple forms, through, for example, the chronicles of Alvar Nuñez Cabeza de Vaca. Shakespeare's *The Tempest* still remains one of the most nuanced explorations of postcolonial relations. Caliban's speech in which he acknowledges the importance of language in his conquest and appropriation constitutes a compelling description of the dynamics of colonial power: 'You taught me language, and my profit

airport, he has become to all intents and purposes, 'Mexican' and is unrecognisable from the aloof Swiss she met in the embassy twenty years before. Herman, thus, also contributes to the process of unsettling of dichotomies that occurs throughout. The process of identity formation in Herman's case, therefore, is closely linked to his trajectories through Africa and Mexico, and cements the connection between self and place that is so vital in Molina's work. It is on this process of identity formation that I would like to focus in the next section.

Self and Place: The Return 'Home'

The final section of the text relates the attempted rape of Hilda by her sister's boyfriend, Enrique, and her subsequent escape over the balcony of the apartment. As a result of her fall, she breaks her leg thereby necessitating her return to Mexico to live in her aunt's house where her brother now resides. It is in this latter stage of the book that the text suggests the possibility of reconciliation between two viewpoints (that of Hilda and Herman) which has been hitherto unimaginable. In narrative terms, the continued and insistently negative imagining of Paris continues as it is the site of a grotesque attempted rape on the fifteen year old Hilda by the predatory Enrique, whose lascivious glances and disturbing comments have troubled her throughout the text. When he cajoles his way into the apartment under pretext and attempts to rape her, her mind takes refuge in her memories of San Juan:

> on't/ Is I know how to curse. The red plague rid you!/ For learning me your language!, Act I, Scene 2, lines 362–4. Fernandez Retamar's positively re-interprets the figure of Caliban as an iconic *mestizo* metaphor for a colonised Latin America. In this way, he refutes José Enrique Rodó's famous adoption of Ariel as a more appropriate symbol for the Americas. See, *Ariel* (Mexico City: Fondo de Cultura Económica, 1984), first published in 1900. See also Roberto Fernández Retamar, *Caliban and Other Essays*, trans. by Edward Baker (Minneapolis: University of Minnesota Press, 1989).

El peruano se estaba bajando el cierre de la chamarra, luchando por quitársela, porque se le había atorado el broche, cuando Hilda comenzó a ver por el balcón, por fin, algo conocido: la noche de San Juan.

Se sintió tranquila, como si el miedo y la tensión la hubieran abandonado. Estaba hueca, como si las manos del peruano la hubieran perforado y le hubieran sacado todo lo que tenía dentro. Comenzaba a flotar como si no estuviera sentada (p.186).

In her turmoil, her mind retreats into her memories of San Juan in order to endure the ordeal:

La oscuridad le impedía ver con claridad, a lo lejos, las copas de los árboles, que no eran los del Bosque de Bolonia sino los del campo de San Juan, pero escuchó la voz de su hermano que la estaba llamando para que saliera a acompañarlo a caminar por el pueblo a esa hora en que los grillos y los pájaros nocturnos comenzaban a cantar (p.186).

She imagines herself lifting off the sofa and reaching the balcony where the text informs us that she runs swiftly towards where the stars are waiting for her. Later it is clarified that she has thrown herself over the balcony, though it is not certain if this is before or after she has been raped, but more probably the latter. When she wakes up she finds herself in hospital and is about to tell her tale to Flora, when Enrique (whom she had not realised was there), interjects to inform them that it was lucky that he found her when he did. All hopes of her story being told and believed, therefore vanish and Hilda retreats to her familiar refrain, 'no me gusta París'. On this occasion, however, her sister finally listens to her and accedes to her request. She is sent home to her aunt, her left leg still in plaster after the 'accident', and thus her Parisian experience ends. There are of course interesting allegorical parallels here, in that Paris is the scene of the rape, as well as the abandonment of Hilda by her mother. Conversely, Mexico is posited as utopian refuge, as it is Hilda's dream of Mexico that 'saves' her from her ordeal with Enrique and enables her to escape. Again, therefore, Paris connotes negativity, loss of identity and violence, evoked in direct opposition to Mexico which, is positioned as Hilda's saviour. Even at this fairly late point in the narrative, therefore, the defining oppositions sustained throughout the novel continue to be upheld. It is on returning to Mexico, however, that these oppositions become definitively unsettled.

On her return to Mexico, we learn that Hilda tells no one about the incident in Paris:

> *Hilda no hablaba con nadie de sus padres, mucho menos del 'accidente'; ni siquiera con sus tíos que veían asombrados su capacidad para guardar rencor; y tampoco tocaba el tema con su hermano, cuando llegaba a verlo. Había enterrado su pasado [...]*
>
> *Durante mucho tiempo después de su regreso de París, soñaba con el peruano o su padre, y en los sueños los confundía como si ambos hubieran sido una sola persona. Despertaba llena de encono por no haber podido reclamarle nada a su padre, y llena de irritación y de rabia por no haber podido decirle a Flora cuánto asco le daba el peruano* (p.187).

In this passage, Hilda relates her personal tale of anguish and abandonment by her parents and links it directly through her dreams to the brutal episode with Enrique in Paris. In this way, the two stories of violence and betrayal converge. Furthermore, it is clear that on an allegorical level, the parallel narratives of Paris and Mexico also become more closely intertwined as the relationship between Hilda's sense of self and her location becomes ever more explicit. The emotions that have been suppressed throughout the text – the agony of abandonment, the frustration, the pain and sense of loss she experiences as a result of her parents' violent marriage and her own banishment to Paris, are finally revealed. This happens in a number of ways but primarily involves the correspondence with her brother, Toni which constitutes a heart-breaking and poignant narrative of abandonment and loneliness. It becomes clear that her emotional anguish has been filtered through the poignant refrain, 'no me gusta París', thus highlighting the ways in which emotion is channelled through experience of place. As her friendship with Herman develops, she is also persuaded to open up about her emotions and reflects on her childhood in a house rotting with violent abuse:

Al oír los detalles de la vida de los hijos de Herman, Hilda comenzó a pensar en la infancia y la adolescencia que habían tenido ella y su hermano. Recordó como escuchaba de niña, por la noche, el llanto de su madre después de una batalla. No la asustaban el ruido ni los golpes sino el llanto, el corazón herido de la madre que sangraba en forma de sollozos, y la ira y la turbación por la impotencia de ella y de su hermano para ayudarla o vengarla. Odiaba aquel silencio que solo permitía oír el desconsuelo.

Pensaba en su padre y lo imaginaba abrazándola, y le parecía inconcebible que aquel hombre, que la levantaba y la ponía sobre sus hombros para que cortara fruta en la huerta de San Juan, tuviera un lado escondido tras la sonrisa de padre y de esposo. Cuantas veces se había preguntado por qué era así. ¿Por qué, en qué momento de su vida se había transformado en aquel monstruo?

El llanto de su madre le llegaba con frecuencia en los sueños tan luego supo que había desaparecido, y en aquella época sus sentimientos hacia ella eran confusos. No sabía si verla como una mujer sometida al abuso de un hombre iracundo que tenía de su lado la fuerza, o como una madre cruel e insensible porque la había abandonado (p.169).

This moving deliberation on her parents' destructive and cruel relationship lays bare her emotional suffering. Hilda's literal displacement to Paris is articulated in direct parallel with the emotional displacement that she must undergo in order to survive. Therefore, the dialectics of self and place, of paramount importance in Molina's work as a whole, emerge here as place becomes a way of negotiating conflicts of identity. The novel continues its process of continual displacement when it discloses that Hilda has trained to be an anthropologist and has rejected a conventional lifestyle to embrace the life of a nomad, wandering the world involved in various diverse projects. This decision is attributed to her inability to forgive her mother for having abandoned her. The novel reveals that two years later, the mother re-establishes contact with both her and Toni but is rejected by Hilda. Her decision to adopt a nomadic lifestyle, therefore, is again, inextricably bound up with the loss of the mother, a connection that remains steadfast throughout. During this nomadic stage, she reconnects with Herman and it is with this encounter that the author chooses to end the novel.

Movement and Flux

The final part of the novel relates Hilda's experiences after her return to Mexico, revealed through her conversations with Herman. We learn that she adapts with great difficulty to life with her aunt and uncle in Hermosillo, and that, ironically, she comes to miss Paris and the freedom she enjoyed there:

> Hilda se aburría con la vida lenta y pequeñita de provincia, donde estaba mal visto que las mujeres salieran solas, donde no había nada que hacer, y donde los hombres, como su novio, se iban al boliche a tomar unas cervezas o al café saliendo del trabajo.
>
> En Hermosillo, donde vivía, no tenía por donde ir ni con quién conversar [...] Extrañaba París, la libertad que le había dado Flora para andar husmeando por todos lados. No sabía estar encerrada en una ciudad con vida de pueblo. Quería irse, huir, salir de allí.
>
> 'No me gusta Hermosillo', se repetía, como cuando le aseguraba a Flora: 'No me gusta París' (p.150).

It seems that a transformation has taken place in that Hilda now is only truly at 'home' when on the move, a lesson she has learned from her stay in Paris. As a result of the primary travelling through the streets of Paris and her secondary travels through Natipah and Flora to the exotic other locations of Malaysia and Algeria, Hilda's identity is now inextricably bound up with the dynamics of movement and flux. Indeed, her response to the trauma of the attempted rape was, of course, to flee, to run and escape, a chain of movement imposed upon her initially by her mother, who insisted she should go to Paris. It has now become an integral part of her self-identity and explains in part, her fascination with Herman, the perpetual traveller. This yearning for an identity characterised by plurality and heterogenity is echoed by her in the text during an earlier exchange: '¿Suizo o mexicano? ¿No era una contradicción ser las dos cosas a la vez? Ella era sólo mexicana' (p.38). The rejection of the singular subject is evident as she is drawn to a subject that seems both familiar and exotic at the same time.

Indeed, the vision of subjectivity that emerges during the final part of the novel seems to revel in the decentred nature of its protagonist. This is illustrated in a number of ways, one of which is her memory of Doña Filotea in Paris, whom she invokes when trying to explain her unease at the thought of a committed stable relationship:

> Se había enamorado a los 19 años, de un muchacho sonorense, directo y sencillo como la gente del norte. Un joven educado a la manera de provincia, quien se había deslumbrado con la frescura de una Hilda inquieta, pero quien no alcanzó a comprender a una Hilda ávida de experiencias e incansable, ni que a su novia le había pasado lo que Doña Filo le había pronosticado una noche en París: nadie podría pegarla al árbol otra vez; menos aún a un árbol que crecía en una población alejada de la ciudad de México, donde había pasado la niñez y parte de la adolescencia, y que no tenía ninguna oferta para retener una rama llegada del extranjero (pp.149–50).

In this passage, the classical metaphor of the tree is invoked as a way of illustrating Hilda's reluctance to become attached ('pegar'). Indeed the verb 'pegar' suggests related notions of sticking or fixing, elements that are rejected out of hand by the rootless Hilda. This notion of rootlessness has been examined at great length and is central to notions of identity as explored by the philosophers, Gilles Deleuze and Felix Guattari.[26] They employ instead the metaphor of the 'root-like' rhizome, which they define in opposition to the idea of the tree as follows: 'any point of a rhizome can be connected to anything other, and must be. This is very different from the tree or root, which plots a point, fixes an order'.[27] In the same way, Hilda's identity is formed via dispersed, transnational routes that connect traumatic experiences in Paris and Mexico, and which are filtered through mediated accounts of other worlds and other places including Malaysia, Africa and Algeria. Hilda emerges at the end of the novel as a travelling diasporic subject whose identity is characterised by a sense of perpetual movement and fluidity. This incessant travelling is set to continue, as evidenced in one of the final exchanges between Hilda and Herman:

26 See their work, *A Thousand Plateaus*. The notion of the 'rhizome' will be discussed in more detail in reference to Sefchovich's novel, *La señora de los sueños*.

27 *A Thousand Plateaus*, p.7.

- ¿Y qué haces? – preguntó Herman.
- Andar en el campo, como tú, supongo. Es mi vida (p.151).

Following the chance encounter with Herman in the airport, many years after their time in Paris, Hilda and Herman commence the conversation that Hilda had always longed for and both recount the stories of their lives to each other. This opening up of communication between them seems to suggest that the 'dos mundos' (p.156) referred to by Herman as distant and unbreachable are, in fact, capable of coming together. The novel thus, ends where it started, immersed in an intense concern with place as Herman and Hilda contemplate their shared surroundings:

> Hacía una noche agradable y fresca cuando Herman puso las botellas de vino en la mesa de la terraza, desde donde el panorama de la ciudad de México era inesperado: se alcanzaba a ver con claridad, allá abajo, la Universidad Nacional, y hacía el centro se distinguía algo que parecía ser la Torre Latinoamericana. Qué grande era la ciudad y que hermosa se veía antes de dormir (p.165).

In the closing pages, her idealised, dream-like lyrical Mexico, is fused with his less romanticised view. Their view which includes the National University and the Latin American Tower, both icons of modernity and progress in a Mexico that is on an ever-continuing path of expansion and *modernización*, crucially brings them together as they make a connection with the past that is forever present: '– Qué vista debe haber tenido Cortés al entrar a Tenochtitlán' (p.165). Their view is the same, forming a crucial link between the two gazes, the colonising gaze of Herman (in parallel with Cortés) is sutured alongside her, more ambivalently positioned gaze, as transnational nomadic Mexican subject.

In this way, the uneasy, tentative dialogue established in the text between Mexico and Paris, Mexico and Asia and Mexico and Africa is reduced to a singular Mexican vision but one that incorporates notions of the past (Tenochtitlán) and the present (the national university, the Latin American tower). Herman, as we have seen, has trodden the well-worn coloniser's path and is now a long-term resident of Mexico.

278

She, on the other hand, retains a strong hostility generally towards stability and place and has embraced a life that involves a constant interaction with the outside world as she has avoided the life that would be deemed suitable for her in her rejection of marriage. In this way, the dichotomies – coloniser-colonised and First-Third – have been challenged by the text's insistence on heterogeneity and plurality. Indeed, Hilda's position is best conceptualised in terms of an axis rather than a specific location. Her identity, therefore, is enabled and empowered by the hybrid interplay of the various discourses of place at play in the text. It operates, as Ella Shohat argues, 'at once within, between, and beyond the nation-state framework' emphasising again her fluidity and mobility.[28] Hilda's subject emerges, then, from the intersection of the various axes of identity that present themselves in the text. Location, Molina seems to suggest, is of paramount importance to identity formation. Indeed, it becomes a useful tool to attack conventional dichotomies that perpetuate age-old beliefs about self and place. As Kaplan points out, 'investigating location becomes an opportunity to deconstruct the binary formations of modernity in favour of the complex, shifting social relations that produce cultures, subjects, and identities in postmodernity'.[29] In the same way, the analysis of the shifting locations of Molina's text serves to deconstruct binary formations of modernity in so far as they relate to the colonial-postcolonial power dynamic. Location, is also pivotal to Sara Sefchovich's innovative look at female identity formation in contemporary Mexico. Furthermore, the enthusiastic embracing of nomadic life connnects Hilda with the protagonist of Sefchovich's novel and it is on this text that I will focus in the second half of the chapter.

28   Cited by Kaplan, *Questions of Travel*, p.186.
29   *Questions of Travel*, p.187.

La señora de los sueños: Nomadic Subjectivity

La senora de los sueños narrates the story of Ana Fernández, a bored, housewife, who is deeply unhappy in her home environment where she takes care of her husband and two children. In order to escape the numbing tedium of her daily routine, Ana begins to read and is transported to the world of her books where she takes pleasure and delight in the diverse lives of many different fictional protagonists. Transposing the lives of her protagonists onto her own, she enacts many of the stories in her own home causing her husband and children to doubt her sanity and to insist upon her seeking psychiatric help. The book alternates between Ana's 'stories' in which she actually becomes the protagonists of the novels she reads, and the sessions with the psychiatrist in which each member of the family in turn tells their version of what has happened to their mother. During these sessions, Ana's husband and daughter are largely hostile to Ana's alarming transformations, her son, Luisito, on the other hand is portrayed as empathetic and loving. As mentioned previously, there are many points of contact between this book and *Muchacha en azul*. First, both books take female angst as their basic premise: Ana Fernández is the clichéd bored housewife and Hilda is the abandoned child, bitter and unjustly treated. Second, both female protagonists take comfort and solace in their fantasies, Hilda in her dreams of the Swiss geologist – Herman Sulzer – and Ana Fernández in the books she devours. Third, *La señora de los sueños* bears testimony to the complete deconstruction of the patriarchal family ideal, a notion similarly undercut in Molina's text. Finally, the critique of Mexican society, so sharply observed through Herman in *Muchacha en azul*, is relayed in this novel through the humorous dynamics of the family unit. Here, the reader is exposed to the vanities and trivial excesses of bourgeois Mexican society, very similar, indeed, to the world exposed by Guadalupe Loaeza in *Compro, luego existo* and examined in Chapter Four.

La señora de los sueños narrates the extraordinary journey of Ana Fernández and constitutes an exploration of alternative subjectivity that is not just about vicarious participation but actual transformation. Indeed, what is perhaps most interesting about the text is the fact that the transformative, rhizomatic identities revealed in the travel sections are constantly brought back 'home', and shown to be in collision with the prevailing family structures. Ana's material reality, therefore, is never allowed to become effaced. On one level, the book, offers a radical new envisioning of subjecthood. On another, this radical new envisioning is deeply problematic, anchored as it is in fictionalised recreations of womens' lives that are rarely progressive in any sense of the term. As we will see, however, I argue that it is not in the actual content of the micro-narratives that the political charge of the text lies, but rather in the way the female subjects of the various stories form cross-cultural alliances that enable not only Ana's empowerment but, more importantly, that of her daughter, Lupe. It is on this process of alliance formation that I would like to focus in this chapter, taking my cue from the work of Gilles Deleuze and Felipe Guattari.

'The problem that has no name'[30]

Ana Fernández is presented to the reader as an archetype: that of the *abnegada mujercita Mexicana*, criticised by Rosario Castellanos in her essays and the focus of much Second Wave feminist political campaigns:

> Yo, Ana Fernández, pobre de mí, soy una mujer que se aburre. La vida me pesa, no hay nada que me interese y no le encuentro sentido a la existencia.
>
> Tengo el alma envejecida, me siento un trapo, una jerga, me estoy secando. Vivo en el hastío mientras las horas van limando los días y los días van royendo los años. Vivo como muerta en esta vida no vivida y se me escurre entre las manos la vida, mi vida.
>
> Nunca hubiera pensado que este vacío podía ser tan fatigoso. Paso tantas horas sin quehacer ni ocupación, los minutos se me hacen eternos inventando con qué llenar el tiempo. Me sé de memoria mi mundo tan estrecho, y no me emocionan sus ruidos y a ciegas encuentro sus rincones (p.13).[31]

Ana is the living embodiment of Betty Friedan's 'problem that has no name', a notion, as we saw in Chapter Four, that came to light during

---

30 This term was made famous, as was outlined in Chapter Four, by Betty Friedan's study, *A Feminine Mystique* (1963). The famous opening lines establish its premise: 'The problem lay buried, unspoken, for many years in the minds of American women. It was a strange stirring, a sense of dissatisfaction, a yearning that women suffered in the middle of the twentieth century in the United States. Each suburban wife struggled with it alone. As she made the beds, shopped for groceries, matched slipcover material, ate peanut butter sandwiches with her children, chauffeured Cub Scouts and Brownies, lay beside her husband at night – she was afraid to ask even of herself the silent question —"Is this all?"' Friedan's *The Feminine Mystique*, as was pointed out in Chapter Four, remains one of the cornerstones of Second Wave Feminism as it formally identified some of the most pressing problems created by changing gender roles after the Second World War and launched NOW (the National Organisation of Women) with a primary goal of offering women choices beyond motherhood and domestic duties. Chapter One of Friedan's text is available online at http://www.h-net.org/~hst203/documents/friedan1.html.

31 All page references are from *La señora de los sueños* (Mexico City: Punto de lectura, 2003) and will appear at the end of quotations in parentheses.

Friedan's exhaustive research into the situation of the middle-class housewife in suburban North America:

> Ama de casa, esa soy yo, ama y señora de mi hogar. Paso el día yendo de un cuarto a otro, aquí tiendo la cama, allá le doy vuelta a la sopa, ahora paso un trapo húmedo y después acomodo, una vez más, los adornos. Esta soy yo, la reina de la casa, la patrona de la licuadora, de la ropa sucia, de los sartenes y la plancha, la mujer libre para elegir si gasto mi tiempo en ordenar o en limpiar, si gasto mi dinero en jitomates o en pan, si gasto mi esfuerzo en el mercado o en el salón (p.14).

Like so many fictional incarnations before her, Ana struggles to survive in a reality that is tedious and soulless.[32] The reference to the beauty salon is also interesting. In Chapter Four, we saw how important this location was for the exploration of Guadalupe Loaeza's bourgeois protagonists, and Castellanos uses the site as a deconstructive tool in her satirical play, *El eterno femenino*, also discussed in Chapter Four. There is also a more sinister edge to Ana's life that begins to emerge when her son, Luisito, the only empathetic member of the family, attests to other aspects of her existence and in particular the control exercised by her husband. In this passage, he describes his father's fervent dislike of his mother's friends with understanding and compassion for his mother:

> Pero yo digo que no es justo, los demás tenemos nuestro quehacer y también amigos y paseos, ella en cambio no tiene amigas porque a él no le gustan y no la deja ir con ellas a tomar café ni que venga a la casa, dice que son puras viejas chismosas y ociosas que pierden el tiempo (p.24).

We learn, therefore, that Ana is not allowed friends, a rather unsavoury reminder of the level of authority enjoyed by her husband, an authority that turns violent at several points in the text. Violence, therefore, forms an integral part of the patriarchal family narrated in this text, forming another connection with Molina's construction of

32 See the plays of Dario Fo and Franca Rame, *Female Parts* and *A Woman Alone*, Rosario Castellanos's short story, 'Lección de cocina', Marilyn French's novel, *The Woman's Room*, Willy Russell's play, *Shirley Valentine*, to name only a few of the many theatrical and literary explorations of the figure of the suffering housewife.

the same, deeply flawed, concept. Ana it would seem, is following the same mould as Castellanos's protagonists, who will take refuge in other pursuits, reading, art, and therefore find an escape route from the oppressive lives they are forced to lead.[33]

In this way, the novel seems to be based on a relatively simple premise – the notion of books as escape. Debra Castillo, in her illuminating reading of the novel, cites Margaret Morse's designation of this as 'attenuated fiction effects', which she defines as 'a partial loss of touch with the here and now'.[34] As with Molina's novel, however, the text's world view is complicated considerably by the stories the author chooses to narrate, and the way in which Ana enters into contact with the worlds described. There are seven stories in total that span various continents and countries – Africa (Morocco), Asia (India), Europe (Russia), America (North, South and Central) – and which incorporate an interesting and diverse array of time-frames, perspectives and stories. There is no obvious link between the stories told, nor is it obvious why Ana might be attracted to the lives narrated within these stories. The first protagonist, Aisha, despite one happy marriage, ends her days as a destitute prostitute in Morocco. Maria Petrovna, the Russian protagonist of story two, enjoys the trappings of wealth and beauty but is frustrated in her personal life and is abandoned by her lover, the famous composer, Franz Liszt. The New York prostitute in story three wanders the streets in a drug-induced haze of disorientation and boredom. Camila, who features in story four, is a scientist who disguises herself as a man in order to live in the wild. She meets Charles Darwin on his travels to the Galápagos Islands and deeply influences his theory of 'natural selection'. Indeed, all references to her are removed from Darwin's work in order to protect him. The story implies that he was deeply ashamed of his attraction toward her, thinking, of course, that she was a man. The unnamed Cuban protagonist in story five – Castro's lover and helper –

---

33   This route is particularly emphasised in the short story, 'Domingo' in which the protagonist, Edith, takes refuge in her painting. See *Álbum de familia* (Mexico City: Joaquín Mortiz, 1971), pp.23–46.

34   'Reading Women: Sefchovich', in *Easy Women: Sex and Gender in Modern Mexican Fiction* (Minneapolis: University of Minnesota Press, 1998), p.153.

lives in Castro's shadow, anonymously, with little or no recognition from the outside world. Keren, the Israeli protagonist in story six, is in many ways, the most fulfilled of the characters outlined in the text. She achieves a measure of self-esteem through her work in the kibbutz and her embrace of religion at the end offers her inner peace. The final story features Maya (later Ananda) who functions primarily as a means to illuminate the work and life of Gandhi in whose entourage she spends most of her life.

There are links between many of the stories but nothing to connect them all, and while some showcase examples of female independence and innovation, most of the protagonists live their lives primarily through the men at their sides (Liszt, Darwin, Castro, Gandhi). Indeed, in these sections, it is clear that the female protagonist is entirely subordinate to the major male character under discussion. This is particularly the case in the stories on Cuba and India in which the protagonists live their lives in the service of the men they adore – Castro and Gandhi respectively. In some stories, there is an emphasis on positive loving mother-daughter relationships (Russian, Moroccan, Israeli). In others, however, this motif hardly figures at all. In some stories, the protagonists are openly promiscuous (Aisha, Keren, the New York prostitute), in others this element barely merits a mention (Galápagos, India). In some, the notion of one true love is exalted (Cuba), in others it is rigorously deconstructed. In short, it is difficult to attempt any coherent assessment of the 'content' of any of the vignettes that make up Ana's escape. Indeed, they seem to constitute a bewildering, confused never-ending narrative that refuses closure or coherence. Instead, what is absolutely clear is the insistence on plurality, heterogeneity and absolute non-conformity to any thematic continuum. The interest in this text, therefore, lies not in what the stories tell us but instead in how they embed themselves as part of Ana's identity, and in turn, how this transforms the material reality of Ana's home. Furthermore, the text ends on a celebratory note, as Ana contemplates with glee the endless possibilities of narrative escape that await her as peace and harmony are restored to her family home. In this way, the book shares another element with *Muchacha en azul* as it closes with another possibility of shared narrative joy. What the micro-narratives also illustrate, then, is the joy of story-telling and the alluring promise of freedom, a concept that reverberates throughout the text. It is this idea of 'freedom' that does connect Ana to the lives of the stories' protagonists and with this idea I will begin my discussion of her first narrative digression.

Nomads and Wanderers

The first story in which Ana takes refuge is the story of the young Arabic girl, Aisha, who leaves her home to enter into an arranged marriage. On her wedding night, Aisha and her husband are attacked by Bedouin nomads and she is taken as part of the bounty by one of the attackers. Mohammad, her new 'husband' is deeply religious, and affected profoundly by a recent trip to Mecca, has decided to keep Aisha pure. After several years living as nomads,[35] they leave the tribe and enter the city in order for him to better pursue his religious convictions. After many journeys, they arrive in Damascus where she lives as a recluse and sees her husband only infrequently. Mohammed is later crushed to death during a pilgrimage and she is left a widow. The narrative then turns in another direction as she is sold to a kind, considerate man, called Yusuf, and lives happily for a time in Granada. When he later dies from grief after the expulsion of the Arabs from Spain, she lives as a prostitute and finally dies destitute. As is apparent from this brief summary, this is a long, detailed story that meanders from place to place, and from man to man, over the course of almost sixty pages. Its form, therefore, is also nomadic, and the tale serves as a template for the other six stories, one of several reasons why I explore it here in depth. Recalling the excess of the descriptions in her earlier novel, *Demasiado amor*, discussed in Chapter One, the story of Aisha here is also excessive on many levels. As mentioned already, there is little in the content of this story to recommend it from a feminist perspective. Recounting the story of a

35   The text does not specify the number of years spent but there are references to several summers and several winters.

286

young girl sold at various points into marriage, it seems instead to highlight the oppressive conditions for women under patriarchal structures that would not seem to suggest its appeal as a means of escape for a woman, like Ana, in surprisingly similar circumstances. However, I would contend, as outlined earlier, that it is not Aisha's story *per se* that is attractive to Ana, but rather the emphasis on nomadic movement, the constant fluidity, the insistence on evolution and change that makes it a rather interesting and innovative arena for the exploration of an alternative subjectivity.

The story includes several long descriptions of Aisha's life in the desert after being abducted by the Bedouin tribe:

> Cuando amaneció, me encontré en un campamento beduino. Había perdido a mi marido, a mi camello y a los objetos que mi madre me había entregado para mi casamiento. Jamás los volví a ver. Después de esperar varias horas bajo el sol del desierto, un hombre llegó hasta mí y me habló: 'De hoy en adelante eres mía, pues yo te robé. Vivirás como nomada y el desierto infinito será tu hogar. No dormiremos dos noches en el mismo sitio ni nos acostaremos jamás en el mismo lugar en que hayamos despertado. Iremos por el mundo buscando agua y alimento, no sentaremos sobre pieles de camella con las piernas cruzadas y esperaremos a que terminen las noches heladas y empiecen los días hirvientes' (pp.35–6).

Aisha is subsequently put at the service of her husband's oldest wife who teaches her how to behave as a Bedouin nomad, and who sings and reads to her to pass the time. In this way, the novel reinforces the importance of the role of teacher played by women in novels in Mexico and reintroduces the motif of the older female teacher that was so apparent in *Muchacha en azul*.[36] In this description, the infinite

---

36 'Me enseñó [...] Me enseñó [...] Me leyó [...] me cantó (p.36)' This description evokes the same motherly warmth Aisha received from her own mother, who is described in similar terms at an earlier point in the story. Molina's text, it should be recalled, also featured women in teacher roles, Madame Anita and Thérèse were teachers and Flora, the elder sister who takes it upon herself at many points in the narrative to educate her younger sibling. This emphasis on the figure of the teacher reinstates the seminal importance of this figure in the Mexican project of national formation: 'It was female schoolteachers drawn from different classes who formed the nucleus of the first women's group to articulate what may be considered a feminist critique of

space of the desert is to become their home and they are to become nomads in a life that is full of endless movement.

The figure of the nomad has been the subject of intense critical interest from a number of different perspectives. Developed extensively by Gilles Deleuze and Felipe Guattari who draw on its diverse etymological roots, the nomad is frequently posited as a symbol of freedom, deterritorialisation and plurality.[37] Caren Kaplan characterises the generalised figure of the nomad as a symbol of hybridity, mobility, and flux. She maintains that 'the metaphorical nomad and theories of nomadology counter assertions of purity, fixed dwelling or being, and totalitarian authorities and social practices'.[38] Furthermore, she suggests that when Deleuze and Guattari 'pose "nomadology" against "history" they evince nostalgia for a space and a subject outside Western modernity, apart from all chronology and totalization'.[39]

society'. 'Introduction', in *Women, Culture and Politics in Latin America: Seminar on Women and Culture in Latin America* (Berkeley: University of California Press, 1990), p.3.

37 Indeed the etymology of the term, 'nomad' constitutes an interesting area of debate. According to Rosi Braidotti, '*Noumos* or plot of land is the etymological root of nomad which means the clan elder who supervises the allocation of pastures to the tribe'. *Nomadic Subjects: Embodiment and Sexual Difference in Contemporary Feminist Theory* (New York: Columbia University Press, 1994), p.26. John D. Erickson writes, 'The word *nomad*, from the Latin *nomad– nomas*, signifying a person belonging to a wandering pastoral people, derives etymologically from the Greek *nemein*, to pasture'. 'Nomadic Thought, Postcolonialism, and Maghrebian Writing', in H.Adlai Murdoch and Anne Donadey (eds), *Postcolonial Theory and Francophone Literary Studies* (Gainesville: University of Florida Press, 2005), pp.67–86, p.67. Critics argue that the concept of power is fundamentally different among these groups and that, 'The segmentary design of nomadic tribal groups, in which the role of the leader is essentially nominal and weak, and whose power depends on persuasion, reflects a structural form that diminishes control', p.68. John Durham Peters writes too on etymology, signalling, in common with Braidotti, the centrality of mobility to identity formation. See 'Exile, Nomadism and Diaspora: The Stakes of Mobility in the Western Canon', in Hamid Naficy (ed.), *Home, Exile, Homeland: Film, Media and the Politics of Place* (London and New York: Routledge, 1999), pp.17–44.

38 *Questions of Travel*, p.92.
39 *Questions of Travel*, p.89.

Sefchovich's text would seem to inscribe a yearning for a space that is anti-chronological and that will liberate both protagonists (Ana and Aisha) from the constraints of their respective lives. This space, in turn, is the desert which posits a different way of envisioning identity that transcends the limiting framework of the nation state and offers a glimpse at an 'other' mode of being. Deleuze and Guattari in their study of Kafka, make repeated reference to the desert as border or margin, linked to 'underdevelopment', *patois* and a 'third world'.[40] In this way, they posit the desert as a utopian, liberating space in which alternative identities may be forged. It is tempting to adopt this conceptualisation of the desert as a template within which we can view Ana's first textual journey. Viewed from this standpoint, the desert is a place, the 'tierra vacía' (p.35) in which she is freed from the constraints of her 'cárcel' (p.24), the word used by her son to describe the closed environment of the home. In contrast, her new desert space is all sky and sand:

> Las arenas formaban y deshacían dunas que el viento empujaba caprichos y el sol caía a plomo haciendo que todo se quejara de calor. La soledad y el silencio profundo eran nuestros acompañantes. Todo era arena y cielo (p.36).

This lyrical, almost utopian, evocation of desert life locates itself firmly within Deleuzian discourses of the desert. The idea of the shifting sands is reminiscent of the appealing notion of 'sand thoughts' which are free from the rational constraints of consciousness and which become possible once an individual is released in the desert.[41]

It is certainly true that the adoption of an 'other' identity – a subject that is free to roam and that is liberated from structures that are otherwise oppressive – offers a 'line of flight' to Aisha, another con-

---

40 *Kafka: Toward a Minor Literature.* Trans. by Dana Polan (Minneapolis: University of Minnesota Press, 1986), p.18.

41 John D. Erickson uses the term to evoke Deleuze and Guattari's description of nomadic thoughts as counterthoughts that are 'by nature violent, redolent of the steppe and the desert, destructive of images', 'Nomadic Thought, Post-colonialism, and Maghrebian Writing', p.73.

cept central to Deleuze and Guattari's visions of nomadology.[42] The journey seems endless and the search for water is never-ending, 'Y de nuevo fueron muchos días y noches de camino bajo el sol y bajo las estrellas, sobre las blandas arenas, comiendo dátiles secos y cebada' (p.45). Deleuze and Guattari identify nomadism as a model of deterritorialisation, which, as Kaplan attests, 'like most Euro-American modernist versions of exilic displacement, stresses the freedom of disconnection and the pleasures of interstitial subjectivity'.[43] She further points out that, 'In going "from one point to another" in the process of distributing "people (or animals) in an open space," nomads have "absolute movement," as distinct from migrants, who move in more determined and located ways'.[44] This absolute movement is signalled in the text, at various points, 'La vida siguió su curso entre las arenas' (p.39), and underlines the ideas of freedom and movement so attractive to Ana trapped in her home. Furthermore, the young Aisha never knows where she is going, another reason she appeals to an imbricated subject like Ana who is trapped in her home and a prisoner of her circumstances.

There are numerous references to the journeys undertaken by Aisha and her husband, Mohammed, but she is rarely aware of where she is going or the purpose of the journey: 'Fuimos por el desierto en largas jornadas ensombrecidas por su silencio. Yo desconocía nuestro rumbo y no lo supe hasta que nos acercamos a él' (p.40). Later, this lack of knowledge is emphasised again:

> Una mañana, antes del amanecer, salíamos de Al-Medina para emprender otra vez el camino. *Tampoco en esta ocasión sabía yo la ruta* que me esperaba que resultó ser la más larga que hubiera andado jamás (p.44, my emphasis).

The journey without end, again recalls Sefchovich's manic consumption of Mexico in *Demasiado amor*, and also Baudrillard's

---

42 'the rhizome is made only of lines: lines of segmentarity and stratification as its dimensions, and the line of flight or deterritorialization as the maximum dimension after which the multiplicity undergoes metamorphosis, changes in nature'. *A Thousand Plateaus*, p.21.

43 *Questions of Travel*, p.89.

44 *Questions of Travel*, p.89.

compelling exploration of the subject in *America* and other texts.[45] In the context of the nomad, of course, this journey without end vividly evokes the notion of deterritorialisation and identity without limits as well as infinite displacement and dispersion. These concepts are central to the way in which Ana's identity begins to slowly transform, and indeed, the possibility of another way of being is subtly suggested in the text itself. When her husband explains to her why she has been kept pure,[46] he outlines his rationale in the following manner:

> Por lo que he entendido de las enseñanzas de Mahoma, se trata de *una nueva manera de ser* y de creer, un código de fe pero también un código de conducta, y al mismo tiempo poesía (p.39).

Being is imagined here as part faith, part poetry, part code of conduct. In collapsing the boundaries between these very different systems, Sefchovich signals a way of being that is pluralist, heterogenous and echoes many of the concepts already outlined in association with nomadic identity. The passage, therefore, suggests an alternative way of being, a way that interrogates the notion of the single unified subject and opens up new possibilities of becoming.

The figure of the nomad, Aisha, functions then, as a symbol of hybridity, countering assertions of unity and positing instead a vision of endless heterogeneity and change. Rosi Braidotti reminds us that

45   In Chapter One, we noted the similarities between the visions of travel espoused by Sefchovich and those of Jean Baudrillard. Caren Kaplan invokes Baudrillard in her discussion of Deleuze and Guattari: 'The site of the desert, traditional home of the nomad, is not unlike Baudrillard's sublime, *sidéreal* space: empty, liberatory, and a margin for linguistic, cultural, and political experimentation'. *Questions of Travel*, p.87.

46   She learns from him that because she is exceptionally good and beautiful, she is to remain pure: 'Tú, Aisha, siguió hablando, eres piadosa y tienes buen carácter. Además tienes bella cara y bella voz. Has aprendido pronto y bien a servirme. Has resistido el polvo que tanto daña los ojos, has comido y dormido bajo las estrellas y te has sabido apretar el cinturon para no sentir hambre cuando escasea el grano. Has soportado las tormentas de arena y también las tormentas de palabras de los beduinos que hablan mucho, creyendo que la belleza del hombre radica en su elocuencia. Te he visto aguantar las injurias de las mujeres iracundas y conservar la calma. He visto todo esto en ti y me ha gustado' (pp.38–9).

'Nomadic consciousness is akin to what Foucault called counter-mmeory; it is a form of resisting assimilation or homologation into dominant ways of representing the self'.[47] Thus the subject, Ana, who 'becomes' Aisha, represents this notion of resistance and asserts herself, like Hilda in *Muchacha en azul*, as defiant rebel. In the next section, I will document how the notion of 'becoming' is developed in the text.

'Becoming Woman'

The process of 'becoming', which invokes de Beauvoir's now famous formulation,[48] is enabled through an intricate textual process that interrogates notions of coherence and linearity. It takes multiple forms but in the first micro-narrative, the story of Aisha, it happens in the following way:

> Esa noche no pude dormir, estuve inquieta y llena de culpa. Se me revolvían en la cabeza las historias que había leído con las caras de enojo de mi hija y las palabras tan feas de mi marido y para cuando amaneció había tomado la decisión de cambiar y ser una esposa como Dios manda.
>
> El problema es que no sé si puedo, porque no sé si sabré cómo se le hace. Creo que para serlo de verdad tendría yo que haber nacido allá, en Arabia, y haber aprendido desde niña, como a su vez habrían aprendido mi madre y mi abuela. Si así fuera, me habría gustado llamarme Aisha, como la esposa favorita del Profeta, y como a ella, a los siete años me habrían comprometido en matrimonio, dátil aún verde como dijo él. Pero eso yo no lo sabría, pues aún tendrían que pasar cinco años para casarme y durante ese tiempo nadie diría una palabra del asunto.
>
> Vivíamos en Taif, la Única, la amurallada, la fresca, la adornada con hermosas palmeras (pp.30–1).

---

47   *Nomadic Subjects*, p.25.
48   As we saw in Chapter Four, 'One is not born, but rather becomes, a woman', Simone de Beauvoir, *The Second Sex* (New York: Vintage Books, 1973), p.301.

292

As this passage demonstrates, the narrative shifts from the perspective of *yo* (Ana) to the first person plural voice of Aisha (and her family in this instance, 'vivíamos en Taif') almost imperceptibly. The lines between the two 'I' voices of the narrative are blurred and fuzzy. At some point in the second paragraph, between her desire to have been born 'en Arabia', and the next paragraph, Ana's voice is fused with Aisha's and their stories become intertwined in a very direct way. The blending of voices, this sense of connection, recalls Hilda and Natipah's dialogues in *Muchacha en azul*, and seem to point again to an idea of global sisterhood and commonality.[49] This idea of connectedness is central also to the other stories that emerge to form an integral part of Ana's transformation.

Having begun the process of dismantling and deconstruction on her first nomadic journey, the text continues its frenetic movement through the lives of six other female protagonists from other points on the globe. What Sefchovich appears to advocate through this original imagining of the subject as a 'nueva manera de ser', is a fundamental break with the concept of the unified, singular subject.[50] Story two tells the story of Maria Petrovna, the Russian artistocrat who has a passionate affair with the musician and composer, Franz Liszt. As in the first story, though, the emphasis on freedom is pronounced: '¡Qué envidia de las señoras rusas que tenían todo el tiempo del mundo para ellas!' (p.93). The collapse of the boundaries between both subjects occurs here too, though in a different way. In this story, it is a more straightforward imagining, a hypothetical scenario rendered by the conditional perfect tense:

Me imagino cómo sería mi vida si yo hubiera nacido en Rusia, el año en que murió el zar Pablo y subió al trono su hijo, el nieto de Catalina la Grande, el heroico y romántico emperador Alejandro I.

---

49 I referred earlier to Mohanty's critique of Morgan's 'reductive utopian vision' of a global sisterhood.

50 This idea resurfaces again in story six which is set in Israel when Keren affirms, 'No sólo inventamos una nueva forma de vida sino también una nueva moral basada en las decisiones democráticas del grupo y vivimos de acuerdo a ella' (p.378).

> Mis padres habrían sido dueños de enormes propiedades en las fértiles estepas ucranianas (p.93).

The movement here to the steppes of the Ukraine, recalls again Deleuze and Guattari's notion of 'an absolute that is manifested locally, and engendered in a series of local operations of varying orientations: desert, steppe, ice, sea'.[51] Having explored the desert already, the steppes of the Ukraine are the setting for the next stage of Ana's subject formation, mirroring the directions taken in Deleuze and Guattari's imaginings. Again, as in the first story, the narrative moves almost imperceptibly from one narrative subject to the next. Over eighty odd pages, Maria's stories of love in Paris and Russia unfold, and Ana voraciously consumes her being, appropriating her loves and revelling in her wealth. Maria's final days are marked by a sense of contentment and fulfillment, of which there are few examples in the book:

> Una sensación de bienestar va inundando mis venas y produciéndome una inexplicable alegría, la de sentirme ya tan por encima del mundo. Ha llegado la hora de irme y quisiera hacerlos dignamente, sin gritos ni lágrimas (p.167).

This story, therefore, constitutes a more straightforward escapist micronarrative in which Ana can immerse herself and remove herself from the more mundane and unremarkable features of her own daily life.

Story three moves to New York and to one of the more disturbing portraits in the book. The notion of freedom, central to the other stories, appears again here but with added emphasis: '¿Por qué no puedo yo tener libertad? ¿Por qué no puedo hacer lo que me gusta?' (p.181). With these questions, it is clear that Ana is still searching for a freedom that eludes her in 'real' life. The entry into the world of the New York prostitute occurs in a similar way as in the other tales, but again with more pronounced vigour:

51   *A Thousand Plateaus*, p.382.

294

Me imagino lo que sería mi vida si estuviera sola, dueña y señora de mi persona y de mi tiempo, en alguna gran ciudad donde pase de todo, donde la prostitución sea total, la luz eléctrica también.
'¿Where you from?'
'New York, she answers with the place she last was, not the place she is made of' (p.181).

In this rather bizarre passage, Ana yearns for freedom and solitude, concepts she associates with prostitution as she sees it as symbolic of total bodily liberty.[52] In the subsequent paragraph, the third person narrative voice disappears and is usurped by another 'I', that of the prostitute: 'Me detengo en los kioskos donde hay montones de revistas pornográficas' (p.182). In this story, just like in the other two, there is an incessant movement, demonstrated by the endless journeys through Manhattan that certainly indicate the prostitute's freedom of move-ment, but also, ironically, her sense of boredom and tedium. In this way, she strikingly resembles Ana.[53] She never stops moving:

Recorro Park Avenue desde la setenta a la noventa. [...] O voy por Madison para ver los aparadores. [...] Voy por la séptima [...] Por la cincuenta y siete [...] Por la ochenta y seis compro manzanas en los puestos de fruta y repaso los discos en las tiendas atestadas de adolescentes. Me gusta caminar (pp.200–1).

The narrative tone is excessive, echoing that of *Demasiado amor* and cementing the idea of travel as the only way of 'becoming': 'Estoy en pleno Soho y sin dinero. Camino y camino' (p.218). The stress on liberty points to the ironies of the use of this term with regard to women's lives whether they are prostitutes or housewives: 'Soy libre,

---

52   This view of prostitution was present too in *Demasiado amor* and is, as we saw in Chapter One, problematic. In both texts, the freedom associated with pros-titution is highly illusory and the full miseries associated with the sex industry are exposed. This happens too in *La señora de los sueños* but with less em-phasis.

53   Debra Castillo draws attention to this irony in her study of the text emphasising that Ana's dream of freedom is projected onto the body of a marginalised, drug-addicted street whore. She points out that, 'the primary emotional characteristic of the prostitute, like the housewife, is her unremitting boredom', 'Reading Women: Sefchovich', p.157.

le digo, no tengo que darte cuentas de mi vida ni decirte dónde ando, ni a ti ni a nadie' (p.220). This categorical insistence on freedom punctuates the story of the prostitute but the story never engages with the ironies it exposes. Lupita attests to her mother's 'crazy' actions: 'Desde que no puede leer, colgó por toda la casa unos letreros que dicen ¡libertad!' (p.243). This frank acknowledgement of the curtailment of her mother's freedom (at this point she is forbidden to read by her husband) echoes the prostitute's similar sentiments.

The novel moves in a very different direction in story four and relates the tale of Camila/Camilo, the young Argentinian scientist and her life spent on the islands of the Galápagos off the coast of Ecuador. This tale has a feminist plot of sorts in that Camila is forced to live life as a man (Camilo) in order to be able to work as a scientist and naturalist on the Galápagos. Here he/she meets Charles Darwin who becomes infatuated with her but who is so ashamed that he is attracted to a male that he severs all contact with Camilo and leaves the island. According to the story, much of the substance of Darwin's theory, in particular the theory of 'natural selection', is attributed not to Darwin but to Camila, a fact that is erased from history because of the confusion and embarrassment over Darwin's desire for him/her. Here again, the recourse to liberty is exalted: 'En otras ocasiones me contaba sobre la naturaleza de su país, que tal como la describía sonaba aburrida y domesticada, ¡a mí que me gusta la naturaleza salvaje y libre! (p.257) The merging of the subjects here reaches a new level of fusion:

> Siento feo de engañar a mi gente, pero ni modo voy a seguir haciéndolo. Todo sería tan fácil si yo viviera en una isla lejana y de difícil acceso, absolutamente sola, sin familia ni nadie que me mande, para poder dedicar todas mis horas a leer. ¿Ha oído hablar de Chatham? Es un lugar de belleza salvaje y sobrecogedora (p.246).

In this passage, Ana explains her determination to continue reading and addresses the reader directly. There follows a long description of the flora and fauna of these islands, which becomes more lyrical as it progresses:

En este extraño lugar hay tortugas, pelícanos, albatros, iguanas y montones de pájaros de plumaje multicolor e inusitada diversidad de picos. Hay playas y también colinas cubiertas de vegetación en cuya cima descansan grises nubarrones de niebla. Este es el sitio de los contrastes: desierto y bosque, jungla y playa, humedad y resequedad, fauna de frío y fauna de calor, de montaña y de mar que habitan juntos y lo mas increíble, que a pesar de ser tan distintos no se atacan entre ellos y miran a los extraños sin el menor temor ni agresividad. Aquí es *mi patria,* un paraíso y un laboratorio para alguien *que como yo,* se dedica en cuerpo y alma, de día y de noche al trabajo de conocer la naturaleza (p.247, my emphasis).

Here the voice of the first person narrator (Ana) has seamlessly merged with the first person narrator (Camilo/Camila), in the space of a few lines and who have been connected via the vivid description of the extraordinary environment of the Galápagos islands.

The same process is repeated in the remaining three stories. In Castro's Cuba where the protagonist is employed by Castro to be his 'eyes and ears' on the streets of the island, the emphasis on movement continues unabated: 'Y no sólo nosotros en la Habana sino en todo el país, desde la punta de Maisí hasta el cabo San Antonio, que yo recorría sin dejar olvidado ningún rincón' (p.325). There is an incessant energy:

¡Cómo trabajé en esos años! Caminaba por las calles de las ciudades, recorría los campos y los pueblos del interior, iba a los juegos de pelota y me montaba en las guaguas, esperaba en la cola de las bodegas y ofrecía mi trabajo voluntario en los círculos infantiles y en los hospitales, participaba en las reuniones de los barrios y en las de las fábricas, todo a fin de oír lo que la gente tuviera que decir (p.327).

In a passage reminiscent of many of the travel sections of *Demasiado amor*, the protagonist moves energetically from place to place and from occupation to occupation. Her freedom of movement in this story is never in question and the narrative voice, unlike that of story three in New York, remains engaged and alert. Here, however, the protagonist is condemned to perpetual movement as a way of distancing her from the figure of Fidel who is embarrassed by their early relationship. In this way, the movement is indelibly connected to the protagonist's lack of stability in her personal life.

In the final two stories, again the protagonists isolate freedom as central to their ideas of happiness and fulfillment. In these stories, religion and the notion of deep faith is central to both their lives. Keren who is committed to the pluralist idea of community through her experience of the kibbutz in Israel, turns to religion by the end of the story. In the final narrative, Maya (who later becomes Ananda), lives in a faith-driven community as a devoted follower of Gandhi. The last story, thus, reinstates the values of freedom, the importance of faith and the necessity for movement that has characterised many of the narratives included. In the final sections, Ana addresses an unidentified reader, yet another subject who may burrow their way into this interconnected alliance of voices across continents and time-frames: 'Lo que sucedió usted lo sabe: aprendí a leer y mi soledad encontró compañía, el silencio se pobló de voces, el vacío se llenó de fantasías' (p.473). The 'vacío' invoked here recalls again the empty land ('tierra vacía', p.35) of the first story explored through the notion of the desert. Here it works in similar fashion as an isolated space, a place outside of chronology and history.

It is worth pausing for a moment in our dissection of the novel to ponder the implications of a narrative like this that privileges notions of freedom and movement (inextricably connected, of course), in the attainment of female subjectivity. Having already invoked Deleuze and Guattari's theories on the nomad in my discussion of the story of Aisha, the subjectivities emerging in the subsequent stories suggest a striking parallel with Deleuze and Guattari's related theories on the rhizome and rhizomatic identity. As outlined in the discussion of Hilda in the first section, the rhizome is employed in direct opposition to the tree: 'There are no points or positions in a rhizome, such as those found in a structure, tree, or root. There are only lines'.[54] Indeed, they suggest a way of being that is rhizomatic, that burrows and fragments, perpetually moving and continuously dispersed. In the following passage, they summarise its principal characteristics:

> unlike trees or their roots, the rhizome connects any point to any other point, and its traits are not necessarily linked to traits of the same nature; it brings into

54   *A Thousand Plateaus*, p.9.

play very different regimes of signs, and even nonsign states. The rhizome is reducible neither to the One nor the multiple. [...] It is composed not of units but of dimensions, or rather *directions in motion*. It has neither beginning nor end, but always a middle from which it grows and which it overspills. It constitutes linear multiplicities with n dimensions having neither subject nor object, which can be laid out on a plane of consistency... (my emphasis)[55]

It would seem to me that this description of the rhizome incorporates many of the key elements present in Sefchovich's evocation of Ana. The idea of directions in motion captures effectively the diverse sets of movements undertaken by Ana as she inhabits the lives of the different protagonists of each story. Ana occupies the middle, and in the process of entering the worlds of the other women crosses multiple lines in an endless exploration of the self. Deleuze and Guattari emphasise the importance of the line, and maintain that:

Unlike a structure, which is defined by a set of points and positions, with binary relations between the points and univocal relationships between the positions, the rhizome is made only of lines: lines of segmentarity and stratification as its dimensions, and the line of flight or deterritorialization as the maximum dimension after which the multiplicity undergoes metamorphosis, changes in nature.[56]

Again, their words address precisely the process that is constructed in Sefchovich's text. According to their logic, Ana, like the rhizome, is in a constant state of motion towards other subjects, travelling across various and diverse lines of flight along which a metamorphosis of her subjectivity occurs. These narrative points are connected in various ways – I noted earlier the more pronounced connections that occur – but there is always a sense of the multiple, the plural and the dispersed subject, 'The tree is filiation but the rhizome is alliance, uniquely alliance'.[57] With this definition, Deleuze and Guattari posit a way of envisioning subjectivity as something constantly evolving, moving towards something else, and thus they elaborate a poetics of resistance through which rhizomatic alliances may resist the classical Western

55   *A Thousand Plateaus*, p.21.
56   *A Thousand Plateaus*, p.21.
57   *A Thousand Plateaus*, p.25.

metaphor of the family tree and destabilise the notion of origins and indeed endings.[58] Taking this notion even further, Kaplan maintains that the 'rhizome constitutes an anarchic relationship to space and subjectivity, resistant to and undermining the nation-state apparatus'.[59] Read allegorically, the juxtaposition between Ana's lines of escape, therefore, may be read as the escape from Mexico, the *patria* that has betrayed her, to travel to other countries forging alliances which offer sustenance and hope. Imprisoned both by family and national structures that are paralysed within a linear logic that debilitates and limits its subjects, Ana burrows her way into other subjectivities, other ways of being. It is in this context, that the rhizome has appeal as a means of escape but also as a way of being that refutes this logic: 'A rhizome has no beginning or end; it is always in the middle, between things, interbeing, intermezzo'.[60] The sense of seamless continuity evoked by this definition is persuasive as an overarching framework within which we may locate the ambivalent figure of Ana. This ambivalence with regard to her role as mother and wife may, of course, be extended to her role as national citizen and her need to escape into other worlds. The link, thus, between nation and family so painstakingly explored in Sefchovich's novel, *Demasiado amor*, is featured here too, albeit in a more muted way.

To return to the text, it is clear that Ana's entry into the lives and lifestyles of Aisha, Maria, the unnamed prostitute, Camila and the others represents a forging of rhizomatic connections that enable her to survive her material reality and transcend its limitations. In this way, Sefchovich proposes a new feminist subjectivity, akin to Rosi Braidotti's term, 'interconnected nomadism'.[61] Braidotti writes enthusiastically about the ideas of Deleuze and Guattari on nomadism which, she maintains, 'entail a total dissolution of the notion of a center and consequently of originary sites or authentic identities of any

58 *Questions of Travel*, p.87.
59 *Questions of Travel*, p.87. I shall return to the connection with the nation in the final section of this chapter.
60 *A Thousand Plateaus*, p.25.
61 *Patterns of Dissonance: A Study of Women in Contemporary Philosophy*, trans. by Elizabeth Guild (New York: Routledge, 1991), p.281.

kind'.[62] She further elaborates, 'nomadic becoming is neither re-production nor just imitation, but rather emphatic proximity, intensive interconnectedness'.[63] Braidotti therefore interprets Deleuze and Guattari's notions on the rhizome as a positive and indeed liberating metaphor for feminist alliance across multiple borders. In this way Braidotti proposes a 'new nomadism' in which ideas function as 'ruses and mobile, specific strategies, which are resistant to systematization', in order to develop 'multiple, transverse ways of thinking women's becoming'.[64] Sefchovich, it could be argued, does precisely this, developing transverse ways of becoming through Ana's temporal occupation and engagement with the multiple female subjects of the inserted stories. The 'emphatic proximity' created between Ana and her fictional selves constitutes a vivid example of Braidotti's nomadic becoming and may indeed be interpreted as a liberating metaphor for feminist alliance. I shall return to the questions of liberation and feminism raised here at the end of my analysis of this novel. At this point, I will turn to the encounter that the novel stages between the fictional heterogenous liberated subject and her material circumstances.

Transformation in Flux

In this section, I would like to consider the implications and effects of the rhizomatic, nomadic process of identity formation that has predominated in the text up to this point. One of the more interesting aspects of Sefchovich's text is the way in which it juxtaposes the rhizomatic subject formation of Ana – as the result of her reading – with a nuanced consideration of her material reality and the changing power dynamics within her family. It must be remembered that the

---

62   *Nomadic Subjects*, p.5.
63   *Nomadic Subjects*, p.5.
64   *Patterns of Dissonance: A Study of Women in Contemporary Philosophy*, p.279.

celebration of female alliance and interconnectedness is enacted to escape the worst excesses of patriarchal power. Ana's 'branching out' into the identities of seven other women, is deployed as a way of contesting systems of domination at home. I would like to assess the extent to which these systems are connected and to address the links evoked between family and nation in Sefchovich's eccentric exploration of female identity.

The figure of the nomadic female who roves along and across diverse lines of subjectivity produces a tension in the text that is generated by the collision between 'home' and 'away', exemplified by the protagonist's incessant movement. It is this tension that keeps the text rooted in a material reality which seeks to engage with real (not just fictional) questions of power and control. The final section describes in detail the changes induced at home within the family as a result of Ana's own transformation through reading:

> He podido vivirlo todo, no perderme nada de la vida. He podido andar y desandar el tiempo al derecho y al revés, subir y bajar por los paisajes y las islas, conocer a los humanos con sus secretos, sus fracasos, sus miedos, sus palabras y su fe.
>
> Mía ha sido la vida del corazón y también la vida regida por la razón, pero no me ha faltado el azar con sus sorpresas. [...]
>
> He vivido en donde he querido: en la India y en Rusia, en Cuba y en Nueva York, a la orilla del mar y en pleno desierto, en las calles de las ciudades y entre las espigas de los campos. He vivido cuando he querido: en los siglos anteriores y en todos los años de este que corre. He vivido con quien he querido: junto a los hombres y mujeres comunes y con los héroes. Grandes maestros me han guiado por el camino de la lucha, por el camino del placer, por el camino del arte y por el camino de la fe. [...]
>
> He recorrido el país donde florece el naranjo y el país de las montañas azules, he estado donde la nieve cae sobre la sierra y allí donde el cielo es más claro. He dormido al pie de un abedul blanco y junto al mar verde y transparente. He caminado por pueblos muy viejos y he esperado en los cafés apenas iluminados. Construí casas, puentes, moví piedras. [...]
>
> Y durante todo este tiempo, un día me olvidé de Su existencia, otro fui una devota creyente. Un día dudé y desesperé de la misericordia divina y otro hallé por fin el camino del Señor.
>
> Sí, eso he hecho yo. Me atreví a ponerme los disfraces, a parecer otras, me atreví a buscar la felicidad como si tuviera derecho a ella. [...]

Dicen que sólo los sueños y los deseos son lo verdadero que tenemos. Ahora el mundo es como yo quiero que sea: un universo de éxtasis, cincuenta universos de éxtasis para mí. ¡Y aún quedan tantos caminos por recorrer!

¿A dónde le parece que podría ir ahora? Después de tanto ascetismo, se me antoja una buena diversión. He pensado en Brasil, con sus negros de nalgas duras, sus playas calurosas y su música alegre. Me gustaría estar allí en pleno carnaval, cuando todo mundo anda en la calle. Yo iría con mi tanga minúscula, bailando sobre uno de esos carros alegóricos que entran al sambódromo... (pp.473–8).

I have quoted this at length from the section entitled, 'El horizonte infinito de Dios', as a way of illustrating a number of important points. First, the emphasis on the first-person narrative seems to constitute an emphatic assertion of identity that had eluded Ana in the early part of the novel. Indeed, the insistent repetition of verb forms in the first person ('olvidé', 'fui', 'dudé', 'desesperé', 'hallé') confirm the narrative of empowerment suggested by Braidotti's positive invocation of the nomad's power. That empowerment is unambiguously present in this final section ('eso he hecho yo'). What is more, while the subject is still irrevocably plural and indeed, infinite, it is not represented as unstable or weak. Second, the book's insistence on the need for further journeys and its elliptical ending ensure that the movement and energy generated by the endless travel in each of the sections is set to continue thereby ensuring travel as a fundamental element in the elaboration of individual consciousness.

One could argue, of course, that this narrative adopts a fairly conventional approach to the age-old 'problem that has no name'. According to this reading, Ana, the bored and frustrated housewife, takes refuge in her books and is transformed as a result. The transformation, however, though psychological is certainly not material. The family structure remains unchanged and the power dynamics at the heart of the structure are untouched. Sefchovich's text may suggest that Ana is a heterogeneous, powerful agent, but it also implies that postcolonial, diasporic heterogeneity may have little to do with feminist oppositional and transnational practices that resist patriarchal power. In this way, the novel could be read as ultimately rather conservative in its cautious recommendation that women escape to their imagination in order to escape the oppressive reality of their lives. This may well be valid as a reading of the work but I would contest that it is undermined, not by the figure of Ana, surprisingly, but rather by the figure of her daughter, Lupe, who, it can convincingly be argued, has undergone a complete social, physical and psychological transformation as the result of her mother's experimentation with fiction. I will focus on the figure of the daughter in the final section of the chapter.

Cross-generational Alliance

The last section of the novel bears testimony to the positive changes wrought in Ana's family circumstances. Her husband is happy and the son remains sympathetic and supportive of his mother. The last words on the subject are assigned to Lupe, Ana's daughter which I reproduce here at length:

> Como verá he adelgazado. No es porque ahora en mi casa medio nos matan de hambre con la nueva forma de comer que inventó mi mamá, espinacas y pan integral, sino porque rompí con mi novio y eso me dolió mucho, hasta el apetito perdí. Yo que pasaba la mitad de mi vida a dieta y sin poder bajar de peso, lo logré ahora por la pura tristeza. Dicen que ya anda con otra, todo mundo lo ha visto, pero según mi jefa es lo mejor para mí: 'no te conviene casarte tan rápido, hay que disfrutar de la vida y esos dolores se curan con el tiempo'. Y la conoce, se pinta sola para eso de echar discursos. Antes yo me enojaba cuando me salía con sus filosofías, hasta le contestaba feo o me encerraba en mi cuarto, pero ahora ya no, simplemente la dejo que hable y no le hago caso. Aunque la verdad, tengo que reconocer que algunas veces las cosas que dice me llegan. [...]
>
> ¿Cree usted que volveré a tener novio? He tratado de renovarme, me corté el pelo en un salón que me recomendaron, hago con más energía los ejercicios en el gimnasio y compré ropa nueva. Mi mamá dice que me veo bien, pero yo me siento rara de estar sola, tenía costumbre de ir y venir con Luis, esperar los fines de semana para pasear juntos. [...]
>
> ¿Sabe lo que me pasó el otro día? Fui al cuarto de mi mamá a buscar unas medias. Ahora ya no lee echada en su cama como antes, sino que acomodó una mesa junto a la ventana y la adornó con macetas que ella misma siembra desde que decidió que le gustaba meter las manos en la tierra. Se arregló un rincón y

allí se siente muy seria haciendo como si estudiara y apuntando montones de cosas. Entonces yo, nada más por ociosa, me puse a ver los libros que estaban encima. Abrí uno al azar y vi una frase que ella había subrayado: 'Nadie posee tanto algo como aquel que lo sueña'. Me dejó pensativa, ¿será cierto que vale tanto la pena soñar? (pp.421–3).

I would argue that it is in these pages that the feminist and political charge of the novel may be located, in that the daughter appears to have changed her life radically as a direct result of her mother's fictional alliances. First, we learn that she has broken up with her boyfriend and thus has postponed, if not indefinitely, certainly for now, the repetition of the pattern that has proved so destructive for her mother. The understated assertions of her mother's wisdom ('algunas veces las cosas que dice me llegan') seem to suggest yet another alliance, but this time, not an illusory one as mother and daughter find a point of commonality and connection. The passage attests to her insecurity at being single again, but significantly, underlines her mother's support in this ('mi mamá dice que me veo bien'). The alliance reaches new heights when, in her mother's room, she enters into her world and realises the importance of dreams. In this last sentence, the alliance between mother and daughter becomes complete and the transformation is finally realised. The resolution of the daughter's story in this way is highly significant in the sense that it exposes the liberating potential of the counternarratives cited in the text thus far. It is thus, not in her mother's generation that the material changes will take place, but in that of her daughter.

The text, therefore, does indeed enact empowerment, but that freedom is anchored in the figure of Lupe, and not in that of her mother. Through the idea of a nomadic consciousness, Sefchovich explores notions of freedom and emancipation for her female prot-agonists while retaining a pragmatic link with material circumstance and feminist politics. I would argue that the emphasis on hetero-geneity in the text and on rhizome/nomadic theory is infinitely appealing in the context of the refashioning of female identity in contemporary Mexico. In this way it is a positive way of exemplifying the possible feminist alliances to which Braidotti refers. However, I would also argue that Sefchovich approaches these notions of plurality and multiplicity with a certain degree of scepticism, which is absent from Braidotti's work. If we return to the first story again and consider Aisha's material reality, this becomes very clear. Aisha, it should be remembered, was first sold into marriage and then abducted and coerced into the nomadic way of life. I would suggest, therefore, that the text celebrates nomadism on one level while utterly deconstructing it as a metaphor of freedom on the other. In this sense, it problematises the more utopian strains of Deleuze and Guattari's thoughts while retaining its central messages of freedom and resistance.

Conclusion

Can it be concluded, then, that Sefchovich and Molina elaborate a feminist poetics of resistance through their innovative exploration of diasporic subjectivity? The answer, as perhaps is to be expected at this stage of a book that isolates ambivalence as a central trope, is an emphatic 'yes' and 'no'. In many ways, their texts do offer a resistant aesthetics that questions the relationship of the female to nation space and to the family through an insistent, often provocative, envisioning of alternative subjectivities. And yet, while collapsing the vestiges of power on the one hand, they uphold them on the other through the inability of the texts to actually realise the emancipatory alliances that might transform the lives of their protagonists. Ana's nomadic wanderings across geographical, temporal and historical divides suggest the possibility for alliances that offer the potential for liberation and fulfillment. On the other hand, she remains firmly within the patriarchal structure of her family albeit with certain minor details rearranged. The escape thus, remains illusory, although the alliances may be real. Similarly, in *Muchacha en azul*, Hilda's enthusiastic embrace of nomadic life and her rejection of the conventional family is much more rooted in the grief at her mother's abandonment than in any notion of freedom and plurality. In this way, the texts suggest alternatives while graphically illustrating the difficulties involved in 'real' as opposed to 'fictional' transformation. Both texts are narratives of the self that refuse closure, and while movement, fluidity and heterogeneity suggest innovative ways of building alliances, it is far more difficult to assess the extent to which they might be mobilised as part of a feminist politics. Transnationality functions as a vehicle through which alternative female identities might be envisioned but is constrained and limited by material realities beyond the protagonists' control. The transformation of subjectivity achieved through transnational dialogues with other women, therefore, is ultimately compromised by structures of power that resist easy displacement. Thus the age-old tension between theory and praxis, in this case explored through fiction, remains.

Conclusion

> If you think you can grasp me, think again:
> My story flows in more than one direction
> A delta springing form the river bed
> With its five fingers spread.[1]

This book has attempted to address the many different ways in which Mexican women writers negotiate the frameworks of power that shape the lives of their fictional characters. The five chapters examined various texts by seven different writers. I began my study by looking at the ways in which Sara Sefchovich and Silvia Molina focus on the role of the nation in the subject formation of their female protagonists in texts that are disquieting and challenging. Chapter Two examined the work of Susana Págano and Brianda Domecq who both explore the liberating potential of fiction as a solution to, and escape from, the self-destructive female subject. Angeles Mastretta places women at the centre of her work and occupies an unrivalled position in the history of Mexican letters. Commercially acclaimed world-wide, she has polarised the critical community, most spectacularly through her controversial winning of the Rómulo Gallegos prize in 1997 for her novel, *Mal de amores*. In Chapter Three, I investigated thoroughly the various stakeholders involved in the competition for literary legitimacy being waged, a competition that is rather emblematically signified by the debate about Mastretta's literary 'worth'. Guadalupe Loaeza and Rosamaría Roffiel explicitly engage questions of class and also sexuality (in the case of Roffiel) in their often harsh exposé of contemporary Mexican society. In Chapter Four, I trace their concerns back to Rosario Castellanos, Mexico's foremost woman writer of the twentieth century, unsurpassed in either output or critical acclaim. Her legacy reaches deep into the contemporary literary community and she

---

1   Adrienne Rich, 'Delta', *Time's Power: Poems 1985–1988* (New York: W.W. Norton and Company, 1989), p.32.

is explicitly invoked in both Loaeza and Roffiel's work. I show how this continuum of gender concern, initiated by Castellanos, is filtered through personal chronicle and political satire, foregrounding the ways in which her profound critiques of patriarchy receive contemporary treatment. Returning to the work of Sefchovich and Molina in the final chapter, I focus, in this instance, on texts that are set (or largely set) outside of Mexico, and that place the dialectic between self and place at their centre. These works exhibit, perhaps, the most optimistic vision of female subjectivity as they chronicle the ways in which fluid, heterogeneous female subjects stake a place for themselves in the national imaginary.

For reasons of space, it has been necessary to limit the study to certain writers. It goes without saying that by choosing Sara Sefchovich, Silvia Molina, Susana Págano, Brianda Domecq, Angeles Mastretta, Guadalupe Loaeza and Rosamaría Roffiel, I have left many other writers out and have barely touched the surface in terms of the sheer number of women writing in Mexico today.[2] The diversity and range of work being produced is extraordinary and among the many writers involved in literary endeavours are poets, playwrights, novelists and chroniclers. They participate actively in various arenas related to writing, including workshops, journalism, academia and

2   It is wise to tread carefully when signalling important omissions. Nevertheless, writers that have also impacted considerably on the literary scene in Mexico since the 1980s include Elena Poniatowska, Carmen Boullosa, Margo Glantz, Esther Seligson, Bárbara Jacobs, Laura Esquivel, Rosa Nissán, María Luisa Puga, Elena Garro, Aline Pettersson, Angelina Muñiz-Huberman, Sara Levi Calderón among others. A whole 'new' generation of writers have become prominent since the 1990s including Ana García Bergua, Ana Clavel, Susana Págano, Eve Gil, Rosa Beltrán and many others. Ana Domenella, Luzelena Gutiérrez de Velasco, Nora Pasternac, Gloria Prado y Graciela Martínez-Zalce (eds.), *Territorio de leonas: cartografía de narradoras mexicanas en los noventa* (México: Casa Juan Pablos Centro Cultural, 2001) offers an excellent overview of writers producing throughout the nineties. It is hoped that the forthcoming project, Nuala Finnegan and Jane Lavery (eds), *The Boom Femenino in Mexico: Reading Contemporary Women's Narrative/El boom femenino mexicano: Aproximaciones a la narrativa de mujeres escritoras contemporáneas* will similarly illuminate this crucial period in Mexican literary history.

310

other fields. The *taller de literatura femenina mexicana* in the Colegio de México has been an important forum for their creative energy but is by no means the only one of its kind.[3] Indeed the history and the effects of the literary workshop network in Mexico is worthy of more critical scrutiny and would benefit from further exploration. As well as the various *talleres*, there are conferences, a very active *Programa Interdisciplinario de Estudios de la Mujer* and the *Centro de Documentación sobre la Mujer*, all of which contribute in different ways to the growing vibrancy of cultural production by women.

In the introduction to this book, I raised the problematic question of how to account for the bourgeois female subject in a third world context. I noted the problems inherent in many of these terms – what does bourgeois mean in a developing world context and where is Mexico located within constantly shifting geopolitical boundaries?[4] As a way of addressing the theoretical conundrum posed by the ontological construct of the 'Mexican woman writer', I suggested turning to the notion of 'supplementarity' as discussed by various writers and critics, some explicitly feminist, others more concerned with categories of subalternity and marginalisation in general.[5] I would like to re-

---

3 The *taller de crítica literaria Diana Morán* is also an important forum, led by many different critics and writers. I noted in my study how many of the writers of the *boom* have been associated at one time or another with the various workshops and centres throughout the country. They include Carmen Boullosa, María Luisa Puga, Elena Poniatowska and Angeles Mastretta.

4 Of course, objections to the term, 'Third World', on the grounds of its colonial perspective, are multiple and various. It is generally acknowledged that the terminology describes an increasingly anachronistic model of the geopolitical world. Mexico is commonly grouped by political scientists and economists as part of a rapidly growing group of 'Newly Industrialised Countries' (NICs), a term that has been in use since the 1970s. Its membership, however controversial, of the North American Free Trade Agreement (NAFTA), links it directly to the powerful economies of Canada and the US to which it is increasingly connected. Mexico, itself, therefore is ambivalently positioned within this new world order. See Fredric Jameson's article, 'Third World Literature in the Era of Multinational Capitalism', *Social Text*, Vol.15 (Fall 1986), pp.67–85.

5 The primary critics invoked in this regard were Homi Bhabha, Jacques Derrida and Gibson-Graham.

turn to this notion in my conclusion as a way of teasing out some of the problems posed by its usage in relation to the women writers studied in the book. In this final section of my study, therefore, I re-examine some of the ideas around supplementarity with specific reference to the work of the seven writers covered in this study.

Supplementarity, Modernity, Power

Given the fragmentation of the cultural field and the general move away from the novel form to which I referred in Chapter Three, the position of the female writer remains theoretically fraught, given the overwhelming evidence of their success in both critical and commercial terms. Indeed, to invoke the categories of 'subaltern' or 'marginalised' seems rather provocative in the context of best-selling celebrity authors, like Mastretta. And yet, as this book has aimed to demonstrate, all of the writers studied here, including those who are prominent as well as others who are less well-known, occupy a highly ambivalent position with regard to the literary 'scene' in which most of them actively participate. To use Mary Louise Pratt's phrase, they seem to have 'one foot in and one foot out'.[6] The characters in their fiction are similarly ambivalent constructs. This is not to imply some reductive autobiographical reading that aligns the characters with their authors, but it does emphasis how ambivalence permeates the worlds of women – both inside and outside these books – in powerful ways. Bhabha memorably described the supplement as 'an adjunct, a subaltern instance'.[7] He added that, 'The supplementary strategy suggests that adding "to" need not "add up" but may disturb the cal-

---

6   In this article, Pratt maintains that, 'women establish a subject position on the borderlands of nationalist ideology, with one foot in and one foot out', 'Criticism in the Contact Zone: Decentering Community and Nation', pp.93–4.
7   *Nation and Narration*, p. 305.

culation'.[8] Applying this principle broadly to the texts and writers covered by this study, some interesting conclusions emerge. First, returning to the idea of success as embodied by many of the writers studied here, including Silvia Molina, Sara Sefchovich, Angeles Mastretta and Guadalupe Loaeza, it might be strongly argued that any subaltern instance occupied by these more established writers has been surpassed. By this I mean that given the commercial acclaim attained by Molina, Sefchovich, Mastretta and Loaeza, any notion of subalternity pertaining to their authority is problematic at best.[9] It is certainly true that Loaeza and Mastretta enjoy best-selling status and are confirmed in their positions as charismatic, enduring and popular story-tellers. However, the critical polarity engendered by their work, their relegation to the league of *literatura lite* and the often blatantly misogynistic language used in attacks on them would seem to point to the fact that they may still be paralysed in a subaltern instance that is not so easily transcended through book sales.[10] Similarly, Sefchovich, given her work as academic, journalist and best-selling author, occupies an uneasy position with regard to authorial status. Her fiction certainly follows a path of readability and accessibility that has proved highly successful. Sefchovich, however, hovers uneasily around the 'subaltern instance', and her disturbed and provocative characters certainly offer evidence of the unsettling effect to which Jean Franco refers:

> many Latin American women writers understand their position to be not so much one of confronting a dominant patriarchy with a new feminine position but rather one of unsettling the stance that supports gender power/knowledge as masculine. The 'unsettling' is accomplished in a variety of ways, through

8   He cites Gasché when he says that 'supplements [...] are pluses that compensate for a minus in the origin'. *Nation and Narration*, p. 305.

9   This idea was suggested to me at a conference when one of the delegates protested against the term 'subaltern' being applied to anyone involved in a *boom*. I find this highly problematic when used with reference to women writers who have struggled for such a long time to be any way part of an established cultural tradition.

10   In Chapter Three, I examined the critical reception of Angeles Mastretta as a way of illuminating this debate.

parody and pastiche, by mixing genres and by constituting subversive myth-ologies.[11]

It is clear that Sefchovich participates in this project of 'unsettling' through her subversive re-working of subjectivity in *La señora de los sueños* and her highly disturbing portrait of the prostitute figure in *Demasiado amor*. In this way, she constitutes a 'plus' that forcefully makes its presence felt, antagonising, as well as interrogating, existing belief systems and thought structures.

Molina is highly successful, and unlike the first three writers mentioned here, is both critically and commercially acclaimed. She is also canonical in a way that eludes the other writers. Her name appears on various prestigious short-lists, she has won many awards and is included in the national literary curriculum, all of which provides telling evidence that she has been accepted. Like Sefchovich, her work also 'unsettles', but not in such a provocative, targeted way. Eschewing controversy, she delves into the worlds of ordinary women's lives, their relationships and personal tragedies in order to explore the everyday drama of contemporary life. By focusing on women in such an intimate way, however, Molina's fiction also troubles the reader and by directly addressing the power dynamics at the heart of these women's tragedies, her work constitutes an unsettling addition to the literary field.

When passing to consideration of Susana Págano, Rosamaría Roffiel or Brianda Domecq, the notion of subalternity emerges again, perhaps as a more obviously evocative label. Págano, writing only since the 1990s, attests to the multiple difficulties facing writers (she does not distinguish between male and female in this regard) who try to have works of fiction published in Mexico. Already a prize-winner with *Y si yo fuera Susana San Juan,* she describes at length her own struggles to have the novel published and the challenges in producing more experimental, less 'readable' work.[12] Rosamaría Roffiel, who places such a clear emphasis on lesbian relationships and the struggle

11   Franco, 'Going Public: Reinhabiting the Private', in *Critical Passions*, p.57.

12   Interview with Ana Cruz García, 'Locura y Feminidad: Representaciones de la loca en la obra de Elena Garro, Susana Págano, Ana Castillo y María Amparo Escandón', Ph.D, University College Cork, 2007, p.138.

of the gay community to be accepted by mainstream society, is clearly writing from a precarious peripheral position and might appropriately be described as occupying the subaltern instance, not yet having found a way to transcend. Her work, while eminently 'accessible' and 'readable', code-words for 'simple' and 'light' as was seen in Chapter Three, exemplifies a new visibility of marginalised categories of society but would, only problematically, be assessed in triumphant terms. It might be argued that Brianda Domecq, with her privileged family background and its consequent advantages with regard to education, could not possibly stake a claim on subaltern status. And yet, her work attests to the silenced voices of powerful, yet marginalised women like the historical figure of Teresa de Cabora and the biblical characters of Eve and Lillith (explored in her short story collection, *Bestiario doméstico*). Indeed, the various other archetypes that populate her fiction would seem to pose the question of status rather poignantly in their incessant quest for recognition and fulfillment. The autobiographical testimony of her kidnapping experience, *Once días y algo más*, examined in Chapter Two, bears witness to the powerlessness experienced by its central character, Leo, in relation to her captors, her family, and the world of letters to which she struggles to gain entry.

It would seem, therefore, that the notion of supplementarity is a useful one when it comes to accounting for the bourgeois female writer in a Third World context such as Mexico. According to Bhabha, the supplementary 'antagonises' as well as interrogates, established modes of power. Thus, it would seem to suggest that these writers and their texts do indeed operate as supplements, in ways that are frequently subversive and always 'unsettling'. This, in turn, might be seen as a victory in the sense that the writers have achieved the acclaim and the status that enables them to transcend traditional biases and prejudice and participate vigorously in the literary arena. Given the polarising nature of the reaction to their work and the rise of terms like *literatura lite*, used to denounce the quality of their work, it would seem prudent to retain the subaltern category as a way of accounting for these writers' positions. It would be regrettable indeed if these well-known figures in Mexican literature were to end up being the losers in a literary game that is currently being played for very high stakes.[13] As I have shown in Chapter Three, this game is far from over.

My readings of the texts engage with theoretical discourses drawn from multiple fields including feminist literary theory, post-colonialism, poststructuralism, psychoanalysis, cultural studies, subaltern studies and many more. That the approach is eclectic is both necessary and politically important. It is no longer desirable or possible for any serious study of women's literature to bypass or evade the role of the culture industries – including publishing and marketing – in literary production, dissemination and consumption. Through a series of text-based studies that locate the texts within the contexts of reception, it is possible to gauge the extent to which these writers have truly 'disturbed the calculation'. That there is no clear-cut subversive result of this disturbance, in terms of feminist politics, should not surprise us. We have seen how difficult it is for women to engage critically with modernity when they are dependent on its power-bases for support and success. On the other hand, these writers' bold excavation of the debilitating effects of modernity, as well as its successes, is to be celebrated. At no other stage in its history has Mexico boasted so many female writers and the volume of books published looks set to increase.

In the introduction, I drew attention to a tension at the heart of poststructuralist feminist analysis which grapples continuously with the notion of the unstable subject. On the one hand, it constitutes one of the central tenets of poststructuralist thought and accounts for much of its progressive nature, given the insistence on the capability for change. On the other hand, this very notion often collides with feminism's drive for political change and its urgent need for the category 'woman' to resist instability. One of the achievements of the writers of Mexico's *boom femenino*, in my opinion, has been to keep that dilemma at the heart of their writing. In other words, by focusing on the material realities of contemporary Mexican women (albeit in fictionalised form), they have raised very pragmatic questions to do with patriarchal power while participating in a nuanced exploration of

13   Some of these issues are explored in Nuala Finnegan, '"Light" Women/ "Light" Literature: Woman and Popular Fiction in Mexico since 1980', *Donaire*, No.15 (November 2000), pp.18–23.

316

the difficulties of 'becoming woman' in the twentieth and twenty first century. They interrogate, antagonise and disturb those modernising structures of power that continue to harm those sectors that inhabit its peripheries. These include women from the privileged classes alongside the many others who suffer from new globalised hegemonic structures and who are central to the concerns of the texts studied here. The characters who populate their texts include prostitutes and deeply unhappy middle-class wives (Sefchovich, Molina), the mentally ill and unjustly incarcerated (Págano), the disaffected underclass that turns to crime (Domecq), the overlooked housewives locked in never-ending cycles of consumption (Loaeza) and the struggle for lesbian women to openly express their sexuality (Roffiel). They also include the rape victims featured in *Amora* and the fluid, plural subjects who are the focus of texts by Sefchovich and Molina. Deeply ambivalent, they wrestle with the more unsavoury extremes of modernity as the struggle for cultural as well as political and economic power continues unabated. As I stated in the introduction, by insinuating themselves into the terms of reference, Mexican women writers thus participate in the crucial project of unsettling dominant discourses as they strive for new ways in which to conceptualise the ambivalent position of Mexican women. The project is not over yet.

Bibliography

Primary Sources by Author

Brianda Domecq

Once días... y algo más (Mexico City: Ediciones Ariadna, 1985). First published 1979.

Bestiario doméstico (Mexico City: Fondo de Cultura Económica, 1982).

La insólita historia de la Santa de Cabora (Mexico City: Ediciones Ariadne, 1998). First published 1990.

De cuerpo entero (Mexico City: UNAM, 1991).

Mujer que publica... Mujer pública: Ensayos sobre literatura femenina (Mexico city: Editorial Diana, 1994).

Achechando al unicornio: La virginidad en la literatura mexicana (Mexico City: Fondo de Cultura Económica, 1998).

A través de los ojos de ella, 2 Vols. (Mexico City: Ediciones Ariadne, 1999).

Un día fui caballo (Mexico City: Instituto de Seguridad y Servicios Sociales de los Trabajadores del Estado, 2000).

Guadalupe Loaeza

Las niñas bien (Mexico City: Cal y Arena, 2000). First published 1987.

Las reinas de Polanco (Mexico City: Cal y Arena, 1989).

Compro, luego existo (Mexico City: Alianza Editorial, 2000). First published 1992.

Sin cuenta (Barcelona: Plaza and Janés, 1996).

Mujeres maravillosas (México City: Océano, 1997).

Detrás del espejo: Entrevistas con grandes intelectuales (Mexico City: Nueva Imagen, 1999).

Los de arriba (México City: Plaza Janés, 2002).

Las yeguas finas (Mexico City: Editorial Planeta Mexicana, 2003).

Angeles Mastretta

La pájara pinta (Mexico City: Altiplano, 1978).
Arráncame la vida (Barcelona: Seix Barral, 1999). First published 1985.
Mujeres de ojos grandes (Barcelona: Seix Barral, 2004). First published 1990.
Puerto libre (Barcelona: Seix Barral, 2002). First published 1993.
Mal de amores (Madrid: Suma de Letras, 2000). First published 1996.
El mundo iluminado (Buenos Aires: Seix Barral, 1998).
Ninguna eternidad como la mía (Madrid: Punto de Lectura, 2002). First published 1999.
El cielo de los leones (Barcelona: Seix Barral, 2004).
La vida te despeina/Life Messes up Your Hair: Mujeres en busca de la felicidad (Mexico City: Planeta, 2006).

Susana Págano

Y si yo fuera Susana San Juan (Mexico City: Tierra Adentro, 1998).
Trajinar de un muerto (Mexico City: Océano, 1999).

Rosamaría Roffiel

Amora (Mexico City: Editorial Planeta Mexicana, 1989).
El para siempre dura una noche (Mexico City: Hoja Casa Editorial, 1999).

Sara Sefchovich

Ideología y ficción en la obra de Luis Spota (Mexico City: Grijalbo, 1985).
Mujeres en espejo: Antología de narradoras latinoamericanas del siglo XX (Mexico City: Folios Ediciones, 1985).
México: país de ideas, país de novelas. Una sociología de la literatura mexicana (Mexico City: Grijalbo, 1987).
Demasiado amor (Mexico City: Alfaguara, 2001). First published 1990.
La señora de los sueños (Mexico City: Alfaguara, 2001). First published 1993.
Gabriel Mistral, en fuego y agua dibujada (Mexico City: Coordinación de Difusión Cultural, Dirección de Literatura/UNAM, 1997).
La suerte de la consorte: Las esposas de los gobernantes de México: Historia de un olvido y relato de un fracaso (Mexico City: Océano, 1999).
Vivir la vida (Mexico City: Alfaguara, 2000).
Veinte preguntas ciudadanas a la parte más visible de la pareja presidencial (Mexico City: Océano, 2004).

Silvia Molina

La mañana debe seguir gris (Mexico City: Joaquín Mortiz, 1977).
Leyendo en la tortuga (Cuernavaca: Martín Casillas, 1980).
Ascensión Tun (Cuernavaca: Martín Casillas, 1981).
Lides de estaño (Mexico City: UNAM, 1984).
El papel (Mexico City: Patria, 1985).
El algodón (Mexico City: Patria, 1987).
Los cuatro hermanos, Leyendas nahuas de la creación (Mexico City: Corunda, 1988).
La familia vino del norte (Mexico City: Cal y Arena, 1988).
El hombre equivocado (coautora) (Mexico City: Joaquín Mortiz, 1988).
Dicen que me case yo (Mexico City: Cal y Arena, 1989).
Imagen de Héctor (Mexico City: Cal y Arena, 1990).
Campeche, punta del ala del país, poesía, narrativa y teatro (1450–1990) (CONACULTA, Letras de la República, 1991).
La creación del hombre, Leyendas nahuas de la creación (Mexico City: Trillas, 1991).
La leyenda del sol y la luna (Mexico City: Trillas, 1991).
El misterioso caso de la perra extraviada (Mexico City: Corunda, 1997; Sámara/SEP, 1992).
Un hombre cerca (Mexico City: Cal y Arena, 1992).
Los tres corazones: Leyendas totonacas de la creación (México Ctiy: Corunda, 1992).
Las dos iguanas, Leyendas mayas de la creación (Mexico City: Corunda, 1993).
Mi familia y la Bella Durmiente: Cien años después (Mexico City: Corunda, 1993).
Circuito cerrado (Mexico City: UNAM-Dirección de Literatura, 1995).
Campeche: imagen de eternidad. Crónica de viaje (CONACULTA: Cuaderno de Viaje, 1996).
Bibliografía contemporánea del estado de Campeche (Gob. del Estado de Campeche, 1996).
El abuelo ya no duerme en el armario (New York: Scholastic, 1996; SEP/Cofunda: Libros del Rincón, 1996).
Encuentros y reflexiones (Mexico City: UNAM – Dirección de Literatura, 1998).
El amor que me juraste (Mexico City: Joaquín Mortiz, 1998).
Marina y el pirata (Mexico City: Ediciones SM, 1998).
El topo y la codorniz (Mexico City: Corunda/DGP, 1999).
Quiero ser la que seré (Madrid: Everest, 2000).
Los gemelos y los dobles (Mexico City: Corunda, 2000).
Las aventuras de don Sebas y campeona (Madrid: Everest, 2000).
Mi abuelita tiene ruedas (CIDCLI/DGP, 2000; CIDCLI/SEP, Libros del Rincón, 2001).
Muchacha en azul (Mexico City: Joaquín Mortiz, Contemporáneos, 2001).

Máscaras prehispánicas (Mexico City: Corunda, 2003).

El diario de Sofía. La gesta histórica de la Batalla del 5 de mayo, narrada por una joven de la época (Mexico City: Planeta, Diarios Mexicanos, 2003).

Le comieron la lengua los ratones (Madrid: Everest, 2005).

Secondary Sources by Author

Brianda Domecq

Finnegan, Nuala 'Reading Ambivalence: Order, Progress and Female Transgression in *La insólita historia de la Santa de Cabora* by Brianda Domecq', *Revista Canadiense de Estudios Hispánicos*, Vol.29, No.12 (March 2005), pp.413–27.

Kelly, Lorraine, 'Fenced In: The Limits of the Female Self in the Work of Brianda Domecq', Ph.D, University College Cork, 2007.

Guadalupe Loaeza

Fernández-Levin, R., 'Trapped in a Gilded Cage: Guadalupe Loaeza's Unhappy Women', in Juan Cruz Mendizábal and Juan Fernández Jiménez (eds), *Visión de la narrativa hispánica: Ensayos* (Indiana: Pennsylvania, 1999), pp.81–96.

http://www.laneta.apc.org/pipermail/boletina/2004-December/000010.html (last accessed 4 April 2007).

http://www.eluniversal.com.mx/notas/344050.html (accessed 3 April 2007).

Lailson, Silvia, 'Aún con resistencias y prejuicios, las editoriales empiezan a publicar literatura lésbica' http://www.jornada.unam.mx/2000/10/02/ lesbianismo3.htm (accessed 4 April 2007).

Meacham, Cherie, 'A Woman's Testimony on the Mexican Crisis: Guadalupe Loaeza's *Sin cuenta*', *Letras femeninas*, Vol.26, Nos.1–2 (2000), pp.111–24.

Shaefer-Rodriguez, Claudia, 'Embedded Agendas: The Literary Journalism of Cristina Pacheco and Guadalupe Loaeza', *Latin American Literary Review*, Vol.19, No.38 (July–December 1991), pp.62–76.

Shaw, Deborah, 'The Literary Journalism of Guadalupe Loaeza and Cristina Pacheco', *Bulletin of Latin American Research*, Vol.18, No.4 (1999), pp.437–50.

Van Loan Aguilar, Julia, 'Humor in Crisis: Guadalupe Loaeza's Caricature of the Mexican Bourgeoisie', *Journal of American Culture*, Vol.20, No.2 (Summer 1997), pp.153–8.

Angeles Mastretta

Newspaper Reports

'Destaca Mastretta en librerías chilenas', *Reforma* (Cultura) 27 December 1996, p.16C.

'Éxito de Libros de Angeles Mastretta en Chile', *Excélsior*, 28 December 1996, p.7B.

'Galardonan en Venezuela a la escritora Angeles Mastretta', *Excélsior*, 2 August 1997, p.4,19ª.

'Mastretta recibirá mañana el Premio Gallegos' *Excélsior*, 1 August 1997, p.6B.

'Mastretta Tiene el Bosquejo de Nueva Obra', *Excélsior*, 2 October 1997, p.6B.

'Novela de Angeles Maestreta[sic] entre los libros más vendidos en Alemania', *El día*, 26 August 1988 (no page number).

'Recibió Mastretta el Rómulo Gallegos por *Mal de amores*', *El nacional* 3 August, 1997, p.11.

'Recibe Angeles Mastretta el Premio Rómulo Gallegos', *Reforma* 13 August 1997, p.5C.

Articles by Author

Anabitarte, Ana, 'Angeles Mastretta: Sólo los besos son más placenteros que las palabras'(Entrevista con la escritora mexicana, autora de *Arráncame la vida*)' http://www.babab.com/no01/angeles_mastretta.htm (last accessed 17 August 2005), pp.1–2 .

Anderson, Danny, 'Displacement: Strategies of Transformation in *Arráncame la vida*, by Angeles Mastretta', *Journal of the Midwest Modern Language Association*, Vol.21, No.1 (Spring 1988), pp.15–27.

Aranda Luna, Javier, 'El periodismo esclaviza más que la literatura: Mastretta', *La jornada*, 10 April 1987.

Arenas Saavedra, Ana, 'El amor como discurso de la postmodernidad en *Arráncame la vida* de Angeles Mastretta', *Revista de Literatura Hispanoamericana*, Vol.46 (January 2003), pp.72–9.

Bradu, Fabienne, '*Arráncame la vida*: Crónica de narrativa', *Vuelta*, Vol.129 (August 1987), pp.59–62.

Brown, Meg H., 'The Allende/Mastretta Phenomenon in West Germany: When Opposite Cultures Attract', *Confluencia: Revista Hispánica de Cultura*, Vol.10, No.1 (1994), pp.89–97.

Bruno, Humberto Isidro, 'Amar a dos hombres y ser feliz: Angeles Mastretta', *Uno más uno*, 27 December 1997, p.16.

'El búho', 'Premio light', *Excélsior*, 20 July 1997, p.10.

Carrera, Mauricio, 'Mujeres poderosas, barcos a la deriva', *Uno más uno* (suplemento sábado), 11 April 1998, p.3.

Coria-Sánchez, Carlos M., 'El discurso feminista de Angeles Mastretta en *Mal de amores*', *South Carolina Modern Language Review*, Vol. 3, No. 1 (Spring 2004), no pagination.

Farfán, Alberto, '¿La Vargas Dulché de intelectuales? Ignorancia y enajenación en los *fans* de Mastretta', *Uno más uno* (suplemento cultural), 21 September 1997, p.26.

García Hernández, Arturo, 'El premio no me hace ni mejor ni peor escritora: Angeles Mastretta', *La jornada* (Cultura), 5 July 1997, p.25.

—— 'La charla sin poses, nítida, ya tenía embelesada a la audiencia'

—— '"¿Éxito Mastretta? Éxito el de *La Tigresa*", dice Angeles', *La jornada*, 17 May 1986 (no page number).

Geibig, Heiko, '*Los de abajo* und *Mal de amores* – zei Beispiele literarischer Arbeit am mexikanischen Revolutionsmythos', in Zimmering, Raina (ed.), *Der Revolutionsmythos in Mexiko* (Würzburg: Königshausen and Neumann, 2005).

Gold, Janet, '*Arráncame la vida*: Textual Complicity and the Boundaries of Rebellion', *Chasqui: Revista de Literatura Latinoamericana*, Vol.17, No.2 (November 1988), pp.35–40.

Guerrero, Gustavo, 'Angeles Mastretta y el triunfo del *best-seller*', *Reforma*, 28 September 1997, p.3.

—— 'Estadísticas del sector editorial: problemas y perspectivas – I', *Libros de México*, Vol.19 (April–June 1996), pp.63–70.

http://www.amazon.com/gp/product/product-description/157322656/ref=dp_proddes (accessed 2 April 2007).

http://www.amazon.com/Arrancame-Vida-Tear-Up-Life/dp/8432216399/ref =pd_bbs_sr_2/104–1846106–3028762?ie=UTF8&s=books&qid= 1175590240&sr=1–2 (last accessed 17 August 2005).

http://www.amazon.com/Lovesick-Angeles-Mastretta/dp/1573226556/ref=sr _1_1/104–1846106–3028762?ie=UTF8&s=books&qid=1175523977 & sr=8–1 (last accessed 03 April 2007).

Isidro Bruno, Humberto, 'Amar a dos hombres y ser feliz: Angeles Mastretta', *Uno más uno*, 27 December 1997, p.16.

Knights, Vanessa, '(De)Constructing Gender: The Bolero in Angeles Mastretta's *Arráncame la vida*', *Journal of Romance Studies*, Vol.1, No.1 (Spring 2001), pp.69–84.

Lavery, Jane, *Angeles Mastretta: Textual Multiplicity* (London: Tamesis, 2005).

—— 'Entrevista a Angeles Mastretta: La escritura como juego erótico y multiplicidad textual', *Anales de literatura hispanoamericana*, Vol.30 (2001), pp.293–319.

Lemaitre León, Monique J., 'La historia oficial frente al discurso de la ficción femenina en *Arráncame la vida* de Angeles Mastretta', *Texto Crítico,* Vol.2, No.3 (July – December 1996), pp.99–114.

Leyva, José Angel, 'El nuevo mundo de Grijalbo', *Libros de México*, Vol.17 (October–December 1989), pp.9–12.

—— 'Por la órbita editoral de Planeta', *Libros de México*, Vol.18 (January–March 1990), pp.5–9.

—— 'Joaquín Mortiz, las grandes transfiguaciones editoriales', *Libros de México*, Vol.31 (April–June 1993), p.12.

Llarena, Alicia, '*Arráncame la vida*, de Angeles Mastretta: El universo desde la intimidad', *Revista Iberoamericana*, Vol.58, No.159 (April–June 1992), pp.465–75.

Maloof, Judy, '*Mal de amores*: Un *bildungsroman* femenino', *Revista de Literatura Mexicana Contemporánea*, Vol.5, No.11 (September–December 1999), pp.101–4.

Peralta, Braulio, 'Adela Palacios dedica su novela a la premiada Angeles Mastretta', *Excélsior*, 5 March 1988, pp.1–3B.

—— 'De su obra *Arráncame la vida*: Mastretta vendió derechos a la TV Venezolana', *Excélsior*, 14 August 1997, p.7B.

—— 'Mi novela es una historia, no un ensayo feminista: Angeles Mastretta', *La jornada*, 11 June 1985 (no page number).

Perera de Moore, 'La paradójica expresión femenina en *Arráncame la vida* y *Mal de amores* de Angeles Mastretta', *Ixquic: Revista Hispánica Internacional de Análisis y Creación,* Vol.3 (December 2001), pp.107–23.

Teichman, Ron, 'Angeles Mastretta: Con la precisión del arrebato', *Nexos* –(April 1987), pp.5–8.

Vega, Patricia, 'Angeles Mastretta, Premio Mazatlán de Literatura 1985 por su novela *Arráncame la vida*', *La jornada*, 6 January 1986 (no pagination).

Susana Págano

Cruz García, Ana, 'La locura femenina: representaciones de la loca en la obra de Elena Garro, Susana Págano, Ana Castillo and María Amparo Escandón', Ph.D, University College Cork, 2007.

Rosamaría Roffiel

Martínez, Elena M., 'Entrevista con Rosamaría Roffiel', *Confluencia*, Vols.8–9, Nos.1–2 (1993), pp.179–80.

—— 'Privileging Lesbian Eroticism: The Works of Rosamaría Roffiel and Nancy Cárdenas', in *Lesbian Voices from Latin America: Breaking Ground* (New York and London: Garland Publishing Inc., 1996), pp.117–41.

Del Campo, Alicia, 'Reterritorializando lo mexicano desde lo feminino en el contexto neoliberal: *Demasiado amor* de Sara Sefchovich', *New Novel Review*, Vol.2, No.2 (1995), pp.61–75.

Other Secondary Sources

Acker, Kathy, *Don Quixote: A Novel* (London: Paladin Books, 1985).

Achebe, Chinua, 'An Image of Africa: Racism in Conrad's *Heart of Darkness*', *Massachusetts Review*, Vol.18, No.4 (Winter 1977), pp.782–94.

Achugar, Hugo, 'Leones, cazadores e historiadores: A propósito de las políticas de la memoria y del conocimiento', *Revista Iberoamericana*, Vol.180 (1997), pp.379–87.

Adorno, Rolena, 'Reconsidering Colonial Discourse for Sixteenth-and Seventeenth-Century Spanish America', *Latin American Research Review*, Vol.28, No.3 (1993), pp.120–4.

Aguilar Camín, Héctor and Meyer, Lorenzo, *In the Shadow of the Mexican Revolution: Contemporary Mexican History, 1910–1989*, trans. by Luis Alberto Fierro (Austin: University of Texas Press, 1993).

Anaya Rosique, José, 'Estadísticas del sector editorial: problemas y perspectivas – I', *Libros de México*, Vol.19 (April–June 1996), pp.63–70.

Allen, Graham, *Intertextuality* (London and New York: Routledge, 2000).

Ahern, Maureen, *Rosario Castellanos Reader: An Anthology of her Poetry, Short Fiction, Essays and Drama* (Austin: University of Texas Press, 1988).

Allende, Isabel, *Cuentos de Eva Luna* (Barcelona: Editorial Sol 90). First published 1989.

—— *La casa de los espíritus* (Barcelona: Plaza and Jones, 1989). First published 1982.

Anderson, Benedict, *Imagined Communities: Reflections on the Origins and Spread of Nationalism* (London: Verso, 1983).

Anderson, Danny, 'Creating Cultural Prestige: Editorial Joaquín Mortiz', *Latin American Research Review*, Vol.31, No.2 (1996), pp.3–41.

Araujo, Helena, *La scheherezada criolla: Ensayos sobre escritura femenina latinoamericana* (Colombia: Universidad Nacional de Colombia, 1989).

Ashcroft, Bill, Griffiths, Gareth and Tiffin, Helen (eds), *The Empire Writes Back: Theory and Practice in Post-colonial Literatures* (London: Routledge and Kegan Paul, 1989).

Assia, Djebar, *A Sister to Scheherezade*, trans. by Dorothy S. Blair (New Hampshire: Heinemann, 1993).

Bartra, Roger, *Blood, Ink and Culture: Miseries and Splendors of the Post-Mexican Condition* (Durham and London: Duke University Press, 2002), pp.104–32.

Baudrillard, Jean, *Cool Memories*, trans. by Chris Turner (London: Verso, 1981).

—— 'Simulacra and Simulations', in Mark Poster (ed.), *Selected Writings* (Oxford: Polity, 1988), pp.169–87.

Barrett, Michèle, *Women's Oppression Today: The Marxist/Feminist Encounter* (London: Verso, 1988).

Barthes, Roland, *S/Z*, trans. by Richard Miller (London: Jonathan Cape 1975).

—— 'The Death of the Author', in David Lodge (ed.), *Modern Criticism and Theory: A Reader* (London: Longman, 1988), pp.166–72.

Bell, Steven, Le May, Albert and Orr, Leonard (eds), *Critical Theory, Cultural Politics and Latin American Narrative* (Indiana: University of Notre Dame Press, 1993).

Benedetti, Mario, *Geografías* (Madrid: Alfaguara, 1984).

—— 'Sudacas del mundo, unios', in *El desexilio y otras conjeturas* (Madrid: El País, 1984), pp.51–2.

Beverly, John, *Subalternity and Representation: Arguments in Cultural Theory* (Durham, North Carolina: Duke University Press, 1999).

Bhabha, Homi K. *Nation and Narration* (London: Routledge and Kegan Paul, 1990).

Blanco, José Joaquín, 'Aguafuertes de narrativa mexicana, 1950–1980', *Nexos*, Vol.56 (1982), pp.23–39.

Bloom, Harold, *The Anxiety of Influence: A Theory of Poetry* (Oxford: Oxford University Press, 1973).

Bonifaz, Oscar, *Rosario* (Mexico City: Presencia Latinoamericana, 1984).

Boullosa, Carmen, *Son vacas, somos puercos* (Mexico City: Ediciones Era, 1991).

Bourdieu, Pierre, 'The Production of Belief: Contribution to an Economy of Symbolic Goods', trans. by Richard Nice, in Richard Collins et al. (eds), *Media, Culture, and Society: A Critical Reader* (London: Sage, 1986), pp.131–63.

Bourdieu, Pierre, with Passeron, Claude, *Reproduction in Education, Society, Culture* (Beverly Hills, California: Sage, 1977).

Bourdieu, Pierre, *Distinction: A Social Critique of Taste*, trans. by Richard Nice (Cambridge, Massachussetts, Harvard University Press, 1984).

Boyle Haberstroh, Patricia and St. Peter, Christine (eds), *Opening the Field: Irish Women, Texts and Contexts* (Cork: Cork University Press, 2007).

Braidotti, Rosi, *Patterns of Dissonance: A Study of Women in Contemporary Philosophy*, trans. by Elizabeth Guild (New York: Routledge, 1991).

—— *Nomadic Subjects: Embodiment and Sexual Difference in Contemporary Feminist Theory* (New York: Columbia University Press, 1994).

Brito de Martí, Esperanza, 'Amor y sexo – liberación o subyugación', *Kena* (August 1972), primera quincena, pp.10–12.

—— 'El amor, los cielos y la mujer emancipada', *Kena* (October 1970), segunda quincena, pp.4–6.

—— 'Cambiemos la imagen de amor', *Kena* (January 1973), primera quincena, p.12.

Brönte, Charlotte, *Shirley* (Oxford: Oxford University Press, 1998).

Brownmiller, Susan, *Against our Will: Men, Women and Rape* (New York: Simon and Schuster, 1975).

—— *Distinction: A Social Critique of Taste*, trans. by Richard Nice (Cambridge, Massachussetts: Harvard University Press, 1984).

Bruce-Novoa, Juan, 'Subverting the Dominant Text: Elena Poniatowska's *Querido Diego*' in Susan Bassnett *Knives and Angels: Women Writers in Latin America* (London: Zed Books, 1990), pp.115–31.

Calvino, Italo, *Six Memos for the Next Millenium* (New York: Vintage Books, 1993).

Campos, Victoria E., 'Toward a New History: Twentieth-Century Debates in Mexico on Narrating the National Past', in Santiago Juan-Navarro and Theodore Robert Young (eds), *A Twice-Told Tale: Reinventing the Encounter in Iberian/Iberian American Literature and Film* (Newark: University of Delaware Press, 2001), pp.47–62.

Castellanos, Rosario, *Rito de iniciación* (México City: Alfaguara, 1997).

—— *El eterno femenino* (Mexico City: Fondo de Cultura Económica, 1975).

—— *El uso de la palabra* (Mexico City: Ediciones de Excélsior-Crónicas, 1974).

—— *Mujer que sabe latín...* (Mexico City: Fondo de Cultura Económica, 1973).

—— *Poesía no eres tú: obra poética, 1948–1971* (Mexico City: Fondo de Cultura Económica, 1972).

—— *Álbum de familia* (Mexico City: Joaquín Mortiz, 1971).

—— *Los convidados de agosto* (Mexico City: Fondo de Cultura Económica 1964).

—— *Oficio de tinieblas* (Mexico City: Fondo de Cultura Económica 1962).

—— *Ciudad Real* (Mexico City: Fondo de Cultura Económica, 1960).

—— *Balún-Canán* (Mexico City: Fondo de Cultura Económica, 1957).

Castillo, Debra A., *Talking Back: Toward a Latin American Feminist Literary Criticism* (Ithaca: Cornell University Press, 1992).

——*Easy Women: Sex and Gender in Modern Mexican Fiction* (Minneapolis: University of Minnesota Press, 1998).

—— Finding Feminisms', in Sara Castro-Klarén (ed.), *Narrativa Femenina en América Latina: Prácticas y Perspectivas Teóricas/ Latin American Women's Narrative: Practices and Theroretical Perspectives* (Vervuert: Iberomamericana, 2003), pp.351–71.

Castillo, Susan and Schweitzer, Ivy (eds), *The Literatures of Colonial Americas: An Anthology* (Oxford: Blackwell, 2001).

Cevallos-Candau, Francisco Javier, Cole, Jeffrey A., Scout, Nina M. and Suárez Araúz, Nicomedes (eds), *Coded Encounters: Writing, Gender, and Ethnicity in Colonial Latin America* (Amherst: University of Massachussetts Press, 1994).

Chakrovorty Spivak, Gayatri, *Outside in the Teaching Machine* (New York: Routledge, 1993).

Chant, Sylvia, 'Urban Livelihoods, Employment and Gender', in Robert N. Gwynne and Cristóbal Kay (eds), *Latin America Transformed: Globalization and Modernity* (London: Edward Arnold, 2004), pp.210–31.

Cixous, Hélène, *Coming to Writing and Other Essays*, trans. by Deborah Jensen (Cambridge, Massachussetts: Harvard University Press, 1992).

—— 'Sorties: Out and Out: Attacks/Ways Out/Forays', in Catherine Belsey and Jane Moore (eds), *The Feminist Reader: Essays in Gender and the Politics of Literary Criticism* (New York: Blackwell, 1997), pp.91–104.

—— 'The Laugh of the Medusa', trans. by Keith Cohen and Paula Cohen, *Signs* (Summer, 1976), pp.875–93.

Clark D'Lugo, Carol, *The Fragmented Novel in Mexico: The Politics of Form* (Austin: University of Texas Press, 1997).

Clendinnen, Inga, 'Preempting Postcolonial Critique: Europeans in the *Heart of Darkness*', *Common Knowledge*, Vol.13, No.1 (Winter 2007), pp.1–17.

Conrad, Joseph, *Heart of Darkness* (New York: Chelsea House Publishers, 1996). First published 1902.

Costantino, Roselyn, 'Resistant Creativity: Interpretative Strategies and Gender Representation in Contemporary Women's Writing in Mexico', Ph.D, Arizona State University, 1992.

Craske, Nikki, 'Ambiguities and Ambivalences in Making the Nation: Women and Politics in 20th Century Mexico', *Feminist Review*, Vol.79 (2005), pp.116–33.

—— '(S)mothering Politics: Motherhood as Political Identity' conference paper, Society of Latin American Studies, University of Liverpool, 14-18 April 1998.

Davies, Lloyd, *Allende: La casa de los espíritus* (London: Tamesis, 2000).

Deane, Séamus (ed.), *Field Day Anthology of Irish Writing* (London, Derry, New York: Faber and Faber, W.W. Norton, 1992).

De Beauvoir, Simone, *The Second Sex*, trans. by H.M. Parshley (New York: Vintage, 1973).

De Beer, Gabriella, *Contemporary Mexican Women Writers: Five Voices* (Austin: University of Texas Press, 1996).

De la Campa, Román *Latin Americanism* (Minneapolis: University of Minnesota Press, 1999).

De la Cruz, Sor Juana Inés, *Los empeños de una casa*, in *Obras Completas*, Vol.4 (Mexico City: Fondo de Cultura Económica, 1951), pp.3–184.

Deleuze, Gilles, *A Thousand Plateaus: Capitalism and Schizophrenia* (Minneapolis: University of Minnesota Press, 1987).

Deleuze, Gilles and Guattari, Félix, *Kafka: Toward a Minor Literature*, trans. by Dana Polan (Minneapolis: University of Minnesota Press, 1986).

De Lizardi, Fernando, *El periquillo sarniento* (Mexico City: Porrúa, 1949).

Derrida, Jacques, *Of Grammatology*, trans. by Gayatri Chakrovorty Spivak (Baltimore: Johns Hopkins Press, 1976).

Dinesen, Isak, *Last Tales* (New York: Random House, 1957).

Dolle, Raymond, 'The New Canaan, the Old Canon, and the New World in American Literature Anthologies', *College Literature*, Vol.17, Nos.2–3 (June–October 1990), pp.196–208.

329

Domenella, Ana, 'Territorio de leonas: Narradoras mexicanas en los noventa', in Ana Domenella, Luzelena Gutiérrez de Velasco, Nora Pasternac, Gloria Prado y Graciela Martínez-Zalce (eds) *Territorio de leonas: cartografía de narradoras mexicanas en los noventa* (Mexico City: Universidad Autónoma Metropolitana, 2001), pp.19–44.

Donadio, Rachel, 'The Chick Lit Pandemic', *New York Times*, 19 March 2006.http://www.nytimes.com/2006/03/19/books/review/19donadio.html ?ex=1178769600&en=87d41ed0116e5353&ei=5070

Douglas, Mary, *Purity and Danger: An Analysis of the Concepts of Pollution and Taboo* (London: Routledge and Kegan Paul, 1969).

Durham Peters, John, 'Exile, Nomadism and Diaspora: The Stakes of Mobility in the Western Canon' in Hamid Naficy (ed.) in *Home, Exile, Homeland: Film, Media and the Politics of Place* (London and New York: Routledge, 1999), pp.17–44.

Dworkin, Andrea, *Woman Hating: A Radical Look at Sexuality* (Boston: Dutton, 1974).

—— *Pornography: Men Possessing Women* (London: Women's Press, 1981).

Eco, Umberto, *Reflections on the Name of the Rose* (London: Secker and Warburg, 1986).

Edwards, Robert, 'Exile, Self and Society', in María-Inés Lagos-Pope, *Exile in Literature* (Lewisburg: Bucknell University Press, 1988), pp.15–31.

Elliott, R.C., *The Power of Satire: Magic, Ritual, Art* (Princeton, New Jersey: Princeton University, 1960).

Erickson, John D., 'Nomadic Thought, Postcolonialism, and Maghrebian Writing', in H. Adlai Murdoch and Anne Donadey (eds), *Postcolonial Theory and Francophone Literary Studies* (Gainesville: Unviersity of Florida Press, 2005), pp.67–86.

Esquivel, Laura, *Como agua para chocolate* (New York: Anchor Books, 1989).

Fanon, Frantz, *Black Skin, White Masks* (London: Pluto Press, 1986).

Feinberg, Leonard, 'Satire: The Inadequacy of Recent Definitions', *Genre*, Vol.1 (1968), pp.31–7.

Fernández Retamar, Roberto, *Caliban and Other Essays*, trans. by Edward Baker (Minneapolis: University of Minnesota Press, 1989).

Finnegan, Nuala, 'Feminine Dis-ease in *Ciudad Real* by Rosario Castellanos', *Hispanic Research Journal*, Vol.2, No.1 (February 2000), pp.45–60.

—— 'Light' women/'Light' Literature: Women and Popular Fiction in Mexico since 1980, *Donaire*, No.15 (November 2000), pp.18–23.

—— *Monstrous Projections of Femininity in Rosario Castellanos's Prose* (Lampeter: Edwin Mellen Press, 2000).

Fo, Dario and Rame, Franca, *Female Parts* (London: Methuen, 1987)

—— *A Woman Alone and Other Plays* (Boston and London: A&C Black, 1991).

Foucault, Michel, *Madness and Civilization: A History of Insanity in the Age of Reason* (London: Routledge, 2001).

—— 'What is an Author' in David Lodge (ed.) *Modern Criticism and Theory: A Reader* (London and New York: Longman, 1988), pp.196–210.

Franco, Jean, 'Globalization and the Crisis of the Popular', in Mary Louise Pratt and Kathleen Newman (eds), *Critical Passions: Selected Essays* (Durham and London: Duke University Press, 1999), pp.208–20.

—— *Plotting Women: Gender and Representation in Mexico* (London: Verso, 1989).

—— *The Decline and Fall of the Lettered City: Latin America After the Cold War* (Cambridge, Massachusetts and London, England: Harvard University Press, 2002).

—— 'What's Left of the Intelligentsia: The Uncertain Future of the Printed Word', in Mary Louise Pratt and Kathleen Newman (eds), *Critical Passions: Selected Essays* (Durham and London: Duke University Press, 1999), pp.182–207.

Franco, Jean, Yúdice, George and Flores, Juan (eds), *On Edge: The Crisis of Contemporary Latin American Culture* (Minneapolis: University of Minnesota Press, 1992).

French, Marilyn, *The Woman's Room* (London: Warner, 1977).

Freud, Sigmund, *The Standard Edition of the Complete Psychological Works of Sigmund Freud*, trans. by James Strachey, 24 Vols. (London: Hogarth, 1953–74), Vols. 4 and 5.

Friedan, Betty, *The Feminine Mystique* (Harmondsworth: Penguin, 1982) First published 1963.

Gallo, Rubén (ed.), *New Tendencies in Mexican Art: The 1990s* (New York: Palgrave Macmillan, 2004).

—— *The Mexico City Reader* (Madison: University of Wisconsin Press, 2004).

García, Brígida, 'Economic Restructuring: Women's Work and Autonomy in Mexico', in Harriet Presser and Gita Sen (eds), *Women's Empowerment and Demographic Processes: Moving Beyond Cairo* (Oxford: Oxford University Press, 2000).

García, Kay S., *Broken Bars: New Perspectives From Mexican Women Writers* (Albuquerque: University of New Mexico Press, 1994).

García Márquez, Gabriel, *Cien años de soledad* (Madrid: Cátedra, 1997) First published 1967.

Garro, Elena, *Inés* (Mexico City: Grijalbo, 1995).

Ghose, Indira, *Women Travellers in Colonial India: The Power of Female Gaze* (Oxford: Oxford University Press, 1998).

Gibson-Graham, '"Stuffed if I know!": Reflections on Post-modern Feminist Social Research', in Linda McDowell and Joanne P. Sharp (eds), *Space, Gender, Knowledge: Feminist Readings* (Oxford: Oxford University Press, 1997), pp.124–46.

Gilbert, Sandra and Gubar, Susan, *The Madwoman in the Attic: The Woman Writer and the Nineteenth Century Literary Imagination* (New Haven: Yale University Press, 1979).

Gillis, Stacy; Howie, Gillian and Munford, Rebecca (eds), *Third Wave Feminism: A Critical Exploration* (New York: Palgrave Macmillan, 2004).

Glad, John, *Conversations in Exile* (Durham: Duke University Press, 1993).

Glantz, Margo, 'Las hijas de la malinche' in *Esguince de Cintura: Ensayos sobre narrativa mexicana del Siglo XX* (Mexico City: Consejo Nacional para la cultura y las artes, 1994), pp.182–3.

Grant, Catherine, 'Authorship and Authority in the Novels of Rosario Castellanos', Ph.D, University of Leeds, 1991.

Grohmann, Alexis, *Coming Into One's Own: The Novelistic Development of Javier Marías* (Amsterdam: Rodopi, 2002).

Gross, Elizabeth, 'The Body of Signification', in John Fletcher and Andrew Benjamin (eds), *Abjection, Melancholia and Love: The Work of Julia Kristeva* (London: Routledge, 1990), pp.80–103.

Gugelberger, Georg M. (ed.), *The Real Thing: Testimonial Discourse and Latin America* (Durham: Duke University Press, 1997).

Haas, William, 'Some Characteristics of Satire', *Satire Newsletter*, Vol.3 (Fall, 1965), pp.1–3.

Haberstroh, Patricia Boyle and St. Peter, Christine (eds) *Opening the Field: Irish Women, Texts and Contexts* (Cork: Cork University Press, 2007).

Haddu, Miriam, *Contemporary Mexican Cinema (1989–1999): History, Space, Identity* (Lewiston: Edwin Mellen Press, 2007).

Hallewell, Laurence, 'The Impact of the Spanish Civil War on Latin American Publishing', in Iliana L. Sonntag (ed.), *Intellectual Migrations: Transcultural Contribution of European and Latin American Emigrés* (Madison: Memorial Library, University of Wisconsin, 1986), pp.139–50.

Hanisch, Carol, 'The Personal is Political', in *Notes from the Second Year: Women's Liberation in 1970* (New York: Redstockings Press, 1970). http://scholar.alexanderstreet.com/pages/viewpage.action?pageId=2259.

Haraway, Donna, 'Situated Knowledges: the Science Question in Feminism and the Privilege of Partial Perspective', in Linda McDowell and Joanne P. Sharp (eds), *Space, Gender and Knowledge: Feminist Readings* (London: Arnold, 1987), pp.53–72.

Harris, Robert, 'The Purpose and Method of Satire', www.virtualsalt.comsatire.htm (accessed 29 August 2006).

Henry, Astrid, *Not My Mother's Sister: Generational Conflict and Third-Wave Feminism* (Bloomington: Indiana University Press, 2004).

Heywood, Leslie and Drake, Jennifer (eds), *Third Wave Agenda: Being Feminist, Doing Feminism* (Minneapolis: University of Minnesota Press 1997).

Hinojosa, Francisco, 'Las editoriales marginales en México (1975–1978)', *Revista de la Universidad de México*, Vol.33, Nos.2–3, pp.62–4.

Horne, Donald, The Great Museum: The Re-Presentation of History (London: Pluto Press, 1984).

Hopenhayn, Martín, *No Apocalypse, No Integration: Modernism and Postmodernism in Latin America* (Durham, North Carolina: Duke University Press, 2001).

http://www.amazon.com/s/ref=nb_ss_b/104–1846106–3028762?url=search-alias%3Dstripbooks&field-keywords=javier+marias (last accessed 3 March 2007).

http://www.ilga-europe.org/content/download/6444/39689/file/World%20legal%20wrap%20up%20survey%20%20November2006.pdf (accessed 4 April 2007).

http://middeast.com/archives/30 (last accessed 24 July 2006).

http://www.santillana.com/co/quienes somos.htm (last accessed 17 August 2005).

http://scholar.alexanderstreet.com/pages/viewpage.action?pageId=2259 (last accessed 17 April 2007).

Humm, Maggie, *The Dictionary of Feminist Theory* (Columbus: Ohio State University Press, 1995).

Ibsen, Kristine, *The Other Mirror: Women's Narrative in Mexico, 1980–1995* (Westport, Connecticut and London: Greenwood Press, 1997).

Jameson, Fredric, 'Third World Literature in the Era of Multinational Capitalism', *Social Text*, Vol.15 (Fall 1986), pp.67–85.

Jones, Ernest, *The Life and Work of Sigmund Freud* (New York: Basic Books, 1955).

Kamel, Rachael and Hoffman, Anya (eds), *The Maquiladora Reader: Cross-Border Organizing Since NAFTA* (American Friends Service Committee, 1999).

Kaplan, Caren, *Questions of Travel: Postmodern Discourses of Displacement* (Durham and London: Duke University Press, 1996).

Kaplan, Caren, Alarcón, Norma and Moallem, Minoo (eds), *Between Woman and Nation: Nationalism, Transnational Feminisms, and the State* (Durham: Duke University Press, 1999).

Kimbrough, Robert (ed.), *Heart of Darkness: An Authoritative Text*, Norton Critical Edition (New York: Norton, 1988).

King, John, 'The Boom of the Latin American Novel', in *Cambridge Companion to the Latin American Novel* (Cambridge: Cambridge University Press, 2007), pp.59–80.

Kinser, Amber E., 'Negotiating Spaces For/Through Third–Wave Feminism, *NWSA Journal*, Vol.13, No.3 (2004), pp.124–53.

Kinsey, A.C.; Pomeroy, W.B. and Martin, E.E., *Sexual Behavior in the Human Female* (Philadelphia: W.B. Saunders, 1953).

—— *Sexual Behavior in the Human Male* (Philadelphia: W.B. Saunders, 1948).

Kliesner, Joseph (ed.), 'The 2006 Mexican Election and Its Aftermath', *Political Science and Politics*, Vol.XL, No.1 (January 2007), pp.11–48.

Knight, Alan, *The Mexican Revolution: Porfirians, Liberals and Peasants*, Vol.1 (Cambridge: Cambridge University Press, 1986).

Krauze, Enrique, *María Félix: Todas mis guerras* (Mexico City: Debolsillo, 2003).

Kristeva, Julia, *Desire in Language: A Semiotic Approach to Literature and Art*. Trans. by Thomas Gora, Alice Jardine and Leon S. Roudiez (New York: Columbia University Press, 1980).

—— *Powers of Horror: An Essay on Abjection*, trans. by Leon S. Roudiez. (New York: Columbia University Press 1982).

Lacan, Jacques, *Ecrits: A Selection* (New York: Routledge, 2001). First edition 1977.

—— *The Four Fundamental Concepts of Psycho-Analysis* (New York: Norton, 1981).

Larraín, Jorge, *Identity and Modernity in Latin America* (Cambridge: Polity Press, 2000).

Larsen, Neil, *Determinations: Essays on Theory, Narrative and Nation in the Americas* (London and New York: Verso, 2001).

Latin American Perspectives. 'Religion, Ideology and Revolution in Latin America', Issue 50, Vol.13, No.3 (Summer 1986).

Levinson, Brett, 'The Limits of Postcolonial theory After Said/Bhabha, or: Is Latin America a Postcolonial Site?', *Journal for the Psychoanalysis of Culture and Society*, Vol.1, No.2 (Fall 1996), pp.144–57.

Lewis, Oscar, *The Children of Sánchez: Autobiography of a Mexican Family* (New York: Random House, 1961).

Leyva, José Angel, 'El nuevo mundo de Grijalbo', *Libros de México*, Vol. 17 (October–December 1989), pp.9–12.

—— 'Joaquín Mortiz, las grandes transfiguaciones editoriales', *Libros de México*, Vol.31 (April–June 1993), p.12.

—— 'Por la órbita editoral de Planeta', *Libros de México*, Vol.18 (January–March 1990), pp.5–9.

Lindsay, Claire, *Locating Latin American Women Writers* (New York: Peter Lang, 2003).

López González, Aralia, *La espiral parece un círculo* (Mexico City: Universidad Autónoma Metropolitana, 1992).

—— 'Quebrantos, búsquedas y azares de una pasión nacional (dos décadas de narrativa mexicana: 1970–1980)', *Revista Iberoamericana*, Vol.59, Nos. 164–5 (July–December 1993), pp.659–85.

López Parada, Esperanza, 'Un escritor ubícuo', *El País*, 6 September, 2006. http://www.elpais.com/articulo/cultura/escritor/ubicuo/elpepicul/20060906elpe picul_5/Tes.

Lorde, Audre, *Sister/Outsider: Essays and Speeches* (Trumansburg, New York: The Crossing Press, 1984).

—— *Uses of the Erotic: The Erotic as Power* (Trumansburg, New York: Out and Out Books, 1978).

Loustanau, Martha, *Mexico's Contemporary Women Novelists* (Massachussetts: Ann Arbor, 1973).

MacCannell, Dean, *The Tourist: A New Theory of the Leisure Class* (Berkeley: University of California Press, 1999).

Macías, Anna, *Against All Odds: The Feminist Movement in Mexico to 1940* (Westport, Connecticut: Greenwood Press, 1982).

Mack, Maynard, 'The Muse of Satire, *Yale Review*, Vol.41 (1951), pp.85–92.

Márquet, Antonio, '¿Cómo escribir un best-seller?: La receta de Laura Esquivel', *Plural: Revista Cultural de Excélsior*, Vol.237 (June 1991), pp.58–67.

McClintock, Anne, 'No Longer in a Future Heaven: Gender, Race and Nationalism' in *Imperial Leather: Race, Gender and Sexuality in the Colonial Context* (New York: Routledge 1994), pp.352–90.

Mernissi, Fatema, *Scheherezade Goes West: Different Cultures, Different Harems* (New York: Washington Square Press, 2001).

Mexican Labour News and Analysis, 3 February 1999, Vol.4, No.4, no page number.

Millán Moncaya, Márgara, *Derivas de un cine en femenino* (Mexico: UNAM and Miguel Angel Porrúa, 1999).

Milliot, Jim, 'How Big is the Market', *Library Journal*, 1 November 2001, p.3.

Mignolo, Water, 'Colonial and Postcolonial Discourse: Cultural Critique or Academic Colonialism?', *Latin American Research Review*, Vol.28, No.3 (1993), pp.120–34.

Mills, Sara, *Discourses of Difference: An Analysis of Women's Travel Writing and Colonialism* (London: Routledge, 1991).

Mohanty, Ann Russo and Lourdes Torres (eds), *Third World Women and the Politics of Feminism* (Bloomington: University of Indiana Press, 1991).

Monsiváis, Carlos, 'Arnaldo Orfila Reynal y la ampliación del lectorado', *Libros de México*, Vol.33 (October–December 1993), pp.31–5.

—— 'San Juanico: los hechos, las interpretaciones, las mitologías' in *Entrada libre: crónicas de la sociedad que se organiza* (Mexico: Ediciones Era 1987), pp.123–50.

Moraña, Mabel, 'El boom del subalterno', *Revista de Crítica Cultural*, Vol.14 (1997), pp.48–53.

Moreiras, Alberto, *The Exhaustion of Difference: The Politics of Latin American Cultural Studies* (Durham and London: Duke University Press, 2001).

Morgan, Robin, *Sisterhood is Global: The International Women's Movement Anthology* (New York: Anchor/Doubleday, 1984).

—— *Sisterhood is Powerful: An Anthology of Writings from the Women's Movement* (London: Vintage, 1970).

Narayan, Uma and Harding, Sandra (eds), *Decentering the Center: Philosophy for a Multicultural, Postcolonial, and Feminist World* (Bloomington: Indiana University Press, 2000).

Los narradores ante el público (Mexico City: Joaquín Mortiz, 1966).

Nash, Dennison, 'Tourism as an Anthropological Subject', *Current Anthropology*, Vol.22, No.5 (October 1981), pp.461–81.

Nesselroth, Peter, *Lautréamont's Imagery: A Stylistic Approach* (Geneva: Droz, 1969).

Nicholson, Linda (ed.), *The Second Wave: A Reader in Feminist Theory* (New York: Routledge, 1997).

Nitze, Wm A., 'Review of *Le Roman de Renard* by Lucien Foulet', *Modern Language Notes*, Vol.30, No.5 (May 1915), pp.45–9.

Noble, Andrea, *Tina Modotti: Image, Texture, Photography* (Albuquerque: University of New Mexico, 2000).

Novy, Marianne (ed.), *Women's Revisions of Shakespeare: On the Responses of Dickinson, Woolf, Rich, H.D., George Eliot and Others* (Urbana: University of Illinois Press, 1990).

O'Connell, Joanna, *Prospero's Daughter: The Prose of Rosario Castellanos* (Austin: University of Texas Press, 1995).

O' Gorman, Edmundo, *The Invention of America: An Inquiry into the Historical Nature of the New World and the Meaning of Its History* (Bloomington: Indiana University Press, 1961).

O'Quinn, Kathleen, '"Tablero de damas" and "Álbum de familia": Farces on Women Writers' in Maureen Ahern and Mary Seale Vásquez (eds) *Homenaje a Rosario Castellanos* (Valencia: Albatros Hispanófila, 1980), pp.99–105.

Orr, Catherine, 'Charting the Currents of the Third Wave, *Hypatia*, Vol.12, No.3 (Summer 1997), pp.29–46.

Paniagua, Lita, 'La lucha por la superación femenina', *Kena* (September 1972), p.4.

Parkinson Zamora, Lois and Faris, Wendy B. (eds) *Magical Realism, Theory, History, Community* (Durham, North Carolina: Duke University Press, 1995).

Passeron, Claude, *Reproduction in Education, Society, Culture* (Beverly Hills, California: Sage, 1977).

Pérez Cruz, Emilio, *Borracho no vale* (Mexico: Plaza y Janes, 1988).

Pérez de Mendiola, Mariana, *Gender and Identity: Formation in Contemporary Mexican Literature* (New York and London: Garland Publishing Inc., 1998).

Poniatowska, Elena, *Ay vida no me mereces!: Carlos Fuentes, Rosario Castellanos, Juan Rulfo. La literature de la onda* (Mexico: Joaquín Mortiz, 1985).

Pope, Alexander, *The Rape of the Lock* (London and New York: Routledge, 1971).

Preminger, Alex and Brogan, T.V.F. (eds), *The New Princeton Encyclopedia of Poetry and Poetics* (New Jersey: Princeton University Press, 1993).

Prada, Javier, 'Las decisiones editoriales', *La Gaceta del Fondo de Cultura Económica*, No.245 (1991), pp.56–7.

Pratt, Mary Louise, *Imperial Eyes: Travel Writing and Transculturation* (London: Routledge, 1992).

—— 'Criticism in the Contact Zone: Decentering Community and Nation', in Steven Bell, Albert Le May and Leonard Orr, *Critical Theory, Cultural Politics and Latin American Narrative* (Notre Dame: University of Notre Dame Press, 1993), pp.83–91.

Puga, María Luisa, *Las posibilidades del odio* (Mexico City: Siglo Veintiuno, 1978).

Rashkin, Elissa J. *Women Filmmakers in Mexico: The Country of Which We Dream* (Austin: University of Texas Press, 2001).

336

Reyes Nevares, Beatriz, *Rosario Castellanos* (Mexico: Departamento Editorial Secretaría de la Presidencia, 1976).

Rich, Adrienne, *Blood, Bread and Poetry: Selected Prose 1979–1985* (New York: Norton, 1994).

—— *Time's Power: Poems 1985–1988* (New York: W.W. Norton and Company, 1989).

Robles, Martha, *La sombra fugitiva: escritoras en la cultural nacional* (Mexico City: UNAM, 1985).

Rodden, John (ed.), *Conversations with Isabel Allende* (Austin: University of Texas Press, 1999).

Rodó, José Enrique, *Ariel* (Mexico City: Fondo de Cultura Económica, 1984). First published 1901.

Rodriguez, Iliana (ed.), *The Latin American Subaltern Studies Reader* (Durham and London: Duke University Press, 2001).

Ruiz Funes, Concepción and Capella, María Luisa, 'No, a los párrafos que enjuician libros: Entrevista con Vicente Leñero', *Revista de la universidad de México* (October–November 1978), pp.12–15.

Rulfo, Juan, *El llano en llamas* (Barcelona: Planeta, 1990).

—— *Pedro Páramo* (Barcelona: Planeta, 1990).

Rupp, Leila J., 'Women's History in the New Millenium: Adrienne Rich's Compulsory Heterosexuality and Lesbian Existence: A Retrospective', *Journal of Women's History*, Vol.15, No.3 (2003).

Russell, Willy, *Shirley Valentine* (London: Methuen Drama, 1988).

Schaefer, Claudia, *Danger Zones: Homosexuality, National Identity and Mexican Culture* (Tucson: University of Arizona Press, 1996).

Seed, Patricia, 'Colonial and Postcolonial Discourse', *Latin American Research Review*, Vol.26, No.3 (1991), pp.181–200.

Seminar on Women and Culture in Latin America, *Women, Culture and Politics in Latin America:* Seminar on Women and Culture in Latin America (Berkeley: University of California Press, 1990).

Serna, Enrique, 'Vejamen de la narrativa difícil', *Sábado*, 18 December 1993, pp.1–3.

Shakespeare, William, *The Tempest* (New York: The Macmillan Company, 1921). Composition date 1610–1611.

Shaw, Deborah, *Contemporary Cinema of Latin America: 10 Key Films* (New York and London: Continuum, 2003).

—— 'Erotic or Political: Literary Representations of Mexican Lesbians', *Travesía: The Journal of Latin American Cultural Studies*, Vol.5, No.1 (June 1996), pp.51–63.

Shaw, Donald Leslie, *The Post-Boom in Spanish-American Fiction* (New York: SUNY Press, 1998).

Showalter, Elaine, *The Female Malady: Women, Madness and English Culture 1830–1980* (London: Virago Press, 1987).

Smith, Sidonie, *Moving Lives: Twentieth Century Women's Travel Writing* (University of Minnesota Press, 2001).

Sommers, Doris, *Foundational Fictions: The National Romances of Latin America* (Berkeley: University of California Press, 1991).

Sommers, Joseph, 'Changing View of the Indian in Mexican Literature', *Hispania*, Vol.47, No.1 (1964), pp.47–55.

——'Literatura e historia: las contradicciones ideológicas de la ficción indigenista', *Revista de Crítica Literaria Latinoamericana* (1989), pp.9–39.

——'El ciclo de Chiapas: nueva corriente literaria', *Cuadernos Americanos*, Vol.2 (March–April 1964), pp.242–261.

——'La novela mexicana, la revolución y la Alianza para el progreso', *La Gaceta* (May 1963), p.3.

Sutherland, James, *English Satire* (Cambridge: Cambridge University Press).

Swanson, Philip, *Latin American Fiction: A Short Introduction* (Oxford: Blackwell Publishing, 2005).

Talpade Mohanty, Chandra, Russo, Ann and Torres, Lourdes (eds), *Third World Women and the Politics of Feminism* (Bloomington: Indiana University Press, 1991).

—— 'Sisterhood, Coalition and the Politics of Experience' in *Feminism Without Borders: Decolonizing Theory, Practicing Solidarity* (Durham: Duke University Press, 2003), pp.106–38.

Tambling, Jeremy, *Narrative and Ideology* (Milton Keynes and Philadelphia: Open University Press, 1991).

Thrall, William; Hibbard, Addison and Holman, Hugh C. (eds), *A Handbook to Literature* (New York: Odyssey Press, 1960).

Tiano, Susan, *Patriarchy on the Line: Labor, Gender, and Ideology in the Mexican Maquila Industry* (Philadelphia: Temple University Press, 1994).

Todorov, Tzvetan, *The Conquest of America: The Question of the Other*, trans. by Richard Howard (New York: Harper and Row, 1984).

Vidal, Hernan, 'The Concept of Colonial and Postcolonial Discourse: A Perspective from Literary Criticism', *Latin American Research Review*, Vol.28, No.3 (1993), pp.113–19.

Villoro, Juan, 'Escribir en México', *Libros de México*, Vol.30 (January–March 1993), p.48.

Volpi, Jorge, *En busca de Klingsor* (Barcelona: Seix Barral, 1999).

Weber, Charlotte, 'Unveiling Scheherezade: Feminist Orientalism in the International Alliance of Women, 1911–1950', *Feminist Studies*, Vol.27, No.1 (2001), pp.125–57.

Weedon, Chris, *Feminism, Theory and the Politics of Difference* (Oxford: Blackwell, 1999).

Wills, Clair, 'Upsetting the Public: Carnival, Hysteria and Womens' Texts' in Ken Hirschkop and David Shepherd (eds) *Bakhtin and Cultural Theory* (Manchester and New York: Manchester University Press, 1989), pp.130–52.

338

Wittig, Monique, *Le Corps Lesbien* (Paris: Les Éditions de Minuit, 1973).
—— *Les Guérillères* (New York: Viking Press, 1971).
Woolf, Virginia, *A Room of One's Own* (England: Hogarth Press, 1929).
—— *Shirley* (Oxford: Oxford University Press, 1998).
Young, Robert, *Untying the Text: A Poststructuralist Reader* (London: Routledge and Kegan Paul, 1981).
Yuval-Davis, Nira, *Gender and Nation* (London: Sage, 1997).
Zimena, María and Toledo, Alejandra, 'Por una literatura fácil', *Macrópolis*, 26 March 1992, pp.32–7.

Films

Allá en el rancho grande (1936), dir. Fernando de Fuentes.
El compadre Mendoza (1933), dir. Juan Bustillo Oro, Juan and Fernando de Fuentes.
Guerrilla: The Taking of Patty Hearst (2004), dir. Robert Stone.
Lola (1989), dir. María Novaro.
Secuestro express (2006), dir. Jonathan Jakubowicz.

Index

Aguilar Camín, Héctor, 43, 149, 166
Aguilar, Julia Van Loan, 184, 186
Álbum de familia, 181–2, 190
Alfaguara, 160–1, 163–4, 166
Allende, Isabel, 112, 137, 145, 163
Amora, 179, 215, 217, 220, 223–4, 228–9, 235, 239–40, 244
Anderson, Danny, 135, 159
Arráncame la vida, 29, 135–9, 147, 151, 160, 165
Arreola Juan José, 158, 168

Balzac, Honoré de, 99, 111
Barthes, Roland, 99–100, 102–3, 110–12, 115
Bartra, Roger, 30, 48, 53, 72–3
Baudrillard, Jean, 39, 290
Beauvoir, Simone de, 223, 292
Beverley, John, 14, 21
Bhabha, Homi, 18, 21, 25, 71, 312, 315
Bjerot, Nils, 104, 120
Boullosa, Carmen, 175–6, 248
Bourdieu, Pierre, 129, 141
Braidotti, Rosi, 291, 300–1, 303, 305, 306

Calvino, Italo, 155–6
Campo, Alicia del 49, 60
Campos, Victoria E., 247, 256
Castellanos, Rosario, 25, 123, 175, 180–3, 188–92, 202–7, 209, 213–14, 216, 218–19, 221–3, 225, 227, 235, 237, 238, 239, 240, 242–3, 282–3, 309
Como agua para chocolate, 137, 145, 162, 179
Compro, luego existo, 185, 190, 191, 200, 214, 280

Cortázar, Julio, 168, 206
Craske, Nikki, 23, 86

Deleuze, Gilles, 250, 277, 281, 288–90, 294, 298–301, 306
Demasiado amor, 30, 32, 34, 54–6, 60, 62, 65, 69–71, 163, 286, 290, 295, 297, 300, 314
Diez-Canedo, Joaquín, 164, 169, 170
Domecq, Brianda, 9, 24, 75–6, 103–4, 108–9, 111, 113, 117, 126, 131, 134, 163, 175, 309–10, 314, 317
Dworkin, Andrea, 224–5

El amor que me juraste, 30, 54, 60, 71
El eterno femenino, 181–2, 188, 190–1, 242, 283,
El para siempre dura una noche, 215, 226, 228
Esquivel, Laura, 137, 162, 175–6, 179
Excélsior, 143, 152, 215

Franco, Jean, 13, 18, 20, 163, 171–2, 177, 313
Friedan, Betty, 219, 282, 283
Fuentes, Carlos, 140, 167–8

Gabriel García Márquez, 140, 145, 168
Grijalbo, 158, 160, 164
Grupo Santillana, 160–2, 166
Guattari, Felipe, 250, 277, 281, 288–90, 294, 298–301, 306
Guerrero, Gustavo, 145–7, 173

Joaquín Blanco, José, 174–5

Kaplan, Caren, 35–6, 52, 59, 60, 262, 279, 288, 290, 300
Kristeva, Julia, 77–8, 82–5

La casa de los espíritus, 137, 145
La insólita historia de la Santa de Cabora, 132, 163
La jornada, 152, 184–5, 212, 214
La Reforma, 152, 184
La señora de los sueños, 30, 163, 247–9, 280, 314
Lacan, Jacques, 20, 107
Las reinas de Polanco, 184–5, 196–7, 202, 207, 209
Loaeza, Guadalupe, 9, 25, 149, 163, 166, 175–6, 179, 180–3, 185–7, 189, 191–2, 194–8, 202, 206, 207–8, 210, 213–15, 228, 237, 244, 283, 309–10, 313, 317
López González, Aralia, 151, 168, 169, 174

MacCannell, Dean, 59–61
Madrid, Miguel de la, 40, 42, 66, 175
Mal de amores, 135–6, 140, 142–3, 147–8, 166, 309
Maquiladoras, 44, 85, 146
Mastretta, Angeles, 9, 25, 29, 72, 134–6, 139, 141–3, 145, 147, 149–50, 152–6, 160, 162–3, 165, 168, 171–7, 309–10, 312–13
Molina, Silvia, , 9, 24–5, 29, 54,62, 175, 247–50, 256, 275, 283–4, 306, 309–10, 313–14, 317
Mondadori, 160–1, 164
Moreiras, Alberto, 14, 26
Mortiz, Joaquín, 10, 58, 160–1, 164–5
Muchacha en azul, 247–50, 280, 285, 287, 292–3, 306

Nexos, 149, 166

Once días y algo más, 75, 93, 103, 131, 315
Onetti, Juan Carlos, 127, 133

Pacheco, Cristina, 175, 212
Págano, Susana, 9, 24, 75–6, 97, 98, 100, 102–6, 109, 111, 126, 133, 134, 309–10, 314, 317
Pedro Páramo, 75, 78, 93, 95
Planeta, 160–2, 164–6
Poniatowska, Elena, 155, 163, 169, 176
Pratt, Mary Louise, 34, 247, 260, 312
Premio Rómulo Gallegos, 140, 142, 144, 148, 152, 154, 309
Puga, María Luisa, 175, 248

Robles, Martha, 139, 143, 155
Roffiel, Rosamaría, 9, 25, 63, 179–83, 215–18, 220–6, 228, 231–2, 237–42, 244–5, 309–10, 314, 317
Rulfo, Juan, 75–6, 78, 87, 89, 93, 96, 98–100, 130, 133, 136, 168

Salinas de Gortari, Carlos, 23, 66, 175
Sarrasine, 99–100, 111
Sefchovich, Sara, 9, 24–5, 29, 35, 40, 62, 68, 163, 175–6, 247–9, 279, 289–91, 291, 299, 300–1, 303, 305–6, 309–10, 313–14, 317
Sheherezade, 75–6, 104, 112–13
Stockholm syndrome, 104, 120

Unomásuno, 184, 211, 212, 214

Vuelta, 148–9

Y si yo fuera Susana San Juan, 75, 77, 93, 96, 133,314

Zapatismo, 9–10
Zapatista, 54, 66, 69